RULES FOR GROWTH

Promoting Innovation and Growth
Through Legal Reform

Published by Ewing Marion Kauffman Foundation
4801 Rockhill Road
Kansas City, Missouri 64110

Printed and bound in the United States of America.

Library of Congress Cataloging-in-Publication Data

2010941516

ISBN 978-0-9831775-0-0 (hardcover)

RULES FOR GROWTH

Promoting Innovation and Growth Through Legal Reform

The Kauffman Task Force on Law,
Innovation, and Growth

KAUFFMAN
The Foundation of Entrepreneurship

Kansas City, Missouri

Contents

Preface

Three years ago the Kauffman Foundation began funding legal scholars and economists to study, research, and write about the way in which the legal system—the contents of specific laws, judicial doctrines, and regulation, as well as the legal processes—affects innovation and growth. This was both a familiar and novel undertaking for many of the scholars involved. It was familiar because for the past several decades, an increasing number of scholars had already been investigating the way in which the law affects economic efficiency, in the sense of improving or adversely affecting the production of goods and services using existing inputs of labor, capital, and ideas. But the initiative also was novel in that it asked the scholars to move beyond the "static" analysis of the extant "law and economics" literature and begin to investigate how the law was affecting what economists call "dynamic efficiency," or the maximum rate at which the production of goods and services can grow with the right institutions and policies in place.

Our Foundation has a special interest in economic growth because our founder, Ewing Marion Kauffman, strongly believed that entrepreneurs were the key to innovation and growth, and that only growth would advance living standards. For many years, we have funded a wide range of researchers concentrating on entrepreneurship and innovation to better understand the growth process. The Foundation's "Law, Innovation, and Growth" initiative represents what we believe is an important extension of research aimed not only at understanding the linkages between innovation and growth, but how the *law and the legal system* affect those linkages, and perhaps, most importantly, what *changes* in the law would be most likely to accelerate growth.

Each summer, as part of the Foundation's initiative, we have convened many of our funded scholars to discuss their ongoing research and how the emerging field of law, innovation, and growth might be best advanced. The third meeting of this annual "Kauffman Summer Legal Institute" was held in July 2010 and formalized these discussions by convening the participants—all well-acknowledged experts in their fields—to present specific proposals for changes in a particular area of the law that, in the author's view, would advance economy-wide innovation and growth. This volume is the product of the work presented at this meeting.

It could not be presented at a more important time in this nation's history. As I write this, the U.S. economy is slowly recovering from the worst recession since the Great Depression. Conventional macroeconomic stimulus measures—more government spending, tax cuts, and monetary easing—have been applied to an extraordinary degree. It is not likely, and in the view of many, not advisable, that much more stimulus will or should be provided. And yet the consensus view seems to be that the U.S. economy, nonetheless, will continue to recover slowly for many years, consigning millions of Americans to unemployment, fear of becoming unemployed, and for those employed, relatively slow annual advances in their compensation.

This is not the kind of economy that we should accept. All economies have rules and institutions that govern the behavior of their actors. The rules that govern the U.S. economy so far have helped guide unprecedented growth and well-being; nonetheless, they could be improved so that our economy can perform even better in the years ahead. This volume provides a roadmap for key policymakers in the legislative, executive, and judicial branches to accomplish that objective *without any additional spending of taxpayer monies or adding to any government deficit.*

The volume also has another important, though narrower, objective, and that is to help redirect and expand the "law and economics" field to refocus on the connections between the law and growth. Given the wealth of experience and prestige of the authors in this volume, we are hopeful that this second purpose will quickly be achieved.

Finally, I want to thank Robert Litan, Kauffman's vice president of Research and Policy, whose energy and continuing intellectual leadership has made the "Law, Innovation, and Growth" initiative and this particular volume possible. I also want to thank Glory Olson for her great work in organizing the summer conference and monitoring the editing of this book; Lacey Graverson, Sarah Gowen, and Matt Rees for the editing itself; Melody Dellinger for designing the book cover; and Barbara Pruitt for managing the publication process.

Carl J. Schramm
President and Chief Executive Officer
Ewing Marion Kauffman Foundation
January 2011

Task Force Members

Robert E. Litan (Task Force Organizer), Ewing Marion
  Kauffman Foundation and The Brookings Institution
Yochai Benkler, Harvard Law School
Henry N. Butler, George Mason University
John Henry Clippinger, Harvard University
Robert Cook-Deegan, Institute for Genome Sciences &
  Policy, Sanford School of Public Policy, Duke University
Robert Cooter, University of California, Berkeley
Aaron Edlin, University of California, Berkeley and
  National Bureau of Economic Research
Nicole Garnett, University of Notre Dame Law School
Ronald J. Gilson, Columbia University
Oliver Goodenough, Vermont Law School
Gillian Hadfield, University of Southern California
Mark Lemley, Stanford Law School and Durie Tangri LLP
Frank Partnoy, University of San Diego School of Law
George Priest, Yale Law School
Larry E. Ribstein, University of Illinois College of Law
Charles F. Sabel, Columbia University
Peter H. Schuck, Yale University
Hal Scott, Harvard Law School
Robert E. Scott, Columbia University
Alex Stein, Benjamin N. Cardozo School of Law, Yeshiva
  University
Victoria Stodden, Columbia University
John E. Tyler, Ewing Marion Kauffman Foundation
Alan D. Viard, American Enterprise Institute
Benjamin Wittes, The Brookings Institution

1 ■ The Importance of Law in Promoting
■ Innovation and Growth

Robert Cooter, Aaron Edlin, Robert E. Litan, and
George L. Priest*

Nobel Laureate and University of Chicago economist Robert Lucas, who received his prize for his theories of how people form expectations about the future and how those expectations arguably should affect economic policymakers, may be remembered by historians more so for one single famous utterance: "Once one starts thinking about [actions to accelerate economic growth], it is hard to think about anything else."[1]

It is not hard to figure out why. Economic growth is the driving force behind improvements in people's living standards. Although measuring economic progress over long lengths of time is fraught with difficulties, it is now the received wisdom that, on

---

* Robert Cooter is Herman Selvin Professor of Law, University of California at Berkeley. Aaron Edlin is both Professor of Economics and the Richard Jennings Professor of Law, University of California at Berkeley, and a Research Associate at the National Bureau of Economic Research. Robert E. Litan is Vice President for Research & Policy at the Ewing Marion Kauffman Foundation and Senior Fellow in the Economic Studies program at the Brookings Institution. George L. Priest is the Edward J. Phelps Professor of Law and Economics and Kauffman Distinguished Research Scholar in Law, Economics, and Entrepreneurship at Yale Law School.

[1] Robert Lucas, "On the Mechanics of Economic Development," *Journal of Monetary Economics* 22, no. 1 (1988): 5.

average, living standards for the world's population barely budged for roughly 2,000 years before the Industrial Revolution of the late 1700s and early 1800s. Only after the remarkable innovations that in retrospect make up that revolution—notably the steam engine and, shortly thereafter, the railroad—did living standards begin to rapidly advance, first in the United Kingdom and the United States, and eventually around the world.

Growth since has been the norm in most locations, though with frequent interruptions in different places and at different times due to wars and civil conflicts, financial crises, and temporary economic downturns. The average American in the early twenty-first century, for example, is roughly seven times better off than he or she was at the beginning of the twentieth century.[2] Similar or even greater advances have been achieved in other developed economies. Even faster progress has been made since as recently as 1980 in large parts of the developing world. The economies of China and India, once thought to be hopelessly moribund, have grown at annual rates of between 6 and 8 percent for more than two decades running, chalking up a record that Lawrence Summers has labeled the most remarkable example of progress in human history.[3] Even portions of Africa, home to some of the poorest nations on earth, began to show sustained vigorous growth in the 1990s and beyond (even through the 2008–9 near-global recession).

Although many concerns remain about how the gains from growth are distributed—a topic we briefly revisit at the end of this introductory chapter—there is little doubt that growth has had broad benefits. One widely used measure of extreme poverty is those who live on less than $1.25 a day. The share of the population in developing countries living below that standard shrank by half, from 52 percent to 25 percent—between 1981 and 2005.[4]

[2] Measured as per capita Gross Domestic Product, see Angus Maddison, *The World Economy: Historical Statistics* (Paris: Organisation for Economic Co-Operation and Development, 2003).

[3] Lawrence Summers, remarks at the Presidential Summit on Entrepreneurship, Washington, DC, April 27, 2010.

[4] World Bank, *Poverty Brief*, March 2010, www.worldbank.org.

That was possible only because the economies in which these people live were able to greatly expand their production of goods and services.

The gains from growth are not exclusively material. Richer societies are also healthier and permit people to live longer. It is no accident that life spans throughout the world, but especially in richer countries, have grown significantly at the same time that output per capita has expanded. With more resources, people and the societies they live in eat better and are able to afford more frequent and better health care, lowering rates of infant mortality and adding years to the average life.

Why do economies grow? This question, which once occupied the attention of the first "economists"—among them, Adam Smith, David Ricardo, and others—has continued to bedevil economists over the past several decades. By and large, economists have been better able to *describe* how growth happens rather than to predict it or to prove that particular policies are responsible for it.

Broadly speaking, the accepted framework for describing growth over the long run (putting aside the inevitable short-run fluctuations due to constant changes in aggregate demand) specifies it as the product of a series of inputs: physical capital (buildings and machines), human capital (human work, adjusted for the skills people bring to their jobs), and "innovation," a catchall term that economists use to capture all growth that is not due to the first two factors. MIT economist Robert Solow won his Nobel Prize for showing in the 1950s that in the United States innovation was by far the most important "factor of production" of the three. Subsequent empirical work by Edward Denison, Robert Barro, and others has confirmed this to be the case in developed economies. There is a broader range of opinion about the relative contribution of the three factors of production in lesser-developed economies, which have the advantage of being able to copy or import cutting-edge technologies from the developed world, and thus seem to rely more heavily on investment in physical capital and education to achieve growth rather than innovation

3

(although this has been changing in parts of the world where innovations aimed at satisfying the wants of low-income individuals are more likely to come from local residents than from abroad).

As important as the construction of the basic growth framework has been, a number of questions remain unanswered. What is inside the "black box" called innovation? What factors influence it and to what degrees? If policymakers had definitive answers to these questions, they would be in a far better position than they are now to boost rates of economic growth on a sustained basis in many different locations.

One standard answer is that innovation is driven by advances in knowledge, which in turn seem to be correlated with spending on research and development, more so by governments (which in principle focus more on basic science where the gains are true "public goods") than by the private sector (where the advances are more applied, and the gains more easily captured by those who discover them, but even then most of these gains, too, accrue to society at large). Any connection between R&D spending and innovation, however, must be loose since there is a large random component to discovery, although in principle—to borrow an analogy from the sport of hockey—it seems logical that more goals are likely to be scored the higher the number of "shots on goal." Still, because not all R&D spending is fungible, any aggregate number for R&D effort is difficult, if not impossible, to adjust for the quality of the researcher or the research itself. More fundamentally, R&D spending is unlikely to translate into new products, services, and modes of production—and thus, to advance growth—unless those innovations are commercialized and then meet the test of the market. Too often, too much attention is paid to just R&D efforts and not enough to commercialization activities; the two may not always be highly correlated. Recently, economist William Baumol has drummed this distinction home by theorizing about the critical role played by "innovative entrepreneurs" in the growth process.[5]

Economists also have sought other keys to unlock the mystery of what accounts for innovation and growth. Perhaps their favorite empirical technique is the "cross-country regression" in which data on GDP for different countries over an extended time period are "regressed" against a number of independent, supposedly causal variables (capital, labor, R&D intensity, and other factors).[6] In principle, these regressions permit the testing of various hypotheses about what factors are correlated with growth, controlling for the influence of a range of other factors. In practice, however, the literature based on these cross-country regressions is far from definitive. Apart from the obvious and unsurprising connections between growth and the basic factors of production already identified, researchers have found, depending on the sample periods and the identities of the countries in the regressions, that growth can be influenced (or not) by such other factors as openness to trade and foreign investment, religious intensity of the population, and measures of violence representing civil conflict or crime, among other variables. Yet another line of research, pioneered by Stanford economist Paul Romer, suggests that growth and innovation may be "endogenous"—that is, innovation is not some independent or autonomous factor that cannot be explained, but instead is the product of, or is heavily influenced by, other factors of production, notably investments in physical and human capital.[7]

This book focuses primarily on still one other broad driving force behind growth—the types and quality of the "institutions" (the formal and informal rules societies set or establish over time)— that either foster or discourage people's engagement in growth-

[5] William J. Baumol, *The Microtheory of Innovative Entrepreneurship* (Princeton, NJ: Princeton University Press, 2010).

[6] Perhaps the most prominent example of such work can be found in Robert J. Barro, *Determinants of Economic Growth: A Cross-Country Empirical Study (Lionel Robbins Lectures)* (Boston, MA: The MIT Press, 1998).

[7] Paul M. Romer, "Increasing Returns and Long Run Growth," *Journal of Political Economy* 94, no. 5 (October 1986): 1002–37; Romer, and "The Origins of Endogenous Growth," *Journal of Economic Perspectives* 8, no. 1 (Winter 1994): 3–22. For a popular guide to Romer's growth theory, see David Warsh, *Knowledge and the Wealth of Nations: A Story of Economic Discovery* (New York: W.W. Norton & Company, 2006).

enhancing activities. The importance of this principle has been explicitly validated by the Nobel prizes given to the several economists who have explained why institutions matter.[8] Economies, like games, cannot function effectively without clear rules set and enforced by someone or some bodies or organizations. Examples include rules of property and contract ultimately enforced by judicial systems, which ensure that those who undertake and succeed at productive endeavors are able to retain a sufficient portion of the gains from their labors to induce them to undertake these actions in the first place.[9]

Yet beyond this basic insight—that certain fundamental "rules of law" should be protected, formally or even informally through norms and customs—not much attention has been paid by economists (or lawyers) to the institutions, laws and legal systems in particular, that are best suited for promoting innovation and economic growth. A noteworthy exception is the running debate between researchers who continue to argue whether Anglo-Saxon legal systems are more conducive to growth (and the coincident development of financial systems) than civil law systems, or vice versa.[10] In principle, so one argument goes, Anglo-Saxon systems rely more on judicial doctrine and administrative rules, and thus are supposedly more flexible and adaptable to change than civil

---

[8] These Nobel Laureates include Douglas North, James Buchanan, and Oliver Williamson.

[9] The vast proportion of the gains from true innovation rightly "leak out" to the rest of the society and greatly exceed the benefits to the innovators themselves. See William D. Nordhaus, "Schumpeterian Profits and the Alchemist Fallacy," Yale Working Papers on Economic Applications and Policy, Discussion Paper No. 6 (2005), http://www.econ.yale.edu/ddp/ddp00/ddp0006.pdf. In contrast, the social benefits of investment in physical capital are not likely to be that much greater than the private benefits to those who undertake the investment.

[10] See, e.g., the work of Rafael La Porta, Florencio Lopez-de-Silanes, and Andrei Shleifer, "The Economic Consequences of Legal Origins," Journal of Economic Literature 46, no. 4 (2008): 285–332 and Edward L. Glaeser and Andrei Shleifer. "Legal Origins," Quarterly Journal of Economics, 117 no. 4 (2002): 1193–1229 (favoring the Anglo-Saxon view); Curtis J. Milhaupt and Katharina Pistor, Law and Capitalism: What Corporate Crises Reveal About Legal Systems and Economic Development Around the World (Chicago: University of Chicago, 2008) and Kenneth Dam, The Law-Growth Nexus (Washington, DC: The Brookings Institution Press, 2006) (challenging the view that legal origins matter); and Mark J. Roe, and Jordan I. Siegel. "Finance and Politics: A Review Essay Based on Kenneth Dam's Analysis of Legal Traditions in The Law-Growth Nexus," Journal of Economic Literature, 47, no. 3 (2009): 781–800 (who support the notion that legal origins matter).

law systems that rest more heavily on less flexible statutes. An opposing view credits the statutory civil law systems with providing more certainty than the judicial/regulatory systems. Others contend that these distinctions are more theoretical than real, and that "legal origins" have very little or no effect on the recent or current growth of economies.[11] Wherever one comes out on this debate—on which we take no position here—it doesn't provide policymakers in any branch of government with clear direction about what *specific rules* are best for growth. The arguments take place instead at a broad systems level and do not provide much practical guidance on the narrower issues that guide the everyday life of citizens and firms in real economies.

A much larger "law and economics" literature has developed over several decades that *has* focused on the economic impact of a broad range of specific rules, but the principal focus of the scholars who have led the way—Aaron Director, Ronald Coase, Richard Posner, Guido Calabresi, and Gary Becker, among others—has been largely about what economists call "static efficiency" rather than "dynamic efficiency" or growth. The distinction is critical. Static efficiency refers to how effective any set of social and economic arrangements is in generating the maximum output of goods and services for any current level of inputs *using existing technologies*. Most of the law and economics scholarship to date has been about figuring out which rules—first in antitrust, then in the basic areas of common law (contracts, property, and torts), and subsequently in virtually every legal field—are most "efficient" in this sense.

Such a task is necessarily forward-looking, though as we will highlight shortly, it does not strictly focus on economic growth in the main sense in which we will use the term here. A useful analogy may be to view law as akin to a guide or a pathfinder in the western part of the United States in the nineteenth century. At any point in time, there was a most efficient direction of transit for a party wanting to travel from, say, St. Louis to San Francisco. The

---

[11] For an excellent guide to this literature, see Roe and Siegel, "Finance and Politics."

various available alternative routes—through New Mexico, Colorado, or Wyoming, for example—each entailed a different set of obstacles or costs: mountains, hostile Native Americans, rivers or deserts to cross, and the like, which changed in various ways over time. The role of the guide was to determine the route that maximized the chances of arrival, preferably at the lowest cost.

Legal rules serve a similar function with respect to economic activity. Rules defined to be "efficient" guide human activity in the direction that will maximize output from existing resources (analogous to the routes in the travel story just described).

This sense of "static" efficiency does not capture, however, the impact of rules on what can be usefully called "dynamic efficiency," or the maximum rate of production of *new* products, services, or modes of operation, given any existing level of resources (capital and labor). Broadly speaking, the law and economics literature has not tackled this much more difficult, and we believe more important, challenge of designing rules to maximize economic *growth* that generates more resources over time for the inhabitants of any society.

In making this distinction between static and dynamic efficiency, we do not dismiss the huge contribution of the law and economics pioneers. They have helped to change legal conversations: from what obligations people owe to each other or what rights people should have, to what the economic impact is likely to be of specifying those obligations or granting those rights. This primarily has been a "positive" conversation in the sense that it is about understanding the consequences of legal decisions. Whether society should actually adopt certain rules, once understanding their likely impacts, is a normative question that, strictly speaking, is not necessarily to be decided with only static economic efficiency considerations in mind. Considerations of how rules affect the distribution of income in general, and which parties or groups stand to gain or lose in particular, are always important as a fundamental matter of political economy.

THE PURPOSE OF THIS BOOK

Our main purpose here is to try to change legal conversations yet again, hopefully in an even more useful direction. We have both positive and normative objectives in mind.

Continuing in the law and economics tradition, it is thus critical to pin down the connection—both the direction (positive or negative) and the magnitude or importance—between certain legal rules and institutions and innovation and growth. But it is also equally important to identify *changes* in those rules—whether they are set by judges, legislators, or regulators—that might plausibly enhance growth on a sustained basis. As Harvard economist Benjamin Friedman has powerfully argued, growth has a critical moral and political dimension as well.[12] In particular, growth acts as a "social lubricant" that eases potential demographic and ethnic tensions within and across societies. Conversely, as history reminds us all too often, the absence of growth can trigger horrible outbreaks of conflict. The clearest example is the global devastation of World War II and the Depression that preceded it.

More pertinent to the matters at hand, growth vastly trumps static efficiency in importance, assuming the two to be in conflict, which they can be in some cases. Take the case of proposals to extend patent lives: These will increase monopoly power of the patent holder and thus distort prices during the extended life of the patent, but in the long run may enhance incentives for invention and thus growth. It is probably more generally true, however, that policies that enhance growth also improve static efficiency, such as when antitrust law (properly applied) enhances competition. In any event, even a highly inefficient economy in the static sense cannot generate the kinds of gains from becoming vastly more efficient that are possible from the gains in wealth generated by sustained growth highlighted at the outset of this chapter. As Cooter and Edlin have put it, sustained growth is

---

[12] Benjamin Friedman, *The Moral Consequences of Economic Growth* (New York: Knopf, 2005).

exponential; improvements in static efficiency, at best, have only multiplicative effects.[13]

This is not to say that growth should be pursued for its own sake without regard to anything else. Economic progress has not been achieved without such "externalities" as air and water pollution, whose ill effects are not well accounted for in the prices of goods and services whose output gets counted in measures of output. There is a deep and growing literature on how best to "internalize" these externalities, whether through well-enforced property rights (as Ronald Coase and his intellectual descendants would argue) or through well-designed taxes and regulation (as many other economists have argued).[14]

Likewise, there are important reasons why societies should take into account how the benefits of growth—namely, incomes and wealth—are distributed across groups and individuals. Distributional or equity concerns are important considerations for their own moral and political reasons. Efforts to improve equity may or may not hurt growth. For example, when government uses tax revenue to improve education and health of the poor, it can lead both to more equitable outcomes and enhance growth by providing more educated, healthy workers and potentially entrepreneurs. Likewise, too much inequality can trigger populist backlashes that may result in growth-penalizing regulatory, trade, and tax policies.[15] Indeed, progressive income taxes, however much they make (after-tax) incomes more equal, also can penalize work and entrepreneurship and thus diminish growth.

---

[13] Robert D. Cooter and Aaron Edlin, "Maximizing Growth vs. Static Efficiency or Redistribution" (working paper, University of California at Berkeley, 2010).

[14] The central assumption underlying Coase's famous theorem—that assignment of property rules has no impact on the allocation of resources—is that transactions costs are essentially zero so that the parties can costlessly rearrange rights to achieve the most welfare-enhancing outcome. In the typical pollution case, however, there may be only one or a few polluters and many harmed parties who cannot costly negotiate with the polluter to quit. In that event, taxes or regulation may be the preferred solution.

[15] See William Russell Easterly, *The White Man's Burden: Why the West's Efforts to Aid the Rest Have Done So Much Ill and So Little Good* (New York: Penguin Group, 2006).

The magnitudes of these effects on growth, both positive and negative, will vary and likely be subjects of continuing dispute. Citizens and policymakers must bring their own value judgments to policy questions and weigh the trade-offs between equity and growth, if there are any.

Nonetheless, while addressing externalities and distributional equity are important objectives, they are not the central focus of this book, which is about growth and how legal systems can best foster it, primarily through boosting innovation. The book also concentrates on the legal system we collectively know best—that of the United States—although many of the suggestions and themes we advance here should be relevant to many other countries at all stages of economic development.

CAN GROWTH CONTINUE?

At various times, critics have questioned whether growth can continue indefinitely—though, importantly, not during and after the 2008–9 recession that has highlighted the importance of growth by its absence. After all, it is argued, the world has only a finite amount of resources (energy-producing sources in particular), and thus, once those are exhausted, must not growth come to a halt? If this is the case, then there would be no point to this book or attempts to design laws and institutions to promote growth.

Fortunately, finiteness in resources does not mean that growth must eventually stop. To see why, it is essential to contrast *inexhaustible ideas* with scarce or exhaustible resources.

Products of the mind—theorems, principles, designs, inventions, expressions, and compositions—can be used without excluding others from using them. Economists call this characteristic "nonrivalry." Looking into the future, nonrivalry implies non-depletion. When anyone from the present generation uses an idea, it remains available for future generations to use. In contrast, scarce "real" resources—like capital, labor, land and fuel—have *rival* uses. When one uses a scarce resource, it is unavailable for others to use. To be sure, some scarce resources renew—like a forest, a river, or grains. But other resources—like oil or iron—deplete irrevocably as they are used.

By making people richer, innovations induce and enable people to consume more goods and services. Some innovations conserve resources, while others hasten resource exhaustion. Many scholars believe that, on balance, the world is depleting its resources at an unsustainable rate. Addressing this danger will require faster innovation or less consumption. Faster innovation, and thus continued economic growth, is obviously the preferred approach of the two. All of the chapter authors proceed on this premise.

THE PLAN OF THE BOOK AND SUMMARY OF RECOMMENDATIONS

The book is divided into several sections, each containing one or more chapters on particular legal topics. The initial section covers legal issues affecting entrepreneurship, including policies toward high-skilled immigrants who have displayed higher propensity to be entrepreneurs than native-born Americans, ways to enhance entrepreneurship in the academic community, and related issues covering the replication of scientific research, which is an important precondition for successful commercialization of new ideas.

Given the importance of finance to the startup and growth of new companies, and hence to general economic growth, the second section includes three chapters devoted to law and finance. Because the taxation of income directly affects how companies are financed, the first of these chapters examines ways to change the federal tax laws to enhance growth. The other finance-related chapters address from different perspectives how changes in the regulation of financial institutions and markets and financial reporting, especially in light of the financial crisis of 2007–8 and its aftermath, could add to growth.

The law affects the ways firms operate in many different ways, and the third section of the book contains multiple chapters addressing various aspects of this broad topic. The subjects in this section include changes aimed at making the market for legal services more competitive, revisions in contracts and tort doctrines, changes in choice of law rules and antitrust law, and at the local level, changes in zoning. Many of the recommendations in this section were vigorously debated among the authors, especially in the case of changes in tort doctrines, where two very different views (by Stein and Parchomovsky on the one hand, and Priest on the other) about how to proceed are found in this volume.

Finally, given that innovation is driven and characterized largely by changes in technology, the fourth section of the book covers emerging legal subjects relating to this subject in particular. One of the new legal areas that has perforce grown up and around the Internet is the area loosely known as "cyberlaw." The first three chapters in this section cover aspects of this subject, ranging from copyright doctrines, to new digital ways to incorporate and govern corporations and other legal entities, to the important issues surrounding identity and privacy on the Internet. The next chapter broadly covers the important topic of intellectual property, with a special focus on possible ways to improve the patent system so that it better promotes innovation and growth. The final chapter in this section examines some of the novel security issues that modern technological innovations force us to confront and looks at the question of how to ensure that growth and innovation do not create conditions that are, in turn, hostile to growth and innovation.

Table 1.1 summarizes the specific legal recommendations advanced in the chapters that follow. The list of suggestions includes changes in judicial doctrine, regulation or administrative action, statutes (at different levels of government), or changes in private law or organization (the kinds of changes required are indicated by the letters next to each item). The recommendations are advanced solely by the authors of each respective chapter, and although the authors in this project may agree with many of them, all of the authors were not asked to and therefore do not endorse each of the items on the list.

The range of pro-growth ideas outlined in the chapters that follow is certainly not exhaustive. Other legal scholars, economists, and interested parties no doubt will be able to add to this list, including reforms that might enhance the effectiveness of the U.S. educational system, the American workforce, and U.S. trade policy, among other topics. Moreover, since we are concentrating here solely on *legal* reforms, we do not examine the host of expenditures, government guarantees, and other reforms that might also enhance growth.

Nonetheless, the wide-ranging discussion of just the legal topics that the subsequent chapters do cover reveals several broad or cross-cutting themes that readers may wish to keep in mind as they read through all or some of the specific essays that follow.

For example, one broad theme running through the recommendations outlined in many of the chapters is that in order to best promote innovation, the legal system—both the rules and the rule-making institutions—must be flexible and adaptable. Rigid rules and processes for generating them can be quickly outmoded by changes in technology. Inflexibility impedes innovation itself.

Second, count on private actors, especially entrepreneurs in a highly entrepreneurial society such as the United States, to constantly try to evade rules that get in their way. These acts of circumvention can be, and generally are, entirely "legal." Whether they are "good" or "bad" however is entirely context specific. Innovations that circumvent inefficient rules that were eventually abolished—such as the long-standing rules that fixed the prices that airlines, trucks, and securities brokers could charge, or the interest rates that banks could pay their depositors—are socially useful and should not be condemned or inhibited. But "innovations" that end-run constructive rules, such as those requiring banks to maintain certain minimum levels of capital to ensure their financial safety and to protect the deposit insurance fund, can be socially destructive. Broadly speaking, it is our view—and we believe the view of the majority of the authors in this volume—that, with perhaps a few exceptions, rules and policy should not prescreen innovations, but rather let the market take the first crack. Only where social ills prove to outweigh the social benefits should regulators constrain, punish, or in extreme cases ban, innovative products and services.

Third, and related to the first two themes, the law must allow for constant uncertainty. Change by definition is uncertain. We can't predict where it will come from and shouldn't try. The chapters on contracts and torts, in particular, urge judges, lawmakers, and agencies not to penalize newness by giving too much deference to existing customs or methods of compliance, while recognizing the benefits that certainty in rules gives to private actors.

Fourth, laws and institutions going forward need to permit collaboration, especially in the age of the Internet, which has dramatically lowered the cost for parties in different cities, states, or countries to work cooperatively together. The creation of new ways for companies to incorporate and be governed digitally, a subject explored by Goodenough in chapter 14, is an example of how changes in the law can do more than permit collaboration; they actually facilitate it.[16]

We conclude the book with some brief thoughts about the political economy of implementing the changes outlined here. We worked on this book during the recovery from what is likely to be the worst recession since the Depression, and even at this writing, the strength and durability of the recovery are open to question. While debate will certainly continue over the effectiveness of the massive fiscal and monetary stimulus implemented during the onset and depth of the recession, the virtue of legal reforms such as those outlined here is that, with few exceptions (such as

---

[16] Successful commercialization of new ideas requires not only collaboration but also trust—what Cooter and Edlin (2010) have called the "double trust dilemma." Combining a new idea with capital requires the innovator to trust the financier not to steal the idea, while the financier must trust the innovator not to steal the money the financier provides. Much commercial law has developed to address these twin challenges.

possibly in the tax arena), they cost governments little or nothing. Indeed, to the extent that legal reforms increase growth, they generate more tax revenue and thus ease budget pressures (which in the wake of the recession and heading into years of baby-boomer retirement are intense). For this reason alone, we believe that policymakers at all levels of government should have some interest in the ideas that follow.

More generally, the authors of this book believe that both scholars of the legal system and legislators and judges who design and implement the system should begin to consider seriously the effects of law on innovation and growth. The ideas presented here and the proposals that follow from them represent a first effort toward that end. Because there is no limit on the extent to which the United States or any other society can grow economically, there is much more to be done. The authors of the book remain committed to the proposition that careful attention in the future to law and its effects on innovation will improve the rate of growth itself, and thus enhance living standards for Americans now and in future generations.

Accordingly, we hope that policymakers at all levels of government will be receptive, at least in principle, to the kinds of ideas broached in this book. We do not expect any of them to be adopted all at once, or even many of them to be implemented. But we modestly hope to have stimulated a much-needed discussion among academic scholars, policymakers, and interested citizens over the linkages between laws, legal systems, and innovation and growth that will be both continuing and beneficial for years to come.

TABLE 1.1 RULES FOR GROWTH:
A SUMMARY OF OPTIONS

Note:
J = changes in judicial doctrine
P = private law/organizational change
R = changes in regulation or administrative actions
S = statutory change

Law and the Entrepreneur

Importing Entrepreneurs: Immigration Reform

- (S) Increase the number and allocation of H1B and EB visas.
- (S) Grant new visas for immigrant graduates of U.S. universities.
- (S) Grant new visas for immigrant entrepreneurs.

Enhancing Academic Entrepreneurship

- (P) Standardize licensing of technologies developed by faculty inventors.
- (P) Create multi-university technology commercialization consortiums to realize economies of scale.
- (P) Use successful serial entrepreneurs to screen technologies for commercialization.
- (P) Allow faculty inventors freedom to license (Free Agency).
- (P) Permit faculty inventors to own all intellectual property in their innovations.

Enhancing Replication and thus Effectiveness of Scientific Research

- (P) Legal obstacles to dissemination, sharing, use and re-use of scientific research should be minimized and require strong and compelling rationale before use.
- (R, S) Government funding agency policy should require openness and sharing of data (including greater enforcement of current sharing policies, promoting public access to final manuscripts by the creation of digital archives, and documenting and disseminating best practices).
- (S) An automatic exception from patent use restriction on code used for academic research purposes should be created.

Law and Finance

Growth-Enhancing Tax Reform

- (S) Shift toward a consumption tax.
- (S) Make research and development (R&D) tax credit permanent.
- (S) Make R&D credit flat rather than incremental.
- (S) Narrow the definition of qualified research to require that research exceed, expand, or refine commonly held knowledge.

Improving Financial Regulation and Reporting

- (R) Accounting rules should require public corporations to list all of their assets and liabilities on their balance sheets.
- (R) Policymakers and regulators should rely more on private market signals (such as those from the credit default swap market) to set and enforce rules.
- (S, R) Regulators could implement rules that rely on market measures of risk instead of measures of risk generated by oligopolistic regulated institutions (such as credit rating agencies).
- (S, R) Policymakers should consider consolidating rather than expanding the number of regulatory agencies.
- (S) Cost-benefit requirement for rule making should be extended to independent agencies.
- (S, R) Regulators should more explicitly consider a range of regulatory options that could achieve a targeted benefit, and adopt an approach that opposes the minimum regulatory cost for a given benefit.
- (R) Regulators should increase disclosure as to how ratings of securities are determined.
- (S, R) The Federal Reserve's independence should be maintained.
- (S, R) Securities class actions should be reformed; shareholders should be allowed to decide whether to keep them at all and, if so, in what form.

Law and Firm Operations

Public and Private Law Production

- (J, S) Open legal markets to competition, initially by creating a federal licensing regime that exempts providers from state-based regulation by the bar and state supreme courts.

- (S) Develop a public-law framework for privately produced legal regimes.
- (S) Reduce barriers to trade in legal regimes in both state-by-state and international transactions.

Contracts

- (J) Induce efficient, transaction-specific investment by both parties.
- (J) Establish a framework for iterative collaboration and adjustment of the parties' obligations under conditions of continuing uncertainty.
- (J) Limit the risk of opportunism that could undermine parties' incentive to make relation-specific investments in the first place.

Torts (Contrasting Recommendations)

- (J, S) Some participating authors favor eliminating courts' reliance on custom in making liability determinations; others disagree.
- (J, S) Some participating authors support using fault only in the context of comparative negligence and otherwise moving toward strict liability; others sharply disagree, believing that further movements toward strict liability would stifle innovation.

Legal Process

- (S) Proposals aimed at increasing growth through a change in law or legal institutions should recognize the existence of multiple jurisdictions and the potential for jurisdictional choice and competition.
- (S) Federal law could impose procedural constraints on state laws blocking enforcement of choice law contracts.

Antitrust

- (R, J) Markets should be defined to include the prospect of global, not simply U.S. domestic, competition.
- (R) The United States should aggressively oppose the application of antitrust laws of other countries that have less economically sound antitrust regimes.
- (S) The United States should expand antitrust laws to prohibit protectionism and industry subsidies wherever they appear.
- (R, J) Special antitrust rules should take account of the unique characteristics of network industries.

Land Use and Zone Laws

- (R, S) Price growth, don't prohibit it; properly calibrated exactions can enable efficient growth by pricing it, thereby forcing developers and consumers to internalize the costs of new development.
- (R, S) Promote interjurisdictional competition, don't stifle it; interjurisdictional competition subjects local governments to some approximation of market competition and may spur regulatory innovations that themselves promote growth and innovation.
- (R, S) Develop alternatives to traditional zoning regulations.

Law and Technology

Cyberlaw

- (S, J) Courts and legislatures should consistently limit the extent to which existing players that own elements of platform technologies use the law to extract value from new parties dependent on those platforms.
- (J) Accept the chaotic, complex, open nature of a system that has been important to innovation and growth; do not try to make order with law.
- (S, J) Employ a narrow construction of scope and applicability of control points based on copyrights or patents (such as employing a broad reading of the *de minimis* doctrine and continuing to expand Digital Millennium Copyright Act exemptions through the Librarian of Congress).
- (S) Create a new kind of injunctive relief in copyright cases that would tie damage-like payments to actual revenue of entrepreneurs who use existing copyrighted materials without permission.
- (S) Eliminate business method patents.

Digital Incorporation

- (S) Authorize a fully digital formation process for corporations and LLCs.
- (S) Authorize a wide range of digital communication as ways in which the formal actions of the corporation and LLC may be taken.
- (S) Authorize the use of software as the original means for setting out agreements and bylaws that govern the actions of LLCs and corporation.

Identity and Privacy

- (R) Subjecting social rule making to scientific and technological modeling and experimentation will spur technological competition and innovation for governance.
- (S, R) Statutes and regulations must encourage and incentivize the innovative use of technologies to create spaces where the expectation of privacy can be met and enforced.
- (S, R) Provide protections to those innovators who take legitimate risks to improve the protection and sharing of private information.
- (R) Establish an open, evolving governance platform for privacy and security that encourages and engages an ongoing series of real world market experiments.
- (R) Encourage the adoption of independent digital auditing and rating mechanisms.

Intellectual Property

- (S, R) Apply evenhandedly a second-pair-of-eyes review (SPER), in which patent applications undergo a second examination, if adopted, to weed out bad patents.
- (R) Change training and incentives so that patent examiners search prior art more effectively.
- (R) The U.S. Patent Office should focus its examination resources on important patents and place less emphasis on the rest; importance would be determined by a tiered review process in which inventors would pay for patent reviews, which would serve as a signal for validity (in theory, by only paying for those they viewed as most important).
- (S) Develop a post-grant opposition process—triggered by competitors—that further scrutinizes a patent and can harness private information from patent competitors; this would signal to the Patent and Trademark Office which patents are the most serious and important.

Secure Platforms for Future Growth

- Develop a comfort level with a certain degree of platform surveillance.
- Develop clear rules assigning liability for platform vulnerabilities that are recklessly introduced or maintained in the system.

- Most challenging, recognize that certain companies, by dint of their businesses, may have unique *affirmative obligations* to the security of platforms.

2 : Producing Law for Innovation[1]

Gillian Hadfield*

I t is a lesson we know well from the events of the past several decades: Whatever their flaws, regulated markets do a better job than central planners in governing the production and distribution of goods and services. They do so because they harness private incentives to seek out the potential for creating value and because they are capable of processing massive quantities of data and responding to complexity. They don't accomplish these goals without legal structure and constraints—to provide the basic framework for transactions and cooperation (property and contract, for example) and to control externalities and exploitation of the disparities created by the unequal distribution of information and resources. But the problem of creating the legal framework to support and regulate markets to produce goods

---

[1] This chapter is largely based on Gillian K. Hadfield, "Legal Barriers to Innovation: The Growing Economic Cost of Professional Control Over Corporate Legal Markets," *Stanford Law Review* 60 (2008): 1689-1732; Hadfield, "The Role of International Law Firms in Harmonizing Legal Regimes," in *Multijuralism: Manifestations, Causes and Consequences*, ed. Albert Breton et al. (Surrey: Ashgate, 2010); and Hadfield, "Law for a Flat World: Legal Infrastructure and the New Economy," 2010, available at works.bepress.com/ghadfield.

* Gillian Hadfield is Kirtland Professor of Law and Professor of Economics at the University of Southern California where she also directs the Southern California Innovation Project. She currently is a fellow at the Center for Advanced Study in the Behavioral Sciences at Stanford University.

and services, while daunting, is still an easier one to solve than the massive one of how to direct individual flows of economic inputs and outputs.

Regardless of how well we have learned this lesson when it comes to goods and services, however, we have yet to recognize that it applies as much to the complex task of producing the legal inputs that structure and regulate markets as it does to the task of producing more familiar economic goods and services. Deciding how to regulate a financial institution to forestall massive coordinated failure is as complex a task as determining how to portion and price the risky assets the institution buys and sells, what algorithms will most efficiently conduct trades, and what organizational structures will create the best incentives. Yet by and large we allocate all the latter tasks to the market—private, generally profit-driven firms and entrepreneurs—and the former task to central planning by public actors: politicians, regulators, and judges. Even the ostensibly private players in the legal field— lawyers—operate within a highly insulated market that leaves it up to judges (but, practically speaking, lawyers themselves) to determine who may provide legal services, where, and through what type of organization.

The neat distinction we take for granted—private actors decide how much to produce and how to price it through decentralized market decision making, while public actors set the rules for markets through deliberative and political decision making—may have served us well in a far less complex economy. And indeed, until the late nineteenth century, the legal needs of a (still heavily agrarian) market economy were largely taken care of by the rules of property and contract generated by common law judges and courts. The rise of mass-market manufacturing, transportation and communications in the late nineteenth century fostered the growth of large-scale federal regulation: The first federal regulatory agency, the Interstate Commerce Commission, was established in 1887 and one of the first major federal regulatory statutes, the Sherman Act, was passed in 1890. But even as the economy grew more complex, the goal for regulation remained relatively simple: control the capacity of large-scale enterprises to increase prices and reduce wages.

The regulatory goals of the twenty-first century are far more complex. We do not want merely to constrain monopoly power; we also want to foster economic growth and innovation to achieve a diverse set of public and private goals. Moreover, the environment in which our regulatory efforts must operate is characterized by high levels of complexity and rapid change. This puts great pressure on the capacity of deliberative central planning to generate the structural and regulatory rules necessary to coax the results we want out of decentralized agents. The information demands alone are staggering and beyond the ken of isolated institutions or comprehensive rational analysis. Again, we know this in the context of ordinary economic production. We call this the "knowledge economy" because information is an increasingly essential input into the production process and a key economic output. In order to compete, producers of goods and services have to be deeply in touch with and capable of responding to exploding amounts of information. To do so, they are moving away from the model of hierarchical organization—the prototypical twentieth-century "managerial enterprise" engaged in the rational top-down planning that Alfred Chandler (1977) described[2]—and toward highly decentralized models that rely on networks, open innovation and flexible alliances in order to harness the capacity to process and respond rapidly to new information.[3] Moreover, they are doing so on a web-based platform that is fundamentally global and not national in structure. And yet we still are looking to centralized bodies such as national and state legislatures, regulatory agencies, and courts to write the rules of the system.

As we explore the nature of the legal rules necessary to achieve the dynamic goals of growth and innovation, we need also to consider the fundamental question of the production methods by

---

[2] Alfred D. Chandler, Jr., *The Visible Hand: The Managerial Revolution in American Business* (Cambridge, MA: Belknap Press, 1977).

which these rules will be generated. Much of our discussion about the rules for growth assumes that the rules can be developed by deliberation and rational analysis—by law professors, economists, judges, regulators, legislators (and their lobbyists)—and implemented by rational processes: voting, agency rule making, judicial argument, and decision. We undoubtedly have to continue to rely heavily on these methods to produce legal rules and procedures to foster growth and innovation. But it is essential—in order to cope with the staggering information and adaptation demands of a high-velocity, innovation-intensive global economy—also to harness for the benefit of legal production the same decentralized and market-based methods we rely on for the innovation and production of ordinary goods and services.

We should be looking for ways to foster the development, for example, of competitive private providers of legal rules and procedures, providers who succeed or fail based on the success of their systems in achieving the goals established for them. Instead of or in addition to the jurisdictional competition between the legislatures of Delaware, Nevada, and Pennsylvania for the business of incorporation and corporate governance systems that Butler and Ribstein discuss in this volume,[4] we also should be looking for competition between "Governance Inc.," "Corporation.com," and "Enterprise Partners." Similarly, instead of competition between California and New York for the business of providing contract law, we should be looking for competition between

---

[3] Todd R. Zenger and William S. Hesterly, "The Disaggregation of Corporations: Selective Intervention, High-Powered Incentives, and Molecular Units," *Organization Science* 8 (1997): 209–22; Bengt Holmstrom and John Roberts, "The Boundaries of the Firm Revisited," *Journal of Economic Perspectives* 12 (1998): 73-94; Timothy J. Sturgeon, "Modular Production Networks: A New American Model of Industrial Organization," *Industrial and Corporate Change* 11 (2002): 451–96; Richard N. Langlois, "The Vanishing Hand: The Changing Dynamics of Industrial Capitalism," *Industrial and Corporate Change* 12 (2003): 351–85; Naomi R. Lamoreaux, Daniel M.G. Raff, and Peter Temin, "Beyond Markets and Hierarchies: Toward a New Synthesis of American Business History" *American Historical Review* 108 (2003): 404–33; and Ronald J. Gilson, Charles F. Sabel and Robert E. Scott, "Contracting for Innovation: Vertical Disintegration and Interfirm Collaboration," *Columbia Law Review* 109 (2009): 431.

[4] Henry Butler and Larry Ribstein, "Legal Process and the Discovery of Better Policies for Fostering Innovation and Growth," this volume, chapter 19.

"Contract Management Ltd." and "Simple Contracting Unlimited." Instead of competition between the United Kingdom's Financial Services Authority and the Securities and Exchange Commission, we should be looking for competition among multiple private, for-profit and nonprofit entities for the business of supplying approved regulatory regimes. And instead of a single monopolized "legal" profession controlled by bar associations, we should be looking for a wide variety of alternative suppliers of legal advice, documents, relationship management, liability predictions, and representation. In this more open and competitive world of legal production, we could turn not only to the expert judgment of traditional legal practitioners operating in law firm partnerships to decide what language to include in a contract or what pretrial motions to bring, but also to data analysis companies that use sophisticated software to analyze liability risks and rewards. We also could turn to not only contracts and threatened litigation to manage business deals, but also to relationship management companies that integrate legal and nonlegal tools to help commercial parties allocate risk, coordinate the efforts, distribute rewards, and resolve disputes. Similarly, we could turn not only to traditional bylaws and board meetings to govern the corporation, but also to digital platforms that coordinate and implement corporate activity.

In this chapter, I first discuss why we need to think of legal infrastructure as economic infrastructure requiring focused economic policymaking, what is wrong with our existing legal infrastructure, and why we need to change our modes of legal production. I then set out a vision of what greater reliance on market-based production of legal infrastructure could look like. Finally, I suggest some concrete steps that policymakers can take to move us toward a more open, competitive system of legal production. These include:

- **Opening up access to the provision of legal services,** initially by creating a federal licensing regime that exempts providers from state-based regulation by the bar and state supreme courts. Among other things, the federal regime should eliminate restrictions on the ownership and management of the providers of legal goods and services to commercial clients and geographical restrictions on where these entities supply their products.

- **Establishing the public law framework necessary to enable competitive private legal providers to emerge.** An easy place to start with this is authorizing private (not necessarily lawyer-owned and managed) firms to supply commercial contracting and recognized incorporation/corporate governance regimes.

- **Reducing barriers to trade in legal services.** In addition to reducing the state-by-state barriers now imposed on the provision of legal services domestically, policymakers also should move to eliminate international restrictions on legal services transactions that cross international borders—protecting overseas legal process outsourcers and law firms, for example, from the threat of unauthorized practice of law charges and obtaining reciprocal trade benefits for U.S. legal providers in foreign markets.

LEGAL INFRASTRUCTURE IS ECONOMIC INFRASTRUCTURE

If the first lesson of the collapse of centrally planned economies during the past several decades was that regulated markets are better at directing resources to produce and distribute value, the second lesson was that markets require a great deal of legal infrastructure in order to function effectively. Comparing Russia and Poland after the fall of the Soviet state, Jeffrey Sachs (a principal economic advisor to both countries in the early 1990s) concluded that "the contrast in reform outcomes . . . revolve centrally around the differing roles of law in the two societies" and that "it is in the legal realm that we find many of the deepest weaknesses and greatest hopes for our age."[5]

---

[5] Jeffrey Sachs, "Globalization and the Rule of Law," *Yale Law School Occasional Papers*, paper 2 (2008), http://digitalcommons.law.yale.edu/ylsop_papers/2.

I define *legal infrastructure* as the set of legal inputs available to the participants in an economy to structure and regulate their economic relationships. This set includes formal legal rules and principles, but it goes well beyond the laws on the books. It also includes:

- the formal and informal elements of procedure for invoking or challenging the enforcement of rules—such as civil procedure and evidence codes;
- the norms and practices, and costs, of legal advising;
- the standard forms and collected contract and other document templates available in legal databases, and the procedures and rules that govern access to those databases;
- the accumulated conventional wisdom about regulatory and dispute-resolution strategies; and
- the stock of knowledge accumulated by legal practitioners through formal education, trade publications, conferences, patterns of training and expertise, and anecdotal experiences.

These features of the legal environment influence the cost and efficacy of any particular legal solution that might appear on the books, and they affect the likelihood of learning about and deploying such a solution. They are inputs to an economic output, namely the structuring of a particular economic relationship.

Why call this legal "infrastructure" and not legal "system" or "regime"? The concepts of legal "system" or "regime" generally refer to the formal elements of a legal environment—and in particular, its formal institutional structures such as the role of the judiciary or constitutional allocation of powers—and focus on the law as seen from the vantage point of the lawyer and judge. These concepts frame deliberative legal analysis, the formal design of legal processes and argument. The concept of infrastructure, in contrast, emphasizes that, like the classical forms of physical infrastructure—highways, railways, electric power grids, telephone lines—and the critical infrastructure of the information economy—the Internet—legal infrastructure "lies beneath" the economic relationships it helps to structure. It is "embedded in other structures, social arrangements and technologies," and while designed, it is ultimately organic and emergent: "Infrastructure does not grow *de novo*; it wrestles with the inertia of the installed base."[6] Perhaps most importantly, the concept of infrastructure shifts the focus away from the perspective of legal analysts and onto the perspective of those who use law to structure their relationships. It emphasizes the pervasive role of law in everyday efforts to coordinate and support cooperative economic activity. If we want to speak to someone in a distant place, our ability to do so is structured by the quality and reach of the voice communications infrastructure. If we want to risk investing time, opportunity, and wealth into a joint venture with someone, our ability to do so is structured by the quality and reach of our legal infrastructure. And like physical infrastructure, what we care about is what we can do and at what cost with the tools actually available to us in this infrastructure, not the blueprint for the system as designed by its engineers. A telephone system is no good to us if it requires an overly expensive handset or if the system has been hacked to broadcast our conversations. Similarly, a legal system is no good to us if it requires overly expensive lawyers, or if in practice the application of legal rules is distorted by graft or incompetence.

Legal infrastructure as I've defined it is economic infrastructure. This is not true of all law, of course. Law also provides the fundamental architecture of democratic political relationships: the rights and duties of citizens and the authority and limits of democratic institutions. But the elements of law on which I want to focus are those that structure and regulate economic relationships—these account for a very large share of law in modern market democracies. It is in this context that I emphasize that legal inputs such as rules of contract or the practices of corporate attorneys are fundamentally economic inputs. It is also in this context that we need to approach the question of legal policy—what

---

[6] Susan Leigh Star and Karen Ruhleder, "Steps Toward an Ecology of Infrastructure: Design and Access for Large Information Spaces," *Information Systems Research* 7 (1996): 111–134.

should our legal rules and institutions look like and how should they be produced?—as a question of economic policy. This is why I take as my starting point in analyzing the production of law the same starting point that we adopt when analyzing how other economic goods and services should be produced: Should this be produced by the state or by the market? If by the market, what is the proper role of government in supporting and regulating this market? In the normative framework we adopt in this book, these are questions that I analyze with reference to dynamic efficiency, innovation, and growth. This is not to deny an important role for political constraints based on the goals of equality, fairness, autonomy, security, dignity, and so on. These are legal objectives that are legitimately produced within accountable political institutions and not private markets. But it is important to see clearly that much of our legal policy is not fundamentally political or jurisprudential; it is economic. There is therefore a much broader scope for market-based legal production than currently recognized.

WHAT DOES OUR EXISTING LEGAL INFRASTRUCTURE LOOK LIKE?

Most people take it as definitional that law is a political, bureaucratic, and judicial product generated by legislatures, administrative agencies, and courts. And indeed, the more formal elements of our current legal infrastructure—legal rules and principles— are largely produced by federal and state governments and judiciaries. There are pockets of nongovernmental rule production. In the financial industry, for example, individual exchanges and the Financial Industry Regulatory Authority (FINRA) generate rules for their members under the oversight of the SEC. Many trade associations, including those for grain, cotton, and diamond merchants, provide systems of contracting and dispute resolution to govern their members.[7] Many think of contracting itself in the Anglo-American tradition—in which contracting parties rather than the state design the rules governing their relationships—as an example of private lawmaking. But these are relatively limited exceptions to the dominant reliance on legislatures, government agencies, and courts to formally generate binding legal rules. This means that nearly all of our legal rules are produced through political and deliberative mechanisms: committees, lobbying, voting, litigation, and formal abstract reasoning. Rules emerge, or do not emerge, based on whether they appeal to voters, experts, and judges—not necessarily on the basis of how well or efficiently they accomplish a task or whether they can survive competition with an alternative that achieves the goals of legal regulation better or more cheaply, or with greater product differentiation. To the extent there is competition, it is regulatory or jurisdictional competition between legislatures and public regulators. While such competition can promote better legal rules,[8] it is important to recognize that it does not follow the same logic or necessarily produce the same results as competition between private profit-maximizing firms.[9]

Legal services are provided in markets—almost all lawyers are private individuals who charge for their services (1 percent are public defenders and legal aid attorneys who may be employed by governments or funded by nonprofit agencies)—but our markets for legal services are among the most closed and highly regulated markets in the U.S. economy. Entry into the legal services markets is heavily restricted: Bar associations and state supreme courts claim regulatory authority over the entire "practice of law," which is vaguely defined but generally amounts to "anything lawyers do."[10] Providers must obtain a law degree, the requirements of which are set by state bar associations, which

---

[7] Lisa Bernstein, "Opting Out of the Legal System: Extralegal Contractual Relationships in the Diamond Industry," *Journal of Legal Studies* 21 (1992): 115; Bernstein, "Merchant Law in a Merchant Court: Rethinking the Code's Search for Immanent Business Norms," *University of Pennsylvania Law Review* 144 (1996): 1765; and Bernstein, "Private Commercial Law in the Cotton Industry: Creating Cooperation Through Rules, Norms and Institutions," *Michigan Law Review* 99 (2001): 1724.

[8] Erin O'Hara and Larry Ribstein, *The Law Market* (New York: Oxford University Press USA, 2009).

[9] Gillian K. Hadfield and Eric Talley, "On Public versus Private Provision of Corporate Law," *Journal of Law, Economics and Organization* 22 (2006): 414–441.

[10] Hadfield, "Legal Barriers to Innovation."

serve as the exclusive accreditation body. Accreditation standards for law schools are significantly more intrusive than other professions such as engineering. Moreover, because a license to practice is dependent on passing an exam set by the bar association, law school curricula are heavily oriented toward achieving educational objectives controlled by lawyers themselves. Collectively, these entry requirements generate a homogenous pool from which the entire industry is supplied—there is little room for entrepreneurial entrants who might devise unconventional methods of achieving the goals of law more quickly, cheaply, and effectively. If a similar regulatory structure had been in place in the 1990s in the "practice of information cataloging and search," we wouldn't have Google. Its founders, Sergey Brin and Larry Page, who were PhD students in engineering at the time, would have been required to obtain advanced degrees in library science before being authorized to develop new methods of organizing and finding information.

Once admitted into the industry, any legal entrepreneurs who have survived the homogenizing forces of law school and the bar exam face further barriers. In the ostensible name of ethics, bar associations (endorsed by state supreme courts) place severe restrictions on the organizational and financial structure of legal businesses. Legal services can only be provided to the market by lawyers who operate within firms owned, managed, and 100 percent financed by lawyers. (Lawyers who are employed by other types of organizations can only provide in-house legal services to their employer.) This means that legal inputs cannot be provided by corporations that are financed with public or private equity or that are created or managed by nonlawyers. Nor can entrepreneurs seek the backing of friends and family, angel investors, or venture capital firms to support the development of new legal business tools, markets, and models. This severely restricts the potential for innovation. Entrepreneurs outside of law who see a better way to do things are prevented even from engaging in a joint venture with lawyers to deliver services. Even law firms owned by lawyers cannot put in place the kind of covenants not to compete that other businesses routinely implement to protect the business against losing customers to departing employees who rely on firm contacts to build their business. This limits the potential for a law firm to build firm capital and diminishes the incentive for the firm to invest in innovation, training, and growth.

Our heavy reliance on government production and a professional monopoly administered by lawyers generates a legal infrastructure characterized by several features that hamper our ability to support innovation and growth. These features include:

Heavy reliance on document/text-based rules: Our legal environment is awash in a high volume of document-based rules. There are more relevant documents, and the length and density of documents such as statutes, legal opinions, and contracts are, by all accounts, much greater today than fifty years ago. (Compare the length of the Glass-Steagall Act of 1933—thirty-six pages—to the length of the 2010 Financial Services Reform Act—almost 2,000 pages.) The problem is not merely volume. Growing specialization within legal practice[11] makes skilled interpretation of many legal documents the province of a shrinking subset of legal experts.

Human capital–intensive craft production: Legal services are characteristically provided on a scholarly craft model: The legal situation facing an individual client is evaluated by an attorney on an individual basis and an individualized strategy or plan is developed and implemented. Lawyers rely heavily on acquired experience and personal judgment in assessing the likely content and consequences of a legal relationship. There is little systematic and quantitative data either available or put to use in developing legal advice or documents. There is minimal use of automated or computer-based methods to produce or deliver legal inputs, such as the predicted effect of different contract clauses or compliance strategies.

---

[11] John P. Heinz, Robert L. Nelson, Edward O. Laumann, and Ethan Michelson, "The Changing Character of Lawyers' Work: Chicago in 1975 and 1995," *Law and Society Review* 32 (1998): 751.

Undiversified production models: With the important exception of in-house counsel (approximately 8–10 percent of the profession), almost all lawyers work in all-lawyer environments where they are exposed to the ideas and problem-solving techniques of people with their same training and intellectual orientation.[12] There are few collaborative enterprises that merge legal expertise with other business expertise. Legal enterprises must be exclusively financed by withheld profits and bank loans, cutting innovators off from large-scale capital markets, private equity, and third-party financing and insurance. This lack of financial diversification limits the risk-bearing capacity of the firm and may account in part for the high levels of risk aversion we see in legal practitioners more generally.

Mandatory rules: Most of the legal rules governing the conduct of a company or organization and available to it for structuring its business dealings are the product of government actors and are by and large mandatory: Their applicability is not a matter of choice for the affected entities. There are important exceptions—such as the choice of state of incorporation or governing contract law—but there is little scope for choosing a regulatory or liability regime. Moreover, with the potential for claims to be framed as legal questions in multiple ways, the set of mandatory rules applicable to a given activity is frequently fragmented and overlapping.[13]

WHAT'S WRONG WITH OUR EXISTING LEGAL INFRASTRUCTURE?

Of course, there is no reason to explore the potential for law to be supplied by competitive private markets if the largely nonmarket

---

[12] Heinz et al.

[13] Robert Kagan, *Adversarial Legalism: The American Way of Law* (Cambridge, MA: Harvard University Press, 2001), 25–29, presents a detailed picture of how multiple federal, state and municipal regulatory agencies, along with federal and state courts, generated a tangled web of litigation and regulatory process that delayed by several years the dredging of the harbor in Oakland, California to accommodate larger containerships.

legal infrastructure we currently have is serving our policy objectives of dynamic efficiency, innovation, and growth. But there are solid theoretical reasons to think it is not, particularly as the new web-based global economy moves into full swing and innovation and dynamic adaptation become key drivers of growth. The transformations in the economy that we have witnessed in the past two decades, with globalization and the migration of much of the organization of work, trade, and communication onto the Internet, also has transformed the nature of what we need law to do in order to support and regulate economic activity.

Compared to the prototypical firm in the early to mid-twentieth century, when our current legal infrastructure was laid down, the prototypical twenty-first century firm demands more and different legal inputs to meet several shifts in the economic demand for law. These shifts include:

Increased firm-boundary crossing: The pervasive shift away from vertical integration to increased reliance on networks, alliances, and global supply chains generates heavy demand for contracting inputs that are capable of managing more complex, flexible, and information-rich relationships. Today the paradigmatic contractual relationship is a joint venture or outsourcing contract, posing very different contracting challenges than the paradigmatic sales contract of the nineteenth and early twentieth century.

Increased jurisdictional boundary crossing: A greater demand for complex contracting inputs is also prompted by the significant increase in cross-border transactions. Regulatory approaches also have to cross jurisdictional boundaries more frequently and in more complex ways as the extent of global interconnection increases.

More pervasive and complex transactions in information: In the new economy, information is a prime object of economic transactions, and information asymmetries are a pervasive attribute of bargaining relationships. But transactions in information or under information asymmetries are especially difficult to structure. There is therefore a greater demand for various forms of protection for intellectual property—particularly IP that is not embodied in a concrete product—and for more tools to address the contracting obstacles information assets pose.

Faster depreciation and obsolescence of legal solutions: The higher velocity of the new economy reduces the lifespan of any particular legal solution, and shifts the relative value of adaptable as opposed to fixed solutions. This requires greater emphasis on dynamic as opposed to static legal analysis.

Increased differentiation of demand: The new economy is characterized by more heterogeneity in products and business relationships. This implies a more differentiated demand for legal solutions. As firms innovate new products and relationships, they face challenges often highly specific to their circumstances. Unlike the sales relationships that dominated the "old" economy, one size does not fit all, or even very many, very well.

Lower margins for legal transaction costs: Legal solutions that have a shorter lifespan and that are developed to address particular rather than standardized products, contexts, or relationships have to be cheaper. The global scale of competition can also put more pressure on transaction costs than was the case in the era of relatively insulated megafirms. And the startups and entrepreneurs who are the lifeblood of the innovation economy lack the scale and financial wherewithal to take on substantial legal expenses.

Greater demand for integration of legal and business expertise: In an economy with high levels of standardization, we can expect legal solutions to effectively capitalize knowledge about the business or regulatory considerations that, for example, a sales contract or employment policy needs to address. But in an environment of heterogeneity and rapid change, the essential problem solving that is at the core of legal work is an ongoing task. This requires legal analysis that is explicitly integrated with all of the elements of business problem solving, rather than unexamined reliance on the solutions found in standardized processes, strategies, and documents.

The changes in what we need in order to address the legal needs of the new economy are now substantially mismatched with what our old-economy legal infrastructure has to offer. The scholarly craft orientation of law implies that lawyers, regulators, judges, and legislators respond to the complexities of the globalizing new economy with the idea that more complexity in the environment must be met with more, and more complex, documents: more words and more specialized drafting. But this is a very costly and slow process and runs counter to factors that are increasing the demand for less costly legal solutions to deal with an increasing number of heterogeneous relationships that are bound to change in short order. Longer, more complex documents and statutes increase the specialization in human capital required to implement and engage in adversarial (often winner-take-all) contests organized around these written materials. But human capital specialization is a key reason why legal markets are noncompetitive—raising the price of legal solutions in a profound way that goes beyond the simple notion that it takes more work to draft 100 pages than it does ten.[14] Greater legal specialization also increases rather than decreases the challenges of integrating legal and business problem solving. This increases the gap between what legal solutions provide and what enterprises and regulators need to address novel, challenging, and rapidly changing environments.

In a competitive environment, we would expect legal providers to adapt to and fix these problems. But the structural features of our legal infrastructure largely prevent competitive responses such as these. Many of the rules are publicly provided and politicians and regulators do not face competitive incentives organized around the efficiency of the statutes and regulations they produce. Because most legal rules are mandatory, there is little scope for businesses or those with regulatory goals to shift to a more productive legal environment. And because of the tight regulation lawyers have imposed on their own profession, there is little

---

[14] Gillian K. Hadfield, "The Price of Law: How the Market for Lawyers Distorts the Justice System," *Michigan Law Review* 98 (2000): 953–1006.

scope or incentive for innovation in even the ostensibly market-based aspects of our legal infrastructure. These are the features of our legal system that are most in need of change in order to promote innovation in the legal infrastructure that will better serve the needs of dynamic efficiency, innovation, and growth.

WHAT WOULD MARKET-BASED LEGAL PRODUCTION LOOK LIKE AND WHY COULD IT DO BETTER?

Market-based production of legal inputs already can be found to some degree in our existing legal system. Private nonprofit organizations such as the American Institute of Architects create and distribute (and sometimes copyright) standard contracting forms for the use of their members and the general public. Commercial entities such as Nolo Press and LegalZoom sell blank documents or software to help people create documents. Most organizations, largely on a contract basis, develop and implement their own internal grievance and human resources procedures. Private dispute resolution services are widely available either as arbitration or mediation. There are market-based document preparers who can fill in documents such as bankruptcy petitions, and e-discovery providers who store and sift through high volumes of electronic documents for litigation purposes.

But these represent ultimately small and still fairly restricted slices of the legal pie. In a world with fewer restrictions on market-based provision of legal inputs, the array of market options would be far greater than it is now. Although one of the key attributes of markets is that they can produce surprising solutions that abstract analysis cannot, we can make some conjectures about what this world would look like.

We would expect a more open legal market to include a variety of providers of legal services, not just JD-trained bar-examined lawyers. Indeed, England and Wales already have eight alternative training and licensing regimes for different types of legal providers, many of whom compete to serve the same clients with legal advice, planning, and representation. Some of these regimes require the traditional university degrees; others are based on community college programs or practical training and experience-based qualification. In this kind of environment, different demand characteristics operating through this market can sort out who works for whom doing what kind of work, increasing the differentiation and variety required by a more heterogeneous economy.

We would expect a more open market also to be characterized by corporate legal providers, not just lawyer partnerships, and by entities that integrate legal services with a broader array of goods and services. Large retailers such as Office Depot, which now provide banking, copying, or postal services, could add to their repertoire legal services such as regulatory information and document filing for small businesses. These services then could be provided by employed professionals who have available to them practices and procedures developed on the basis of market testing and data and backed by the quality incentives and malpractice liability of a large organization, rather than the resources and experience of relatively isolated solo practitioners or small local partnerships. The megafirms now providing e-discovery services on a national (if not global) scale, but limited to document storage and filtering, could integrate these services with legal expertise, likely informed not only by traditional legal judgment based on human capital, but also on large-scale data analysis. Legal process outsourcers such as CPA Global would not be required, as they now are in most states, only to provide services under the supervision of a licensed attorney who retains them, assumes liability for them, and serves as a middleman. In a less restrictive environment they could compete head-to-head for clients on a bundled or unbundled basis. This is especially important for startups, as well as small and medium-sized businesses that lack large legal departments. Faced with regulatory, contract, or litigation concerns, these smaller entities could turn to lower-cost and differentiated sources of information and advice (summaries of the law, legal research, document selection, and advice in preparation comparable to accounting advice on taxes, for example), and likely obtain delivery in formats that are better attuned to their needs and budget.

More radically, greater market-based provision of law would also include a greater role for private for-profit and nonprofit entities in providing legal rules.[15] While there is an extensive role for private contracting, private contracts still are subject to state-provided rules of validity, interpretation, and enforcement. But a market-based provider of such rules with an incentive to gain market share and access to investment capital to devote to the costly process of designing better solutions could conceivably shift the entire function of designing and managing contractual relationships away from adversarial dickering over contract language and toward creative multipronged methods for allocating risks, coordinating activities, adapting to change, and resolving disputes. A private competitive corporate governance regime—supplying the rules that are now supplied by state legislatures—could conceivably offer dramatically different models for creating and managing the corporation. In this volume, for example, Oliver Goodenough describes a privately provided digital corporate governance platform that incorporates and then coordinates the relations among owners, managers, and agents. Many of these functions could be performed via algorithms, including algorithms that organically adapt to changing conditions and environmental feedback. Developing systems like this requires entrepreneurial energy, creativity, and investment capital—things lacking from our current deliberative and public systems of law production.

Shifting the provision of the rules governing contractual and corporate governance relationships to more market-based providers is a relatively easy step. Farther on the horizon we can imagine, however, a greater role for privately provided regimes to substitute for or complement existing publicly provided securities,

---

[15] Gillian K. Hadfield, "Privatizing Commercial Law" Regulation 40 (2001); and Hadfield, "Delivering Legality on the Internet: Developing Principles for the Private Provision of Commercial Law," *American Law and Economics Review* 6 (2004): 154.

environmental, product safety, intellectual property, and other regulation. Organizations in this world would choose their regulator from a competitive array of providers, including private providers. Legal scholars already are discussing the potential for a "portable" securities regulation scheme under which issuers select their regulatory regime from those offered by participating countries, regardless of where they physically issue securities.[16] Expanding the set of available regulators to include private providers requires rethinking the role for public actors in this process, shifting that role from the detailed enactment of thousands of pages of statutory and regulatory provisions to the certification and oversight of competitive private regulatory bodies.

In the United States, securities regulation has included government oversight of self-regulatory bodies such as stock exchanges and broker-dealer associations since the passage of the Securities Exchange Act of 1934. Other professions, including the legal profession, are also private sources of self regulation. There are two key, related, differences between our existing self-regulatory model and the model of competitive private regulatory bodies that I am envisioning. First, self regulation generally refers to a membership organization's regulation of its members. FINRA, for example, regulates those who are members of the New York Stock Exchange. This ties the provision (and hence incentives) of the regulatory product to the provision of the underlying product—in the case of the NYSE, access to a dominant exchange. Second, and related, the providers of regulation are generally monopolists within a broadly defined field. The NYSE might compete with other exchanges for business, but there are no competing regulatory providers for those who want to be members of the NYSE. These features of self regulation weaken the market incentives directed toward better regulation, and raise an almost insurmountable barrier to deauthorizing a private regulator gone

---

[16] Stephen J. Choi and Andrew T. Guzman, "Portable Reciprocity: Rethinking the International Reach of Securities Regulation," *Southern California Law Review* 71 (1998): 903; Roberta Romano, "The Need for Competition in International Securities Regulation," *Theoretical Inquiries in Law* 2 (2001): 387; and Howell E. Jackson and Eric J. Pan, "Regulatory Competition in International Securities Markets: Evidence from Europe in 1999: Part I," *Business Law Review* 56 (2001): 653.

astray: Deregistering the NYSE as an authorized exchange because of regulatory failures is probably not on anyone's reform agenda. In a more open system of privately supplied regulatory systems, the provision of regulatory services could be provided separately from membership in an underlying economic entity. We could expect to see the emergence of regulatory service firms, specializing in the design and implementation of regulation to achieve publicly established performance goals. These firms would compete, and would be exposed to the risk of product innovation and cost reduction from other regulation providers and new entrants. We would expect them to rely more on the tools of the marketplace to develop their "product"—investing in research, testing products in the market, collecting and analyzing data, retaining a wide variety of specialists—than on the (often weakly funded and weakly researched) governmental processes of hearings, committee meetings, and rule making that self-regulatory membership organizations often employ.

The regulation of the legal profession embodied in the United Kingdom's Legal Services Act of 2007 is an example of this new model: a publicly accountable and appointed body (the Legal Services Board, which must be dominated by nonlawyers) manages the designation and oversees the performance of private regulators. Any entity may apply to be an approved regulator. While the current set of eight approved regulators reflects significant continuation of historical models of self regulation by membership organizations engaged in differentiated activities—the Solicitors Regulatory Authority regulates solicitors and the Bar Council regulates barristers—it is clear that the new model will allow alternative regulators, which are not membership organizations, to seek approval and compete for the business of licensing practitioners. Indeed, the Institute for Legal Executives, which sets out an alternative non-University path to qualification to perform many of the same tasks historically performed by solicitors, although also a membership organization, is clearly a step in this direction. More generally, given the erosion of limitations on the scope of approved practice for members of these different legal professions—barristers in England now may contract directly with clients and need not be retained exclusively by a solicitor, while solicitors and legal executives now may gain rights of audience in some higher level courts—these multiple professional bodies (as well as new entrants) can begin to compete and differentiate across training and regulatory requirements. This competition can reduce the need for excessive and expensive training of those who provide many legal services.

On the farthest horizon, we can envision a world in which specialized private regulatory services firms (not industry membership organizations) design and implement regulations in a wide variety of areas such as health care, environmental protection, intellectual property, product safety, and workplace conduct. In this world, public regulators—legislators and administrative agencies—could focus on identifying performance and outcome targets for regulation and monitor the success of the regulatory body at a relatively macro level. Private firms seeking status as approved regulators would have to demonstrate success in achieving regulatory objectives and would then compete for the business of those who require, in turn, regulatory approval.

WHAT DO WE HAVE TO CHANGE TO FACILITATE MORE MARKET-BASED PRODUCTION OF LAW?

Three essential changes are needed to move toward a greater role for market-based production of law:

1) Open legal markets to competition.
2) Develop a public-law framework for privately produced legal regimes.
3) Reduce barriers to trade in legal services.

I discuss each of these changes in turn.

1) *Open legal markets to competition, initially by creating a federal licensing regime that will exempt legal services supplied to commer-*

cial clients from state-by-state bar and state supreme court regulation.

Opening legal markets to competition requires a substantial shift in the U.S. regulatory environment. The current state-by-state regulatory regime is a major obstacle to reform. Not only is the potential for reform highly fragmented, it is dominated by the voting interests of individual lawyers (who, for example, can have a private interest in expanding the scope of unauthorized practice rules to protect market share) and the deliberative reasoning of those trained in legal analysis. The point that legal infrastructure is, in large part, economic infrastructure is one that a profession at least rhetorically organized around concepts of rights, justice, and due process is likely to have difficulty hearing. More importantly, state judiciaries and bar associations are not really designed to be policymaking institutions, much less economic policymaking institutions. They often lack full-time leadership (like law firm managing partners, most of those who participate in the leadership of bar associations continue their practice) and they lack expert policy staff and resources to devote to policy, particularly data collection and analysis.

At a substantive level, the state-by-state licensing regime limits the potential for significant innovation in legal production by limiting the mobility and scale of legal businesses. Although these limits are routinely ignored in large corporate practice and recent rule changes have softened their edges, on the books it is nonetheless an unauthorized practice of law for a New York lawyer to "practice law" on behalf of a California client or in Californian proceedings involving a New York client. This obviously limits the mobility of individual practitioners. Moreover, by burdening the achievement of scale in the distribution of legal services, state-by-state licensing has a significant impact on the development of innovations such as data-intensive methods for improving on the anecdotal judgment that now drives the human-capital intensive craft model of legal production. It also restricts the development of web-based tools to deliver legal services. Although online providers (such as LegalZoom and Intuitowned MyCorporation.com) can provide documents online and conduct guided interviews to assist users in the completion of the documents, these providers cannot enrich their offering with legal advice, either through data-driven analysis of interview answers or a "chat with a lawyer now!" link on the website. Not only would the provider have to be fully owned, managed, and financed by lawyers in order to provide that service, it would have to ensure that a client in Idaho only received advice from a lawyer licensed to practice in Idaho.

To open competition in legal markets, it is therefore critical to establish a national regulatory regime guided by both legal and economic policymakers. Preempting state regulation, perhaps initially for only subsets of lawyers (such as those providing services to corporations only), is a necessary step both to reduce the fragmentation of the industry and to shift regulation onto an economic policy–based footing. Such a regime should drop the requirement of lawyer ownership, control, and financing of legal businesses and sharply curtail the scope of activities for which formal legal training and bar admission is required. Arguably, business consumers of legal services—particularly larger businesses and those with expert in-house purchasers of these services—should not be under any limitation on who they can hire, domestic or foreign, to perform "legal" work. Where necessary, consumer protection can be much more carefully targeted than it is now; much of the consumer protection that lawyers' regulation now claims it seeks to provide can be provided by existing protections rooted in laws against false advertising, negligence, and related issues. Competition and differentiation in training and practices can be further encouraged by allowing multiple competing national bodies to provide accreditation and licensing where needed. And all limitations imposed on the practice of law by professional associations or accrediting bodies should be subject to ordinary application of antitrust law. Recent restructuring of the legal system in the United Kingdom, where many of these reforms have already been implemented, provides a useful model for the development of a much more competitive and innovative legal market in the United States.

2) Develop a public-law framework for privately produced legal regimes.

Like markets for other goods and services, markets for legal goods and services require a legal framework in which to operate. To move in a policy direction toward a greater role for market-based production of legal goods and services (including formal rules and procedures) does not imply disconnecting entirely from public provision. It merely shifts the locus of public provision back a level, in the same way that the well-understood effort to "privatize" the production of steel in formerly communist states shifts the role of government upstream—out of the daily determination of production volumes and pricing and into the determination of ownership rights over a manufacturing facility, contract dispute resolution, and employment regulation.

In order to create a reasonably competitive market in private contract law systems, for example, we would require publicly provided law that recognized the authority of the private provider to be the exclusive provider of "contract law" for its customers. Note that this is more than providing contract terms: It means establishing the framework in which obligations and commitments become binding on the parties and the basis on which obligations and commitments are implemented, as well as the scope of the authority for the provider to act to manage and adjust the parties' relationship. It also requires enabling private providers to issue orders resolving a contractual dispute (examples include paying damages, delivering promised goods, participating in information exchanges, or resolution procedures) enforceable in state-provided courts. This is what the Federal Arbitration Act (FAA) in the United States accomplishes now: It makes an arbitrator's resolution of a case as effective as if it were resolved by a state court itself. Arguably this is all that we require of the public-law framework to make private contracting systems effective. The fact that we have yet to see robust private contracting providers in the nearly 100 years of experience with the FAA, however, suggests that more may be needed to support the creation of such a system. Public law would have to make it clear, for example, that providing such a system is not an "unauthorized practice of law" (as some may argue is now the case under existing state-by-state professional regulation), enabling corporate entities with public financing and nonlawyer owners and managers to participate and to provide the service across state lines. That such restrictions have constricted the scope for arbitration as an alternative system is evident in the fact that in some cases arbitrators are required to be licensed attorneys,[17] and in many states lawyers have argued and state supreme courts have agreed that representing a party in an arbitration is "the practice of law" and hence nonlawyers and out-of-state lawyers may not provide this service.[18]

Building the framework to support a competitive market in bankruptcy law or corporate law would also seem to be relatively straightforward. In the case of bankruptcy, it would require federal courts to recognize bankruptcy contracts[19] as effectively displacing federally provided default rules. In the case of corporate governance, it would require individual states to recognize incorporation under a privately provided legal regime (governing, for example, duties of directors and meeting requirements) as being as effective as incorporation under the legal regime provided by another state. This would imply according the benefits of incorporation to those who chose the incorporation regime as against third parties, such as tort claimants (who would not be able to sue individual shareholders for their losses in the absence of reasons to pierce the corporate veil), and interpreting contractual or statutory obligations (such as taxes) based on corporate form or bank-

---

[17] See FINRA, Code of Arbitration Procedure for Customer Disputes (FINRA Manual), §10211 available at http://finra.complinet.com/en/display/display_main.html?rbid=2403&element_id=4096.

[18] See, e.g., *Rappoport v. Florida Bar*, 540 U.S. 967 (2003); Florida Bar re Advisory Opinion on Non-Lawyer Representation in Securities Arbitration, 696 So.2d 1178, 1180 (Fla. 1997); Virginia State Bar, UPL Opinion 214 (April 8, 2008) available at http://www.vsb.org/site/regulation/upl-opinion-214.

[19] Alan Schwartz, "Contracting about Bankruptcy," *Journal of Law, Economics & Organization* 13 (1998): 127–146.

ruptcy status to apply equally to corporations formed, liquidated, or reorganized under private as well as under public legal rules.

It is conceivable that a market for privately provided corporate governance, bankruptcy, or contracting regimes would require some form of intellectual property protection to generate appropriate incentives to invest in potentially appropriable system design—as Ribstein (2010) argues.[20] And we should expect that a competitive market for private legal regimes would require the oversight of antitrust law and other regulations intended to balance market power or protect consumers against fraud. But these issues should be approached on the same terms that we approach them when we are deciding how best to structure and regulate private markets for ordinary economic goods and services, such as business consulting or computer operating systems.

The much harder case for public framework development arises when there are substantial public interests affected by the content of the private legal regime. Environmental regulations, for example, clearly cannot simply be shunted off to the elections made by the entities that would be subject to the regulation: With no political oversight, those regulations would quite predictably offer next to no environmental protection for the benefit of the public generally. But it is conceivable that we could design public law requirements for a private regime, such as a targeted level of industrial pollution. The key would be to allow and facilitate competition between regulatory bodies and minimize capture by regulated entities. We would also have to address the question of how "conflicts of law" would be resolved in these noncontractual settings where we cannot rely on a negotiated *ex ante* "choice of law" by all involved parties. (Compare, O'Hara, and Ribstein 2009). Understanding how to resolve these difficult design issues is probably beyond the reach of our existing state of knowledge— and the recent regulatory failures attributable in part to self regulation in the financial industry certainly emphasize how difficult the design problem is—but the prospect for building these

---

[20] Larry Ribstein, "The Death of Big Law," *Wisconsin Law Review* (forthcoming).

markets to better meet the demands of increasingly more complex economic activity is something that should be seriously addressed by policy analysis and debate.

3) Reduce barriers to trade in legal goods and services.

Just as domestic restrictions on the practice of law need to be dismantled in order to promote more competitive production of legal inputs, so too do international restrictions need to come down in order to support a truly global market for legal inputs. The global base for the economy and the fundamentally multijurisdictional nature of a growing share of economic activity makes reduction in the barriers to mobility of legal inputs a critical reform for the twenty-first century. But globalization of trade in legal services lags far behind globalization more generally. Most countries have strict local requirements that erect substantial barriers to entry by foreign providers. These restrictions significantly repress the economic incentives for legal practitioners to invest in the invention of transborder legal solutions to address the key feature of the globalizing economy.[21] General counsels of some of our most innovative companies complain that they have no choice but to rely on a "patchwork of providers" to resolve the multijurisdictional issues they face, often long before they achieve the kind of scale that could justify hiring armies of lawyers from different countries: today's innovative firms are "Global from Day One." And even when scale is not the problem, the absence of providers capable of developing solutions to multijurisdictional legal problems—such as those faced by Google distributing YouTube in more than 100 countries around the globe, each with its own laws on privacy, intellectual property, defamation, and national security—is a significant obstacle to growth and innovation.[22]

Around the world, domestic lawyers are protected by requirements that in order to provide services within their borders or on

---

[21] Hadfield, "The Role of International Law Firms."

[22] Hadfield, "Law for a Flat World."

issues related to domestic laws, they must possess a local law degree and pass a local qualifying examination (generally available only in domestic languages). Some countries impose citizenship or residency requirements, or demand that legal providers operate a physical office in the country (inhibiting electronic services). Local restrictions on advertising abound in the United States but they often are even more restrictive in other locations, preventing lawyers from advertising specialties, for example. The effect is to limit competition. Organizational restrictions—such as requirements that lawyers operate only in partnerships, preventing the employment of a lawyer by another lawyer, and prohibiting multiple offices—limit the capacity for growth of law firms to meet global demand. The European Union has reduced many of these barriers, prohibiting differential restriction on the practice of law by lawyers from one member country in another member country. But these benefits do not extend to countries outside the EU.

Domestically, an easy first step to globalizing legal markets would be to eliminate U.S. restrictions on the purchase of overseas legal services by U.S. corporations. This is emerging as a significant issue for U.S. companies as they increasingly seek to reduce burgeoning legal expenditures through the use of low-cost and data-intensive legal services provided by legal process outsourcers such as CPA Global, which is headquartered in the United Kingdom but maintains a large office performing legal support work in India. These companies review, organize, and draft documents, manage contracting processes, conduct legal research, prepare deposition summaries, and more. Currently, such outsourcing is required by state bar association rules to be channeled through and supervised by state-licensed lawyers. Again, federal law may be required to cut through this limitation, reducing the cost of supervision and expanding the availability of these low-cost services to small and medium-sized businesses that lack the in-house resources to perform supervision of offshore legal work.

Internationally, any efforts to open up U.S. markets to offshore providers should also seek reciprocal benefits in other countries. Legal services are covered by the General Agreement on Trade in Services (GATS), thus requiring WTO member states to take steps to ensure that licensing requirements are based on objective criteria and are not overly restrictive. Arguably, then, the framework is already in place to promote these efforts. But on the basis of the assertion that law is fundamentally political in nature and that the independence of the legal profession is a pillar of democratic governance, legal professions worldwide thus far have faced little difficulty protecting restrictive practices from scrutiny. This is why I emphasize that a large share of legal infrastructure is fundamentally economic infrastructure—distinct from the political components of a legal system that are indeed critical to effective democracy.

SUMMARY

A clear recognition of the economic impact of legal policy is essential for the production of the legal infrastructure necessary to promote dynamic efficiency, innovation, and growth in a global economy. Having grown up largely under the stewardship of lawyers informed by distinctively legal analysis, and in the context of a far more stable, homogeneous, and vertically integrated economy, our existing legal infrastructure is increasingly ill suited to meet the needs of our new globalized and increasingly web-based economy. So long as we rely exclusively on lawyers, judges, bureaucrats, and politicians to design our legal rules, and allow lawyers to severely restrict competition in legal markets, we are unlikely to see the kind of entrepreneurial innovation in legal rules, practices, and procedures necessary to meet the rapidly changing demand for the legal inputs that structure and regulate activity in the new economy. A greater role for market-based production of legal inputs promises to harness greater resources and diverse ways of thinking about how to do what law aspires to do more effectively and at lower cost. Some of the reforms needed to open up our legal markets to the kind of competition we need are relatively straightforward to identify and implement, such as eliminating the state-by-state restrictive regulation of legal markets by lawyers and judges who lack both the resources and the orientation (as well as the legitimacy) to approach the task as the problem of economic policy that it is. Other relatively straightforward reforms involve the facilitation of markets for privately provided regimes in areas such as commercial contracting, corporate governance, and bankruptcy. The broader challenges are to design the appropriate framework law to create and oversee competition among private regulatory bodies in a wider range of areas that reach beyond the contracting interests of commercial parties—to areas touching more directly on the public interest such as intellectual property, environmental regulation, and product safety. We should not be surprised if the task is daunting, however; the very reason the task is so necessary is that the complexity of the world that law structures and regulates is already outstripping the capacity of conventional political, bureaucratic, and judicial methods of producing law (as we have witnessed with recent efforts to reform the regulation of massively complex systems such as health care and the financial industry). Matching the radical innovations we have witnessed throughout the global economy, we need to find a way to harness the creativity and investment potential of markets to generate radical innovations in the production of law.

3 ■ Universities and Economic Growth: ■ The Importance of Academic Entrepreneurship

Robert E. Litan and Robert Cook-Deegan*

Though economists continue to debate how best to promote economic growth, there is at least some broad agreement about some elements that contribute to it. Roughly speaking, the growth of the *output* of any economy is a product of the growth of its key *inputs*: physical capital, "human" capital (labor hours adjusted for skill), and a catch-all term labeled "innovation" (or "multifactor productivity" in economic jargon). Furthermore, there is a general agreement that of these three factors, physical capital is probably the least important, and that the sum of the other two—advances in skill levels of people and innovation—are the dominant driving forces.

Given the role of universities in education and in knowledge creation, it is readily apparent why they play an essential role in economic growth. They add to skills of the labor force by disseminating existing and new knowledge through their traditional teaching functions. Although much of the benefit of added skills

* Robert M. Cook-Deegan is a Research Professor of Public Policy; Research Professor, Department of Internal Medicine, School of Medicine; Research Professor, Department of Biology; and Director, Center for Genome Ethics, Law and Policy, Institute for Genome Sciences & Policy at Duke University.

accrues to individual students—especially if they are taught not only specific content but how to learn new content and skills continuously throughout their working lives—there are important benefits for society as a whole of having a more skilled workforce. Generally speaking, more skilled workers are more adaptable and are able to learn and apply new skills as economies change and grow and, in the process, work requirements change. Skilled workers also have the tools to be more resourceful entrepreneurs—those who found new businesses—who are important drivers of innovation and job creation.

But universities, especially "research universities," do a lot more than teach. Through the research of their faculty (and sometimes their students), universities develop new knowledge, which is the basis for the innovation that economists now widely agree is the most important driver of growth in the long run. Some new knowledge is only distantly related to the marketplace for lengthy periods, until enterprising researchers and/or entrepreneurs find ways to combine or refashion it to generate new products, services, or ways of producing them. Examples include fundamental theorems in math and sciences. In other cases, however, university-generated knowledge is more applied in nature at the outset and, with some further experimentation and refinements, can be more quickly disseminated throughout society.

Indeed, university-generated knowledge cannot benefit society, not just in the countries of origin but eventually elsewhere throughout the world, unless it is disseminated. University research reaches others through academic publications, instruction, meetings and symposia, and today, increasingly, via the Internet. When transmitted this way, knowledge is a true "public good," available to anyone, including those who find useful ways of combining the "new" with what they already know or is otherwise publicly available to develop and market some new commercial applications.

Increasingly, universities also engage in commercialization of the innovations developed by their faculty, either by licensing technologies to ongoing businesses or through the launch of new enterprises, in which faculty may—and often do—take a leading role. Some contest whether commercialization should be a university function at all, however. Perhaps the broadest claim is that universities exist to further the creation of new *basic* knowledge, and it is not their role or that of their faculty to engage in commercialization. Based on this view, some worry that commercial activities distort the research interests and detract from the time that faculty members have to give to their basic research and instructional activities. Moreover, it is sometimes claimed that commercialization can distort the values and culture of the university, its faculty, and its leaders.

Universities' primary goals are and should always continue to be the discovery and dissemination of new knowledge. But at the same time, universities are not monasteries. New knowledge for its sake cannot benefit human beings unless it also is applied to real world problems and challenges, and when this is done, the results must be disseminated to society. In market economies, dissemination is often best accomplished when innovations are commercialized, for it is the infusion of human and financial capital that enables innovations to "scale." To take the academic inventors out of this process can significantly reduce the likelihood that discoveries in the lab will be turned quickly to constructive uses by the larger society that exists outside university walls.

Presuming there is a dichotomy between basic and applied knowledge, moreover, is quite frequently a deep conceptual mistake. Some fields of academic research are indeed quite remote from application, but most are not. In the life sciences, in particular, most research is conducted squarely in what Donald Stokes termed "Pasteur's Quadrant," where research is both scientifically valuable and also immensely practical. Most university research is supported by public funds precisely because it promises to contribute to a government mission, such as health, national defense, energy production, or environmental protection. One common pathway entails commercialization of a product or service arising in research funded by government or nonprofit organizations.

In fact, the notion that universities must play an integral role in the commercialization of faculty-generated innovations has been national policy for some time. In 1980, Congress codified this notion in the Bayh-Dole Act, which among other things explicitly grants universities, small businesses, or nonprofit institutions rights to retain intellectual property (IP) in inventions funded by the federal government.

Scholars continue to debate the effectiveness of Bayh-Dole, a subject explored in more detail shortly.[1] Two features of the Bayh-Dole Act are, however, not much in dispute: it made policies far more consistent among agencies, reducing the need for costly and protracted case-by-case negotiation; and it set strong default rules for ownership of intellectual property, again avoiding transaction costs. The act thus increased the efficiency of commercializing technologies arising from federal funding.

Federal funding for research is itself a policy central to achieving social benefit through translation into goods and services. Federal funding of university research has resulted in numerous and important commercial applications. As just one illustration, consider the list of the fifty most important innovations and discoveries funded by the National Science Foundation in its first fifty years, according to the NSF itself in 2000. Although this *Nifty Fifty* list includes some huge basic advances—such as the discovery that the universe is expanding at an accelerating rate—most items on the list are innovations that have been commercialized or have become platforms for many commercial products and services and are widely in use: barcodes, CAD/CAM software, data compression technology used in compact discs, and perhaps most sig-

---

[1] For an excellent summary of the literature on this question, see Frank T. Rothaermel, Shanti D. Agung, and Lin Jiang, "University Entrepreneurship: A Taxonomy of the Literature," *Industrial and Corporate Change* 16, no. 4 (2007): 739-40.

[2] National Science Foundation, *Nifty Fifty* (2000), available at www.nsf.gov/od/lpa/nsf50/nsf-foutreach/htm/home.htm.

nificant of all, the Internet (which the NSF funded along with DARPA, a defense research agency).[2] Not all of the *Nifty Fifty* innovations are high tech, however, but their importance is indisputable. These include yellow barrels used on the sides of highways to slow down out-of-control vehicles before they hit barriers and walls, and the American Sign Language Dictionary, which has changed the lives of the Deaf and hard of hearing.

Another, more recent accounting of the importance of university-generated innovations is reflected in an analysis of the top 100 "most technologically significant new products" listed each year in *R&D* magazine. Fred Block and Matthew Keller report that universities and federal laboratories have become much more important sources of the top 100 innovations over the last thirty-five years.[3] In 1975, for example, they note that private firms accounted for over 70 percent of the R&D 100, while the academic institution share was just 15 percent. By 2006, just three decades later, these two shares were reversed: academia contributed over 70 percent of the top 100 innovations, while private firms accounted for about 25 percent. Presumptively, the primary reason for the turnaround is that after the Bayh-Dole Act of 1980, academic institutions became far more active in research with potential commercial outcomes. The real story is more likely, however, that the huge growth of federal funding for research over the six decades after World War II took a couple decades to begin to translate into commercially significant innovation, and such federal funding for research will continue to be a crucial federal policy affecting the national innovation system.

University-generated innovations should be even more important to the U.S. economy and society in the years ahead. As Jonathan Cole states in his impressive history of universities in

---

[3] Fred Block and Matthew Keller, "Where Do Innovations Come From? Transformations in the U.S. National Innovation System, 1970-2006." (Washington, DC: The Information Technology and Innovation Foundation, 2008).

[4] Jonathan Cole, *The Great American University: Its Rise to Preeminence, Its Indispensable National Role, Why It Must Be Protected* (New York: Public Affairs, 2009), 4.

the United States, *"In the future, virtually every new industry will depend on research conducted at America's research universities."*[4] (emphasis added) Moreover, the federal government is heavily involved in bringing this future about. In 2009, the various federal agencies channeled approximately 60 percent of the $147 billion they spent on research and development—or roughly $90 billion—directly to U.S. universities.[5]

Given the importance of university research to many commercial goods and services, it is critical that university-generated innovation is quickly and efficiently commercialized, for it is often primarily through commercialization that the benefits of innovation are widely disseminated and translated into increases in GDP (and other measures of welfare). This chapter argues that although there is much to applaud in the current system of federal research support and commercialization, like any system or process, it can be improved. Indeed, the innovative process itself requires those within it never to be totally satisfied with the way things are, and to be constantly on the lookout for ways to do better. Indeed, all those participating in the system need constantly to learn from experience, based on careful analysis of what works and what does not.

Special attention is given here to one important aspect of the commercialization of university innovation: the process governing the licensing of intellectual property rights in innovations developed by faculty inventors. The chapter outlines several reasons why this process at most universities is suboptimal and offers several possible improvements. All of them involve changes in the relationships between faculty inventors and their universities. The federal government, as a principal funder of university research, is in a position to accelerate these changes, if it so chooses.

---

[5] National Science Foundation, *Science and Engineering Indicators 2010*, Chapter 4.

THE COMMERCIALIZATION OF UNIVERSITY-GENERATED INNOVATION: NOT ALL IT CAN BE

By at least one well-accepted measure—revenues from licensing agreements—universities have had increasing success commercializing the innovations of their faculty members. According to the Association of University Technology Managers (AUTM), which compiles these data for most universities annually, universities earned $1.9 billion in licensing revenues from faculty-generated IP in 2008, up from just $221 million in 1996, when these data were first available.[6] The top ten university earners over the entire 1996-2008 period are listed in table 1.

How important are these figures? One conventional way to answer that question is to compare licensing revenue to invested funds from all sources (not just federal government support) in order to compute a "rate of return." Table 1 also lists these rates of return for the top ten schools for the thirteen-year period, which range from lows of 0.3 percent (for the University of California system and the University of Washington) to a high of 4.3 percent for the top-earning school, NYU.[7] Admittedly, these rates of return are imperfect measures because they do not take account of the different kinds of research on which the faculty at different universities are engaged. For example, almost by definition, if a school is focused largely on basic research that is not likely to have any immediate commercial payoff, then its rate of return will be close to zero. At the other end of the spectrum, if much of the research is concentrated on projects likely to have more immediate commercial uses, then rates of return should be higher. In addition, a university may be engaged largely in basic

---

[6] Association of University Technology Managers, *AUTM U.S. Licensing Activity Survey*, available at www.autm.net/Licensing_Surveys_AUTM.htm. The AUTM data are not a complete census as participation is voluntary, but since they cover virtually all of the top research universities, the reported licensing figures are likely to come close to an actual total for all university licensing revenues.

[7] The average annual rates of return are calculated by dividing total licensing income by total research expenditures for each university, and then dividing that figure by thirteen, or the number of years in the 1996-2008 period.

research, but have one or two commercial "big hits" that bump up the reported return for the school as a whole. Only very few university inventions become financial blockbusters, and the returns are highly skewed; luck plays a large role in those "home run" financial successes. The rates of return shown in table 1 are not adjusted for these differences in research types and outputs, and in the absence of other data, it is impossible to do so.

Moreover, in all fairness, licensing revenue certainly is not and should not be the only measure of the effectiveness of university research and its dissemination. The better metrics for success would be measures of how knowledge, not money, changes hands to foster innovation. Much of what universities produce are true public goods. The knowledge from faculty research finds its way into the research of others, thus changing the way firms and other organizations operate. And people trained in academe go on to found businesses or bring their expertise to private firms that innovate. These impacts do not readily show up in market transactions or prices, and even when the knowledge and the people have direct commercial benefit, their contributions cannot be easily attributable to any particular research finding. Indeed, as William Nordhaus has shown, inventors generally capture for themselves only about 4 percent of the value of their inventions.[8]

Licensing revenues are nonetheless a useful indicator of commercial success, indeed more useful than some other hard counts of research output, such as papers published in prestigious journals (many of which may have no commercial value), or numbers of patents filed or issued. It also would be useful to have measures of the numbers and performance of companies launched by university faculty members, but such data are generally not available. MIT did study the number of firms and jobs associated with its faculty and alumni and found that MIT alumni had founded

---

[8] William D. Nordhaus, "Schumpeterian Profits and the Alchemist Fallacy," Yale Working Papers on Economic Applications and Policy, Discussion Paper No. 6 (2005), http://www.econ.yale.edu/ddp/ddp00/ddp0006.pdf.

[9] Edward B. Roberts and Charles Eesley, "Entrepreneurial Impact: The Role of MIT," 2009.

25,800 active companies that employed 3.3 million people, generating annual world sales of $2 trillion. This production is equivalent to the eleventh-largest economy in the world.[9] But such studies are few and far between, and MIT is an unusually productive entrepreneurial institution by any account.

Even with all of the foregoing caveats, the rates of return reported in table 1 are quite low. Collectively, they indicate either that most research by most universities has very little commercial value, or that the commercial potential is there but is far from being fully realized. Both of these assertions could be, and probably are, true. In fact, there are three reasons—in addition to any inferences about suboptimality that may be drawn from the rates of return—for believing that more innovations developed by university faculty could be commercialized more quickly and effectively.

First, by one industry-specific output measure—the number of drugs approved for marketing by the Food and Drug Administration—compared to federal support of university research devoted to or related to the development of new drugs, performance looks less than stellar. Whereas federal funding for health-related research, which is primarily channeled to university faculty through the National Institutes of Health, has increased substantially—from under $20 billion in 1993 to almost $30 billion in 2008—the number of new FDA-approved drugs has dropped fairly consistently since 1996, when it peaked at over fifty, to just fifteen in 2008.[10] Many factors contribute to this drop in new drug approvals, but the underlying point is that a rise in R&D expenditure and drop in new drug approval happened during the same period, suggesting that federal research support for the health sciences, which is the dominant way in which federal university-research dollars are spent, has been becoming less commercially productive.

---

[10] See Robert E. Litan and Lesa Mitchell, "A Faster Path from Lab to Market," *Harvard Business Review* (January/February 2010): 7.

Admittedly, the pattern of declining productivity is just part of the broader story of the pharmaceutical industry, which from 1993 to 2004 increased its R&D spending by 147 percent, but increased the number of new drug applications to the FDA annually only by 38 percent.[11] Clearly, there is something at work that is causing health sciences research, however it is funded and pursued, to become less productive of commercially valuable drugs and biologics. Perhaps it is just a process of diminishing returns. But there also may be underlying inefficiencies in the research and commercialization process in both private industry and on campus, as well as legal and regulatory impediments.

With respect to universities in particular, there are additional reasons for believing that the current commercialization process is suboptimal. For starters, with some notable exceptions, university technology licensing offices (TLOs) or technology transfer offices (TTOs), the bodies that have come to have sole responsibility on university campuses for licensing faculty-generated innovations, are not all equally well funded or staffed. Most such offices have to ration the attention they are able to give to university faculty. Furthermore, in principle, a successful TTO employee should have the same skill set as a partner in a private venture capital firm. In practice, this is rarely possible because VCs pay their staff and partners much more than a university could afford or justify.

In addition, some university faculty do not technically comply with their employment contracts that require them to use the TTO for licensing, and instead commercialize their innovations "through the back door," in part for the reason just stated, and also because TTOs themselves have their own bureaucratic tendencies. Indeed, the extent to which this occurs is an indicator of the suboptimality of the current university commercialization system.

---

[11] U.S. Government Accountability Office, *New Drug Development: Science, Business, Regulatory, and Intellectual Property Issues Cited as Hampering Drug Development Efforts*, November 2006.

How much back-door activity takes place? This is difficult to answer with any precision, since many faculty innovators will be reluctant to admit this is what they are doing, and universities may have difficulty finding out. Nonetheless, the best research on this subject, by Jerry Thursby, Anne Fuller, and Marie Thursby, suggest that the volume of back-door patenting and thus, by implication, commercialization is substantial. The university can elect to forego patent rights, leaving them to the faculty inventor, or research may have taken place abroad or under terms giving faculty ownership rights, so not all such cases represent "back-door" commercialization. The frequency of apparent back-door commercialization seems high enough, however, to suggest that it is a very real phenomenon. In their study of eighty-seven research universities, this research team found that almost 38 percent of the more than 5,800 patents in their sample are not assigned solely to the university, which the authors note is surprising in light of the standard faculty employment contract that expressly requires that universities own faculty inventions when university resources are used in the research.[12]

In effect, back-door commercialization acts as a safety valve, but it is an inefficient one. Not every faculty innovator who is frustrated with the university's TTO will take the risk or go to the effort of commercializing "in the dark" and instead will simply take his or her place in the queue at the TTO. When this happens, useful commercialization activity may be slowed or halted.

Finally, and perhaps most importantly, the licensing systems that universities have established are structured to generate suboptimal results. Since the passage of Bayh-Dole, virtually all research universities have centralized licensing activities and decisions in their TTOs. Universities apparently did this to realize economies of scale in licensing; to comply with Bayh-Dole reporting requirements; to assure that faculty members reported their discoveries to the universities so that universities could thus accurately keep

---

[12] Jerry Thursby, Anne Fuller, and Marie Thursby, "U.S. Faculty Patenting: Inside and Outside the University," *Research Policy* 38 (2009): 14-25.

tabs on royalties they were owed under faculty employment agreements; to coordinate patenting decisions when multiple faculty and students were involved; to coordinate licensing arrangements when faculty from other universities were coinventors; and presumably out of a belief that TTOs would accumulate more knowledge about the most advantageous licensing opportunities than individual faculty members.

All these were and are worthy reasons for centralization. But centralization also had the likely unintended effect of creating a monopoly bureaucracy that leaves faculty inventors with little choice about how, to whom, and at what pace to license or otherwise commercialize their innovations. If universities applied the same model to faculty research, it would mean that all faculty members would be required, by contract, to first obtain the approval of a central "publications office" that would coordinate the submission of articles to journals and books to publishers. It almost goes without saying that faculty would not stand for such an approach to their publications, nor would universities voluntarily adopt it for fear of frustrating the dissemination of research results to the academic community and the wider public. Yet when it comes to commercial activity, universities have taken a very different approach.

It has not always been this way. Prior to the passage of Bayh-Dole in 1980, few academic institutions—Wisconsin's independent Wisconsin Alumni Research Foundation (WARF) established in 1925 being the notable exception—had formal TTOs, inside or independent of the university. Only after Bayh-Dole was enacted did universities gradually begin to centralize the commercialization functions that the act legitimated. Now, as noted, virtually all research universities have a TTO, which in the typical case has exclusive control over the licensing and commercialization activities related to innovations developed by university faculty.

In theory, of course, TTOs can be structured or can operate in such a way as to facilitate rather than hinder licensing and commercialization. There are examples where this in fact is the case. But monopolies, especially those wielding legal rights to that status by virtue of university employment contracts, also have well-known incentives to behave suboptimally.

Perhaps most recognized is the incentive for monopolies to reduce output. In the university commercialization context, this tendency manifests itself in the limited attention, given limited resources, that TTOs have to give to all innovations developed by university faculty, and the inherent need therefore to focus on only a few potential "winners." But with talent and experience no better than private venture firms, and without the same or similar gain-sharing incentives for success that motivate general partners of VC firms (who typically take 20 percent of the profits of the enterprise), there is no reason to believe that the TTOs can be any more effective than the market itself in determining the true winners. This leaves potentially many innovations by faculty members not given favored treatment by the TTO staff in bureaucratic limbo until someone in that office can give them proper attention, if ever. Indeed, the well-known tendency toward bureaucracy and inefficiency of monopolies, to which TTOs certainly are not immune, aggravates this problem.

The monopoly that each TTO has over its university's licensing and commercialization of faculty inventions also leads to a potentially even more significant *systemwide* flaw. Given their exclusive control over licensing, TTOs are required to be jacks-of-all-trades and thus cannot, without ignoring innovations across many technologies by many different faculty members, specialize in one or a few technologies. Even in cases where TTOs choose to specialize in their search for "home runs," they cannot exploit any economies of scale since, with all research universities relying on their own TTOs for licensing, there is no opportunity for all of them to offer their services to faculty of other academic institutions (a situation that can be remedied under at least one of the reform options outlined below). The net result is that the market for the licensing of university-developed technologies is highly and almost certainly inefficiently fragmented.

In sum, despite the clear progress that universities have made since 1980 in commercializing innovations by their faculty, there are several reasons for believing that they could do even better. Rates of return on research investment, however imperfect as a measure of success, are disappointingly low. Research productivity in one particular field where university research is amply supported by the federal government—pharmaceuticals—has been declining. Most technology transfer offices are underresourced and cannot effectively compete in the market for talent in identifying promising commercial opportunities. And perhaps most important, the university technology licensing market is structured to inhibit competition, which almost certainly leaves some commercial opportunities on the shelf while slowing others from reaching the marketplace and consumers. Finally, although it has not been said to date but should be obvious, no system in any organization can be perfect. The search for improvements is or should be never ending.

None of this is to suggest that fixing the technology transfer model will necessarily improve the productivity of pharmacological research in particular, where the productivity statistics are especially disturbing. Much more far-reaching changes in the structure of that particular industry are probably necessary.

Possible Reforms

The suboptimal performance of university commercialization operations as a whole not only hurts society, but also universities and faculty innovators. A more efficient system would generate more commercially useful products more quickly, which not only would help consumers, but also bring greater revenue more quickly to universities and to faculty innovators whose employment contracts typically give them some share in the royalties or revenues when their technologies are commercialized. University faculty are not in a position to change the status quo, however, since no single faculty member has enough bargaining position to compel his or her university employers to change the system in any meaningful way. Why then, do university leaders follow a path that seemingly is not in their own interest?

This important question is not well addressed in the literature, so it is possible here only to speculate on the possible reasons. One possible answer is that, at least for universities that have had some commercialization successes such as those listed in table 1, university presidents and trustees probably are pleased with their performance and thus unlikely aware that they could do even better. This is true even though there is no evidence that a university's ranking on the top ten list of cumulative licensing revenue has anything to do with the effectiveness of its TTO. One or a few blockbuster innovations may account for most of the revenue, and these events are more likely to be random than the product of successful staff work at the TTO. Nonetheless, for reasons already given, the current monopoly TTO structure is not well suited to quickly identifying and speeding the commercialization of even these random successful innovations.

Universities with far less success at commercial licensing may also be unaware of how much better they might do under different arrangements. While perhaps disappointed at their relative (and absolute) lack of success at commercialization, their leaders may attribute this result also to randomness of a different sort: their faculty, either because of disinterest in commercially relevant research or because they have just been unlucky, haven't yet had the big hits that drive commercial success.

Another factor at work may be the fact that technology transfer officials have no interest in calling attention to university presidents or other university leaders the suboptimality of the current system, assuming they believe this to be the case. Indeed, there is little evidence that technology transfer officials even believe the current system is suboptimal in any way. But for those few who might recognize this to be the case, it still is not in their self-interest to want to disturb the status quo, especially in any way that might compel them to compete against other licensing agents.

The Great Recession and its aftermath, however, may induce some university leaders and/or trustees to begin searching for ways to improve commercialization outcomes. With the drop in university endowments caused by the decline in equity and real estate values, the corresponding falloffs in wealth among alumni donors, and the potential decline in federal research monies post-stimulus due to continuing budget pressures, universities will be looking even harder for other ways to raise funds (other than by raising tuition even more than otherwise would be the case). One obvious target is increased revenue from technology commercialization.

An intensified focus on commercialization could be a mixed blessing. It could reinforce TTOs' incentives and tendencies to concentrate their time and efforts on what they believe are home run opportunities, to the detriment of perhaps many other singles and doubles. Certain licensing agents in a freer market can be expected to behave in the same fashion, but at least they would be competing against each other for deals, and thus some agents who might not have access to the true home runs would be content to work on the doubles and singles if they only had the chance. Given the difficult economic circumstances confronting universities, it is possible that leaders of some of them would recognize the advantages of harnessing free-market forces in licensing, or at the very least, be open to some fundamental rethinking about the ways they want to commercialize their faculties' inventions in the future.

In that spirit, some ways to improve upon the current university technology licensing system are catalogued and discussed below. It bears emphasis that each of these ideas can be implemented by universities on their own—primarily through changes in their relationships and legal agreements with their faculty. This section closes, however, with some thoughts on how the federal government, as a significant funder of university research and as the originator of the concept that universities have a right to commercialize federally funded research (under the Bayh-Dole Act), might encourage universities to adopt one or more of these ideas.

Standardized or "Express" Licensing

One method to make licensing more efficient and provide stronger incentives to faculty innovators, who may be closer to market opportunities than less-specialized TTO staff, to explore commercially relevant opportunities (either by starting their own companies or licensing their technologies to existing enterprises) is to standardize the license agreements themselves. This would eliminate the need for potentially time-consuming and costly negotiations between university TTO staff, potential licensees, and faculty inventors.

The University of North Carolina implemented its form of this idea in early 2010 for start-up company licensees only through its "Express License Agreement." The Express License can be chosen by any UNC faculty member, student, or staff who is a founder of a company using IP rights owned solely by the university, and after a detailed business plan is reviewed and approved by the TTO. Key provisions of the standard agreement include a 1 percent royalty on products requiring FDA approval and 2 percent for all other products. In addition, the standard agreement requires the licensee to make a cash payout of 0.75 percent of the company's fair market value upon its merger, stock or asset sale, or initial public offering. The license also encourages the licensee to make products available for humanitarian purposes in developing countries.[13]

Something like the UNC Express License should be easily replicable at other universities and also federal labs. Admittedly, one limitation of the idea is that it presumes capability within the university's TTO to evaluate the innovator's business plan. Not all TTOs are well equipped to do this. One way to address this potential problem is for universities wanting to use the Express License approach to establish an outside panel of experienced

---

[13] Joseph M. DeSimone, William R. Kenan, Jr., and Lesa Mitchell, *Facilitating the Commercialization of University Innovation: The Carolina Express License Agreement* (Kansas City, MO: Ewing Marion Kauffman Foundation, April 2010), www.kauffman.org.

entrepreneurs (comprising alumni and local residents with interest in the university) to review these plans.

One other possible objection, which on closer inspection may be an advantage, is that since the standard license would be available only for startups, it might bias university faculty, staff, and students toward launching new companies, which is likely to be a riskier source of revenue, rather than licensing to existing companies. The advantage of such a bias, however, is that the payoff to the launch of a new business, if it succeeds, may be much larger than any royalty that might be realized from a license to an already established company.

To help ensure the best possible outcome for the university, innovators, and society, it therefore is in universities' best interest—regardless of which, if any, of the reform ideas outlined here (or others) they may wish to adopt—to provide entrepreneurial training and mentoring to faculty and students who want to launch a business around their innovations. There are successful models of this idea at multiple universities—MIT, Washington University of St. Louis, the University of Miami, and the University of North Carolina, among others—that can and should be replicated.

Multi-university Technology Commercialization Consortiums

TTOs have inherent difficulties realizing economies of scale, both because of resource limits at their universities and also because of the broad range of technologies developed by the faculty at their universities. Licensing and commercialization activity thus cries out for specialized providers—those who can serve a sufficient volume of similar innovations to develop expertise and realize some economies of scale.

One way of doing this would be for university TTOs to join forces, either in full-scale mergers or in less-than-full-scale joint ventures. Such consortia could be developed along regional lines, within specific technological fields, or both. A single consortium could replace an individual TTO, or a single TTO might join multiple consortia. Obviously, there are many different possible combinations of these alternatives.

While participation in one or more consortia would enable universities to better realize economies of scale and the advantages of specialization, this option has its drawbacks. It may be difficult specifying *ex ante* rules for distributing the gains from various royalty or equity participations arrangements, and possibly also for splitting expenses. Likewise, there may be disputes over these matters *ex post* in individual cases where faculty members from different universities in a consortium are involved in creating the innovation. At the same time, these issues may be no more difficult than is the case now, where faculty from multiple universities share in the invention and the universities involved have to decide how to split the IP rights and any related gains.

The advantages of the consortium option(s) may be enhanced if the consortia also adopt a standardized license for startups. This would combine the benefits of both approaches while eliminating at the outset some potential disputes or negotiating difficulties that otherwise could later arise.

Commercialization Decision Making by Successful Entrepreneurs

A more far-reaching reform would devolve decisions about which university-developed innovations to commercialize, in what order and in what manner, to a special board of successful entrepreneurs who have close affiliations with the university. Successful alumni are obvious candidates, but so also are successful local entrepreneurs who care about and have worked with or supported the university.

The case for doing this should be obvious, regardless of what other reforms might be adopted. Successful entrepreneurs, especially if they have backgrounds in areas of innovation developed by university faculty, almost certainly have more experience and expertise in commercialization than the typical employees of the university TTO (unless, by chance, those employees have had successful entrepreneurial careers themselves, which is surely the exception and not the rule). If none of the permanent members of the special board have sufficient expertise to evaluate a particular technology, they and the university should have the ability to recruit ad hoc members who would have such knowledge.

It is important that the board be more than advisory, but actually have a decision-making role. For this purpose, it probably will be necessary to compensate the board members in some manner, though given their ties to the university some members are likely to donate any such amounts back. Faculty members may be included on the selection boards, but priority should be given to "star scientists," or those relatively few faculty members who have also had successful entrepreneurial careers.

Turning the decision making over priorities and deal structures for commercialization activities to a board of entrepreneurs would, of course, fundamentally change the function of university TTOs. While they may continue to perform ministerial functions relating to licensing, their focus instead (assuming they would continue to exist) would turn to education of faculty members about the entrepreneurial process. However, as suggested as part of the next option, it is not clear that TTOs are best equipped to provide this service, and if not, it should be outsourced to more capable hands.

Choice in Licensing (or "Free Agency")

As meritorious as they may be, however, neither consortia nor the standardized license get at the root cause of most of the likely underperformance of university commercialization efforts. That is, neither option would break up the monopoly control each university TTO has over its own faculty, which as argued above has likely led to excessive bureaucracy and slowed or inhibited the commercialization of innovations that TTOs deem not to be potential home runs.

The solution to these problems is to let the market decide—more than it does now—which innovations should be commercialized and at what pace, rather than gatekeeper TTOs. In particular, the third reform option offered here would grant faculty (or staff and student) innovators the same freedom in choosing the licensing agent for their innovations that they now have in choosing where to publish their research. This would require, of course, a change in the standard university faculty employment agreement, but it would extend only to the licensing decision and not affect the university's financial and reporting arrangements with respect to faculty innovations, and would not require statutory change or altering the fundamentals of the Bayh-Dole framework.

Freeing up the market in technology licensing should bring big benefits to all parties concerned. It would provide much stronger incentives for faculty to commercialize their discoveries more quickly, eliminating the potentially long waits at the TTO to get recognition. This would generate benefits for society, for faculty innovators, and for the universities who will share in their success. Choice in licensing would also encourage specialization and thus economies of scale among licensing agents, whether or not they are affiliated with universities. Some universities might even decide to drop their TTOs, merge or pool them with other research institutions, or significantly reduce their staff as a result and thereby save money and generate better returns. Or, universities could decide to keep their TTOs to compete with other licensing agents and/or transform them into technology consulting offices that would give advice to faculty about the commercialization and licensing process.

Several objections to the so-called "free agency model" in technology commercialization can be anticipated. One question that may arise relates to who will pay for patent filing fees in a system of free agency. Under the current system, a faculty or staff innovator who can persuade the university TTO that a patent should be filed will have that cost underwritten by the university itself. But under free agency, might faculty inventors have no ways other than by digging into their own pockets to fund their patent filings, in which case IP might be underprotected?

The answer to this question is that markets would (and should) determine how patent filings are funded. The university could often retain ownership while delegating some choice of technology licensing authority to faculty. Some nonuniversity licensing agents or attorneys may choose to take royalties or a small equity interest in the innovator's company as payment for patent filings that innovators cannot fund themselves. Since there are many such potential agents, competition among them can be counted on to protect innovators. Alternatively, even under free agency, faculty innovators would retain the right to choose their own university's TTO, or any new commercialization consortia that may be formed in a freer and more competitive environment, and any one of these entities could front the costs of the patent filing. Moreover, in many cases, the university does not pay patent prosecution costs even now, but rather the licensing firm pays those costs.

Another possible objection to free agency is the belief that many faculty innovators need the guidance of their TTOs since they are unlikely to have significant experience in this area or as entrepreneurs more broadly. It is precisely for this reason, however, that it is important that universities more generally help train and mentor entrepreneurial faculty. But this training need not be done by the TTO; indeed, there should be a presumption against this since TTO staff members are not likely to have the requisite entrepreneurial experience.

Furthermore, the notion that many faculty innovators need the helping hand of TTOs in licensing is wrong often enough that an alternative is prudent policy. There are cases where faculty does need TTO expertise, but other cases when faculty expertise far outstrips TTO capacity. Current policy only makes sense in situations where the TTO adds value. Consistent with the "80/20" rule applicable in so many other realms of life, a relatively small group of the most successful serial faculty innovators are probably

---

[14] See, e.g. Lynne Zucker and Michael Darby, "Star Scientists, Innovation and Regional and National Immigration" (working paper no. 13547, National Bureau of Economics Research, 2007).

responsible for most of the successful innovations university TTOs are now licensing. Indeed, such "rock star" scientists have been demonstrated to be critical to the economic success of the local areas where they live and work.[14] These individuals are not likely to be in need of the counseling that TTOs provide; to the contrary, many of these innovators are likely to have more experience and a stronger social network than TTO staff members. As for other faculty members with less commercial experience, in a free market, many would almost surely do what consumers who are looking for a doctor, a repair specialist, or an auto mechanic routinely do: they ask others (in the university case, most likely, more senior or more experienced faculty innovators) for their suggestions. In addition, in a freer market, it is likely that information providers would build Internet-accessible databases and rating services of the most effective licensing agents, generally and in particular technological fields.

A third potential concern is whether free agency complicates the commercialization of innovations developed by faculty innovators from multiple laboratories within a university, or from multiple universities. In particular, with innovators having the right to choose their licensing agents, will this lead to more disputes over ownership of the IP, which would slow commercialization? Although it is difficult to know the answer to this question with any precision, there are reasons to doubt that free agency would lead to significantly more intra- or interuniversity disputes. Problems of attributing IP to different inventors and universities already exist under the current system, with TTO offices and university general counsel having to resolve them. Indeed, the nature of research is evolving to bigger teams and more institutions involved in invention and its commercialization. The problem of multiagency is very real and likely to intensify, but it is not necessarily a problem solved by centralization at the university level, which is the current default framework.[15]

---

[15] In the intrauniversity case, which is frequent, however, the university administration does have many channels to address the problem without "taking it to the outside."

Of course, if free agency were to lead to more cross-university faculty collaborations—some of which may result in IP ownership disputes—this is not necessarily a bad outcome. To the contrary, the more cross-fertilization of ideas takes place, the more innovative the entire university ecosystem is likely to be. Having to resolve some increased level of IP disputes seems a price worth paying for more commercialized innovation.

In the end, opponents to free agency have a difficult question to answer: why only in the particular case of technology licensing, but not in research, should faculty members lack the freedom to choose the best method for advancing their innovation (especially when the exercise of choice does not disrupt the university's royalty or gain-sharing arrangement in the faculty member's contract)? To be more precise, on what grounds can monopoly and central control in this narrow sphere of highly expert activity be justified (when the presumption in virtually every other sphere of economic activity favors competition)? At the very least, opponents to free agency would seem to have the burden of proof in carrying the day on each of these questions.

Inventor IP Ownership

The final, and arguably most extreme, option for accelerating the university commercialization process is for universities to give up their IP rights in faculty inventions, or at least not to pursue them so aggressively (as has been the norm in a number of universities). This could easily be accomplished by revising the standard university faculty employment contract so that any university rights to inventions under Bayh-Dole would be assigned on a royalty-free basis to faculty, staff, or students.[16]

Letting faculty inventors have full rights in their innovations clearly would provide the maximum incentives possible for rapid

---

[16] Some reform advocates argue that even under the current standard employment contract, universities cannot claim ownership of the IP of faculty innovators, even those who conduct their research using university resources. This hot-button issue is not addressed here, except to note that if this position were upheld by a court, universities could override any such ruling by revising their faculty contracts to make it explicit that universities have full rights to the IP.

commercialization, and for that reason the idea should be seriously considered, though perhaps on an experimental basis, or in cases where that appears to be the optimal solution because of the nature of the invention and the inventor. The major reason for proceeding incrementally is that universities need to test both whether giving up their IP does in fact lead to more commercialization—which is a social good—but also whether faculty inventors, so legally empowered, would feel morally obligated to share with their universities some of their private gains from commercializing their innovations. This has happened already under the existing system, and it is likely that loyal faculty would continue sharing their wealth if they had full rights to the IP. Even if, on a per-transaction basis, faculty givebacks were not as generous as the current standard royalty arrangements, if university assignments of IP rights to faculty led to more commercialization, the "pie" of what there is to share would grow, and universities, individually and collectively, would be better off. Only by experimenting with this option can universities learn whether this would be true.

There are some powerful counterarguments to taking faculty free agency to the level of ownership that must be acknowledged. One is that some faculty will selfishly abuse the system. This is probably the case, but faculty who want to remain part of a university are subject to many other criteria for evaluation of their performance. Another objection is that the university itself is responsible for creating the environment in which creative innovation takes place, and it deserves part of the reward. This argument is sound, but the formulas used for allocating licensing revenues among faculty inventors, departments, schools, and overall university coffers are the real focus for revenue sharing, and this could be done with faculty ownership as well as institutional ownership, as a condition of the faculty employment agreement. If the real driving force is "star" scientists as much or more than "star" universities, then the current default ownership policies are suboptimal.

Role of Federal Policy

Each one or all of these reform options can be adopted by universities on their own. But given the broad social interest in more rapid commercialization of faculty-generated innovation, coupled with the substantial federal taxpayer commitment to university research, the federal government has good reasons for wanting to encourage universities to adopt one or more of the foregoing reforms (or perhaps different ones).

There are several possible ways for the government to go about this. One "soft" option would be for the funding agencies, in consultation with the Department of Commerce, to issue guidance about implemention and interpretation of licensing procedures and terms. The National Institutes of Health has done this, in effect, for research tools and for genomic inventions.[17] Perhaps the broadest approach would be for the Commerce Department, which has rule-making authority implementing the provisions of Bayh-Dole, to issue a proposed rule, meant to apply to all federally funded research, to encourage more effective commercialization of faculty-generated innovations. That rule might outline a "default" standardized license that universities could decide to adopt, while making clear that although Bayh-Dole gave universities the rights to the IP from faculty innovations, it does not confer on universities the exclusive rights to control licensing. However, the Commerce Department does not have the legal authority to overrule Bayh-Dole and thus require universities to give up their IP rights to faculty inventors. As just noted, this is something that universities can do voluntarily.

Individual federal agencies that fund university research—notably the Department of Energy, the National Science Foundation, the Department of Defense, and the National

---

[17] For research tools, see National Institutes of Health, "Principles and Guidelines for Recipients of NIH Research Grants and Contracts on Obtaining and Disseminating Biomedical Research Resources: Final Notice," *Federal Register* 64, no. 246 (December 23, 1999): 72090-72096, http://www.ott.nih.gov/pdfs/64FR72090.pdf. For genomic inventions, see National Institutes of Health, "Best Practices for the Licensing of Genomic Inventions—Final Notice," *Federal Register* 70, no. 68 (April 11, 2005): 18413-18415, http://www.ott.nih.gov/pdfs/70FR18413.pdf.

Institutes of Health—could go further and condition their grants on universities adopting any one of the first four proposals (the notion that the government would condition a grant on universities giving up their IP rights is almost certainly too extreme). As a step in this direction, they could at least open the door to experimentation. Of course, Congress could impose similar conditions in its annual appropriations to these and other funding agencies, and through oversight of the federal funding agencies.

CONCLUSION

Universities are critical to economic growth in a number of ways: through the students they teach and equip with skills; through the production of new knowledge, both basic and applied; and through the commercialization of research by some faculty members.

The Bayh-Dole Act was enacted in 1980 explicitly to promote economic growth through the last of these channels. It appears to have been effective in stimulating universities to pay more attention to commercialization opportunities. At the time, the act unintentionally led to the centralization of commercialization decisions in licensing offices that have gained de facto monopoly control over the licensing of faculty-developed innovations.

This chapter has outlined several reasons why this system is not as effective as it could and should be in bringing to market innovations developed at universities. It has outlined several reforms that individually or in combination could speed commercialization of new technologies, thereby accelerating economic growth and benefiting society, innovators, and the universities that employ them.

TABLE 1. LICENSING INCOMES AND RESEARCH EXPENDITURES, TOP TEN UNIVERSITIES

1996-2008 (CUMULATIVE)

School Name	Licensing Income (billions of dollars)	Research Expenditure (billions of dollars)	% Return Annual Average
New York University	1.49	2.67	4.3
University of California System	1.40	33.28	0.3
Northwestern	0.96	3.81	1.9
Emory University	0.76	3.48	1.7
MIT	0.49	12.23	0.3
University of Minnesota	0.42	6.01	0.5
University of Washington	0.41	9.25	0.3
University of Florida	0.41	4.76	0.7
Florida State University	0.37	2.05	1.4
Wake Forest University	0.36	1.43	3.4

Source: AUTM Licensing Survey, 1996-2008

4 ■ U.S. Policy Regarding Highly Skilled ■ Immigrants:
Change Whose Time Has Come

John E. Tyler and Peter H. Schuck*

I. INTRODUCTION

Highly skilled immigrants to the United States (HSIs), particularly those with graduate degrees in science, engineering, technology, and math (STEM) fields, have helped catalyze innovation, economic growth, jobs, wealth, and advances in human welfare. America has been attractive to HSIs and other innovators at least in part because of its fundamental freedoms, market-friendly values, and reliable infrastructure. But this past success provides no assurances for our future. Consider three questions.

First, could our nation have achieved substantially more if our policy had focused more deliberately on HSIs' potential economic contributions? Second, how can the United States ensure that

* John Tyler is Vice President and Secretary of the Ewing Marion Kauffman Foundation. Peter Schuck is Simeon E. Baldwin Professor Emeritus of Law at Yale University and visiting professor at New York University School of Law. The authors are grateful for the assistance of David Back and the comments and feedback of their colleagues on the Kauffman Task Force for Economic Growth. A longer version of this chapter also appears in the January 2011 symposium edition of the *Fordham Urban Law Journal.* The authors are grateful to the Foundation and Fordham for their respective permissions and to those from each who contributed to editing, cite checking, and otherwise improving both piece.

we continue to benefit from HSIs in the face of increased competition from other countries seeking to attract (or retain) them? And finally, is our economic leadership being compromised by clinging to old policies not well adapted to current and future circumstances?

In this chapter, we marshal data and evidence demonstrating that HSIs spur innovation and entrepreneurship, particularly in STEM fields. We also show that new approaches could better deploy these talents and increase economic growth. Among changes that we advocate are allowing state and local governments to target their efforts to recruit and arrange for permanent or at least provisional visas to HSIs; guaranteeing such visas to HSIs who receive degrees, particularly at the graduate level, from U.S. universities in STEM disciplines; and adopting a new system that uses points, an auction, and/or job creation potential to direct visas to HSIs who can advance innovation, entrepreneurship, and economic growth.

Part two of this chapter identifies economic problems that new HSI policies might address. Part three summarizes current U.S. policies regarding HSIs. Part four advances specific proposals to increase economic growth, innovation, jobs, wealth, and human welfare through a more effective approach to HSIs.

2. UNDERSTANDING HOW HSIS CAN HELP EXPAND THE U.S. ECONOMY

The United States can use HSI policies to address at least two macro-level economic problems: sluggish economic growth with too few new firms and jobs; and competition from increasingly educated and productive countries in the developed and developing worlds.[†]

2.1. HSIs are Innovative and Entrepreneurial

HSIs innovate and engage in entrepreneurial activity, particularly in STEM industries, at levels disproportionate both to their presence in the population and to native-born Americans, generating new firms, jobs, and economic growth.

2.1.1. Measuring HSI Innovation by Education Levels and Patenting Activity

Researchers often consider two indicators of innovation in the United States: education in a STEM discipline and patenting activity.[1] They find a correlation between advanced education in a STEM field and "high rates of entrepreneurship and innovation,"[2] high rates of patenting activity by foreign-born inventors relative to their presence in both the general population and the workforce more specifically, and substantial spillover effects or indirect benefits.

For instance, increasing the number of H-1B visas strongly correlates with an increase in the number of patent applications filed in the United States, while times of decreased H-1B visas show decreases in the number of patent applications with immigrant filers.[‡3] Moreover, innovation by noncitizen residents, as measured by patent applications, appears to be twice the rate of their presence in both the population and workforce.[4] In addition, immigrants with bachelor's degrees were granted patents at twice the rate of native-born Americans with bachelor's degrees with the difference rising to almost three times when comparing those with graduate degrees. The differences in patenting activity were less pronounced when the comparison is with scientists and engineers but such immigrants still received about 20 percent more patents than native-born scientists and engineers.[5]

---

† Although many studies show that legal immigration in general improves job growth and economic development, particularly in disadvantaged areas (Herman and Smith, 2010, see endnote 32), we focus here on HSIs.

‡ For instance, non-citizen U.S. residents were named on 7.3 percent of patent applications filed in 1998 with the World Intellectual Property Organization from the United States. The rate increased to 13.8 percent in 2003, rose to 23.5 percent in 2005 and then to 24.2 percent in 2006 (Wadhwa et al., 2007a, see endnote 15), thereby doubling and then tripling along with the number of available H-1B visas between 1999 and 2003 (NFAP, 2010, see endnote 32).

In addition to contributing directly to U.S. innovation, HSIs also contribute in the form of "spillover" effects[6]—that is, indirect benefits to native-born workers and the broader population. Spillover benefits include helping achieve critical mass in researching specialized areas and providing skills that complement native-born researchers.§ Some commentators contend that immigrants crowd out native-born STEM innovation by interfering with access to graduate education,[7] taking jobs,[8] and depressing wages.[9] On the other hand, several researchers find no evidence that increasing the number of H-1B visas reduced innovation by nonimmigrant researchers, as measured by patent applications.[10] Still others have found either no crowding out or even an affirmative crowding *in*, a positive spillover effect.[11]

Ultimately, because knowledge is fundamentally cumulative, iterative, and arguably infinitely expandable, whatever crowding out may occur must be weighed against the widely distributed, substantial benefits produced by the quickened pace of scientific progress and discovery. The United States, then, benefits from having foreign-born people create and pursue their ideas and innovations here,[12] but we have not adequately pursued the potential for those benefits. Policy changes that encourage HSIs to work here are likely to increase overall U.S. innovation and, by extension, economic growth and job creation.

2.1.2. HSIs Start and Grow Firms and Create Jobs

HSIs have contributed significantly to U.S. economic growth over time,[13] and they have a "striking propensity" to start and grow companies that create jobs, particularly in technology fields.[14] HSIs have been integrally involved with founding about one-quarter of the technology and engineering companies started between 1995 and 2005 that comprise the Dun & Bradstreet Million Dollar Database.[15] Other research corroborates this 25

---

§ Hunt and Gauthier-Loiselle found that a 1 percent increase in immigrant college graduates is associated with a 12-15 percent increase in total patenting per capita, thereby implying spillover effect. Their correlations are even more substantive for graduate education and for science and engineering fields more particularly (2009, see endnote 1).

percent ratio, including studies of Silicon Valley,[16] biotech companies in New England (Immigrant Learning Center 2007),[17] and publicly traded companies that receive venture capital.[18]

The consistent finding that immigrants create a quarter of businesses is particularly impressive when compared with their presence in the population and workforce. Immigrants start companies at twice their share of both the U.S. population and workforce, and at more than two-and-a-half times the proportion of legal immigrants in the overall population.** However, these comparisons may actually *understate* immigrant entrepreneurial activity for at least two reasons: the lag effect, and evidence of even higher rates of firm formation.

With regard to lag effect, it would be unusual for immigrants to found their companies in the year in which they arrive in the United States because most immigrants come to America to study or work, rather than to start companies.[19] Also, it generally takes time for the ideas, networks, and other entrepreneurial factors to coalesce and motivate visa holders to start a company.[20] For these reasons, a more accurate analysis would compare immigrants as founders or cofounders of companies begun between 1995 and 2005 with the proportion of immigrants in the population in earlier years, such as 1990, when immigrants were less than 8 percent of the overall population,[21] or in 1995, when they were just over 9 percent of the population.[22] Comparing immigrants in this way, they arguably founded companies at about three times the rate of their overall presence in the United States during the relevant years.

** Immigrants, legal and illegal, comprise only about 12 percent of both the overall United States population and workforce (Hunt and Gauthier-Loiselle, 2009; Robert W. Fairlie, PhD, *Estimating the Contribution of Immigrant Business Owners to the U.S. Economy, prepared for the SBA Office of Advocacy,* November 2008), with legal immigrants at just under 9 percent (United States Census Bureau; United States Department of Homeland Security Office of Immigration Statistics). (The illegal population has declined somewhat since 2007.) One study showed that immigrants started businesses at a monthly rate of about 530 per 100,000 compared with 280 among native born people, or just under a two-to-one ratio (Herman and Smith, 2010), while another study found immigrants to be 30 percent more likely than native born people to start a business (see Fairlie, 2008).

Moreover, some studies indicate that immigrants have founded substantially more than 25 percent of companies;†† indeed, some data suggests double that rate.‡‡ If these higher rates are accurate, and if the lag effect is ignored so that 2008 is the relevant year for comparing population (12 percent), workforce (12 percent), and legal presence in the population (9 percent), then the rate of immigrants involved with founding companies is three to five times their presence in the relevant comparison population. If the lag effect is also factored in so that the relevant population comparison years are 1990 and 1995, then the relative rate of new company involvement becomes five to six-and-a-half times, an astonishing statistic.

This phenomenon is critical for our nation's economic growth because new firms disproportionately create new jobs. For instance, firms between one and five years old account for about two-thirds of net new job creation[23] with firms between three and five years old generating about 10 percent of net new jobs even though they comprise less than 1 percent of the total number of companies.[24] Because about one-third of all new firms close by year two and about half do not survive to age five, the firms that do reach age five are largely responsible for that net new job creation. Obviously, a continuous procession and a large number of new firms are needed to sustain or expand on that job creation trend. Yet in recent decades, the United States has experienced a consistent pattern of about 500,000 new firm starts each year, despite sharp changes in economic conditions and markets

---

†† If narrowed to technology companies, immigrants were part of starting 40 percent of publicly traded venture backed technology companies started between 1990 and 2007 and 47 percent of privately held venture backed companies (Anderson and Platzer, 2006, see endnote 14). Foreign-born people could have had a role in founding up to 40 percent of New England's biotechnology companies, instead of only 25.7 percent of them (Monti et al., 2007, see endnote 25).

‡ About 52 percent of technology and engineering companies started in Silicon Valley between 1995 and 2005 had at least one immigrant founder (Wadhwa et al., 2007a, see endnote 15). This ratio falls slightly to 47 percent of Silicon Valley technology and engineering companies started between 1980 and 2005 (Ibid.).

and the presence of longer cycle changes in population and education.[25]

It is in U.S. economic and policy interests, then, to find ways to increase the number of firm starts and their survival rates. As the rest of the world has discovered, attracting and retaining entrepreneurial HSIs could produce more new firms that contribute more net new jobs and grow into mature firms.

2.2. The United States Faces Increasing Competition for HSIs

Competition in knowledge-based, STEM industries is increasing from both developed and developing countries, endangering U.S. leadership in innovation.[26] Other countries have raised their standard of living, improved educational quality, provide attractive environments for professional growth and development, and produce more sophisticated products and services. Although many of the factors that contribute to this competition and affect U.S. stature in the world economy are beyond our control, there is much that policymakers can do, including altering immigration policy to target HSIs most likely to contribute to economic growth.[27]

Science and technology are no longer the exclusive province of developed nations as many parts of the developing world now view science and technology as "integral to economic growth and development," and they are building "more knowledge-intensive economies in which research, its commercial exploitation, and intellectual work would play a growing role."[28] They also have increasingly opened their markets to trade and foreign investment, improved relevant infrastructures, stimulated research and development, and expanded higher education that produces more scientists and engineers. China and developing countries in Asia have been particularly aggressive in these fields, as have Brazil and South Africa. More intense competition from the European Union, Israel, Canada, and Australia adds to the competitive pressure.[29]

An objective indicator of these developments is the United States' declining share of global research and development activity,§§ of the number of researchers,*** and of the volume of patenting activity††† and degree production in STEM disciplines.‡‡‡

In addition, other nations' immigration policies are often more welcoming and less restrictive than U.S. policies.[30] Other nations offer streamlined processes for hiring foreign workers and potential entrepreneurs,[31] special visa and entry requirements for immigrants who may be entrepreneurs,[32] and fewer barriers to HSIs employment.[33]

The United States is no longer the only or even primary option for HSIs seeking to find work or start and grow companies.[34] Foreign-born students and workers now frequently return to their home countries for reasons that include increasingly sophisticated work, including in primary research and development in such industries as aerospace, medical devices, pharmaceuticals, and software;[35] growing demand for their skills;[36] a belief that their home country offers better long-run career opportunities;[37] a belief that the U.S. economy will soon lag global growth rates;[38] and a higher standard of living and social status for successful people in their home country compared with the United States.

Our policies and procedures must adapt to this new reality. We can no longer expect to satisfy our unfulfilled high-skill labor and innovation needs at our will and discretion.[39]

---

§§ The North American share of global R&D activity between 1996 and 2007 dropped from 40 percent to 35 percent while the Asia/Pacific region increased its share from 24 percent to 31 percent (NSF, 2010).

*** The United States, European Union, and China all had about 1.4 million researchers in 2007. The number of researchers in the United States and European Union grew by about 40 percent between 1995 and 2007, but China's growth in these years was 173 percent (NSF, 2010).

††† Moreover, in 2009, non-natives obtained more patents than did Americans, further confirming that U.S. innovation is declining (West, 2010, see endnote 12).

‡‡‡ Only 16 percent of U.S. students receive science or engineering degrees compared to 38 percent in Korea, 33 percent in Germany, 28 percent in France, 27 percent in England, and 26 percent in Japan (West, 2010).

Even so, this worldwide competition can benefit us. The global marketplace is not a zero-sum game. Instead, economic growth here and abroad will create complementary new jobs, innovations, and opportunities. Moreover, robust entrepreneurial economies abroad may presage greater political stability there, relieving the strain on U.S. economic and other resources. And because the world still looks to us as an engine for economic growth, global competition can benefit the United States and its enterprises. Our current immigration policies are inhibiting America's economic strength and leadership.[40]

3. OVERVIEW OF CURRENT U.S. POLICY REGARDING HSIs

The most relevant visa programs for HSIs to work or start businesses in the United States are the H-1B and the EB series.

3.1. H-1B Nonimmigrant, Temporary Visa Program

The H-1B is a temporary work visa for specialty jobs requiring theoretical and practical application of a body of specialized knowledge and requiring at least a bachelor's degree.[41] The visa requires a sponsoring employer and permits the holder to work in the United States for up to three years with the potential to renew once for an additional three years.[42] §§§ Since 1990, those receiving H-1B visas have been allowed to choose to apply for permanent residency, which can lead to citizenship,[43] but of course they do not always receive one of the limited number of such visas.

Current law allocates 65,000 H-1B visas, with an additional 20,000 available since 2004 for those receiving advanced degrees from U.S. universities.[44] At different times, Congress has changed the

---

§§§ Recipients of these visas are determined on a first in/first out basis among qualified applicants or by a lottery when there are more applications filed prior to the fiscal year than there are visas available (73 Federal Register 15,389 at 15, 389-92) (March 24, 2008) (to be codified at 8 C.F.R. pt. 214).

cap in response to economic conditions. The chart below shows the applicable cap and the number of H-1B visas issued.[45]

Fiscal Year	Number of H-1B Visas Authorized Per Fiscal Year	Number of H-1B Visas Issued Per Fiscal Year
1990-1996	65,000	Less than 65,000
1997-1998	65,000	65,000
1999-2000	115,000	115,000
2001	195,000	163,000
2002	195,000	79,100
2003	195,000	78,000
2004-2010	65,000	65,000

Historically, about 163,000 applicants annually have sought these visas, so demand has generally overwhelmed supply,[46] and the annual quota was often exhausted within the first few months of availability, if not sooner.[47]

The current cap on H1-B visas, while too low, is not the most significant factor limiting applicability of this visa. As of November 12, 2010, only 47,800 H1-B visa cap eligible petitions had been filed under the first category, and only 17,400 had been filed under the second category.[48] The recent economic downturn certainly explains part of this decline, but many in Congress (and not only congressional Democrats) were dissatisfied with the terms of the visa—even before the recent downturn.

The H-1B visa program has other substantial drawbacks. For instance, labor unions oppose H-1B visas for a variety of reasons, including their belief that visa holders compete with American workers and are vulnerable to employer exploitation because the visas are temporary, can only be renewed with the employer's cooperation, may not lead to permanent employment, and do not allow spouses to work in the United States. Republicans are more concerned about the temporary nature and limited number of the H-1B visas and the uncertainty that these factors create for their workforce. Employers like Google complain that the HSIs the company wants most to recruit often resist H1-Bs for this reason.[****]

Both parties agree on the need to expand, and perhaps even uncap, the number of permanent visas for HSIs, particularly in STEM fields, and during the 111th Congress, Representative Zoe Lofgren (D-Calif.) was developing legislation to accomplish this goal.[††††]

Some consider the most significant drawback of the H-1B visas to be the worker's lack of employment mobility; indeed, some have characterized this condition as a form of indentured servitude.[49] Certainly, it interferes with efficient labor markets.[50] The H-1B visa holder cannot change employers without initiating the entire process again and jeopardizing his presence in the United States, unless the worker convinces his or her new employer to sponsor him/her.[51] Those seeking permanent residency also depend on the sponsoring employer, so they may feel compelled to accept lower compensation, work longer hours, and tolerate otherwise intolerable and unacceptable conditions and behavior by employers.[52] Along these lines, some argue that H-1B holders are a source of "cheap labor" that reduces compensation for native workers in the same jobs,[53] and that they take jobs from American citizens.[54] What seems clear, however, is that the direct impact of the relatively small number of H-1B visa holders on the overall civilian workforce is negligible.[‡‡‡‡] In fact, as we have seen, these visa holders may actually create jobs.[§§§§]

[****] Interview with a staff member of the Subcommittee on Citizenship, Refugees, Immigration, and Border Security, House Judiciary Committee, August 5, 2010.

[††††] Ibid.

[‡‡‡‡] New H-1B visa holders constitute only 0.06 percent of a civilian workforce of 154 million (NFAP, 2010). Over six years and assuming efficient visa processing, there would be about 510,000 H-1B workers in the United States at any given time—only about 0.3 percent of the U.S. civilian workforce.

[§§§§] Studies report that employers hire an additional four or five for each H-1B worker they bring here (Herman and Smith, 2010; NFAP, 2010; Kerr and Lincoln, 2008, see endnote 1).

More relevant to our purposes, the lack of mobility inhibits H-1B holders from starting and growing companies and creating new jobs, unless they can do so outside of their regular employment or employer sponsorship. The inability to fully focus on and dedicate time and attention to a new company limits prospects for success and growth.

3.2. EB Series Immigrant, Permanent Resident Visa Program

The EB visa series, which generally affords permanent resident or "green card" status, contains five categories. The EB-1 targets "priority workers."[55] ***** The EB-2 applies to professionals with advanced degrees or people with exceptional ability.[56] ††††† The EB-3 covers skilled or professional workers with a bachelor's degree but not otherwise qualified under EB-1 or EB-2, skilled workers with at least two years of training or experience, and unskilled workers.[57] The EB-4 applies to ministers and other religious workers.[58]

The EB-5 or "investor" visa is available for people who invest at least $1 million and create or sustain at least ten full-time jobs or who invest $500,000 in a "targeted employment area"‡‡‡‡‡ and create or sustain ten jobs.[59] The EB-5 also requires direct involvement by the investor in supervising operations.[60] Unlike the other EB categories, the EB-5 is a conditional visa that lasts for only two years.[61]

***** EB-1 workers must meet one of three criteria: have extraordinary ability in sciences, arts, education, business, or athletics; be an outstanding professors or researchers; or be a manager or executive subject to international transfer (8 USC § 1153(b)(1); 8 CFR § 204.5(b)(2)).

††††† EB-2 visa holders claiming "exceptional ability" must satisfy one of three criteria: have exceptional ability in sciences, arts or business; be an advanced degree professional; or be a qualified physicians who will practice in underserved areas of the United States (8 USC § 1153(b)(2); 8 CFR § 204.5(k)).

‡‡‡‡‡ The EB-5 category also has a regional center pilot program in which 3000 of the EB-5 visas are reserved for investors targeting one of the 90 government-designated regional centers (8 USC § 1153(b)(5); 8 CFR § 204.6). Under this program, permanent residence is available if certain requirements are met and the conditional period has passed (8 USC § 1153(b)(5); 8 CFR § 204.6).

No more than 7 percent of the EB series visas may go to citizens of any one country annually.[62] Therefore, countries like India and China receive the same number of EB series visas in each year as Malawi, Liechtenstein, Luxembourg, and Costa Rica.[63]

The United States issues approximately one million permanent resident visas (green cards) each year.[64] Currently, about 40,000 visas are available for people with extraordinary ability (EB-1), 40,000 for professionals with advanced degrees (EB-2), and 10,000 for investors (EB-5).[65] This is only about 9 percent of the annual allotment of permanent resident visas.[66] Because these allotments must cover spouses and unmarried children,[67] *HSIs themselves only comprise about one-third of the visa recipients in these categories— and a paltry 3 percent of the green cards issued annually.* Compared with the U.S. workforce of 154 million people, the allotment of relevant EB visas increases that workforce by 0.08 percent each year. Considering the infusion of innovation, new firms, new jobs, and other benefits contributed by HSIs to the U.S. economy, this increase is vanishingly small and the foregone benefits (opportunity costs) correspondingly huge.

There is also a category of investor visas referred to as the E-2, which affords temporary status for foreign-born persons from countries with relevant treaties and whose sole purpose for coming to the United States is to direct and develop a "real operating commercial enterprise".[68] §§§§§ E-2 visas are not capped, but they are only valid for up to five years with indefinite renewals possible as long as eligibility continues and the treaty remains.[69] Approximately 150,000 holders of E-2 visas employ more than one million people in the United States.[70] Two notable differences between the EB-5 and E-2 visas are that the E-2 is limited to treaty countries, and it does not allow the visa holder to petition for permanent residency.

---

§§§§§ An E-2 visa holder is not eligible for permanent status and must establish intent to leave as part of his or her application (8 USC § 1101(a)(15)(E)(ii); 8 CFR § 214.2(e)(2)). About 150,000 E-2 visa holders employ over one million people in the U.S. (Mold, 2010, see endnote 68).

4. PROPOSED CHANGES IN U.S. POLICY

The pace, strength, and magnitude of our economic growth will be shaped by U.S. policy regarding HSIs. A major constraint is that U.S. immigration policy allots a very large share of permanent visas to family members without regard to their skills.[71] Current policy shows only a negligible interest in highly skilled labor and the economic benefits that it tends to generate.[72] Giving greater weight to economic growth and entrepreneurship will require major reforms and new priorities, principles, and approaches. Merely tinkering around the edges may produce incremental improvements, but more far-reaching changes are required to yield larger gains. More than family-oriented policies (and especially refugee/asylee policies), immigration policy that is oriented toward innovation, growth, and entrepreneurship can be measured in its effects, diversified in its targeting, and adapted to the changing macro needs of our economy.

Several of the recommendations below suggest the need for a new class of "provisional" visa that would permit the holder to work in the United States as long as they satisfy certain conditions such as English fluency, a STEM graduate degree, no criminal record, etc. Unlike "temporary" status that requires a later bureaucratic decision to be rendered permanent, the holder of a "provisional" visa automatically transitions to permanent status after passage of specified time(s) and having met additional expectations, such as regular employment or starting and growing a business, etc. Some of these conditions are discussed below. Properly designed, a provisional visa can be better than a temporary visa characterized by uncertainty and delays in processing renewals (when available) or by the need to start over when applying for permanent status. A provisional visa could also minimize certain social risks relating to uncertainties about whether the holder will in fact make the anticipated contributions to economic growth while avoiding the use of welfare benefits.******

4.1. Intensive Recruiting Efforts

To the extent that our current system considers economic factors at all, it relies on employers to recruit for their specific labor needs, but this reliance may not always suffice to produce the desired scale of economic growth and innovation that goes beyond the needs of specific, existing employers. Therefore, states and local communities should also be encouraged to actively advertise for and recruit HSIs with preferred characteristics, experiences, and skills, such as in life sciences, clean energy, or other disciplines that they deem important to their area's economic future. Such recruitment overseas was common in the nineteenth century when states advertised extensively in Europe to attract foreign workers,[73] and some has occurred more recently during tight labor markets. To be sure, the skills sought during the nineteenth century were much lower and they also were recruiting to populate a relatively empty continent. Although the number of such entrepreneurs to be recruited may not be large, their effect on the economy is likely to be disproportionately great. Of course, such recruitment will be of limited use if visa allotments for HSIs remain as under current policy.

Among those who might be recruited are immigrants who have demonstrated entrepreneurial success or capacity for scaling high-growth companies. Congress could create a provisional visa, with permanent status conditioned on satisfying specific criteria such as experience starting and scaling companies that reach defined levels of revenue, profit, and employees; or commercializing university research results to specified degrees of marketability or utility. Although the criteria for this visa should be demanding and reasonably detailed, formal educational requirements should not be used to exclude successful entrepreneurs who have followed nontraditional paths to starting and growing

---

****** Papademetriou and his colleagues advocate a provisional system that combines the H-1B and EB series 2 and 3 levels because such a such a large percentage of EB series visas—90 percent—are awarded to workers adjusting from temporary status (Papademetriou et al., 2009, endnote 77). Orrenius and Zavodny call for a system through which provisional visas are auctioned to employers (Orrenius et al., 2010, endnote 6).

companies. Even so, foreign graduates of U.S. universities are most likely to contribute to and take advantage of the qualities of America that foster innovation and entrepreneurship.

4.2. Recruit Graduates of U.S. Colleges and Universities

Many advocates of economic growth propose allowing almost all foreign-born graduates of U.S. universities to stay in the United States,[††††††] another form of recruiting. The United States makes a substantial economic and training investment in foreign students.[‡‡‡‡‡‡][74] It should reap, rather than export, the benefits delivered by a high-quality American education and experience. Foreign graduates of U.S. university programs can contribute significantly to a pipeline of talent for high-skill labor, innovation, firms, and jobs.[75]

In addition, economic communities and networks develop around strong academic programs and their graduates, both native- and foreign-born. Silicon Valley, Boston's Route 128, and the Research Triangle are only the best-known examples.[76] It is foolish and self-defeating to force foreign-born graduates of U.S. schools to abandon their professional communities, thus denying these communities the fruits of their labor in educating them at great cost.

Therefore, the United States should award a green card or at least a provisional visa as described above to any foreign-born person who earns a graduate degree from a U.S. university, particularly in a STEM discipline, provided that they meet other nominal criteria such as English fluency, no criminal record, job offer, etc. At a minimum, degree recipients should have more than one year after graduation within which to qualify for alternative visa

---

[††††††] Among these supporters are Mayor Michael Bloomberg, Craig Barrett from Intel, Senators Schumer and Graham, Robert Litan and Tim Kane from the Kauffman Foundation, Vivek Wadhwa, and many others (West, 2010; Kerr and Schlosser, 2010; Alden, 2010; Herman and Smith, 2010; Wadhwa, et al. 2009c).

[‡‡‡‡‡‡] For instance, graduate students generally and regardless of citizenship can receive free tuition to PhD programs, grants for research, and funding for teaching positions (West, 2010).

status by starting a company, creating jobs, working in a STEM job, or otherwise.

Variations on this theme could specifically target those who may be most likely to advance innovation and economic growth. For instance, the STAPLE Act proposes offering visas to those who earn a doctorate from a U.S. university in various STEM disciplines.§§§§§§ Given the disproportionate numbers of foreign-born people with doctorates or in doctoral programs who have founded STEM-oriented firms in the United States or who work at STEM-based firms, this approach would be fruitful. Another variation extends the offer to those who earn a master's degree in a STEM discipline from a U.S. university, as those with either master's or doctorate degrees in science or engineering are more likely to be involved with patenting activity.[77] Approximately 260,000 foreign-born students were enrolled at various stages of graduate STEM programs at U.S. universities in the 2005-6 academic year.[78]

A provisional visa for STEM graduates, rather than a temporary visa, might be more politically attractive and practical. Even well-designed temporary visas can be unpredictable and subject to exploitation and abuse.[79] As discussed below, temporary visas also can inhibit entrepreneurship. A provisional visa for graduates addresses those problems while also requiring that the graduate demonstrate that permanent residence is deserved, which balances against the "supply shock" risk and permanent increase in the labor market that accompanies an immediate green card.[80]

If a visa for STEM graduates does not provide for permanent residence, portability between employers or to entrepreneurship must be permitted at a minimum. The H-1B limits portability partly to allow the sponsoring employer to recoup its expenditures in recruiting and bringing the immigrant to the United States, but this rationale does not apply to students. Portability to a new employer allows the labor market to operate more

---

§§§§§§ *The STAPLE Act*, HR 1791, 111th Cong. (2009-10).

efficiently,[81] while portability to self-employment or entrepreneurship acknowledges that foreign students do not necessarily plan to start businesses at the outset but evolve into the idea.[82]

4.3. A Point System

Many immigration specialists and some legislators, including the late Senator Edward Kennedy, have advocated a system that awards points based on an applicant's potential contributions, including to economic growth.[83] Such a system could be used to identify entrepreneurs in emerging, strategic industries such as clean energy technologies.[84] It could be particularly effective as the global "race" for talent intensifies ("as it is widely projected to do").[85] Papademetriou cautions, however, that point systems are not intended for government to undertake job matching or to meet specific needs of specific employers within narrow timeframes.[86] Other nations have been using point systems for decades to target and attract immigrant entrepreneurs and innovators.

In addition to conventional point categories such as educational attainment, a U.S. system targeted on economic growth through innovation and entrepreneurship could award points and establish weights for attributes or experiences such as degrees in STEM disciplines; the nature of the degree (e.g., bachelor's, master's, doctoral); post-doctoral experiences; mentoring relationships and recommendations; previous time spent in the United States or engaged with U.S. business operations; actual committed investment capital and/or credit extension; patent applied for and received; licenses granted or received—regardless of patenting activity; economic and humanitarian outcomes and effects of the licenses; and experience with beginning a business(es), attracting financing, putting together and working with a founding team, and/or growing and scaling a business(es). A point system might also consider the viability of a business plan as evidenced by enforceable capital or credit commitments, employees hired, and/or contracts with customers to receive the relevant goods or services. Applicants might even be awarded points based on the amount that they or their sponsor are willing to pay the United States government for the visa.

Among the advantages of a point system are the political confidence and appearances of impartiality inspired by using objective selection criteria and data readily tied to the economy, labor markets, economic growth, and competitiveness objectives.[87] Among the disadvantages are an inability to adjust quickly to market changes and business cycles as long as Congress retains authority for determining selection criteria and allocating values,[88] but this disadvantage could be minimized if Congress delegated to an agency to determine the weightings in light of changing conditions.

4.4. Auction Systems

Immigration visas are scarce resources worth a great deal of money to those who obtain them. Indeed, these visas in a sense are windfalls to the immigrants who are fortunate and patient enough to win them over other applicants. As a matter of fairness, it is not at all clear why the full value of this windfall should go in the first instance to the immigrant; the society that enriches him, even as he is enriching it, has a strong claim to part of that value.

In this spirit, a number of economists—most notably Gary Becker, Barry Chiswick, Richard Freeman, Gordon Hanson, and Julian Simon—have proposed auctioning visas to the highest bidders who satisfy other economic (e.g., minimum bids) and noneconomic (e.g., noncriminal conduct) criteria.[89] Any such auction should be designed to achieve certain fairness and credibility constraints,[90] such as consistency, transparency, objectivity, and being well- and clearly defined. These features are all too lacking in the current system, which strongly favors those who happen to have family members, friends, and a lawyer already in the country.[91] A well-designed auction, then, might achieve at least as much as the current system.

It could allow sponsors, employers, family members, and even humanitarian organizations to bid on behalf of individuals,[92] or individuals could bid for themselves on behalf of their own entrepreneurial venture.[93] The government might even finance bids by low-income but credit-worthy, high-skill applicants out of a fund created from auction proceeds.[94]

Moreover, the bid amount need not be the only or decisive criterion in the awarding of visas. Depending on the weight society wishes to place on other criteria, the bid could be one factor among many with certain specified thresholds that must be met as a condition for the visa's validity.[95]

Such a system has several advantages. First, it would allow the market to measure the value of the underlying visa and the opportunities it presents to different applicants—an attractive approach for a capitalist system. Second, the amount of each bid would reveal that bidder's self-assessed productivity potential in the United States, an assessment backed by cash such that the winners are likely to be the most productive additions to the U.S. economy and society.[96] This information, along with other, noneconomic information, is socially valuable when it comes to selecting what is inevitably a limited number of immigrants.[97] Third, an auction would enable the government, and thus taxpayers, to recover the surplus—the difference between the costs of running the system and the value that bidders place on the visas—while shifting those costs to those who will benefit most from the visas in the first instance. Finally, as mentioned above, the government could use auction proceeds for social purposes.[98]

Critics may contend that an auction system would unfairly benefit those who can come up with the bid amount or who are connected with people who can finance it. Their rhetoric might depict the scheme as "selling the Statute of Liberty." This is a false critique, however, as it also applies to the current system, which greatly advantages those who have family members in the United States, the contacts to find an employer sponsor, or the financial resources to hire an expert lawyer.[99] One way of meeting this objection—and a good idea in its own right—is to experiment with auctions by using them, at first, only for a limited number of visas rather than moving directly to an auction system for all of them. An obvious place to start would be to eliminate the current "diversity visa" category and allocate those 50,000 visas annually through an auction.[100]

4.5. Start-Up Visa Act

Senators John Kerry (D-Mass.) and Richard Lugar (R-Ind.) introduced a bill to create an EB-6 category that grants two-year visas to immigrants who meet certain capital-raising thresholds from "qualified" venture capitalists or "super angels".******* They can qualify for permanent residency if they meet additional capital-raising or revenue-generating benchmarks and add at least five full-time jobs for nonfamily members. The proposed Start-Up Visa draws against the 10,000 visas allotted to the EB-5 investor visa.†††††††

The Start-Up Visa could be useful, but it is unlikely to have a lasting, material effect or grow the economy or produce new jobs on the scale of other strategies. For instance, less than 1 percent of new businesses receive angel or venture capital investment at the outset.[101] Thus, the act assumes a reasonably mature business ready to operate in the United States.[102] Only about 16 percent of the fastest-growing companies receive any venture capital funding at all.[103] The bill's proposed requirements also assume the existence of a network that includes United States citizens who are, or have access to, venture capitalists or super angels even before the person arrives in the United States, which further restricts the eligible applicant pool. This requirement also gives the venture capitalist or super angel additional leverage over the potential immigrant entrepreneur to demand more favorable financial terms, ownership interest, and other concessions.

******* *Start-Up Visa Act of 2010*, S 3029 and HR 5193, 111th Cong.
††††††† Ibid.

Finally, temporary visas limit entrepreneurial activity for at least two reasons. First, the temporary status creates uncertainty for possible capital sources. Investors and creditors willing to accept normal market risks may be less inclined to tolerate enhanced risks of deportation or nonrenewal if, for instance, the business hires only four employees instead of five or generates only $900,000 in revenue instead of $1 million. Such risks may cause investors and creditors to charge a price premium or make other risk-reducing demands, which will increase barriers to success and thus jeopardize permanent status.

Second, as noted earlier, very few new ventures succeed. About one-third of the 500,000 firms created each year will close within the first two years and only about 50 percent will make it to year five. Temporary status or conditions based on success may perversely induce people to sustain failed businesses rather than moving on to the next venture. Consequently, visas designed or intended to promote otherwise promising entrepreneurial activity should not unduly punish the prospects of failure beyond normal market conditions.

Therefore, while the Start-Up Visa legislation may provide some opportunities and even be an improvement, other paths seem more likely to maximize opportunities for HSIs to expand our economy.

4.6. A Job Creators' Visa

Another promising approach would create a provisional visa based on jobs created rather than investments. Robert Litan proposes allowing H-1B or student visa holders an additional six to twelve months to start at least one company and hire and retain at least one nonfamily member.[104] If they satisfy that threshold, he proposes an additional three to five years within which to employ and retain an average of five to ten nonfamily members for at least an average of three years, after which they would receive permanent residency status. Although this approach may suffer from some of the disadvantages just discussed, it does not unnecessarily tie the foreign-born entrepreneur to a single employer or even to the same employees. Nor does this approach restrict the applicant to starting only one company or keeping that company alive when the market otherwise suggests its demise.

4.7. Improve Existing Programs

Current restrictions in the number of available visas and the time required to process petitions, particularly for permanent residency status, harm the economy, damage American competitiveness, and reduce potential job creation and innovation.[105] At a minimum, the current allocations of H-1B and EB series visas should be increased and lengthy processing times for approving permanent residency should be reduced.

4.7.1. Modify Allocations

In the years before the economic downturn, demand for H-1B and EB series visas had exceeded supply.[106] The resulting denials and delays represent significant opportunity costs that increasing caps (or eliminating certain of them) and provisional characteristics could remedy. Congress should consider increasing the allocation of HSI visas, including by returning H-1B visas to at least the level of the early 2000s, tying visa allotments to changes in the overall population or civilian workforce or to changes in the gross domestic product, which has risen 64 percent in the last two decades,[107] or tying caps to the preceding year's usage.‡‡‡‡‡‡‡[108]

At a minimum, Congress should remove the 7 percent cap on immigrants from any one country receiving an EB series visa.[109] This cap inhibits the ability to attract skills sets, networks, and other capabilities intended to advance the U.S. economy. Restrictions by country or region perversely deny the United

---

‡‡‡‡‡‡‡ Hunt and Gauthier-Loiselle suggest that patent activity per capita would increase by six percent for every one percent increase in immigrant college graduates in the United States, and that such activity would increase by 12 percent for every 1 percent increase in foreign-born graduate degree recipients (Hunt and Gauthier-Loiselle, 2009). Maskus found that for every 100 foreign students who receive doctorates in science or engineering from a U.S. university, there are an additional sixty-two future patent applications (NFAP, 2010, citation omitted).

States access to contributions and innovations that those cut off by the cap would have made.[110]

To the extent there are concerns about increasing the number of immigrants beyond current allocations, room could be found by eliminating the so-called "diversity visa" program[111] under which 50,000 visas a year are available for applicants and their families from certain low-admission states and regions. The program suffers, however, from very practical problems that undermine its usefulness, particularly when balanced against the value of targeting HSIs and economic growth. Diversity visa holders often lack technical education or usable skills, and they usually lack any network or resources within the United States to help them acclimate and adjust to their new home. As a result, they and their families are less likely to contribute to economic growth. Moreover, the program is ripe for abuse through the submission of multiple applications under derivatives of the person's name, use of falsified documents, sales of successful applications to others in their country, and corrupt governments that may intercept and redistribute visas or destroy them.[112] Diversity visas are of doubtful economic, social, political, and ethical value, and the allocation could be better used to test some of the recommendations in this chapter.

Congress should experiment with a certain number of H-1B visas that would not be tied specifically to any particular employer or that the commitment be for one year. This change would not only address criticisms about H-1B holders being cheap and exploited workers and native-wage depressors, but also recognize that promotions, raises, and other indicia of upward mobility are now more frequently available across firms rather than within them.[113]

4.7.2. Accelerate Processing

The processing time for green cards and temporary skills-based visas can take *up to twenty years*.[114] The uncertainty, unfairness, and inefficiency inherent in such long waits affect the would-be immigrants, family members, employers, investors, creditors,

and others, and surely inhibit innovative thinking and investment of human and financial capital in productive ways.[115]
Processing times can be reduced by hiring more people, organizing them more efficiently, and updating technology. Increasing
fees and/or revenue from the point system or auction programs
proposed above could help to defray the costs of a faster
system.[116]

5. CONCLUSION

A U.S. economy that needs innovation and economic growth is
ill-served by law, standards, and systems designed to further outdated goals and dubious policies. A blatant disconnect exists
between our current HSI system and the demands of economic
growth through innovation and entrepreneurship.

Yet, a vast number of HSIs is waiting to contribute to these goals.
In many ways, HSIs are low-hanging fruit. Why, then, have policymakers failed to reap these potential rewards? What is the
source of lethargy and tolerance for an unambiguously deficient
system? Policy regarding HSIs and corresponding benefits for
innovation, our economy, and human welfare should not be held
hostage to the contingencies of reforming other parts of our
immigration system.

Immigration, particularly by HSIs, has been both "engine and
fuel" for the U.S. economy by providing knowledge, technology,
and even capital. HSIs invigorate national and global commerce
and trade and in doing so contribute disproportionately to
American jobs, wealth, and human welfare. Current HSI policies
and standards do not adequately serve these essential goals.

ENDNOTES

[1] William R. Kerr and William F. Lincoln, "The Supply Side of Innovation: H-1B Visa Reforms and U.S. Ethnic Invention" (Working Paper 09-005, Harvard Business School, 2008); Jennifer Hunt and Marjolaine Gauthier-Loiselle (2009), *How Much Does Immigration Boost Innovation?* Institute for the Study of Labor, Bonn, Germany, January 2009.

[2] Vivek Wadhwa, AnnaLee Saxenian, Ben Rissing, Gary Gereffi, *Education, Entrepreneurship, and Immigration: America's New Immigrant Entrepreneurs, Part II*, June 2007 (Study II; hereinafter "Wadhwa et. al 2007b").

[3] Kerr and Lincoln, 2008.

[4] Hunt and Gauthier-Loiselle, 2009.

[5] Ibid.

[6] Pia M. Orrenius and Madeline Zavodny, *Beside the Golden Door: U.S. Immigration Reform in a New Era of Globalization* (Washington, DC: The AEI Press, 2010); Hunt and Gauthier Loiselle 2009.

[7] George J. Borjas, "Do Foreign Students Crowd Out Native Students From Graduate Programs?" (working paper 10349, National Bureau of Economic Research, March 2004).

[8] Neeraj Kaushal and Michael Fix, "The Contributions of High-Skilled Immigrants," Migration Policy Institute, *Insight* no. 16 (July 2006).

[9] George J. Borjas, "Immigration in High Skill Labor Markets: The Impact of Foreign Students on the Earnings of Doctorates," (working paper 12085, National Bureau of Economic Research, March 2006).

[10] Hunt and Gauthier-Loiselle, 2009; Kerr and Lincoln 2008.

[11] Orrenius et al., 2010; Kerr and Lincoln, 2008; Kaushal and Fix, 2006.

[12] Darrell M. West, *Brain Gain: Rethinking U.S. Immigration Policy* (Brookings Institution Press, Washington D.C., 2010); Hunt and Gauthier-Loiselle, 2009; Arlene Holen, "The Budgetary Effects of High-Skilled Immigration Reform," Technology Policy Institute, March 2009; Kerr and Lincoln, 2008; Kaushal and Fix, 2006.

[13] Wadhwa et al., 2007b.

[14] Stuart Anderson and Michaela Platzer, "American Made: The Impact of Immigrant Entrepreneurs and Professionals on U.S. Competitiveness," National Venture Capital Association, 2006.

[15] Vivek Wadhwa, AnnaLee Saxenian, Ben Rissing, Gary Gereffi, *America's New Immigrant Entrepreneurs*, January 4, 2007 (Study I; hereinafter referred to as "Wadhwa et al., 2007a").

[16] AnnaLee Saxenian, "Silicon Valley's New Immigrant High-Growth Entrepreneurs," *Economic Development Quarterly* 16, no. 1 (2002).

[17] Daniel J. Monti, Laurel Smith-Doerr, and James McQuaid, *Immigrant Entrepreneurs in the Massachusetts Biotechnology Industry*, Immigrant Learning Center, June 2007.

[18] Anderson and Platzer, 2006.

[19] Vivek Wadhwa, "A Reverse Brain Drain," *Issues in Science and Technology* (Spring 2009): 45-52, http://ssrn.com/abstract=1358382 (hereinafter referred to as "Wadhwa, 2009a"); Wadhwa et al., 2007b; Anderson and Platzer, 2006.

[20] Herbert J. Schuetze and Heather Antecol, "Immigration, Entrepreneurship and the Venture Start-up Process," in *The International Handbook Series on Entrepreneurship, Vol. 3: The Life Cycle of*

Entrepreneurial Ventures, ed. Simon C. Parker (New York: Spring Science+Business Media, 2006), 10735.

[21] Susan J. Lapham, *We the American Foreign Born*, U.S. Department of Commerce, Bureau of the Census, (1993), 2 fig. 1.

[22] John A. Camarota, *Immigrants in the United States, 2007: A Profile of America's Foreign-Born Population*, Center for Immigration Studies, 2007.

[23] Dane Stangler and Robert E. Litan, "Where Will the Jobs Come From?" *Kauffman Foundation Research Series: Firm Formation and Economic Growth* (Kansas City, MO: Ewing Marion Kauffman Foundation, 2009).

[24] Ibid.; Dane Stangler, "High Growth Firms and the Future of the American Economy," *Kauffman Foundation Research Series: Firm Formation and Economic Growth* (Kansas City, MO: Ewing Marion Kauffman Foundation, 2010).

[25] Dane Stangler and Paul Kedrosky (2010), "Exploring Firm Formation: Why is the Number of New Firms Constant?" *Kauffman Foundation Research Series: Firm Formation and Economic Growth* (Kansas City, MO: Ewing Marion Kauffman Foundation, 2010).

[26] Ivan Light, forward to *Transnational and Immigrant Entrepreneurship in a Globalized World*. ed. Benson Honig, Israel Drori, and Barbara Carmichael (Toronto: University of Toronto Press, 2010), ix-xvi; Benson Honig, Israel Drori, and Barbara Carmichael, preface to *Transnational and Immigrant Entrepreneurship in a Globalized World*. ed. Benson Honig, Israel Drori, and Barbara Carmichael (Toronto: University of Toronto Press, 2010), xvii-xxiv.

[27] West, 2010; Orrenius et al., 2010; Peter H. Schuck, "The Morality of Immigration Policy," *San Diego Law Review* 45 (November/December 2008): 865-897; Monti et al., 2007.

[28] U.S. National Science Foundation, "Overview," *Science and Engineering Indicators 2010* Washington, DC: NSF, 2010) http://nsf.goiv/statistics/seind10/c/cs1.htm; U.S. National Science Foundation, "Chapter 3: Science and Engineering Labor Force," *Science and Engineering Indicators 2010* (Washington, DC: NSF, 2010) available at http://nsf.goiv/statistics/seind10/c/cs1.htm.

[29] NSF, 2010; West, 2010.

[30] Edward Alden, "U.S. Losing Ground in Competitive Immigration," *World Politics Review*, July 27, 2010.

[31] Review and Outlook, "The Other Immigrants: Low Quotas, Long Lines Hurt U.S. Competition for Human Capital," *The Wall Street Journal*, November 18, 2009 (hereinafter "Review, 2009"); NSF, 2010; Schuetze et al., 2006; Orrenius et al., 2010; Lesleyanne Hawthorne, "The Growing Global Demand for Students as Skilled Migrants," Migration Policy Institute, July 27, 2010.

[32] Schuetze et al., 2006.

[33] Anderson and Platzer, 2006; NSF, 2010; Schuck, 2008; Schuetze et al., 2006.

[34] Wadhwa, 2009a; Review, 2009; National Foundation for American Policy, "H-1B Visas by the Numbers: 2010 and Beyond," NFAP Policy Brief, March 2010; Richard T. Herman and Robert L. Smith, *Immigrant, Inc.: Why Immigrant Entrepreneurs are Driving the New Economy (and how they will save the American worker)*, (Hoboken, NJ: John Wiley & Sons, Inc., 2010); Kaushal and Fix, 2006.

[35] Wadhwa, 2009a.

36 Vivek Wadhwa, AnnaLee Saxenian, Richard Freeman, Gary Gereffi, and Alex Salkever, *America's Loss is the World's Gain: Americas New Immigrant Entrepreneurs Part IV*, March 2009 (Study IV; hereinafter referred to as "Wadhwa et al., 2009b").

[37] Ibid.; NFAP, 2010; Alden, 2010.

[38] Vivek Wadhwa, AnnaLee Saxenian, Richard Freeman, and Alex Salkever, *Losing the World s Best and Brightest: Americas New Immigrant Entrepreneurs Part V,* March 2009 (Study V; hereinafter referred to as "Wadhwa et al., 2009c").

[39] NSF, 2010; Demetrious G. Papademetriou, Doris Meissner, Marc R. Rosenblum, and Madeleine Sumption, "Aligning Temporary Immigration Visas with U.S. Labor Market Needs: The Case for a New System of Provisional Visas," Migration Policy Institute, July 2009; Demetrios G. Papademetriou and Stephen Yale-Loehr, *Balancing Interests: Rethinking U.S. Selection of Skilled Immigrants* (Washington, DC: Carnegie Endowment for International Peace, 1996).

[40] Schuck, 2008.

[41] 8 USC § 1101(a)(15)(H)(i)(B).

[42] 8 USC §§ 1184(c) and 1184(g)(4); 20 CFR § 655.731; 8 CFR § 214.2(h)(9)(iii)(A)(1).

[43] 8 USC § 1184(h).

[44] 8 USC §§ 1184(g)(1)(A)(vii) and 1184(g)(5)(C).

[45] Madeline Zavodny (2003), "The H-1B Program and Its Effects on Information Technology Workers," Federal Reserve Bank of Atlanta *Economic Review* Third Quarter (2003): 111; Anderson and Platzer, 2006; NFAP, 2010; NSF, 2010.

[46] Vivek Wadhwa, AnnaLee Saxenian, Ben Rissing, and Gary Gereffi, "Skilled Immigration and Economic Growth," *Applied Research in Economic Development* 5, no. 1 (May 2008): 514.

[47] NFAP, 2010; Anderson and Platzer, 2006.

[48] See http://www.uscis.gov/portal/site/uscis/menuitem.5af9bb95919f35e66f614176543f6d1a/?vgnextoid=4b7cdd1d5fd37210VgnVCM100000082ca60aRCRD&vgnextchannel=73566811264a3210VgnVCM100000b92ca60aRCRD.

[49] Norman Matloff, "On the Need for Reform of the H-1B Non-Immigrant Work Visa in Computer-Related Occupations," University of Michigan Journal of Law Reform 36 (Summer 2003): 815-913.

[50] Papademetriou et al., 2009.

[51] 8 USC § 1184(a), (n).

[52] West, 2010; Orrenius et al., 2010; Papademetriou et al., 2009; Matloff, 2003.

[53] Huma Khan, "Shooting Itself in the Foot: Is U.S. Turning Away Entrepreneurs?" *ABC News Politics,* April 21, 2010; Matloff, 2003; West, 2010.

[54] Khan, 2010; David Adams, "The Immigrant Answer to Recession," *PODER360*, April 30, 2001, Http://www.poder360.com/article_detail_print.php?id_article=4207; Matloff, 2003.

[55] 8 USC § 1153(b)(1); 8 CFR §§ 204.5(h)(2), (i), and (j).

[56] 8 USC § 1153(b)(2); 8 CFR § 204.5(k).

[57] 8 USC § 1153(b)(3); 8 CFR § 204.5(i)(2).

[58] 8 USC § 1153(b)(4); 8 CFR § 204.5(m)(5).

[59] 8 USC § 1153(b)(5); 8 CFR § 204.6(f).

[60] 8 USC § 1153(b)(5); 8 CFR § 204.6.

[61] 8 USC § 1153(b)(5); 8 CFR § 204.6.

[62] 8 USC § 1152(a)(2).

[63] Herman and Smith, 2010.

[64] Ibid.

[65] 8 USC § 1151(a)(2); 8 USC § 1151(d)(1)(A).

[66] Herman and Smith, 2010; Castillo, 2010.

[67] 8 USC § 1151(d)(1); 8 USC § 1153(d).

[68] 8 USC § 1101(a)(15)(E)(ii); 8 CFR § 214.2(e)(2).

[69] Nelson A. Castillo, "Gaining Access to the United States by Investing," *PODER360*, April 30, 2001, http://www.poder360.com/article_detail_print.php?id_article=4207.

[70] Nina Mold, "Guest Commentary: New Visa Holders Won't Create More Jobs Than E-2 Investors," *naplenews.com*, April 13, 2010.

[71] Schuck, 2008; Peter H. Schuck, "Immigration: Importing and Assimilating Diversity," in *Diversity in America: Keeping Government at a Safe Distance*, (Cambridge, MA: The Belknap Press of Harvard University, 2003), 75133; Schuetze et al., 2006; Papademetriou and Yale-Loehr, 1996; West, 2010.

[72] West, 2010; Orrenius et al., 2010; Alden, 2010.

[73] Demetrious G. Papademetriou, "Selecting Economic Stream Immigrants through Points Systems," Migration Policy Institute, May 18, 2007 (hereinafter referred to as "Papademetriou, 2007b"); Aristide R. Zolberg, *A Nation by Design: Immigration Policy in the Fashioning of America* (Cambridge, MA: Harvard University Press, 2006).

[74] West, 2010; Borjas, 2004; Monti et al., 2007.

[75] West, 2010.

[76] Orrenius et al., 2010.

[77] Hunt and Gauthier-Loiselle, 2009.

[78] Vivek Wadhwa, Guillermina Jasso, Ben Rissing, Gary Gereffi, and Richard Freeman, *Intellectual Property, the Immigration Backlog, and a Reverse Brain Drain: Americas New Immigrant Entrepreneurs Part III*, August 2007 (Study III; hereinafter referred to as "Wadhwa et al., 2007c").

[79] Papademetriou et al., 2009; Orrenius et al., 2010.

[80] Borjas, 2006.

[81] Papademetriou et al., 2009.

[82] Gerry Kerr and Francine K. Schlosser, "The Progression of International Students into Transnational Entrepreneurs: A Conceptual Framework" in *Transnational and Immigrant Entrepreneurship in a Globalized World*, ed. Benson Honig, Israel Drori, and Barbara Carmichael (Toronto: University of Toronto Press, 2010), 122144.

[83] Demetrios G. Papademetriou, Statement Before the Subcommittee on Immigration, Citizenship, Refugees, Border Security, and International Law of The House Judiciary Committee, U.S. House of Representatives, May 1, 2007. (hereinafter referred to as "Papademetriou, 2007a"); Schuck, 2003; Papademetriou and Yale-Loehr, 1996.

[84] Papademetriou, 2007a.

[85] Ibid.

[86] Ibid.; Papademetriou and Yale-Loehr, 1996.

[87] Papademetriou, 2007b.

[88] Orrenius et al., 2010.

[89] Schuck, 2003; Orrenius et al., 2010.

[90] Ibid.

[91] Schuck, 2003.

[92] Ibid.

[93] Orrenius et al., 2010.

[94] Schuck, 2003.

[95] Ibid.

[96] Schuck, 2003; Orrenius et al., 2010.

[97] Ibid.

[98] Schuck, 2003.

[99] Ibid.

[100] Ibid.

[101] Paul Kedrosky, "Right-Sizing The U.S. Venture Capital Industry," Ewing Marion Kauffman Foundation, June 10, 2009.

[102] Robert E. Litan, "Visas for the Next Sergey Brin," *The Wall Street Journal*, March 8, 2001, A19.

[103] Kedrosky, 2009.

[104] Litan, 2010.

[105] NFAP, 2010; Anderson and Platzer, 2006; Herman and Smith, 2010.

[106] Wadhwa, et al. 2007c; Orrenius et. al 2010.

[107] Review, 2009; NFAP, 2010; West, 2010; Orrenius et al., 2010.

[108] Papademetriou and Yale-Loehr, 1996.

[109] Orrenius et al., 2010.

[110] Papademetriou and Yale-Loehr, 1996.

[111] Schuck, 2003; Orrenius et al., 2010; 8 USC § 1153(c).

[112] Schuck, 2003.

[113] Papademetriou and Yale-Loehr, 1996.

[114] NFAP, 2010; Wadhwa et al., 2007c; Review, 2009.

[115] NSF, 2010; Wadhwa et al., 2009c; West, 2010; Papademetriou, 2009; Alden, 2010.

[116] Schuck, 2003.

5 : How to Improve Five Important Areas of Financial Regulation

Hal Scott*

T his chapter analyzes five important issues in financial regulation, most of which have been dealt with by the Dodd-Frank Act, and makes suggestions about the proper way to resolve them. First, it examines systemic risk, the major reason for regulating the financial system. The focus is on what to do about the three Cs of systemic risk: connectedness, contagion, and correlation. Second, it argues for more expansive use of cost-benefit analysis, using the consequences of the failure to do so with respect to Section 404 of the Sarbanes-Oxley Act as an example of why a better approach is needed. Third, it discusses the importance of securitization to the housing markets and how disclosure, alignment of incentives, and the role of the credit rating agencies should be treated. Fourth, it discusses the threat to the independence of the Federal Reserve System posed by the financial crisis and Dodd-Frank. Finally, it examines the negative impact securities class actions may be having on the competitiveness and efficiency of U.S. capital markets.

* Hal S. Scott is the Nomura Professor of International Financial Systems at Harvard Law School and the Director of the Committee on Capital Markets Regulation.

THE THREE CS OF SYSTEMIC RISK

The major rationale for regulation of the financial system has always been avoidance of systemic risk. Systemic risk comes in three flavors, all of which were on display during the financial crisis, the three Cs: connectedness, contagion, and correlation. Connectedness, or interconnectedness as it is often called, involves the problem that the failure of one institution (A) can cause the failure of another institution (B) because B has an exposure to A that exceeds B's capital. Contagion occurs when the failure of one institution causes the creditors of other institutions to withdraw funding for fear that their institutions will be next—the classic bank run. Correlation involves the same external event, e.g. the bursting of the house price bubble, having an impact on a wide set of institutions similarly exposed to that event. This section discusses the nature of each of these varieties of systemic risk and then turns to what the recent Dodd-Frank bill has done to contain or minimize them.

Connectedness

A chain reaction of bank failures traditionally focused on the payment system. Continental Illinois Bank, a Chicago bank, almost failed in the mid-1980s. Continental served as a payments correspondent to many small banks (making and receiving payments on their behalf). As a result, Continental held sizable uninsured deposits of these banks; in many cases the amount of such deposits substantially exceeded the capital of the depositor banks. If Continental had failed, those banks would have failed as well. Section 308 of the FDIC Improvement Act of 1991 gave the Federal Reserve Board certain powers to deal with the general problem of interbank credit. It permits the board to limit the credit extended by an insured depository institution to another depository institution. This may be feasible with respect to placements (actual loans) by one bank to another since the amount of credit extended is known in advance and fixed for a given term. However, such exposures are much more difficult to control when they arise from payment flows, as was the case with

Continental. Every time Continental received a wire transfer for the benefit of a customer of a small bank, the small bank had a risk of Continental's failure, and the small bank has no practical way to control the size of wire transfers received by its customers. The prospect of a chain reaction of small banks from the failure of Continental resulted in its rescue by the FDIC.

An even more serious version of the payment system chain reaction problem was presented by the possible failure of a payments clearinghouse in the United States, the Clearinghouse Interbank Payment System (CHIPS). As of 2009, there were 48 CHIPS participants, the majority of which were foreign banks from nineteen countries. CHIPS transfers in 2009 were about $1.4 trillion per day, and the average transfer was about $4.3 million. Under CHIPS rule 13, the failure of one bank to settle causes its positions with other banks to be deleted and unwound, causing the potential failure of other banks with net debit positions with the other banks. Before 2001, this was a very substantial problem—indeed it was commonly understood that such a chain reaction of failures would have to be forestalled by some form of public rescue. Large net positions resulted from an end-of-day settlement system, the exposures building up during the day. After 2001, CHIPS changed its basic mode of operation, converting to a continuous settlement system, leaving the end-of-day exposures quite modest in relation to the capital of participants. Payment system issues were not a problem during the financial crisis.

In the financial crisis, we instead saw a new version of the chain reaction problem, interconnectedness through derivatives. The concern was that the default of an institution on its counterparty obligations with respect to derivative contracts, particularly credit default swaps, could result in the failure of other institutions. It is more difficult to estimate the size and consequences of derivative counterparty default than of interbank deposit default. The chain may be longer, as the failure of one bank could lead to the failure of a counterparty, which in turn could lead to the failure of counterparties to the first counterparty and so on. Second, the actual losses of counterparties depend on the value of their positions, and collateral they hold, but these values are hard to estimate, particularly in an impaired market. Fear of such a chain reaction was prevalent in the recent crisis but the extent to which the fear was based on reality has yet to be determined. There were many problems in unwinding Lehman's large derivatives book when it declared bankruptcy but its failure did not trigger the failure of any of its derivative counterparties.

AIG's own failure was certainly caused by its derivative positions—as a writer of credit default swaps (CDS) on collateralized debt obligation (CDO) portfolios, its exposure increased as the value of CDO portfolios decreased, triggering calls for increased collateral, which it was eventually unable to meet. What is not clear is whether any of AIG's derivatives counterparties would have failed if AIG had failed. There is substantial evidence that Goldman Sachs, one of AIG's largest counterparties, would not have failed. It held cash collateral against AIG's failure to honor its CDS obligations, and covered possible shortfalls in the amount of collateral through hedges, through the purchase of CDS contracts written on AIG itself, with collateral on these contracts as well. A report by the Special Inspector General for the Troubled Asset Relief Program (SIGTARP) on the government's investments in AIG indicated that Goldman Sachs, a major counterparty, would have been made whole in the event of an AIG default.[1] Of course, other AIG counterparties, which included foreign banks, may have had more unprotected exposures—the history on this has yet to be fully written.

Contagion

A second form of systemic risk comes in the form of contagion. This has traditionally manifested itself in the form of a bank run. When Bank A fails, depositors in Bank B fearing that if A fails B might fail as well, withdraw their funds from B, thus causing B to fail even though B has sufficient capital. This can occur because

---

[1] U.S. Office of the Special Inspector General for the Troubled Asset Relief Program, *Factors Affecting Efforts to Limit Payments to AIG Counterparties* (Washington, DC: November 17, 2009), 16–17.

B's assets are less liquid than the withdrawn deposits and what assets can be sold must be sold quickly at fire-sale prices. There is substantial academic debate about whether such bank runs represent rational, nearly simultaneous reassessments of bank risk by banks' short-term creditors,[2] or indiscriminate withdrawals from institutions regardless of their underlying financial strength.[3] Either way, however, bank runs have plagued the banking systems of many countries for centuries.

Two principal antidotes involving public intervention have been devised to deal with the problem: deposit insurance and the lender of last resort power of a central bank. Deposit insurance meant that depositors with deposits below deposit insurance limits have nothing to fear from the failure of their bank. So seeing Bank A fail, the depositors of Bank B are much less likely to withdraw funds. The deposit insurance ceiling has been set to cover a large portion of the deposits of individuals who might be prone to making irrational judgments about the implications of the failure of Bank A for the failure of their own banks. The second antidote gave the central bank the power to loan to banks experiencing irrational runs, to be the lender of last resort to such banks. Such central bank liquidity replaced the withdrawn deposits, provided that the bank experiencing the run had adequate collateral (which meant sufficient capital) to pledge against the value of the central bank loan.

Significant bank runs were not a feature of the financial crisis; instead there were runs on nonbank financial institutions (which some call the shadow banking system, though this term is quite vague). The assisted acquisition of Bear Stearns, under which the Federal Reserve loaned $29 billion to JP Morgan on a nonrecourse

---

[2] For a discussion of this view, see, for example, Gary Gorton, "Banking Panics and Business Cycles," *Oxford Economic Papers* 40 (1988): 751, http://www.som.yale.edu/faculty/gbg24/Banking%20Panics%20and%20Business%20Cycles.pdf.

[3] See, e.g., Ted Temzelides, "Are Bank Runs Contagious?" *Business Review*, November/December 1997 (Philadelphia, PA: Federal Reserve Bank of Philadelphia), http://www.philadelphiafed.org/research-and-data/publications/business-review/1997/november-december/brnd97tt.pdf.

basis, was triggered by the combination of a run on Bear and the fear that the run could become contagious, triggering runs on other investment banks. The run on Bear and other banks principally manifested itself through the refusal of short-term repo funders to renew their funding. There was no deposit insurance to protect the exposure of these creditors, and at the time of the Bear run the Fed had not yet created a liquidity facility to act as lender of last resort for nonbanks (it created the Primary Dealer Facility for this purpose shortly thereafter). There is a dispute over whether Bear did have adequate collateral to back a Fed loan if such a loan had been available. The Bear assisted acquisition seemed to quiet the fear of contagion, at least for several months.

Runs did occur in the wake of the Lehman failure. First, other investment banks experienced funding difficulties as their CDS spreads dramatically widened after the Lehman failure. At that point, however, the Primary Dealer Facility permitted the Fed to supply funding to these banks, averting the consequences of a run. While the Fed has claimed that such funding was adequately collateralized, there is concern that this may not have been the case in some instances. Second, the Reserve Primary Fund, a money market fund with significant holdings of Lehman commercial paper, failed to honor its obligations at par, thus "breaking the buck." This triggered a run on other money market funds that was only averted by a combination of the supply of Fed liquidity and FDIC guarantees (the equivalent of unlimited deposit insurance). The Lehman case is actually a combination of the connectedness and contagion problem—the Reserve Primary Fund's failure to honor money market deposits at par was caused by its overexposure on Lehman commercial paper—connectedness. But its failure to honor its deposits at par caused runs on other funds not connected to Lehman—contagion.

Correlation

A third form of systemic risk is correlation. An external event can have a large impact on the financial system if important financial institutions have taken similar risks and are therefore all impacted by the external event. This is the story of the housing bubble, because various institutions had made loans or invested in securities whose values depended on residential real estate prices. Real estate exposure was the primary cause of the failures or near failures of several banks, perhaps most notably Washington Mutual and Wachovia. Similar real estate exposures also contributed to the capital weakness of the nine banks that initially received funds from the Troubled Asset Relief Program (TARP). Finally, high correlations between the riskiness of different CDOs—whose values were also largely dependent on real estate prices—also led to significant losses during the crisis in this roughly $4.7 trillion market. Although many valuation models used by banks to price CDOs had predicted relatively low correlations between the prices of different CDOs (due to diversification in their underlying mortgage-backed securities), the unprecedented declines in house prices caused many of these models to fail, with banks suffering large correlated losses across their CDO portfolios as a result.[4]

Dodd-Frank Measures to Limit Systemic Risk

In the broadest terms, the provisions of Dodd-Frank requiring more capital for systemically important financial institutions are aimed at minimizing systemic risk by making institutions less leveraged and therefore less prone to insolvency.[5] This makes chain reactions less likely because counterparties are better able to absorb losses. It also addresses correlation risk because with higher capital buffers, all financial institutions should be better able to absorb external shocks. These capital provisions are probably least effective in controlling contagion, however, since even well-capitalized institutions with relatively illiquid assets compared to liabilities are unable to withstand runs. Dodd-Frank

---

[4] See, e.g., Felix Salmon, "Recipe for Disaster: The Formula that Killed Wall Street," *Wired*, February 23, 2009.

[5] See, e.g., Dodd-Frank Wall Street Reform and Consumer Protection Act §§ 115(a)-(b) (2010) [hereinafter Dodd-Frank]; ibid. §§ 171(a)-(b).

does not determine how much capital will be required, or what counts as capital, matters principally determined by the Basel Committee for Banking Supervision for banks, with additional requirements imposed by the Fed for systemically important non-banks.[6] The Basel Committee is also focusing on liquidity requirements, which are more relevant to contagion.[7] Government-determined risk-based capital requirements sound good but are extremely difficult to devise given the ever-changing dimensions of risk—more should be done to strengthen market discipline in this area.

One major problem with the Dodd-Frank approach is the need for the Financial Stability Oversight Council to determine what qualifies as systemically important nonbanking financial institutions, which will be subject to heightened capital (and supervision).[8] In the case of banking organizations, these requirements apply to firms with $50 billion or more in assets.[9] This determination is fraught with difficulty. The inquiry must be focused on chain reactions or contagion since correlation risk by its very nature affects an overly broad range of institutions to single out some as systemically important. If institutions prudently limit their exposures to each other (a matter further discussed below), which "risk management 101" requires them to do anyway, then no institution should cause or suffer from chain reactions; perhaps, then, the quality of risk management is the key. If the focus is on contagion, and institutions comply with risk-based capital and liquidity requirements, it is hard to see what else the FSOC would be looking for. Further, there is a real danger that branding of institutions as systemically important could create significant moral hazard as creditors assume such institutions will be bailed out if they get into trouble. And the designated institutions will thereby enjoy a cheaper cost of capital, which is on net likely to

---

[6] Ibid. § 171(b).

[7] Basel Committee on Banking Supervision, *Strengthening the Resilience of the Banking Sector*, December 2009, 11, http://www.bis.org/publ/bcbs164.pdf.

[8] Dodd-Frank, § 115(a)(1).

[9] Ibid. § 115(a).

outweigh the increased cost of heightened capital and supervisory requirements. This creates a competitive disadvantage for those institutions not anointed as systemically important.

Connectedness

Focusing specifically on the chain reaction problem, there are two important promising provisions of Dodd-Frank. First, the legislation requires standardized and liquid over-the-counter derivatives contracts to be centrally cleared, thus mandating that these contracts be subject to risk-reducing clearinghouse requirements, such as margin requirements, and that any default of a clearing member is collectivized through all clearinghouse members absorbing the loss.[10] Many important details of this requirement will have to be determined by regulation, but given the key role counterparty exposures on derivatives play in the chain reaction problem, this is a welcome measure. As with CHIPS, however, one will now have to deal with the risk of a clearinghouse collapse and the fact that important clearinghouses will almost certainly have to be bailed out. This makes regulation of systemically important clearinghouses crucial, which the legislation fortunately leaves in large measure to the Fed, rather than just to the Securities and Exchange Commission and Commodity Futures Trading Commission, who are less qualified to deal with systemic risk. Second, Dodd-Frank provides that the Fed require large banks and systemically important nonbanks to limit their credit exposure (broadly defined) to other institutions to no more than 25 percent of their capital stock and surplus, thus significantly expanding current lending limits.[11] These exposures will be difficult to determine given the problems of valuing derivative positions, noncash collateral, and hedging offsets, but the fundamental approach is quite sound.

---

[10] Ibid. § 723(a).

[11] Ibid. §§ 165(e)(2)-(3).

Contagion

With respect to contagion, no specific new measures are formulated by Dodd-Frank although the new resolution procedures that extend the current FDIC-type procedures to systemically important nonbanking firms create a framework under which new approaches may be devised.[12] Numerous possibilities can be explored, ranging from bail-ins of creditors in a prepackaged bankruptcy to priorities for short-term creditors, thus forestalling the possibility of runs.[13] However, there is one provision of Dodd-Frank that makes future contagion more likely: the requirement that the Fed get the approval of the secretary of the treasury before fashioning emergency liquidity facilities of the kind that it devised in the crisis.[14] This is discussed at more length under Fed independence.

Correlation

With respect to correlation risk, the FSOC is supposed to monitor macroeconomic developments to identify potential shocks that could affect a wide number of institutions (such as asset bubbles) and then make recommendations as to what to do about them.[15] There is healthy debate among economists as to whether bubbles can be identified, and certainly doubt as to whether the FSOC would have sufficient confidence in their determination to curtail them. The verdict on this approach is clearly out.

Regulatory Structure

A final point with respect to systemic risk under Dodd-Frank: the failure to reform the regulatory structure by consolidating the

---

[12] Ibid. §§ 202-06.

[13] For a discussion of the bail-in proposal, see, for example, Wilson Ervin, "Are We Ready for the Next Crisis?" (Credit Suisse, March 2010), 8-9. For a discussion of the proposal giving higher priority to short-term creditors, see Oliver Hart and Luigi Zingales, "Curbing Risk on Wall Street," *National Affairs* (Spring 2010), http://nationalaffairs.com/publications/detail/curbing-risk-on-wall-street.

[14] Dodd-Frank, § 202(a)(1)(A)(i).

[15] Dodd-Frank, § 112(a)(1)(C).

regulatory agencies will hinder any implementation of the plans to detect and control systemic risk. The Committee on Capital Markets Regulation recommended that the United States have one regulator, along the lines of the United Kingdom's Financial Services Authority (FSA), the Fed, and possibly a separate consumer and investor protection agency.[16] The Paulson blueprint adopted a similar approach.[17] Instead, several new agencies have been created: the FSOC, the Consumer Financial Protection Bureau, and the National Office of Insurance. The only consolidation has been the minor merger of the Office of Thrift Supervision into the Office of the Comptroller of the Currency.[18] Our fragmented regulatory structure will pose increasing problems of coordination, opportunities for regulatory arbitrage, and problems falling through the cracks. The FSOC is not the solution; if everyone is responsible no one is responsible. Compare the lessons learned by the United Kingdom from the crisis. Concerned by the coordination of just two regulators, the FSA and the Bank of England, the United Kingdom has effectively abolished the FSA, converting it into a subsidiary of the Bank of England.[19]

COST-BENEFIT ANALYSIS AND SOX 404

Numerous commentators have noted the importance of using cost-benefit analysis (CBA) as a critical disciplining tool in the regulatory process,[20] and Executive Order 12,866[21] stipulates that CBA be applied in the case of any "significant regulatory action"

---

[16] See, e.g., Committee on Capital Markets Regulation, *The Global Financial Crisis: A Plan for Regulatory Reform* (Cambridge, MA: May 2009), 209 [hereinafter CCMR Plan for Regulatory Reform]; Committee on Capital Markets Regulation, Recommendations for Reorganizing the U.S. Financial Regulatory Structure (Cambridge, MA: January 14, 2009), 5 [hereinafter CCMR Recommendations for Regulatory Structure].

[17] U.S. Department of the Treasury, *Blueprint for a Modernized Financial Regulatory Structure* (Washington, DC: Treasury Department, March 2008) [hereinafter Paulson Blueprint].

[18] Dodd-Frank, §§ 312-13.

[19] George Osborne, Chancellor of the Exchequer speech at The Lord Mayor's Dinner for Bankers and Merchants of the City of London, June 16, 2010, http://www.hm-treasury.gov.uk/press_12_10.htm.

and submitted in a report to the Office of Information and Regulatory Affairs (OIRA), the interagency coordinating body.[22] Nevertheless, independent agencies have historically been exempt from the provisions of Executive Order 12,866 and are not officially obliged to provide CBA analyses of their regulatory rule making to OIRA.[23] Section 404 of the Sarbanes-Oxley Act (SOX), which was designed to check the soundness of internal procedures for financial reporting, is arguably one of the most prominent examples of regulators' failure to justify their actions in cost-benefit terms. SOX 404 has widely come to signify an overly burdensome and expensive regime that may have set the compliance bar too high to be an efficient and cost-effective method of fraud prevention, particularly for smaller market players. By enacting regulatory reform and subjecting independent agencies' financial regulations—including those implementing SOX 404—to more comprehensive CBA and to OIRA review, financial agencies could likely retain many of the intended protections of existing rules, but do so within a more rational and efficient regulatory framework. This section discusses SOX 404 in cost-benefit terms as an example of the broader problem of rationalizing independent agency action.

SOX 404 Overview

The Sarbanes-Oxley Act[24] was the culmination of swift (perhaps too swift) Congressional reaction to the corporate governance

---

[20] For a general background on the evolution of the use of cost-benefit analysis in the United States, see Cass Sunstein, "Cost-Benefit Default Principles," *Michigan Law Review* 99 (2001): 1651, 1660–63. For a discussion of cost-benefit analysis in the SEC regulation context, see Edward Sherwin, "The Cost-Benefit Analysis of Financial Regulation: Lessons from the SEC's Stalled Mutual Fund Reform Effort," *Stanford Journal of Law, Business & Finance* 12 (2006): 1.

[21] Executive Order no. 12,866, 58 *Federal Register* 51735 (September 30, 1993).

[22] Ibid. § 6(a)(3)(B)(ii).

[23] Executive Order no. 12,291, 46 *Federal Register* 13193 (February 17, 1981); Executive Order no. 12,866, §3(b). It should be noted that Executive Order no. 12,866 does require each independent agency to provide OIRA with a regulatory agenda detailing its legislative actions under preparation or review, as well as its significant legislative actions. Executive Order no. 12,866, §4(b), 4(c)(1). The SEC's submissions have not usually included a cost-benefit analysis, however. Sherwin, "Lessons," 12.

and accounting scandals that contributed to the fall of industry giants Enron and WorldCom, denting investor confidence in the integrity of the U.S. securities markets. Section 404 of SOX requires the management of public companies and their outside auditors to evaluate the effectiveness of internal controls over financial reporting. The SEC has stated that Section 404 procedures are intended to help companies detect fraudulent reporting early and deter financial fraud, thereby directly improving the reliability of financial statements.[25] Specifically, a company's management must state whether internal controls are effective and note any significant deficiencies or material weaknesses. An external safeguard is provided by an independent auditor's attestation of management's assessment, pursuant to guidance issued by the Public Company Accounting Oversight Board (PCAOB), an independent board established under SOX to provide guidance for auditors of public companies.[26]

Costs and Benefits of SOX 404

It has been noted that the SEC does not have an official program for CBA and the CBA that is conducted does not match the rigor expected by Executive Order 12,866.[27] Indeed, the U.S. Court of Appeals for the D.C. Circuit in two decisions has chastised the

[24] *The Public Company Accounting Reform and Investor Protection Act of 2002*, Public Law 107-204, 107th Cong., 2d sess., *U.S. Statutes at Large* 116 (2002): 745.

[25] Management's Report on Internal Control Over Financial Reporting and Certification of Disclosure in Exchange Act Periodic Reports, Exchange Act Release No. 33-8238 (Aug. 14, 2003).

[26] Committee on Capital Markets Regulation, Interim Report 117 (Cambridge, MA: November, 2006) [hereinafter CCMR Interim Report]. In July 2007, the PCAOB approved Auditing Standard 5 for public companies, which superseded earlier guidance (Auditing Standard 2) that had been provided by the PCAOB. Similarly, the SEC also issued guidance for management, to complement PCAOB guidance. Commission Guidance Regarding Management's Report on Internal Control Over Financial Reporting Under Section 13(a) or 15(d) of the Securities Exchange Act of 1934, Exchange Act Release Nos. 33-8810, 34-55929 (June 27, 2007). The PCAOB and SEC Guidance put in place a "top down risk assessment" that seeks to base the compliance with SOX 404 on risk-based criteria.

[27] See generally Sherwin, "Lessons," 17. Indeed, general lack of CBA analysis in the area of banking and capital markets regulation has been broadly noted for some time. Robert W. Hahn, *An Analysis Of The First Government Report On The Benefits And Costs Of Regulation* 10 (working paper no. E-98-05, Belfer Center for Science & International Affairs, 1998), http://papers.ssrn.com/sol3/papers.cfm?abstract_id=167048.

SEC for failing to take CBA into account in its rule making. In 2005, for example, the D.C. Circuit struck down an SEC rule requiring at least 75 percent of the directors on mutual fund boards to be independent, and for there to be an independent chairman.[28] When the SEC attempted to pass the rule again, it was once more invalidated by the D.C. Circuit court on the same grounds.[29] The SEC's reluctance to espouse rigorous CBA in promulgating rules with significant compliance costs and market impact contrasts with the practice of international financial regulators, for whom CBA is a critical aspect of rule making. The United Kingdom's Financial Services Authority, for example, routinely uses CBA in the exercise of its regulatory functions.[30]

Nowhere is this lack of rigorous CBA analysis more apparent than in the implementation of SOX 404, which has been widely criticized as being overly costly.[31] To illustrate, the SEC initially estimated that SOX 404 compliance would cost the average company roughly $92,000;[32] however, a 2006 Financial Executives International report estimated that in the first year of SOX 404 reporting, an average company paid around $4.36 million to meet its compliance requirements, including the vastly increased costs created by the obligation to procure an auditor attestation report.[33] And though the average recurring SOX 404 cost has come down somewhat in the wake of 2007 SEC reforms to SOX 404—the SEC estimates that mean recurring compliance costs decreased from $2.87 million in 2006 to $2.33 million in 2008 for Section 404(b) companies—first-year compliance costs have not

---

[28] *Chamber of Commerce v. Securities Exchange Commission*, 412 F.3d 133, 143 (D.C. Cir. 2005).

[29] *Chamber of Commerce v. Securities Exchange Commission*, 443 F.3d 890, 908 (D.C. Cir. 2006).

[30] Financial Services Authority, *Central Policy, Practical Cost-Benefit Analysis For Financial Regulators: Version 1.1* (London: FSA, June 2000), http://www.fsa.gov.uk/pubs/foi/cba.pdf.

[31] Stephen Bryan and Steven Lillian, "Characteristics of Firms with Material Weaknesses in Internal Control: An Assessment of Section 404 of Sarbanes Oxley" (working paper, March 2005), http://ssrn.com/abstract=682363.

[32] House Committee on Financial Services, *Sarbanes Oxley at Four: Protecting Investors and Strengthening Markets: Hearing Before the House Committee on Financial Services*, 109th Cong., 2006, 37.

declined significantly.[34] In addition to direct reporting costs, it has been estimated that public companies also face large indirect costs incurred as a result of managerial attention being focused on SOX compliance rather than on decisions regarding the business and investing activities of a firm.[35]

The expense burden has been felt more acutely by smaller companies. For example, it has been estimated that compliance costs for firms with less than $700 million of market capitalization averaged 0.46 percent of revenues, more than five times more on a relative basis than firms with greater than $700 million in market capitalization (0.09 percent of revenues).[36] Moreover, the 2007 regulatory SOX 404 reforms have not had a statistically significant effect on recurring compliance costs for companies with public float of $75 million or less.[37] Indeed, since the enactment of SOX 404, the SEC has granted a series of exemptions and extensions to smaller public companies, although in October 2009, the SEC announced that even these smallest public companies must begin to comply fully with SOX 404 for annual reports of fiscal years ending after June 15, 2010, without further exceptions or exemptions.[38] However, Congress overrode this requirement by including a provision in the Dodd-Frank Act that exempts com-

---

[33] Financial Executives International, *FEI Survey on Sarbanes-Oxley Section 404 Implementation*, March 2006. The FEI survey reports a single cost estimate for reporting member companies (ranging from less than $25 million in market capitalization to greater than $25 billion). It has been reported that there was an average increase in audit fees of $2.3 million in 2003-2004. See Susan W. Eldridge and Burch T. Kealey, "SOX Costs: Auditor Attestation Under Section 404," June 13, 2005, 3, http://ssrn.com/abstract=743285.

[34] U.S. Securities and Exchange Commission, Office of Economic Analysis, *Study of the Sarbanes-Oxley Act of 2002 Section 404 Internal Control over Financial Reporting Requirements* (Washington, DC: SEC, Sept. 2009), 4–5, http://www.sec.gov/news/studies/2009/sox-404_study.pdf [hereinafter "SEC Study"].

[35] Bryan and Lillian, "Characteristics of Firms," 3.

[36] Charles River Associates International, *Sarbanes-Oxley Section 404 Costs and Implementation Issues: Survey Update*, December 2005.

[37] SEC Study, 4–5.

[38] U.S. Securities and Exchange Commission, "Small Public Companies to Begin Providing Audited Assessment of Internal Controls Over Financial Reporting in Nine Months," news release, October 2, 2009, http://www.sec.gov/news/press/2009/2009-213.htm.

panies with market capitalizations of less than $75 million from having to comply with the SOX 404(b) provision that requires independent auditor attestation as to the adequacy of management's evaluation of internal controls.[39] This legislative override was fortunate, since small firms' compliance burden under SOX 404 would have been likely to reduce the competitive appeal of the U.S. capital markets as a viable arena for small firms raising capital, and for small business investors that may be unwilling to see the value of their investments disproportionately eroded through higher regulatory costs. By requiring a study in the Dodd-Frank Act of how to reduce compliance burdens for companies with market capitalizations between $75 million and $250 million, legislators also correctly recognized that many of the same cost-benefit issues that apply to the smallest companies are relevant for moderately larger firms as well.[40]

Despite these high costs, it remains empirically unclear whether adherence to SOX 404 achieves its intended benefit: reduced incidence of fraud or opaque and aggressive accounting practices by public companies. First, an empirical study suggested that average market reactions to announcements of accounting restatements since 2001 have decreased notably, suggesting that the market views an increasing number of such restatements as immaterial (and therefore, arguably not justified by the increased costs of SOX 404).[41] Second, the number of restatements revealing misreporting appears relatively low. It has been noted that only 38 percent of restatements from July 2002 to September 2005 had a market impact in excess of $5 million, and 12.6 percent of restatements resulted in a negative market impact of greater than 10 percent of company value.[42] Finally, even when there is actual reporting of fraud, heightened internal controls appear not to be

---

[39] Dodd-Frank, § 989G(a).

[40] Dodd-Frank, § 989G(b).

[41] Susan Scholz, "The Changing Nature and Consequences of Public Company Financial Restatements 1997-2006" (Washington, DC: U.S. Department of the Treasury, April 2008).

[42] CCMR Interim Report, 130-31.

the most effective way of detecting it. A 2008 study found that 46.2 percent of the initial detection of occupational frauds was due to tips, compared to 23.3 percent by internal controls.[43]

Future Reform

As described, the implementation of the SOX 404 regime has generated considerable controversy because the approach of imposing broad compliance costs on U.S. listed companies may not be justified by the benefits.

On the narrow topic of SOX 404, the Committee on Capital Markets Regulation has proposed that SOX 404 be implemented with a stronger focus on materiality to govern which internal controls should be most stringently examined.[44] While the 2007 guidance issued by the SEC and the PCAOB has gone far in underscoring the role of risk-based compliance, for example, to some extent in its reshaping of the term "material weakness,"[45] it has not gone far enough. Nor has CBA generally improved at either the SEC or PCAOB. The SEC's new Office of Risk Assessment, as led by Professor Henry Hu, may improve matters, but does the SEC really have the culture or capacity to do serious risk-based, e.g. cost-benefit based, regulation? Two broader potential reforms may help address this problem.

First, the scope of Executive Order 12,866, with OIRA review, should be extended to independent agencies. This type of review would mandate more rigorous CBA from all independent agencies, and go a long way toward rationalizing the U.S. regulatory process. For financial regulation specifically, this reform would bring the SEC in line with its international counterparts like the United Kingdom's FSA and also complement the methodology

---

[43] Association of Certified Fraud Examiners, *Report to the Nation on Occupational Fraud and Abuse*, 2008, U.S. Department of the Treasury.

[44] CCMR Interim Report, 131.

[45] Commission Guidance Regarding Management's Report on Internal Control Over Financial Reporting Under Section 13(a) or 15(d) of the Securities Exchange Act of 1934, Exchange Act Release Nos. 33-8810, 34-55929 (June 27, 2007).

behind risk-based oversight that imposes greater costs for greater regulatory risks. While there could be a concern that control by OIRA could threaten the independence of these agencies, it could be argued that independence is undesirable if it leads to unjustified regulation.

Second, beyond applying CBA in the context of OIRA review, regulators should more explicitly consider a range of regulatory options that could achieve a targeted benefit, and adopt the approach that imposes the minimum regulatory cost for a given benefit.[46] Had the SEC applied this approach to the implementation of SOX 404, it might have realized that it could have achieved the same level of fraud reduction through less-costly rules. This approach of minimizing costs for a given benefit, coupled with expanded OIRA review and mandatory CBA, would do much to improve the current financial regulatory structure.

SECURITIZATION

Securitization is a financial innovation of the 1970s with great economic value. Before the advent of the financial crisis, private securitizations—as opposed to those affected by the government-sponsored enterprises (GSEs), Freddie Mac and Ginnie Mae—dominated the market. While there were clearly deficiencies in the process—particularly the near-complete reliance on credit rating agency (CRA) ratings and inadequate disclosure—underwriting standards were set in response to the demands of private investors rather than bureaucratic imperatives. It is important to revitalize the private securitization market and to diminish the role of the GSEs so that underwriting standards, and thus mortgage lending, are responsive to market forces. But there is a need for added regulation of these markets to promote more transparency. Whether originators should be required to keep skin in the game is unclear, however. When armed with more information in the future, investors, who have been burned badly in the

---

[46] CCMR Plan for Regulatory Reform, 27, 32.

past, should be a more powerful force in disciplining bad securitized products and will rely much less on the analysis of credit rating agencies.

Importance of Securitization

Securitization is the process of converting a pool of financial assets into tradable obligations backed by identifiable cash flows. Issuers like banks raise funds via securitization to improve their capital and liquidity positions, and to transfer risk. Investors benefit from securitization because it gives them a wider choice of high-quality investments. Further, the demand for securitized products drives the supply of funds in the underlying markets, thereby improving the allocation of capital. On average, U.S. financial institutions securitized approximately 46 percent of the total credit they originated from 2005-7.[47] Because of the general benefits of securitization, a poorly functioning securitization market could pose a significant risk to economic growth.

The Current State of the Securitization Market

The global financial crisis has devastated the private market for securitized debt. Residential mortgage securitization volumes, not backed by Fannie Mae or Freddie Mac, collapsed from $744 billion in 2005 to $8 billion during the first half of 2009.[48] Throughout the financial collapse and afterwards, the federal government essentially became the only securitizer of mortgage loans; from 2006 to 2009, Fannie Mae and Freddie Mac's share of securitization grew from 39 percent to 72 percent of all domestic mortgage originations, while mortgages insured by the FHA have increased from 3 percent to 22 percent of total origination volumes over the same period.[49] Including the Federal Housing Administration and the Department of Veteran Affairs, the

---

[47] Securities Industry and Financial Markets Association, *Restoring Confidence in the Securitization Markets*, December 3, 2008, http://www.sifma.org/capital_markets/securitization-report-exec-summary.shtml.

[48] Jenny Anderson, "Debt-Market Paralysis Deepens Credit Drought," *New York Times*, October 6, 2009, http://www.nytimes.com/2009/10/07/business/economy/07shadow.html?_r=2&ref=business.

federal government backed 94.6 percent of all mortgage origination activity in 2009, and 96.5 percent of all new home loans in the
first quarter of 2010.[50] And in the aftermath of the crisis, the government has not only been involved on the origination side of the
securitization market; since the collapse of Lehman Brothers in
September 2008, the Federal Reserve has purchased over $1 tril-
lion in mortgage-backed securities (MBS) issued by the GSEs.[51]
This MBS purchasing activity by the Federal Reserve during the
last two years is highly significant: the Fed's purchases of MBS
comprise roughly half of its over $2 trillion balance sheet,[52]
and nearly 10 percent of the entire stock of outstanding U.S.
mortgage debt.[53]

Because Fannie and Freddie dominate the mortgage-underwrit-
ing market, private-sector standards for underwriting do not currently exist. Moreover, as a result of the crisis, the GSEs have
demanded that banks conform their loans to standards that often
may have little or nothing to do with the creditworthiness of the
borrower but are driven by excessive aversion toward risk—
bureaucrats do not want to be criticized for making bad loans. For
example, the full documentation requirement of the GSEs has
begun to exclude some high-quality self-employed borrowers
from the mortgage market, and the stricter appraisal requirements under the GSE Home Valuation Code of Conduct have significantly increased the difficulty of getting appraisals.[54] This
general tightening of the availability of credit does not reflect consideration of the factors in the more nuanced market-based

---

[49] Republican staff of the House Committee on the Budget, *A Roadmap for America's Future*, 111th Cong., 2d sess., January 2010, http://www.roadmap.republicans.budget.house.gov/Plan.

[50] Nick Timiraos, "Fannie, Freddie Fix is Federal Hot Potato," *Wall Street Journal*, May 24, 2010, http://online.wsj.com/article/SB10001424052748704167704575258503544541716.html?KEY-WORDS=Fannie+Mae+Freddie+Mac.

[51] "Exit, Pursued by a Bear," *Financial Times*, May 31, 2010, http://www.ft.com/cms/s/3/4a67d702-6cd1-11df-91c8-00144feab49a.html.

[52] Ibid.

[53] Federal Housing Finance Agency, *Enterprise Share of Residential Mortgage Debt Outstanding: 1990-2009* (Washington, DC: FHFA, 2009) http://www.fhfa.gov/webfiles/15556/Enterprise%20Share%20of%20Residential%20Mortgage%20Debt%20Outstanding%201990%20-%202009.xls.

approach recommended by the American Securitization Forum, which includes over 150 relevant predictors of loan performance, including loan type, lien position, loan term and amortization type, borrower information, property characteristics, and many others.[55]

In addition to impeding the operation of markets, the GSEs have been responsible for $226 billion of combined capital destruction since the end of 2007 and have required $148 billion of government capital support.[56] The GSEs have been backed by an initial $200 billion per institution, but still potentially face even greater losses than that.[57] Indeed, these large and growing taxpayer losses from the activities of the GSEs already have eclipsed the most recent estimates of roughly $66 billion of private sector losses from the entire TARP program.[58]

CRITICISMS OF THE REGULATION OF THE SECURITIZATION MARKET IN LIGHT OF THE FINANCIAL CRISIS

Among the criticisms of securitization markets are lack of disclosure requirements, poor incentive structures, and the failure of the credit ratings process.

---

[54] Jack M. Guttentag, "What Should Be Done With Fannie and Freddie?" The Mortgage Professor, *Yahoo! Finance*, July 22 2010, http://finance.yahoo.com/expert/article/mortgage/257571.

[55] For a complete list of these market based criteria, see American Securitization Forum, ASF RMBS Disclosure and Reporting Packages 36-81 (July 2009), http://www.americansecuritization.com/uploadedFiles/ASF_Project_RESTART_Final_Release_7_15_09.pdf.

[56] Federal Housing Finance Agency, *Conservator's Report on the Enterprises' Financial Performance: Second Quarter 2010* (Washington, DC: FHFA, 2010), 9, http://www.fhfa.gov/webfiles/16591/ConservatorsRpt82610.pdf.

[57] James R. Hagerty and Jessica Holzer, "U.S. Move to Cover Fannie, Freddie Losses Stirs Controversy," *Wall Street Journal*, December 28, 2009, http://online.wsj.com/article/SB126168307200704747.html.

[58] Congressional Budget Office, *The Budget and Economic Outlook: An Update* (Washington, DC: CBO, Aug. 2010) 18, http://www.cbo.gov/ftpdocs/117xx/doc11705/08-18-Update.pdf.

Disclosure Requirements

A fundamental problem in the securitization process was the lack of disclosure to the market of granular information about the composition of the pools of assets in securitization deals. Without such information, investors cannot properly value their investments.

Past regulations, primarily SEC Regulation AB which allowed but did not require dealers issuing mortgage-backed securities to provide granular loan-level data, have failed to provide investors with sufficient disclosure on securitization deals. As the Committee on Capital Markets Regulation noted, numerous securitization-related data for investors have historically not been made available to them, thus making accurate analysis of these instruments far more difficult.[59] The SEC's proposed new approach (released in April 2010) is commendable insofar as it seeks to improve standardized loan-level disclosure in ABS offerings;[60] it also appears to be consistent with the Dodd-Frank Act's similar new requirement for additional asset-level disclosures in securitizations.[61] This increased transparency should protect ABS investors, and also enable market participants—not just ratings agencies with preferred access to information—to more accurately evaluate securitization offerings.

Despite the progress made by the SEC in reforming Regulation AB, however, regulatory reform of ABS disclosure processes has been the subject of regulatory turf wars. Most notably, in early 2010, the FDIC has attempted to regulate the ABS disclosure process through its role in determining bankruptcy remoteness.[62] Although the Dodd-Frank Act commendably assigns promulgation of ABS disclosure processes to the SEC,[63] there is nothing in

---

[59] CCMR Plan for Regulatory Reform, 147.

[60] U.S. Securities and Exchange Commission, *Asset-Backed Securities, Exchange Act Release* nos. 33-9117, 34-61858, http://www.sec.gov/rules/proposed/2010/33-9117.pdf. Note that this proposed rule is along the lines suggested by the Committee. See, e.g., CCMR Plan for Regulatory Reform, 151.

[61] Dodd-Frank, § 942(b).

the act to suggest that the FDIC cannot continue to use its bankruptcy remoteness authority to regulate ABS disclosure. However, several factors suggest that regulating ABS disclosure would be better left to the SEC. First, it is the SEC's statutory responsibility to set disclosure and transparency requirements for primary and secondary issues, including of ABS.[64] Additionally, the SEC has substantially more experience than the FDIC in this area and is better equipped to exercise continued oversight over these disclosure requirements. While the Committee on Capital Markets Regulation, as well as the Paulson blueprint, called for meaningful regulatory consolidation,[65] given that this option was not followed, leaving regulation of these disclosures to the SEC is the most sensible option.

Incentives of Originators

Insufficient alignment of incentives between originators and investors in securitized products may have played a role in the recent credit crisis.[66] More specifically, numerous commentators have noted that the "originate-to-distribute" model in U.S. securitization markets caused mortgage lenders and securitization originators to excessively focus on up-front fees collected from direct lending or from structuring deals, without paying sufficient attention to the underlying quality of assets.[67] Investors, in

---

[62] Federal Deposit Insurance Corporation, *Advance Notice of Proposed Rulemaking Regarding Treatment by the Federal Deposit Insurance Corporation as Conservator or Receiver of Financial Assets Transferred by an Insured Depository Institution in Connection with a Securitization or Participation After March 31, 2010*, 4, http://www.fdic.gov/news/board/DEC152009no5.pdf.

[63] Dodd-Frank, § 942(b).

[64] Ibid.; Securities Act of 1933 § 7; Securities Act of 1934 § 13(a).

[65] See e.g. CCMR Plan for Regulatory Reform, 203. See also CCMR Recommendations for Regulatory Structure; Paulson Blueprint; and Chris Dodd, Chairman, Senate Committee on Banking, Housing, and Urban Affairs, "Summary: Restoring American Financial Stability – Discussion Draft 5," November 10, 2010 [hereinafter Dodd Discussion Draft] (discussing consolidating bank regulatory power in a newly created Federal bank regulator).

[66] CCMR Plan for Regulatory Reform, 129.

[67] European Central Bank, *The Incentive Structure of the 'Originate and Distribute' Model* (Frankfurt: ECB, 2008), http://www.ecb.europa.eu/pub/pdf/other/incentivestructureoriginate-distributemodel200812en.pdf.

turn, were subsequently burned when asset quality deteriorated and they had not obtained sufficient recourse against originators to recoup their losses, particularly in the case of securitizations backed by the riskiest mortgage products. Of course, if investors had had more information and not left all evaluation of their investments to the credit rating agencies, investor demands might have disciplined the originators.

The most common proposal to remedy this possible misalignment of incentives in the securitization process has been to create fixed retention thresholds for originators; the Dodd-Frank Act, for example, sets this threshold at 5 percent of the overall issue, subject to exceptions depending on the underwriting quality of the underlying assets.[68] While such proposals could potentially help improve originator-investor incentive alignment, setting a fixed percentage threshold for retention in all securitizations is an overly inflexible approach given that different deals pose different levels of risk. Insofar as Dodd-Frank allows deviation from the fixed 5 percent threshold contingent on underwriting quality, it introduces a desirable degree of flexibility into the process.[69] By exploring other methods of incentive alignment like restrictions on high-risk mortgage products from entering the securitization market, and strengthening of representations, warranties, and repurchase obligations by originators, regulators could introduce further flexibility.[70] To this end, Dodd-Frank has given the new Consumer Financial Protection Bureau broad discretion to promulgate rules restricting high-risk products at the origination phase (a useful power if reserved only for true outlier products),[71] but it does not strengthen originators' representations and warranties (though it does require that these representations and warranties be more fully disclosed).[72]

---

[68] Dodd-Frank, § 941(b).

[69] Dodd-Frank, § 941(b); see also CCMR Plan for Regulatory Reform, 142.

[70] CCMR Plan for Regulatory Reform, 141–42.

[71] Dodd-Frank, § 1011(a).

[72] Ibid. § 943.

Credit Rating Agencies

While CRAs have been broadly criticized since the financial crisis for their role in underestimating risks across a variety of rated assets, arguably nowhere has this failure been as pronounced as in their failure to rate securitized assets accurately. Since the third quarter of 2007, CRAs have downgraded substantial percentages of their ratings for residential mortgage-backed securities (RMBS) and CDO securities, even for those securities with the highest investment-grade ratings.[73] The impact of these ratings failures has been catastrophic because of the unprecedented scope of structured credit issuance in the years leading up to the financial crisis; from 2005 to 2007, CRAs facilitated the issuance of over $6.5 trillion into global credit markets.[74] Because of these failures, and despite some recent efforts by the SEC to improve various dimensions of the credit rating process,[75] there have been numerous broader proposals in the wake of the crisis to improve regulation of CRAs.

There are three broad themes that should guide the regulation of CRAs both domestically and internationally.[76] First, policymakers should seek to develop globally consistent standards for CRAs and enforce these standards at the highest governmental level (not, for example, at the state level in the United States). CRAs, like the investors they serve, operate globally, and regulating them at an international level would ease the burdens of compliance with new regulation, as well as the use of credit ratings themselves. Likewise, placing enforcement powers with the highest level of governments worldwide would promote consistent enforcement and avoid an inefficient and confusing patchwork

---

[73] CCMR Plan for Regulatory Reform, 155.

[74] Ibid. at 154.

[75] See U.S. Securities and Trade Commission, *Proposed Rules for Nationally Recognized Statistical Rating Organizations*, Exchange Act Release No. 34-57967 (Washington, DC: SEC, June 16, 2008) (proposing new rules applicable to NRSROs, many of which were adopted in February 2009 substantially as proposed or as modified in response to comments).

[76] Note that these three themes are largely distilled from the recommendations proposed in CCMR Plan for Regulatory Reform, 171–72.

approach to their regulation. The recent G20 agreement on several of these points represents progress in this direction,[77] though there is much more work to be done.

Second, governments should seek to separate themselves from the ratings process to the greatest extent possible. Governments should not interfere with how CRAs set ratings to ensure the functioning of market processes in ratings determination; nor should they seek to restructure the conflicts of interest in the issuer-pays CRA business model by giving itself the power to assign CRAs to issuers, as was proposed in the Franken Amendment to the U.S. Senate financial reform bill. Although the Franken Amendment was fortunately not adopted in the final Dodd-Frank legislation, the Dodd-Frank bill does unfortunately increase the scope for government interference in the credit ratings process by giving the new Office of Credit Ratings within the SEC wide authority to promulgate rules related to rating methodology.[78] Governments should also seek to reduce statutory and regulatory reliance on CRA ratings. There is no reason why reliance on privately determined CRA ratings should be hardwired into federal regulations, and the government should not support a private oligopoly in the credit rating industry, particularly where reliance on such ratings has proved extremely harmful in the recent past. On this score, Dodd-Frank justifiably requires that CRA-issued ratings be "purged" from statutes, with the relevant agencies required to promulgate their own standards for measuring creditworthiness.[79]

Finally, governments should seek to increase disclosure as to how ratings are determined, particularly for complex structured credit products. Doing so will enhance investors' ability to monitor more accurately the meaning of changes in credit ratings. By the same token, governments should not grant CRAs informational advantages over other market participants, as in the U.S. govern-

---

[77] G20, *Declaration on Strengthening the Financial System* 6 (April 2, 2009).

[78] Dodd-Frank, § 932(a)(8).

[79] Dodd-Frank, § 939.

ment exemption of CRAs from Regulation FD, which generally prohibits material information from being selectively disclosed to particular analysts. Governments should not support a private oligopoly in this industry, particularly when investors with access to the same information could perform independent evaluation of the data relevant to credit performance. In the United States, the Dodd-Frank Act delivers on both of these dimensions, by increasing the amount of disclosure for rating methodologies[80] and by eliminating the Regulation FD exemption for CRAs.[81]

FEDERAL RESERVE INDEPENDENCE

The independence of the Federal Reserve System (the Fed) is crucial to the U.S. economy. Its independence has allowed it to take necessary but unpopular measures to fight inflation and to be an aggressive, but again unpopular, lender of last resort when necessary, as in the recent financial crisis. Central bank independence is normally thought to involve independence from the administration or government, not independence from a legislative body.[82] Of course, in most Western democracies this distinction is without a difference since the administration controls the parliament—indeed, the administration is formed from the parliament. However, in the American democracy of checks and balances, the administration and the Congress each pose their own threats to Fed independence. Going forward, the threat from Congress may become the more significant one.

Crisis Response [83]

During the crisis, the Fed was an aggressive lender of last resort. It first cut its borrowing rate, then its discount window penalty rate to make it more acceptable for banks in trouble to borrow

---

[80] Dodd-Frank, § 932(a)(8).

[81] Dodd-Frank, § 939B.

[82] For a general discussion of the issue of central bank independence, see generally Sylvester C. Eijffinger and Jakob de Haan, "The Political Economy of Central-Bank Independence" (Princeton Special Papers in International Economics no. 19, 1996).

without fear that borrowing would signal their weakness. It created several new liquidity facilities and extended access to the discount window to primary dealers, including investment banks. In response to the run on the money market funds, it made loans to banks to buy unsecured and asset-backed commercial paper, and to special-purpose vehicles to buy certain assets from money market funds. It attempted to counter the severe dislocation in the securitization market by making loans to holders of asset-backed securities and became a major purchaser of the direct debt obligations and mortgage-backed securities of the government-sponsored entities (GSEs) Fannie Mae, Freddie Mac, and the Federal Home Loan Banks. In the process, the Fed balance sheet ballooned to over $2 trillion in 2009 compared with $852 billion in 2006, at the same time reducing the fraction of those assets in the form of U.S. Treasury securities (Treasuries) to 29 percent in June 2009 from 91 percent in 2006. Although traditional loans by a lender of last resort are sufficiently collateralized to prevent moral hazard for borrowers and to reduce risk to the central bank, it is increasingly clear that in many cases the collateral taken by the Fed was inadequate.[84] Many of these liquidity measures were taken with the prompting of Secretary of the Treasury Hank Paulson, who knew he could not get the Congress to appropriate funds for such programs[85]—this occurred only in October 2008, when the Congress enacted TARP when the economy was on the brink of disaster because of the possible collapse of major financial institutions despite the heroic measures taken by the Fed.

These crisis measures not only increased the Fed's risk, but the resulting shortage of Treasuries also hindered the Fed's ability to

---

[83] Much of this section is based on, and some is taken verbatim from, Glenn Hubbard, Hal Scott, and John Thornton, "The Fed's Independence is at Risk," *Financial Times*, August 21, 2009.

[84] See, e.g., Caroline Salas et al., "Fed Made Taxpayers Unwitting Junk-Bond Buyers," *Bloomberg*, July 1, 2010. For a discussion of Bloomberg's ongoing lawsuit to require the Fed to increase its disclosure of collateral for emergency loans during the crisis, see Josh Gerstein, "Bloomberg Notches Win in Fed FOIA Fight," *Politico*, August 23, 2010, http://www.politico.com/blogs/joshgerstein/0810/Bloomberg_notches_win_in_Fed_FOIA_fight.html.

[85] Henry Paulson, *On the Brink* (New York: Business Plus, 2010), 240-41.

conduct monetary policy. In order to counter the potential infla-
tionary impact of its credit expansion (a concern during much of
the crisis), the Fed sought to sterilize its expansion of "crisis credits" by selling Treasuries. But since its supply of Treasuries had
dwindled through its purchases of other assets, the Fed requested that the Treasury Department sell special issues of Treasuries
under the Supplementary Financing Program—not to raise revenue for the U.S. Treasury but simply as a measure to sop up
excess liquidity. As of June 2009, the Supplementary Financing
Account of the Treasury Department was about $200 billion,
almost half the size of the Fed's Treasury holdings.

Most of the Fed's lending was done under the authority of
Section 13(3) of the Federal Reserve Act, which permitted the Fed
in "unusual and exigent circumstances" to lend to "any individual, partnership or corporation," against notes that are "secured
to the satisfaction of the Federal Reserve Bank." Many, including
former Reserve Board Chairman Paul Volcker, questioned the
Fed's authority to engage in much of the lending.[86]

Loss of Independence and Dodd-Frank

When the Congress took up legislative reform in the summer of
2009, Fed bashing, particularly from Republicans, was all the
rage. It was the Fed that had bailed out the evil financial institutions on Wall Street. While Chairman Frank of the House
Financial Services Committee held the line against curtailing Fed
power (apart from consumer protection authority), and even
expanded it with respect to systemic risk regulation, the Senate
was a different story. The first proposal by Chairman Dodd of the
Senate Banking Committee would have taken away much of the
Fed's existing supervisory and regulatory power.[87] As the year
progressed, however, Fed bashing declined and Chairman
Dodd's subsequent proposals moved closer to those of the House.

---

[86] See, e.g., John Brinsley and Anthony Massucci, "Volcker Says Fed's Bear Loan Stretches Legal Power," *Bloomberg*, April 8, 2008.

[87] See Dodd Discussion Draft (discussing stripping the Federal Reserve of most of its bank regulatory powers and vesting them in a newly created Federal bank regulator).

So how does the Fed's independence fare under Dodd-Frank? First, the Fed's role in controlling systemic risk is now largely shaped by a new agency, the Financial Stability Oversight Council (FSOC), a ten-member group chaired by the secretary of the treasury, composed of regulators plus one nonregulator appointed by the president.[88] The remit of the FSOC is quite broad. The general counsel of the Federal Reserve Bank of New York suggested that the FSOC could even make monetary policy recommendations to the Fed.[89]

The Fed has an increased role in supervision, retaining its role as supervisor of all state banks and bank-holding companies, but getting added power to supervise on a consolidated basis all bank-holding companies with $50 billion or more of assets and any nonbank financial institution (NBFI) that the FSOC believes is systemically important.[90] How many NBFIs will be so designated remains to be determined. The Fed has also been given more power to regulate systemically important derivatives clearinghouses, which will play an increased role in general under Dodd-Frank.[91] The Fed in partnership with the FSOC is the systemic risk regulator. With more responsibility comes potential blame if it fails to prevent future crises, thus making the Fed more mindful of its political environment.

A major strength of the Fed has been its research capacity and *esprit de corps* of influential and able economists. Until now, no other agency has come close to matching these resources. However, Dodd-Frank has created a potentially powerful competitor to Fed research in the form of a new Office of Financial Research.[92] With competing centers of knowledge, Fed policy recommendations may be more contested.

[88] Dodd-Frank, §§ 111-12.

[89] R. Christian Bruce, "Oversight Council Might Urge Rate Hikes, New York Fed Official Tells Bar Organization," *BNA's Banking Report*, August 10, 2010.

[90] Dodd-Frank, § 113 (for non-bank financial institutions), § 165 (for banks with over $50 billion in assets).

[91] Ibid. § 805.

Fed monetary policy has been restricted by the narrowing of its authority under Section 13(3). No longer can the Fed make a one-off loan to a corporation as it did in the JP Morgan Chase acquisition of Bear Stearns or to the receivership it created in the case of AIG. Further, new mandates for adequate collateral no longer leave this issue to the sole discretion of the Fed. Under Dodd-Frank, Fed emergency lending procedures will be subject to new rules requiring that collateral with a "lendable value" be assigned to each facility, that this lendable value be "sufficient to protect taxpayers from losses," and that these procedures be terminated in a timely and orderly fashion.[93] Additionally, while such programs are in effect, the Fed must provide reports on the value of the collateral posted for emergency lending programs to the relevant House and Senate committees every thirty days.[94]

Most significantly, Dodd-Frank requires Treasury Department approval of Fed emergency lending facilities and submits these procedures to more extensive congressional oversight.[95] This measure was suggested by the administration in its June 2009 financial reform proposal and was not resisted during the legislative process by the Fed, which at various periods was fighting what it perceived were bigger battles over its supervisory jurisdiction. Some would point to the crisis and say this is not a problem. After all, it was Secretary Paulson who was encouraging the Fed to create new facilities to stave off the collapse of the financial markets. But that was then. Can we be assured that in a new crisis the secretary of the treasury will do the same, or in light of the criticism (unfair in my mind) of these facilities in the recent crisis, will a new secretary and his or her president want to shoulder responsibility for bailing out Wall Street? Also, remember that Paulson was running the financial show, not the White House. This situation is unlikely to repeat itself. The need for prior

---

[92] Ibid. § 152.

[93] Ibid. § 1101(a)(6).

[94] Ibid.

[95] Ibid.

approval represents a major incursion on the Fed's role as lender of last resort. The Congress should have stopped with the requirement of more adequate collateral.

Finally, the Fed will be subject to more extensive and frequent audits by the comptroller general.[96] The specific purpose of these audits is to monitor the Fed's operational integrity, accounting practices, and procedures for emergency lending activities.[97] Although the new procedures represent a greater degree of transparency in Fed practices, they do not reach the extent of transparency proposed in Rep Ron Paul's (R-Texas) "Audit the Fed" bill, which proposed opening Fed Open Markets Committee meetings to increased scrutiny. While the proposal passed the House, it ultimately failed in the conference committee that produced Dodd-Frank.[98] Even the more limited form of audit in Dodd-Frank, however, makes it is possible that some degree of heightened scrutiny may reduce the Fed's willingness to make politically unpopular but necessary policy decisions.

Conclusion

The Fed's independence has been seriously eroded by the crisis. With respect to monetary policy, its lender of last resort authority has been significantly curtailed and its independent monetary policy tools were compromised by its shortage of Treasuries. This is not presently a problem as it seeks to buy Treasuries to fight deflation but could be a problem if the focus turned to inflation and its shortage of Treasuries made it dependent on Treasury Department initiatives like Supplemental Financing. Further, the FSOC, as bubble-burster-in-chief, may put pressure on the Fed to burst bubbles, whereas before Dodd-Frank this was left entirely to the Fed without a new agency to put pressure on it. Finally, the Fed will be more rigorously audited and its enhanced role in

---

[96] Ibid. § 1102(a).

[97] Ibid.

[98] Ron Paul, *Audit the Federal Reserve*, http://www.ronpaul.com/legislation/audit-the-federal-reserve-hr-1207/.

supervision may expose it to further political attacks. Most of the Fed's problems lie not with the Administration, but with the Congress—a Congress that sees political profit in reining in Fed independence.

SECURITIES CLASS ACTIONS

Securities class actions are a unique American invention that demonstrates that not all inventions are a good thing. They negatively impact the competitiveness of the U.S. capital market because they are often not in the interest of shareholders.[99] Class actions generally result in institutional shareholders suing themselves while giving lawyers over 25 percent of the settlement amount. All shareholders pay for something they did not do and could not control. Certain shareholders recover because they happen to have engaged in stock transactions during the class period; in other words, recoveries are essentially random. The only justification for such class actions is deterrence, but it is hard to see how shareholder liability will deter bad management, particularly since it is almost always the consequences of disclosing a wrongdoing itself (e.g., the significant loss of firm value, reputational damage, and executive firings) rather than penalties imposed in shareholder lawsuits that provide any relevant deterrence for management.[100] Furthermore, the United States has a massive federal and state enforcement of securities laws. Given that these actions primarily affect shareholders, I would allow shareholders to decide whether to keep them at all and, if so, in what form.

Current Role of Securities Class Actions

Class actions present a very tangible liability risk for issuers operating in the U.S. capital markets, with one recent study estimating that an average public company faces a nearly 10 percent

---

[99] CCMR Interim Report, 71.

[100] See Hal S. Scott, *International Finance: Transactions, Policy, and Regulation* 17th ed. (Eagan, MN: Foundation Press 2010), 71.

probability of becoming subject to a securities class action in the course of a five-year period.[101] Moreover, the measure of liability faced in such suits can be both unpredictable and extensive. In 2005, U.S. public companies paid out more than $3.5 billion to settle securities class action lawsuits, not including the $6.2 billion settlement reached with WorldCom at the end of that year.[102] Excluding the exceptional sums involved in the Enron and WorldCom settlements, the average settlement in 2005 was $71.1 million—an increase of 156 percent over the $27.8 million average settlement in 2004.[103] The years 2005–7 saw eight of the decade's nine billion-dollar settlements. In 2008 and 2009, average figures for class action settlements were less dramatic, but nevertheless totaled an average of $28.4 million and $37.2 million for 2008 and 2009 respectively (with total settlement value of $2.75 billion for ninety-seven total settlements in 2008 and $3.83 billion for 103 settlements in 2009).[104]

Predictably, issuers in the United States are paying vastly more than their counterparts in other countries to insure against the liability risks from shareholder class actions. For example, figures show that the cost of Directors and Officers (D&O) insurance in the United States is 125 percent higher than it is in Europe,[105]

---

[101] Elaine Buckberg et al., *Recent Trends in Shareholder Class Action Litigation: Are WorldCom and Enron the New Standard?* (White Plains, NY: National Economic Research Associates, 2005), 2.

[102] PricewaterhouseCoopers Advisory, *2005 Securities Litigation Study* (2006), 18. A similar study by the National Economic Research Association excludes data related to both WorldCom and Enron, as well as any settlements reached by year-end 2005 but not yet finalized. Because this approach omits from the 2005 calculations many large settlements, it suggests a much smaller growth in the average settlement value between 2004 and 2005—approximately 28 percent. Although the NERA study suggests that, underneath the megasettlements, there may be some stabilization occurring in average settlement values, it also shows the scope of the upward shift in these values. According to NERA's study, the average settlement value for the period 1996-2001 was $13.4 million. The average settlement value for the period 2002-5 was $22.7 million. Buckberg et al., 6.

[103] Ibid.

[104] Ellen Ryan and Laura Simmons, *Securities Class Action Settlements: 2009 Review and Analysis*, Cornerstone Research, 2009, 2.

[105] Memorandum from Advisen and Association of Insurance and Risk Managers (AIRMIC), received August 19, 2010.

potentially setting high expense burdens for U.S. issuers compared to international competitors. This is likely one important reason why U.S. public capital markets have been gradually losing their competitive advantage to other international financial hubs and to private U.S. capital markets. By way of example, in 2009, foreign companies raised over twice as much equity in the private U.S. markets as in the public markets ($7.3 billion private vs. $3.1 billion public, or 70 percent private share of total global IPOs in the United States) compared to a historical average of 64 percent private from 1996-2006.[106] Further, the U.S. share of equity globally raised in public markets was 24.4 percent in 2009, below the historic average of 32.2 percent for 1996-2006.

Notwithstanding the above, high-profile incidences of corporate misfeasance, seen in the cases of Enron, WorldCom, and Tyco, as well as more recently in the securities swindles perpetrated by Bernie Madoff and Allen Stanford, underscore the importance of a strong framework for the enforcement of the antifraud provisions of U.S. securities regulation. Indeed, in the wake of the financial crisis, regulators appear to be taking a tougher approach to investor protection in the securities markets, even in jurisdictions such as the United Kingdom that traditionally have relied on a more principles-based, "light touch" approach to regulation.[107] Although securities class actions and the associated large settlements and damages awards might seem to provide effective deterrence against wrongdoing, commentators and practitioners alike have expressed considerable doubt about whether they do so in practice.[108] As briefly detailed below, class actions' punitive effects and the resulting allocations of wealth between actors in

---

[106] Ibid.

[107] Kate Burgess and Brooke Masters, "Insider Trading: a Bigger Bite," *Financial Times*, May 12, 2010, http://www.ft.com/cms/s/0/bbc0ee56-5dfa-11df-8153-00144feab49a.html.

[108] John C. Coffee, "Reforming the Securities Class Action: An Essay on Deterrence and its Implementation" (working paper no. 293, Columbia Law and Economics, October 2006), http://ssrn.com/abstract=893833; *Merrill Lynch, Pierce, Fenner & Smith, Inc. v. Dabit*, 126 S. Ct. 1503, 1510 (2006) (arguing that securities litigation "presents danger of vexatiousness different in degree and in kind from that which accompanies litigation in general" (quoting *Blue Chip Stamps v. Manor Drug Stores*, 421 U.S. 723, 739 (1975))).

the securities market have been analyzed as largely inefficient, undermining both the health and competitive pull of the U.S. securities markets.

Governance and Cost Benefit in Class Actions

The basic legal regime for bringing securities class actions in the United States is governed by Rule 23 of the Federal Rules of Civil Procedure, and by the Private Securities Litigation Reform Act of 1995 (PSLRA).[109] The regime allows an attorney to bring a claim against an issuer on behalf of an entire class of investors who purchased the securities issued and suffered a loss on their investments as a result of an issuer's alleged misconduct. Accordingly, a claim may be brought on behalf of an entire, indeterminate class of plaintiffs, subject to the requirement that there be a "lead" plaintiff, judged to be someone best representing the interests of the class.[110] Under Rule 23(b)(3), the basis for the vast majority of securities class actions, the class certification extends to cover all members of the investor class, unless one specifically "opts out" from proceedings, either to pursue a claim independently, or to drop out of the litigation altogether. There are a number of problems with this approach.

First, the alignment of interests between plaintiffs and their representative attorney is far from clear. The large number of plaintiffs involved, some of whom may never be aware of the suit[111] and may only leave the class when they expressly opt out of it, creates the risk of a principal-agent conflict of interest between plaintiffs and the class attorney. Class members (with the possible

---

[109] *Private Securities Litigation Reform Act*, Public Law 104-67, 104th Cong., 1st sess., *U.S. Statutes at Large* 109 (2005): 737 (codified as amended in scattered sections of 15 and 18 U.S.C.). One of the stated purposes of the PSLRA was to provide greater discipline in bringing shareholder suits, with a more stringent check on bringing suits, with changes in an issuer's stock price, without further investigation of culpability, being an insufficient basis on which to bring a claim. H.R. Rep. No. 104-369, at 31 (1995).

[110] Private Securities Litigation Reform Act of 1995 § 101(a).

[111] In suits filed under Rule 23(b)(3), class members must receive "the best notice practicable under the circumstances, including individual notice to all members who can be identified through reasonable effort." Fed. R. Civ. P. 23(c)(2)(B).

exception of the lead plaintiff) will likely not have chosen the attorney, and do not have access to effective coordination mechanisms for exerting control and direction over attorney conduct. Nevertheless, they are bound by the final settlement or judgment.[112] Commentators have therefore suggested that such class actions are susceptible to a heightened risk of collusive conduct between defendant issuers and plaintiff attorneys (agreeing to an early settlement that spares the uncertainty of trial and generates lucrative fees for the plaintiffs' lawyer).[113] Indeed, NERA found the ratio of settlements to investor losses in 2002, 2003, and 2004 to be 2.7 percent, 2.9 percent, and 2.3 percent, respectively. Moreover, plaintiffs often do not collect whatever settlement amounts they are awarded; one recent study found that only 40-60 percent of potentially eligible plaintiff shareholders collected any proceeds at all after a settlement award is reached.[114] Meanwhile, plaintiffs' attorneys are customarily awarded between 25 percent and 35 percent of any recovery (although this percentage may be declining),[115] indicating high agency and transaction costs in such litigation.

Further, the process of bringing securities class actions has given rise to a number of unsavory and abusive practices. Until the passage of the PSLRA in 1995, it was common for professional plaintiffs to own small pools of shares in large firms that enabled them to bring class action suits, in return for kickbacks from attorney firms.[116] Similar abusive practices have continued since the passage of the PSLRA, however, perhaps most notably as reflected in the indictment and conviction of several partners and lead

---

[112] See generally John C. Coffee, Jr., "Class Action Accountability: Reconciling Exit, Voice, and Loyalty in Representative Litigation," *Columbia Law Review* 100 (2000): 381.

[113] Bruce L. Hay and David Rosenberg, "'Sweetheart' and 'Blackmail' Settlements in Class Actions: Reality and Remedy," *Notre Dame Law Review* 75 (2000): 1377, 1389.

[114] Francis E. McGovern, *Participation Rates in Private Securities Litigation Settlement Distributions* (May 6, 2010).

[115] Buckberg et al., 6.

[116] Russell Kamerman, "Securities Class Action Abuse: Protecting Small Plaintiffs' Big Money," *Cardozo Law Review* 29 (2007): 853, 858-9.

plaintiffs of the firm Milberg Weiss on conspiracy charges related to an alleged $250 million kickback scheme for lead plaintiffs in shareholder class actions.[117] Since the passage of the PSLRA, attorneys have also engaged in so called pay-to-play practices that involve attorney firms making large payments to the campaign funds of state officials in return for being appointed as counsel for suits brought by state pension funds.[118]

Second, notwithstanding the large settlements involved and the nuisance value of such claims, securities class actions have limited deterrence benefit. This is in part because individual directors and officers are not usually personally liable for the amount of the claims,[119] leaving the punitive burden to fall on the shoulders of shareholders, who do not have day-to-day control over the decisions of the directors and officers of an issuer. It is also due to the fact that much of the deterrence against management misconduct arises from the prospect of disclosure of such conduct itself, and not from the resulting shareholder lawsuits, as discussed above.

Proposals for Reform

One potential solution to the efficiency and governance concerns set out above would be to give shareholders the choice of amending their bylaws to prohibit class action suits in favor of alternative dispute resolution, such as arbitration, or through some variation on current class action procedures.

---

[117] U.S. Attorney, Central District of California, "Milberg Weiss Law Firm, Two Senior Partners Indicted in Secret Kickback Scheme Involving Named Plaintiffs in Class-Action Lawsuits," news release, May 18, 2006, http://online.wsj.com/public/resources/documents/milberg-press05182006.pdf; "New York Attorney Sentenced in Kickback Scheme," *New York Times*, November 1, 2008, http://www.nytimes.com/2008/02/11/business/worldbusiness/11iht-kickbacks.5.9951917.html.

[118] See, e.g., Mark Maremont, Tom McGinty, and Nathan Koppel, "Trial Lawyers Contribute, Shareholder Lawsuits Follow," *Wall Street Journal*, February 3, 2010, http://online.wsj.com/article/SB10001424052748703837004575013633550087098.html?mod=WSJ_hpp_RIGHTInDepthCarousel.

[119] Individuals may be liable where the business is insolvent and where there is insufficient D&O insurance to cover the value of the claim, as happened in the case of WorldCom, for example, where outside directors paid $25 million each to settle the claim.

There are several potential drawbacks to subjecting more share-holder disputes to arbitration. First, shareholders would have to approve this dispute resolution mechanism through a proxy vote amending the bylaws of their corporation. Whether a present group of shareholders should have the right to bind all existing and future shareholders through such a vote may be debated, although this is the effect of all bylaw amendments. Second, the general counsel's office of the SEC issued an opinion in 1990 that the limited instances in which the Supreme Court has allowed mandatory arbitration of claims under the securities laws, as between brokers and their customers, should not be extended to the context of issuer-shareholder disputes.[120] While there is no legal reason that the SEC general counsel may not revisit this interpretation of the Supreme Court's arbitration jurisprudence—an interpretation that I regard as wrong—it is unclear whether the SEC would do so. As a more general matter, arbitration usually affords plaintiffs and defendants fewer procedural protections than does litigation, and plaintiffs generally lose the opportunity to appeal. And consumer advocates have made arguments against arbitration proceedings in other contexts (such as broker-age and credit card disputes), arguing that it favors repeat indus-try players over consumers.[121] Despite these potential problems with arbitrating shareholder disputes, the benefits of reducing burdensome shareholder class action litigation could be substan-tial, and at the very least, shareholders will be no worse off for having the right to choose.

Another alternative would be for shareholders to determine through their bylaws that shareholders be required to bring opt-in, rather than opt-out, class actions. Under Rule 23 of Civil Procedure, class actions proceed on the basis of an inclusive model, under which investors are automatically included unless they expressly opt out of proceedings. As commentators have noted, opting out is rare in securities actions,[122] leaving a large

---

[120] Ibid. at 111; Thomas L. Riesenberg, *Arbitration and Corporate Governance: a Reply to Carl Schneider, Insights* 4 (1990): 2.

[121] Kara Scannell, "SEC Explores Opening Door to Arbitration," *Wall Street Journal*, April 16, 2007.

class of investors who have little control over proceedings, or in some cases, no knowledge of or interest in their conduct. Basically, small shareholders do not care whether or not the litigation proceeds because they have so little to recover. But their automatic inclusion makes the litigation viable for the plaintiff attorneys.

The main advantage of allowing shareholders to opt into class action suits is that only shareholders who affirmatively want a class action suit would be part of one; investors who believed participating in a class action was not in their interest would not join the class, or those who were indifferent also would not be included. Additionally, an opt-in approach allows only those participating in the class to be bound by the ruling, leaving the remainder of the class with the possibility of pursuing a suit if they wish to do so.

This approach may also be more palatable to courts than arbitration. Rather than requiring shareholders to waive their right to bring class actions, switching to an opt-in regime just alters the procedure under which they are conducted. Moreover, opt-out regimes are used in other countries. For example, the United Kingdom, Sweden, and Spain use a system of group litigation in which potential claimants must affirmatively opt into a suit in order to participate.[123] In addition, the Fair Labor Standards Act in the United States also provides for an opt-in regime.[124] A switch to opt-in class actions is similar to other types of predispute agreements courts often enforce, such as waiving a jury trial or specifying a choice of forum or choice of law. The case for an opt-in regime is particularly strong when the shareholders affirmatively opt for such a system through the proxy vote procedure.

---

[122] Theodore Eisenberg and Geoffrey Miller, "The Role of Opt-Outs and Objectors in Class Action Litigation: Theoretical and Empirical Issues" (Cornell Law School Legal Studies Research Paper Series, Research Paper No. 04-019, March 2004).

[123] See Peter Mattil and Vanessa Desoutter, "Class Action in Europe: Comparative Law and EC Law Considerations," *Butterworths Journal of International Banking and Financial Law* (2008).

[124] 29 U.S.C. § 216(b).

CONCLUSION

This chapter has offered ideas in five important areas of financial regulation: control of systemic risk, the use of cost-benefit analysis, the revitalization of the private securitization market, the preservation of Fed independence, and the use of securities class actions. The first four subjects have been dealt with in the Dodd-Frank Act but often in a non-optimal fashion. Many of the shortcomings could be fixed through implementing regulation. Securities class actions have been a troubling feature of our public equity markets for a long time and shareholders need, in their own self-interest, to be more active in shaping their use.

6 ■ How Financial Regulation Might Harness
■ the Power of Markets

Frank Partnoy*

One of the major themes of this volume is the importance of sustained growth and dynamic efficiency, as opposed to static efficiency. In the past, static efficiency analyses of financial markets generally have led to one of two conclusions: (1) financial innovation is an unalloyed good, and financial markets must be left unfettered, free from the regulatory intrusions of mandatory disclosure and securities litigation; or (2) financial innovations are a source of deadweight loss and danger, and financial markets must be tightly regulated to constrain agency costs and control externalities.

As I understand it, one goal of "Rules for Growth" is to reach beyond static analyses, to find more sophisticated and helpful ways of thinking about the ongoing relationship between legal rules and sustainable growth. In this respect, financial innovation presents particularly difficult challenges. Although much

* Frank Partnoy is the George E. Barrett Professor of Law and Finance, University of San Diego School of Law. I am grateful to the Kauffman Foundation for support and to participants in the Third Annual Kauffman Summer Legal Institute on Rules for Growth for helpful comments and suggestions. I particularly want to thank Robert Litan, who has inspired and encouraged my work in the financial regulatory area for more than a decade, and George Priest, whose efforts to keep my intellectual follies in check began failing when I was his student, well before that.

financial innovation (automated payment processing, online transacting, and low-cost hedging with "plain vanilla" derivatives) is beneficial for growth, other innovation (undisclosed synthetic collateralized debt obligations, LIBOR-cubed swaps, and bonds with payments based on the number of wins by a professional basketball team) is of more questionable benefit.

Financial innovation differs from other forms of innovation in that it—like many of its products—tends to be derivative. The over-the-counter derivative markets, at roughly $600 trillion in notional amount, are by far the largest markets in the world, financial or otherwise. Significant portions of that derivative activity have led to a misallocation of capital, including most prominently the use of super senior tranches of synthetic collateralized debt obligations to shift the risks associated with subprime mortgages to and from financial institutions in ways that were hidden from financial market participants. Standardized derivatives play a valuable role in an economy, but over-the-counter derivatives are less useful and more dangerous.[1]

Moreover, the interplay between financial regulators and financial markets over time adds a layer of complexity to the analysis. Markets constantly search for regulatory arbitrage, so that many costly rules, even those with sensible static efficiency rationales, can have short useful lives. In addition, regulators are either inherently at a disadvantage, given the disparities in pay and expertise between government and financial services, or are subject to the industry revolving door that creates strong incentives to deliver economic rent instead of optimal policy. Given these complexities and challenges, it can be nearly impossible to draw conclusions about what kinds of rules best resolve the double trust dilemma that arises when new ideas and capital are combined.

---

[1] See Robert E. Litan, "The Derivative Dealers' Club and Derivatives Markets Reform: A Guide for Policy Makers, Citizens and Other Interested Parties," *Brookings Working Paper* (2010), http://www.brookings.edu/papers/2010/0407_derivatives_litan.aspx.

The most salient examples arise from the recent financial crisis, which has spurred reform efforts in numerous areas related to financial markets, ranging from consumer protection to corporate governance to derivatives. The proposed reforms in the Dodd-Frank Wall Street Reform and Consumer Protection Act (Dodd-Frank Act),[2] which became law on July 21, 2010, are sprawling and unrelated. Some are directed at problems related to the crisis. Most are not.

Overall, the reforms are a hodgepodge, lacking a consistent intellectual theme. In this chapter, I argue in favor of one unifying principle for financial regulation and reform, a core set of ideas to use in sketching a road map for new financial rules for growth. That basic principle is simple: Financial regulation should harness the power of markets.

Ironically, in recent decades, as financial markets have become more liquid, financial regulators have relied less on markets for regulatory purposes. This move away from market reliance has limited innovation and economic growth. It has locked regulators into relying on outdated and inaccurate balance sheets, on incompetent fraud investigators, and on undisciplined rent-seeking gatekeepers.

From a theoretical perspective, this move away from markets is a perversion of Ronald Coase's argument that transactions could take place either within markets or firms, depending on costs.[3] From a practical perspective, it has led to misallocation of and distortions in the cost of capital. Moreover, this regulatory move, particularly as it relates to reliance on credit rating agencies, was a core cause of recent financial crises. Whereas market forces might naturally have performed a regulatory or quasi-regulatory function, regulatory intervention has prevented these forces from acting to discipline or deter deleterious private action.

---

[2] Dodd-Frank Wall Street Reform and Consumer Protection Act of 2010 (Dodd-Frank Act), H.R. 4173, 111th Cong., (2d. Sess. 2010).

[3] Ronald Coase, "The Nature of the Firm," *Economica* 4 (1937): 386.

In this chapter, I consider three examples of the shift away from market-based regulation, in the areas of accounting, enforcement, and regulatory reliance. First, a rules-based approach centered on financial market gatekeepers, such as audit firms, has come to dominate accounting and mandatory disclosure, particularly for balance sheet reporting, resulting in disclosure that is not useful for market actors. Second, government agencies have come to dominate the investigation and prosecution of financial fraud, as legislative and judicial changes have limited the market incentives of, and scope of efforts by, the plaintiffs' bar and the private attorney general enforcement role. Third, prudential regulation has come to depend on regulated institutional measures of risk, particularly those embodied in credit ratings, even when market-based measures of risk are demonstrably more accurate and reliable.

In each of these three areas, regulators could harness the power of markets by changing rules to stir innovation and improve economic growth. First, regulators could require that companies create new "real" market value-based balance sheets to go alongside, or replace, their "fictitious" ones; such financial statements would force directors and officers to determine which assets and liabilities were reflected in equity prices, an exercise that would pressure them to allocate capital more efficiently. Such efforts would move the focus of accounting away from regulatory intermediaries in the direction of reality-based market forces.

Second, regulators could revitalize reliance on private enforcement of legal claims. I suggest two possible ways to do this: by incentivizing private litigants and by encouraging the creation of "synthetic common law." Incentivizing private financial fraud enforcement would pressure corporate actors to internalize more of the costs associated with fraudulent or manipulative activity. Likewise, specifying common law menus of hypothetical results to govern future disputes would increase certainty and reduce costs in transacting complex financial contracts. In general, a shift to privately enforced standards could leverage the Holmesian notion of law as a prediction of what a judge will do to govern the conduct of market actors in a more efficient manner.

Third, regulators could implement rules that rely on market measures of risk, instead of measures of risk generated by oligopolistic regulated institutions. Such changes would reduce the distortions that arise from "regulatory licenses," the entitlements to comply with regulation that have become the primary business of gatekeepers such as credit rating agencies. Specifically, I argue that market measures such as credit default swap spreads are viable substitutes for credit ratings.

ACCOUNTING: REQUIRE REAL BALANCE SHEETS, TO GO ALONG WITH FICTITIOUS ONES

The first proposal is that Congress should harness the power of free, well-functioning markets by requiring that public corporations, particularly financial institutions, include all of their assets and liabilities on their balance sheets.[4] Transparency is one of the central pillars of a well-functioning market, and it is central to overcoming the double trust dilemma.

Congress recognized the importance of transparency in 1933 and 1934, when it implemented a two-pronged approach to shine sunlight on the markets with (1) a requirement that companies disclose material facts, and (2) an enforcement regime for companies that do not make such disclosures. That approach was the backbone of economic growth for decades. Now that the markets have once again swung far from transparency and balance sheets have been opaque and fictitious, Congress should implement a similar regime to require that (1) balance sheets are a clear picture of a corporation's financial health, and that (2) there are consequences for companies that hide their debts.

---

[4] This proposal is derived from a recent white paper I coauthored with Lynn Turner, former chief accountant at the Securities and Exchange Commission, on off–balance sheet accounting. See "Bring Transparency to Off–Balance Sheet Accounting," *Roosevelt Institute White Paper*, March 2010, http://www.rooseveltinstitute.org/policy-and-ideas/ideas-database/bring-transparency-balance-sheet-accounting.

As in the 1920s, the balance sheets of major corporations recently have failed to provide a clear picture of the financial health of those entities. Banks in particular have become predisposed to narrow the size of their balance sheets, because investors and regulators use the balance sheet as an anchor in their assessment of risk. Banks use financial engineering to make it appear they are better capitalized and less risky than they really are. Most people and small businesses include all of their assets and liabilities on their balance sheets. But large financial institutions and public corporations do not.

This story began in the 1980s, when the derivatives market was relatively small and off–balance sheet transactions were largely unknown. The Financial Accounting Standards Board, the group that publishes most accounting guidance, suggested that banks should include swaps on their balance sheets.

The accountants' argument was straightforward. Banks already accounted for loans as assets, because the right to receive payments from a borrower had positive value. Banks already accounted for deposits as liabilities, because the obligation to pay depositors had negative value. A swap, the FASB argued, was no different: it was simply an asset and a liability paired together, like a house plus a mortgage, or a car plus a loan. (The asset part of the swap was the money owed by the counterparty; the liability part of the swap was the money owed to the counterparty.)

The FASB's premise was simple, common sense. When most people and businesses prepare financial statements, they list *all* of their actual assets and liabilities. The reason is straightforward: The government, creditors, and investors want to see the entire picture. Individuals and small business owners cannot hide some of their debts merely by relabeling them.

But banks foresaw that the burgeoning business of swaps would inflate the size of their balance sheets if they were reported as assets and liabilities. Banks wanted to profit from trading swaps, but they did not want to include swaps in their financial statements. Instead, they argued to the FASB that swaps should be treated as off–balance sheet transactions. In 1985, the banks formed a lobbying organization called the International Swap Dealers Association. That group, now widely known as ISDA, pressed the FASB to exempt swaps from the standard approach to assets and liabilities. The banks argued that swaps were different, because the payments were based on a reference amount that the swap counterparties did not actually exchange. ISDA was a forceful advocate, and the banks persuaded the FASB to abandon its argument.

ISDA and the banks have continued their lobbying efforts to keep swaps and other derivatives off–balance sheet, as they argued more generally for deregulation of these markets. As a result, banks and corporations that trade swaps do not play by the same rules as other individuals and businesses. Banks are permitted to exclude their full exposure to swaps from their financial statements, and instead report only the "fair value" changes in those swaps over time. Such reporting is like an individual reporting only the change in their debt balances, instead of the debts themselves.

A similar analysis applies to off–balance sheet treatment of deals that used "Special Purpose Entities," or SPEs. An SPE is a corporation or partnership formed for the purpose of borrowing money to buy financial assets. Historically, under accounting rules adopted by the American Institute of CPAs, corporations were required to consolidate any SPEs they used to finance assets. During the 1970s, if a transaction was a financing, both the assets being financed as well as the financing had to be reported on the balance sheet. During the following two decades, the finance industry lobbied for changes that would permit them to avoid consolidating SPEs for many transactions. In general, the revised approach required that a corporation include the assets and liabilities of another entity in its financial statements only if it had a "controlling interest" in that entity. Importantly, the banks and Wall Street quickly sidestepped these rules by engineering transactions in which the sponsor did not have legal control, but still had economic control and would suffer losses from a decline in the assets' value. The rationale was that if a bank did not have a legally controlling interest in an SPE, the liabilities of the SPE could remain off–balance sheet. The key question was: what was "control?"

That vexing question led many companies, most notoriously Enron, to create SPEs in which they held just a sliver of ownership, and therefore, they argued, did not have control. Enron's infamous Jedi and Raptor transactions were designed to take advantage of the so-called "3 percent rule," an accounting pronouncement that essentially permitted companies with less than 3 percent ownership of an SPE to keep the SPE's assets and liabilities off–balance sheet.

Enron became the poster child of off–balance sheet liabilities, and the FASB responded to public outrage about Enron's hidden liabilities by adopting FIN 46 and later a watered-down version called FIN 46(R), a new rule with a new acronym. FIN 46(R) recast the guidance on SPEs by creating a new definition of "Variable Interest Entity," or VIE. The new guidance ostensibly was designed to limit the kinds of accounting shenanigans that had permitted Enron to hide so many liabilities. But FIN 46(R), like the earlier rules, continued to focus on "control." In simple terms, if a bank did not have control of a VIE, it could keep that VIE's liabilities off–balance sheet.

In the aftermath of Enron, banks responded to this new guidance cautiously at first. During the early 2000s, there was a lull in off–balance sheet deals. But by 2004–5, banks were using new forms of financial engineering to create VIEs that, like Enron's SPEs, remained off–balance sheet. The FASB was aware of these problems, but decided not to rewrite FIN 46(R). By 2008, VIEs were even more common than SPEs had been a decade earlier. And the financial crisis did not reduce their use.

Congress should address the problems associated with the accounting treatment of swaps and VIEs by adopting a general requirement that companies record all of their gross liabilities in their financial statements. This provision should include all liabilities for which a company will use its assets to pay or liquidate those liabilities. It should include all liabilities that are, in substance, a financing of assets, regardless of legal form. Most crucially, Congress should require that balance sheets include assets and liabilities associated with swaps and VIEs. Without such transparency, regulators and investors who look at the reported assets and liabilities of financial institutions are looking at a mirage. It should not be a radical request to ask that financial statements of banks reflect reality.

Lynn Turner and I previously have detailed how Citigroup's financial statements did not accurately describe that bank. Instead, even during 2006–9, Citigroup's balance sheet presented a picture of a stable institution, with solid asset growth, relatively stable liabilities, and increasing net equity. That picture was a fiction. A similar analysis holds for other major financial institutions.

Accordingly, we have proposed the following language to require that corporations, and particularly banks, account for off–balance sheet liabilities:

> *The Securities and Exchange Commission, or a standard setter designated by and under the oversight of the Commission, shall, within one year from the enactment of this bill, enact a standard requiring that all reporting companies record all of their assets and liabilities on their balance sheets. The recorded amount of assets and liabilities shall reflect a company's reasonable assessment of the most likely outcomes given currently available information. Companies shall record all financings of assets for which the company has more than minimal economic risks or rewards.*

The motivation behind our proposal is simple. Abusive off–balance sheet accounting was a major cause of the financial crisis. These abuses triggered a daisy chain of dysfunctional decision making by removing transparency from investors, markets, and regulators. Off–balance sheet accounting facilitated the spread of the bad loans, securitizations, and derivative transactions that brought the financial system to the brink of collapse.

Banks argue that recording all liabilities will be too difficult, or will introduce too much volatility. They also argue that some contingencies have such low probabilities that they should not appear in financial statements. With respect to difficulties, banks already are required to assess material liabilities; recording them involves merely reporting a number they already have calculated for internal purposes. With respect to volatility, it is true that balance sheet valuations would become more volatile, but that is because they are more accurate. In any event, regulatory tools can be based on lagged reported balance sheet information, to reduce volatility, if such a reduction is warranted. Finally, low probability events are precisely those that should be included on balance sheets. Imagine how bank boards would have assessed the risks of their institutions if they had been required to record a probability-weighted estimate of the losses they would incur if housing prices declined by 30 percent.

In sum, companies should include swaps on their balance sheets. Companies should record all assets and liabilities of VIEs, in amounts based on the most likely outcome given current information. Companies should report asset financings on the balance sheet (not as "sales"). Congress should adopt a legislative standard requiring such disclosures (mere "guidance" from the accounting industry is not enough). These changes would lead to more meaningful financial statements, and therefore would better support sustainable growth.

ENFORCEMENT: REVITALIZE RELIANCE ON PRIVATE ACTORS

The second proposal is that policymakers should rely more on private market-driven actors in enforcing legal rules. The two specific areas of focus are securities litigation and arbitration of financial contract disputes.

First, during the past decade, both judges and legislators have limited the scope of private litigation in the securities area. The combination of the recent Supreme Court decisions in *NAB* (restricting foreign-cubed claims), *Dura Pharmaceuticals* (restricting loss causation claims), and *Stoneridge* (restricting aiding-and-abetting liability) have sliced the expected value of traditional securities litigation by perhaps half or more. Many scholars have supported these limitations, as part of the general policy move in favor of tort reform.

My specific recommendation is to revitalize reliance on private enforcement of antifraud standards by repealing these limitations on such enforcement. This recommendation is general, though three specific areas of focus would be the aforementioned Supreme Court decisions.

One reason to strength private enforcement is that enforcement by regulators has been less than optimal, for two reasons. First, it has been misdirected. Second, it has been ineffectual. Regulators have targeted only a relatively small number of cases, with limited success. Prosecutors have brought simple actions based on facts that are not representative of the most deleterious conduct. Examples include the prosecutions of Frank Quattrone, Martha Stewart, Jeffrey Skilling, as well as the recent SEC complaint filed against Goldman Sachs based on the Abacus 2007-AC1 synthetic collateralized debt obligation. Prosecutions based on obstruction of justice or false statements deter only obstruction and lying, not financial fraud. Likewise, focusing on representations peculiar to a particular CDO might affect those representations, but it will not be relevant to the underlying problems associated with CDOs.

Of course, private litigators have been criticized for similar reasons. But those criticisms have a different basis. One argument is that recoveries are circular, and merely involve collecting from one set of shareholders to pay other (or often the same) shareholders, with the net loss in social utility from the transfer made to the attorneys and the costs associated with the litigation.

Others argue that private litigation serves a deterrent function, though there is disagreement about whether the benefits of deterrence outweigh other costs.

Hal Scott has addressed these arguments in his chapter, and several commentators at the 2010 summer conference also criticized the role of the plaintiffs' bar as antigrowth. In response, I want to focus the debate on the incentives of plaintiffs' lawyers as contrasted to prosecutors, and the reasons why plaintiffs' lawyers might behave in the deleterious way critics suggest. Critics of the plaintiffs' bar, and even defense attorneys, do not claim that plaintiffs' lawyers are economically irrational in targeting specific conduct. To the contrary, plaintiffs' law firms resemble hedge funds more closely than regulators in their decision making. Because of the contingent nature of their recovery model, they react quickly and strongly to financial incentives. This reaction is both positive and negative: If cases are attractive financially, they will be pursued more aggressively; if they are not, they will not be filed or will be abandoned as soon as it becomes apparent they have negative expected value. Cases based on stock option backdating and structured finance were prominent examples: When it became apparent that stock option backdating cases had positive expected value, more than 100 were filed; yet the expected value of complex structured finance suits is less clear, and those suits are relatively uncommon.

A regulatory structure that controlled the incentives of the plaintiffs' bar could more easily create incentives for those actors to file (or not to file) appropriate cases. Yet regulators have largely abandoned this function. Judicial approval of settlements is mostly perfunctory; indeed, judges recently have shown more skepticism of government litigation than private litigation (with the Securities and Exchange Commission being the most notorious). Regulators rarely partner with private litigants in U.S. courts (Israel is a counterexample, where regulators and securities class action lawyers can work together pursuant to statute). Private and public litigation each can follow the other, but rarely work in tandem.

My point is not necessarily that regulatory policy should encourage or deter lawsuits. Instead, my point is that regulation should harness the market incentives of the plaintiffs' bar. Consider the SEC's lawsuit against Goldman Sachs based on the Abacus CDO. In that instance, instead of picking a particular targeted CDO and firm based on a dubious rationale, regulators could encourage or assist private litigants. Instead of selectively disclosing particular documents in public hearings, which generate political capital but matter little to policy, Congress or the SEC could publicly disclose all of the documents relevant to a class of conduct and hold a public forum for the plaintiffs' bar to discuss and consider causes of action.

Critics of the plaintiffs' bar should consider whether it is really the nature of the plaintiffs' bar they are criticizing or, instead, whether the problems arise from the institutional incentives created by the judicial system. If legal rules (particularly as implemented by judges approving settlements) established better incentives, parties would not have reason to engage in the practices that most trouble critics. Proponents of markets should not criticize market actors for responding to incentives. The solution is not to attack the market actors; it is to realign the incentives.

The recent bias against private rights of action is ironic given the growth of the regulatory state and the multiplication of legal rules, particularly in the areas of banking and securities. As the system has become more rules based, officers and directors understandably have focused more on complying with rules than on achieving the objectives of transparency and accuracy in financial statements. A market-based private enforcement regime could help shift the thinking of officers and directors away from simply complying with rules and instead in the direction of acting in a way they believe a judge would find acceptable at some future date. Moving toward standards enforced *ex post* (and away from rules specified *ex ante*) would help develop a culture of ethics in financial statements. This is particularly important given the failure of regulators to spot and remedy problems at major financial institutions. Without a robust private enforcement regime, a rules-based culture of financial innovation will always be one step ahead of the regulators.

The second enforcement topic is related to the first. The adjudication and enforcement of financial contract claims and disputes have evolved away from market-based enforcement in a similar way as legal rules in securities litigation. Complex financial disputes are rarely resolved through litigation, lawsuits involving swaps and other derivatives are rare, and there is virtually no case law for financial market participants to look to in resolving claims arising from the financial crisis, particularly claims based on individual negotiated derivative contracts. Substantive common law, which previously had provided guidance based on litigation decisions by private actors, has been disappearing.

Accordingly, a second proposal for revitalizing reliance on private actors in enforcement would be to encourage the selection of "synthetic common law" in contracts. I have set forth and defended this proposal at length elsewhere,[5] but I mention it briefly here because it fits analytically with the argument in favor of increased regulatory reliance on plaintiffs' bar. (More general arguments about the efficiency of markets for legal rules have been made more forcefully and eloquently by George Priest and Gillian Hadfield.)[6]

By "synthetic common law," I am referring to the notion that private parties might opt to create and use a body of law that does not actually exist. For example, suppose two parties negotiating a contract are considering which body of law should govern any future disputes. In the past, they have chosen New York law, as have most parties in their area of practice, but a recent New York case has been decided in a way the parties agree should not

[5] See Frank Partnoy, "Synthetic Common Law," *University of Kansas Law Review* 53 (2005): 281.

[6] See, e.g., See George L. Priest, "The Common Law Process and the Selection of Efficient Rules," *Journal of Legal Studies* 6 (1977): 65 (supporting efficiency conclusion with the argument that inefficient rules are more likely to be litigated, and then changed); Gillian K. Hadfield, "Bias in the Evolution of Legal Rules," *Georgetown Law Journal* 80 (1992): 583 (arguing efficiency conclusion holds only on average and cases are not a random sample).

govern their contractual relationship. California law includes a few cases in subjects similar to the parties' area of practice, with reasoning and outcomes that they find acceptable, but those decisions are nearly a century old, and the parties worry that a judge might decide a future dispute based on different principles. Courts in a few other states have published decisions in related areas, but nothing directly on point.

What should the parties do? My argument is that they should create, perhaps with regulatory encouragement (it is a public good that likely would be underprovided), a synthetic common law regime. Private synthetic law associations would be established, consisting of experts in individual fields of law. Those associations would publish menus of cases. The cases would involve simplified facts in particular areas of practice and would focus on the issues that, in the judgment of the association (and of parties who would choose that association), most likely would arise in future disputes. The cases could include published state and federal cases, or examples based on such cases, or even stylized Restatement-like versions of such cases with certain facts changed or omitted. Numerous associations would compete for a particular contract. Private parties might simply list, or check a box for, cases they selected to govern disputes under the contract.

The association would then commit to resolve disputes based on those cases. The association might describe, or even commit to, its anticipated mode or process of reasoning in any future dispute. The reputation of the association over time would be based on the extent to which it was able to keep its commitments. The association could incorporate information gleaned from actual cases it adjudicated into new synthetic common law for future parties to choose. Associations would compete for business over time. As with arbitration, courts would have limited review of association judgments.

From the perspective of private parties, synthetic common law would be no more complex *ex ante* than arbitration. Parties would simply select an association to adjudicate their disputes, and then select from that association's menu of cases a particular set of cases to govern their contract. The association would adjudicate any disputes based on the selected menu of cases, and the selected mode of legal reasoning, if applicable.

Note that synthetic common law is a hybrid of common law and the alternatives to common law. It contains some of the public aspects of common law and statutory law (e.g., limited judicial review, real common law cases forming the basis for synthetic cases included on a particular menu), as well as nongovernmental aspects of private law and private adjudication (e.g., synthetic common law associations are private entities). Synthetic common law also involves both *ex ante* and *ex post* specification of legal rules: the governing legal rules (e.g., cases) are specified *ex ante*, as they are in statutory and private law, whereas the results in particular cases are decided *ex post*, as in common law or private adjudication. Synthetic common law draws advantages from each.

Synthetic common law has certain advantages over common law, particularly in complex areas. Synthetic common law cases need not evolve over time in order to reflect social practice. A filter limits synthetic cases, just as one limits common law cases, but it does not depend on the potentially abnormal behavior of parties other than the contracting parties. Real cases and controversies are often based on disputes in which parties are behaving in an economically irrational manner. Numerous real cases are litigated because one or more parties misperceive the probability of recovery, the likelihood of victory, or both. Most importantly, the case or controversy filter is incredibly costly. The synthetic common law filter costs very little.

Synthetic common law likely would be fairer than common law, because it would avoid judicial temptation to create new law. The value of common law rules depends on their consistency (i.e., cases that are consistent with each other) and stability over time (i.e., the "stickiness" of precedent). Synthetic common law, because it is created all at once, is far more likely than common law to be consistent. Moreover, because synthetic common law cases will not change, absent agreement of the parties, during the life of the contract, they are guaranteed to be stable over time.

Synthetic common law *by definition* is replicable because the rules selected by the parties cannot change during the life of the contract, regardless of the views of particular judges. Synthetic common law eliminates the possibility that prospective overrulings or transformative rulings by judges will change the law relevant to any dispute between the parties. Under synthetic common law, private parties can avoid a bad case simply by not checking that particular box.

The number of competing synthetic common law regimes is virtually unlimited. Competition among synthetic common law associations would eliminate problems associated with the common law mode of legal reasoning. Successful associations would develop reputations for deciding cases using a particular mode of reasoning; they might even advertise a particular type of legal reasoning methodology.

In difficult areas of commercial law, where some cases may seem irreconcilable even after years of legal commentary, parties using synthetic common law could reconcile such difficult cases simply by deleting problematic sections. Hard cases may be useful for law professors and students, but private parties likely will not find the intellectual challenge of such precedents, as originally written, to be worth their commercial while. If a particular passage in a case seems troubling or confusing, the parties could simply delete it. Whereas common law in the United States now performs poorly in generating a public record of legal rules, synthetic common law guarantees an adequate number of on-point cases. If the parties do not believe the cases cover a specific point, they can change or add a case.

Because synthetic common law is a public good, like common law, it is subject to tragedy-of-the-commons limitations. Just as government attempts to ameliorate this problem for common law, it might do the same for synthetic common law, either by subsidizing its formation or providing a framework to give private parties assurance that their choices of synthetic common law would not later be limited by changes in actual statutory or common law. Without such assurances, parties would be unwilling to invest in a synthetic common law regime. Perhaps this is one reason why parties have not already adopted elements of synthetic common law.

Looking to market actors—whether to enforce antifraud rules *ex post* or to establish adjudicatory regimes *ex ante*—is a pro-growth strategy. Two perhaps underappreciated areas in which regulators might look more to market actors in the dispute resolution setting would be rules that better align the incentives of the plaintiffs' bar and harness those incentives, and rules that encourage the creation of synthetic common law.

REGULATORY RELIANCE: USE MARKET-BASED MEASURES OF RISK

Finally, I want to propose that regulators harness the power of markets by making financial regulation depend on market measures of risk. As with the other topics discussed in this chapter, reliance on markets is a mechanism for bridging the gap between ideas and capital, for encouraging the pro-growth allocation of capital to its highest use.

One of the Dodd-Frank law's most important provisions is a requirement that regulators remove many references to credit ratings from their rules.[7] Some regulatory judgments continue to depend on credit ratings and credit rating agencies, but generally regulators must remove references to the ratings of Nationally Registered Statistical Rating Organizations (NRSROs) and find viable replacements. The law does not say what the replacements should be.

---

[7] Dodd-Frank Act of 2010, Sec. 939(a-f).

My argument is simple: regulators should use market measures instead of ratings. Specifically, instead of relying on credit ratings and credit rating agencies (or institutions generally), regulators should rely on market measures of credit risk. In some areas, the markets for credit defaults swaps, and CDS prices, are potentially viable substitutes. In other areas, credit spreads based on bond prices—or "price talk" for not-yet-issued securities—might be viable. As a general matter, the point is that regulators should harness the power of financial markets, including prediction-like markets, because market prices will better reflect relevant risks than institutions such as credit rating agencies.[8]

CDS might not seem an obvious source of regulatory guidance. In a typical CDS transaction, one counterparty (the "buyer of protection") agrees to pay a periodic premium to the other counterparty (the "seller of protection"). In return, the seller of protection agrees to compensate the buyer of protection in the event a reference entity specified in the CDS contract experiences a default or similar "credit event." For simple CDS, the reference entity might be a corporation or government entity. For more complex CDS, the reference entity might be a portfolio of structured finance instruments. The various CDS terms usually are documented through a standard form agreement created by the International Swaps and Derivatives Association.

One of the most important terms in a CDS agreement is the definition of "credit event," the definition of which has become largely standardized. The most common credit event is the failure to pay by the reference entity. Other credit events include bankruptcy or "restructuring," which can vary depending on the parties' preferences as to how much interest reduction or maturity extension they wish to specify in the CDS agreement.

---

[8] I first proposed this market-based argument in 1999, and have revisited it several times since then. "The Siskel and Ebert of Financial Markets: Two Thumbs Down for the Credit Rating Agencies," *Washington University Law Quarterly* 77 (1999): 619. The data in this section is derived from my most recent research on alternatives to credit ratings, coauthored with Mark Flannery and Joel Houston. See "Credit Default Swap Spreads as Viable Substitutes for Credit Ratings," *University of Pennsylvania Law Review* 158 (2010): 2085.

CDS "prices," as measured in the market, represent the size of the premium paid by the buyer of protection, and are generally known as CDS "spreads." CDS spreads change over time based on supply and demand for particular CDS contracts. CDS spreads are analogous to insurance premia, and reflect market participants' assessment of the risk of a default or credit event associated with the underlying obligation.

In general, CDS are widely and deeply traded, and reflect market information about the credit risk of underlying financial obligations; several studies have shown that CDS markets generally reflect valuable information. Broad market participation suggests that CDS prices should convey information about counterparties' assessments of this risk. Notwithstanding the evidence that CDS markets generally reflect valuation information, regulators and market participants have resisted moving away from reliance on NRSRO credit ratings toward reliance on CDS spreads.

In recent coauthored work with Mark Flannery and Joel Houston, we presented evidence that credit default swaps based on financial institution obligations are potentially useful for regulatory purposes, as well as by private investors. Overall, the data show that changes in CDS spreads reflect information more promptly than changes in credit ratings, even during periods of intense market discord. CDS spreads increased during 2007 and 2008, as information became available showing that the probability of defaults by financial institutions was increasing. During this same period, credit ratings nevertheless remained relatively unchanged. We concluded from this data that CDS spreads are superior to credit ratings in reflecting information because of their market-based nature. In other words, markets (credit default swaps) responded to new information, while institutions (credit rating agencies) did not.

Specifically, during January 2006 through June 2007, CDS spreads traded in a fairly narrow range. The average spreads for the BBB group generally were between 40 and 50 basis points, while the spreads for the AAA and AA groups were between 10 and 20 basis points. Indeed, from early 2006 until early 2007, CDS spreads actually declined somewhat, reflecting a period of calm.

Then, beginning in March 2007, CDS spreads increased and became more volatile. The movements at this time were relatively small, particularly when compared to more recent volatility, but they correspond to two important early events in the financial crisis. First, various measures of subprime mortgage risk, including the ABX indices, had begun to increase in early 2007. The ABX indices, also published by Markit, reflect CDS spreads for mortgage-backed securities themselves, as contrasted to the obligations of the financial institutions we are examining. Second, New Century Financial, a prominent subprime mortgage broker, filed for bankruptcy protection on April 2, 2007. Although market participants did not yet know how much various financial institutions were exposed to subprime mortgages, the increase in risk was associated with an increase in both the level of CDS spreads on financial institutions and the volatility of CDS spreads. This increase was reflected in increased CDS spreads during March and April 2007.

Nevertheless, despite this negative information, average CDS spreads overall had increased only slightly by the end of June 2007. Average spreads for AAA and AA firms were just under 20 basis points and the spreads for the A and BBB firms were 25 and 47 basis points respectively. On an aggregated basis, the CDS spreads for all financial firms did not signal a warning of the troubles ahead until March 2007 at the very earliest, and even that signal was a quiet one.

The reaction of CDS spreads during July 2007 through the end of 2008 was more dramatic. Negative information was disclosed throughout the summer and fall of 2007, and CDS spreads increased to reflect that information. By the beginning of 2008, average spreads exceeded 100 basis points in each of the categories, and by June 2008 they exceeded 200 basis points. At the end of 2008, the average CDS spreads for the AA, A, and BBB firms were 340, 377, and 842 basis points, respectively.

Overall, two conclusions emerge from the CDS spread data history. First, CDS spreads responded quickly to the events surrounding the financial crisis beginning in 2007. Second, credit ratings became disconnected from market-based measures of information, such as CDS. Credit ratings remained largely unchanged through these periods, even as disclosures about the increased riskiness of rated financial institutions increased dramatically. Credit ratings did not respond to available information about financial institution credit risk, especially beginning in mid-2007.

One might argue that high credit ratings were justified throughout this period, notwithstanding the negative news, because they reflected the high probability of government intervention and rescue. This argument is convenient in hindsight, but has no support in the data. With respect to major financial institutions, credit rating agencies did not supply a government intervention rationale during this time period, and, more importantly, the likelihood of government intervention was not constant across either periods or firms.

To the extent credit ratings might seem preferable because of their stability; there is a simple way to mediate any unwanted volatility in a market-based measure: use a rolling average. Rolling average CDS spreads based on thirty-day or ninety-day periods would make manipulation of these markets difficult, if not impossible, and would mute any short-term volatility, or avoid, at least partially, the cyclicality associated with ratings. Regulation can be anti-cyclical even if the market measures it is based on are pro-cyclical. More fundamentally, stability is not attractive for regulatory purposes if that stability masks underlying real volatility in the markets. As is the case with the other areas discussed in this chapter, reality is better than fiction.

CONCLUSION

The recent financial crisis has made legislators and regulators skeptical of markets, and policy proposals have reflected that skepticism. However, one lesson from the crisis is that markets could have provided important regulatory tools, which might have prevented or ameliorated the collapse. Regulators should recognize these potential benefits, and should implement pro-growth rules designed to harness the power of financial markets.

7: Tax Policy and Growth

Alan D. Viard*

As discussed in Chapter 1, long-term economic growth is heavily influenced by capital accumulation and technical innovation. This chapter discusses the potential role of a move from income to consumption taxation in promoting capital accumulation and the potential role of research tax credit reforms in promoting innovation.

BACKGROUND: THE LONG-RUN FISCAL IMBALANCE

Choices about tax policy structure, particularly major issues such as the role of income and consumption taxes, cannot be properly examined without first looking at the federal government's severe long-run fiscal imbalance. As is widely recognized, the growth of Social Security, Medicare, and Medicaid is slated to dramatically outstrip the growth of revenue over the upcoming decades. The discussion below focuses on the alternative fiscal scenario set forth in a 2010 report by the Congressional Budget Office titled "The Long-Term Budget Outlook," which most analysts accept as a reasonable description of current policy.[1]

---

* Alan D. Viard is a resident scholar at the American Enterprise Institute for Public Policy Research.

Under this scenario, non-interest federal spending rises from 22.9 percent of GDP (itself unusually high, due to the recession, financial-sector bailout, and stimulus spending) in 2010 to 26.4 percent of GDP in 2035. Social Security accounts for part of the increase, rising from 4.8 to 6.2 percent of GDP. But its role is eclipsed by that of medical spending. Medicare roughly doubles as a share of the economy, from 3.6 to 7.0 percent of GDP. Medicaid and related spending also posts rapid growth, from 1.9 to 3.9 percent of GDP, partly due to the March 2010 health care reform law. These programs account for more than all of the growth in non-interest spending, as other programs shrink from 12.5 to 9.3 percent of GDP.

The Congressional Budget Office's alternative fiscal scenario assumes that federal revenue settles down at 19.3 percent of GDP, its average value in recent decades. (Revenue is an unusually low 14.9 percent of GDP in 2010, reflecting the recession and the stimulus tax cuts). The gap between non-interest spending and revenue gives rise to large deficits, with the resulting debt obligations triggering large interest outlays that further add to the deficit. In 2035, publicly held debt is projected to be a staggering 185 percent of annual GDP, up from 63 percent in 2010. Interest on the debt is forecast to be 8.7 percent of GDP, which combined with the excess of non-interest spending over revenue, results in a deficit of 15.9 percent of GDP. Of course, the situation only becomes worse after 2035.

These projections are not intended to describe what will actually happen, but rather what *would* happen if current policies were maintained. The projections demonstrate that current policies are unsustainable and must be modified. It will be necessary to restrain the growth of Social Security and (especially) medical spending relative to its current policy path, increase revenue relative to its recent share of GDP, or both.

---

[1] Congressional Budget Office, *The Long-Term Budget Outlook* (Washington, DC: Government Printing Office, 2010).

Economic growth is likely to be stronger to the extent that the fiscal gap is addressed through spending restraint rather than tax increases. Depending on the specific provisions, though, spending restraint can have distributional and other disadvantages. I argued, in Viard 2009, that spending restraint should be a major part of the response to the fiscal imbalance. But I also noted that it is politically impossible to close the fiscal gap solely on the spending side and that revenue will need to rise, as a share of GDP.[2]

Because this chapter is devoted to tax rather than spending policy, I do not further address spending restraint. Instead, I consider the ways in which the tax system can be reconfigured to minimize any drag on economic growth, even as the overall tax burden increases. I first discuss a possible shift to consumption taxation and then consider more modest measures, related to the research tax credit, that can be pursued within the current income tax system.

POTENTIAL ADVANTAGES OF CONSUMPTION TAXATION

Many countries obtain some of their revenue from consumption taxation, although most of them also raise some revenue from income taxes. The widespread use of consumption taxation reflects the recognition of its potential economic advantages over income taxation.

The fundamental difference between income taxation and consumption taxation is that consumption taxation provides more favorable treatment of capital accumulation. Unlike consumption taxation, income taxation imposes a penalty on saving.

To illustrate this point, consider two individuals, Patient and Impatient, each of whom earns $100 of wages today. Impatient wishes to consume only today, while Patient wishes to consume only at a future date. Savings can be invested by firms in

---

[2] Alan D. Viard, "Four Long-Term Fiscal Realities," *Business Economics* 44 (2009): 143–49.

machines that yield a 100 percent rate of return between now and the (potentially distant) future date. In a world with no taxes, Impatient consumes $100 today. Patient lends the $100 to a firm, which builds a machine that yields a $200 payoff in the future; the firm then pays Patient back her $100 loan and $100 interest, allowing her to consume $200 in the future.

What happens in a world with a 20 percent income tax? Impatient pays $20 tax on his wages when they are earned and consumes the remaining $80, which is 20 percent less than in the no-tax world. Patient also pays a $20 wage tax and lends the remaining $80 to the firm. On her $80 loan, she earns $80 interest and is repaid $160 by the firm, reflecting the payoff on machines. However, a $16 tax is imposed on the $80 interest. Patient is left with $144, which is 28 percent less than in the no-tax world, compared to a mere 20 percent reduction in Impatient's consumption. Under the income tax, Patient faces a higher percentage tax burden solely because she consumes later.

Consumption taxation yields a more neutral outcome, at least if the tax rate remains constant over time. Consider a consumption tax imposed directly on individuals at a 25 percent rate, which means that the tax is 20 percent of the combined amount devoted to consumption and the tax. (For example, a taxpayer who consumes $100 pays $25 tax, which is 20 percent of the $125 total spent on consumption and the tax.) After earning $100 of wages, Impatient consumes $80 and pays $20 tax. Patient lends her entire $100 to the firm; she owes no tax because she has not yet consumed. On her $100 loan, she earns $100 interest and accumulates $200, reflecting the payoff on machines. She consumes $160 in the future and pays $40 tax. Each worker's consumption is reduced by 20 percent, relative to a world with no taxes. Because both workers face the same percentage tax burden, the consumption tax does not penalize saving.

It is interesting to compare the consumption and income taxes to a wage tax. Under a wage tax, Impatient would still pay $20 tax up front. Patient would also pay $20 up front, save the remaining

$80, and (because the wage tax does not apply to investment income) ultimately consume $160. In this simple example, the wage tax is equivalent to the consumption tax. More generally, though, the consumption tax differs from the wage tax in two important respects. First, if the machine had yielded above-normal returns, greater than the minimum return required to induce Patient to finance the investment, the government would capture 20 percent of those extra returns under the 20 percent consumption tax, but not under a wage tax. Notice that taxing the extra returns does not discourage investment, because they are a surplus above the minimum needed to induce investment. Second, the introduction of a new consumption tax would raise additional revenue by taxing consumption financed from capital accumulated before the tax took effect, although transition relief might be adopted to ease that burden.

In short, a consumption tax and a wage tax, unlike an income tax, impose a zero *marginal* tax burden on *new* investment. But the consumption tax, unlike the wage tax, collects some revenue from investment because it taxes above-normal returns from new investment and (subject to transition rules) taxes payoffs from investments made before the tax took effect.

Despite common assertions to the contrary, consumption and income taxes are fundamentally similar, apart from their treatment of capital accumulation. Both tax systems penalize work relative to leisure. Consumption taxation has no advantage over income taxation in taxing drug dealing and other illegal transactions, nor is it generically less susceptible to evasion. There is also no competitiveness advantage from the manner in which consumption taxation treats imports and exports.

Some simulation studies have found that a full switch to consumption taxation would significantly expand the U.S. economy in the long run, by increasing capital accumulation. Auerbach (1996) estimated long-run output gains of 2.7 to 9.7 percent from various proposals to replace the income tax with a consumption tax.[3] The President's Advisory Panel on Federal Tax Reform in

2005 estimated a long-run increase in output of up to 6.0 percent from replacing the income tax with a progressive consumption tax.[4] In 2001, David Altig, et al., estimated long-run output gains ranging from 1.9 percent to 9.4 percent for various consumption tax proposals.[5] The long-run output gain is associated with an initial reduction in living standards, however, as households reduce their consumption and increase their saving. These simulations are not universally accepted as an accurate description of economic behavior because they assume, rather than prove, that households make saving decisions in an optimizing manner. But the studies suggest potential gains from replacing the income tax with a consumption tax.

By considering the replacement of the *current* income tax system with consumption taxation, the studies may understate the relevant stakes involved in completely switching to consumption taxation. As the tax system expands to become a larger share of GDP in upcoming years in response to the fiscal imbalance, the gains from fully replacing income taxation with consumption taxation will increase.

The gains would be diminished, however, if only part of the income tax was replaced. As discussed below, partial replacement is politically more likely and more in accord with international experience. Because the most common way to incorporate consumption taxation into a tax system is to adopt a value added tax (VAT) alongside an income tax, I first consider that possibility.

---

[3] Alan J. Auerbach, "Tax Reform, Capital Allocation, Efficiency and Growth," in *Economic Effects of Fundamental Tax Reform*, ed. Henry J. Aaron and William G. Gale (Washington, D.C.: Brookings Institution, 1996), 29–73.

[4] President's Advisory Panel on Federal Tax Reform, *Simple, Fair, and Pro-Growth: Proposals to Fix America's Tax System* (Washington, D.C.: Government Printing Office, 2005), http://govinfo.library.unt.edu/taxreformpanel/final-report/index.html.

[5] David Altig, Alan J. Auerbach, Laurence J. Kotlikoff, Kent A. Smetters, and Jan Walliser, "Simulating Fundamental Tax Reform in the United States," *American Economic Review* 91 (2001): 574–95.

ADOPTION OF A **VAT** ALONGSIDE THE **INCOME TAX**

The VAT is best understood as a modification of a retail sales tax. While a sales tax is collected only on the final sale to a consumer, a VAT is imposed and collected at each stage in the production of goods and services. This collection structure helps prevent the tax from being evaded at the retail level, an important consideration at high tax rates. Each firm is taxed on its sales, whether to consumers or to other firms, but effectively deducts its purchases from other firms. The most common implementation method employs invoices to show the tax paid on purchases and charged on sales, which creates a paper trail that aids enforcement. Like the retail sales tax, the VAT is a real-based tax that applies only to the sale of goods and services, with no tax on, or deductions for, financial transactions such as loans and stock purchases.

Figure 1 illustrates the relationship of the VAT to the sales tax in an economy with two firms and two individuals. Firm A produces a machine that it sells for $100 to Firm B and pays $70 of wages to Jones, its employee. Firm B buys the machine for $100, pays $40 wages to its employee Smith, and produces $150 of consumer goods. Jones buys $90 of the consumer goods and Smith buys the remaining $60.

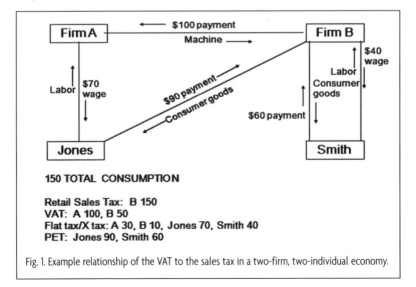

150 TOTAL CONSUMPTION

Retail Sales Tax: B 150
VAT: A 100, B 50
Flat tax/X tax: A 30, B 10, Jones 70, Smith 40
PET: Jones 90, Smith 60

Fig. 1. Example relationship of the VAT to the sales tax in a two-firm, two-individual economy.

Under a retail sales tax, tax would be collected from Firm B on the $150 of consumer goods that it sold. Under a VAT, tax is collected from Firm A on the sale of the $100 machine and from Firm B on its $50 value added ($150 sales to consumers minus $100 machine purchase). Because the sale of the machine washes out, the VAT is equivalent to the sales tax.

The adoption of a VAT (or a sales tax) is likely to lead to a one-time increase in the consumer price level. Consider a worker who produces 100 apples. With no taxes, the worker is paid a wage equal to the consumer price of 100 apples; if apples sell for $1, the worker is paid a $100 wage. Now, suppose that a 10 percent VAT is adopted. If the Federal Reserve's monetary policies keep the *tax-inclusive* consumer price of apples unchanged at $1, then the firm clears only 90 cents for each apple sold, with the other 10 cents paid in VAT. Because the 100 apples produced by the work-er are worth only $90 to the firm, the market-clearing wage falls to $90. Because apples still cost $1, including tax, the worker's real disposable income is 90 apples.

The problem is that it may be difficult to reduce nominal wages. If the worker's wage remained rigid at $100 rather than falling to the new market-clearing level of $90, firms would pay 100 apples to workers while also paying 11 apples (10 percent of the total of 111 apples) to the government. Firms would lay off workers until the marginal product of workers rose to 111 apples. To avert these job losses, the Federal Reserve would be likely to "accommodate" the VAT, allowing the tax-inclusive price of apples to rise to $1.11, so that real wages could fall without a reduction in nominal wages.

It is important to realize that the individual income tax does not cause a similar increase in the price level and that replacement of the income tax would therefore not mitigate the price increase resulting from the introduction of the VAT. With a 10 percent indi-vidual income tax, the 100 apples are still worth $100 to the firm and the worker receives the same $100 wage as in the no-tax world. Of course, the worker pays $10 of the $100 as income tax, so that disposable income is $90, which is enough to buy only 90 apples. Although the individual income tax reduces the worker's real *after-tax* wage from 100 to 90 apples, it does not reduce the real wage paid by the firm to the worker. Rigidity of the nominal wage paid by the firm to the worker therefore poses no problem and no price increase is required. The difference is that the income tax is collected from the worker out of the wage payment received from the firm, rather than being collected from the firm.

If a VAT is adopted, it would be important for the Federal Reserve, Congress, and the President to reach an early and public agreement on the extent to which the Federal Reserve would accommodate the VAT. If the tax was accommodated, steps would need to be taken to minimize the economic disruption from the one-time price level increase; if the tax was not accommodated, steps would need to be taken to reduce wage rigidity and facilitate the necessary nominal wage decline.

It is virtually certain that a VAT (or a sales tax) will not be adopted as a full replacement for the income tax. As a proportional tax on consumption, a VAT would be burdensome to the poor. Although the problem could be addressed to some extent by providing rebates, a complete replacement of the income tax by a VAT would still shift the tax burden downward in the income distribution. The VAT is therefore better suited as a partial replacement of the income tax. This conclusion is consistent with the international experience, as most countries that impose a VAT also have an income tax. A number of public figures have recently suggested consideration of a VAT (generally without making an outright endorsement), but always in the context of retaining the income tax.

The adoption of a VAT would raise a number of other issues. One concern is that the VAT would be relatively invisible to consumers, making it a money machine that would ease any pressure for spending restraint. The visibility of the tax could be enhanced, however, by listing it separately on customer receipts, as is done in Canada. On a broader level, though, the presence of both the income tax and the VAT could still make spending increases easier than they would be with either revenue source alone. Other issues concern the tax treatment of financial institutions and state and local governments. Because these issues have been extensively discussed elsewhere, I do not examine them here.

A partial-replacement VAT offers one way to reap economic gains from moving toward consumption taxation. Larger gains may be possible, though, from complete replacement of the income tax system with a consumption tax. As the above discussion suggests, the full-replacement consumption tax would need to be more progressive than the VAT. Such consumption taxes exist, but they are much less familiar than the VAT and pose their own potential challenges. I now explore those options.

COMPLETE REPLACEMENT OF INCOME TAX WITH PROGRESSIVE CONSUMPTION TAX

The leading options for progressive consumption taxation are the Bradford X tax and the personal expenditures tax (PET). The two taxes attain progressivity in quite different ways and have different strengths and weaknesses.

Mechanics of X Tax and PET

The X tax is a modification of the "flat" tax, which is in turn a modification of the VAT. Robert Hall and Alvin Rabushka (1983) proposed a two-tier VAT that they called the flat tax.[6] Firms compute value added, as they would under a VAT, but deduct their wage payments to obtain a remainder called "business cash flow." Workers are then taxed on their wages. The total tax base is the same as under a VAT (or a sales tax). Because the VAT is a consumption tax and the flat tax is simply a two-part VAT, the flat tax is also a consumption tax. Like the VAT, the flat tax is a real-based tax.

---

[6] Robert E. Hall and Alvin Rabushka, *Low Tax, Simple Tax, Flat Tax* (New York: McGraw Hill, 1983).

Figure 1 (page 185), applies the flat tax in the simple economy. Firm A is taxed on $30 cash flow ($100 value added minus $70 wage payment) and Firm B is taxed on $10 cash flow ($50 value added minus $40 wage payment). Smith and Jones are taxed on the wages they receive.

The purpose of taxing wages and business cash flow separately is to promote progressivity. Firms are taxed at a single flat rate—say, 25 percent—on business cash flow, while workers are taxed at that same rate on wages above a substantial exemption amount. Workers with earnings below the exemption amount pay zero tax, those with incomes moderately above the exemption amount pay a small fraction of their wages in tax, and those with very high earnings pay close to 25 percent. That pattern ensures some degree of progressivity across workers. Meanwhile, consumption financed from business cash flow is taxed at the full 25 percent with no exemption, because business cash flow, which is attributable to above-normal returns and capital in place when the reform is introduced, is likely to accrue to relatively affluent households.

Due to its administrative similarity to the current income tax system, the flat tax is often mistakenly thought to be a type of income tax. For further confirmation that the flat tax is a consumption tax, introduce a 20 percent flat tax into the previous example of Impatient and Patient, both of whom are assumed to be above the exemption level.

Impatient pays $20 tax on his wages and consumes his remaining $80. Patient pays $20 tax on her wages and lends the remaining $80 to the firm. So far, the flat tax looks like an income tax, because Patient has been taxed on her wages without having consumed anything. The picture changes, though, when we walk through the remaining steps. The firm uses the $80 loan to buy a $100 machine; under the flat tax, a $100 machine costs only $80, because the firm immediately deducts the $100 of wages paid to build the machine and thereby reaps a $20 tax savings. In the future, the machine yields a $200 payoff, on which the firm pays

$40 tax. With the remaining $160, the firm pays Patient her $80 principal plus $80 in interest. Patient then consumes the entire $160, because interest is tax-exempt under a flat tax.

Because Patient's consumption under the flat tax matches the $160 attained under a direct consumption tax and differs from the $144 attained under an income tax, the flat tax is, from an economic perspective, a consumption tax rather than an income tax. Two features of the flat tax together make it a consumption tax. First, firms immediately expense, rather than depreciate, investment outlays, so the firm is not required to capitalize and depreciate the wage costs of building the machine, as it would have to do under an income tax. Second, households pay tax only on wages, not on capital income.

The flat tax's exemption amount for workers may not provide sufficiently progressivity. Bradford (1986) therefore proposed that the tax be modified to feature a full set of graduated marginal tax rates.[7] Under Bradford's proposal, which he called an X tax, workers with earnings below the exemption amount pay no tax (and may receive refundable tax credits), the highest earners face a marginal tax rate equal to the firms' tax rate, and workers with intermediate wages face intermediate marginal tax rates.

The personal expenditures tax (PET), which is sometimes called a consumed-income tax, takes a different approach. Each household files an annual tax return on which it reports wage income, deducts all saving (deposits into savings accounts, asset purchases, amounts lent to others, and payments made on outstanding debts), and adds all dissaving (withdrawals from savings accounts, gross proceeds of asset sales, amounts borrowed from others, and payments received on outstanding loans). The resulting measure equals the household's consumption, which is taxed at graduated marginal tax rates based on the level of consumption. No tax is imposed at the firm level. The PET is a real-plus-

---

[7] David F. Bradford, *Untangling the Income Tax* (Cambridge, MA: Harvard University Press, 1986), 81-82.

financial tax because it taxes households on inflows from financial transactions and allows them to deduct the corresponding outflows. Figure 1 (page 185), shows that the PET imposes tax on each individual, based on his or her consumer spending.

Evaluation of X Tax and PET

Aside from their progressivity, both the X tax and the PET have other advantages over the VAT. Both taxes are more visible than the VAT because households must file annual tax returns. Also, both taxes avoid the one-time increase in the price level because, like the current individual income tax, they collect wage taxes from workers rather than from firms. Of course, the X tax and the PET differ along many dimensions. Many of the differences arise from how the two taxes treat financial transactions. To understand these differences, it is useful to review the relationship of real production and financial transactions.

Firms and workers engage in real production by using labor and capital to produce goods and services, generating wages for workers and capital income for firms. Financial transactions then take place. In one set of financial transactions, firms allocate the income and cash flow generated by production to households. Firms obtain funds from households by issuing stock and bonds, pay funds to households in the form of interest and dividends, and retain funds on behalf of stockholders. These transactions do not change the total cash flow or income generated by the firms' real production. A second set of financial transactions, such as borrowing and lending, occur between households. These transactions also result in zero aggregate net cash flow and income in a closed economy; for example, when a lending household receives interest income, the borrowing household incurs negative interest income (interest expense).

A real-based tax system tracks only the production activity of firms and workers while a real-plus-financial tax system also tracks the financial transactions. Because a real-based system does not track capital income or business cash flow to their final recipients, it can tax those items only at a flat rate at the firm level.

To employ graduated rates based on a household's annual income or consumption, a real-plus-financial approach that tracks all flows to the final household recipients is necessary. Of course, tracking financial flows adds complexity.

At one extreme, the real-based nature of the VAT eliminates the need for household returns, but forces all consumption to be taxed at a single flat rate. At the other extreme, the real-plus-financial nature of the PET permits graduated tax rates tied directly to annual consumer spending, but requires households to file annual tax returns reporting a wide array of financial transactions. (The current tax system takes a similar approach to the taxation of income.) The X tax follows an intermediate strategy, adopting the real-based approach of the VAT, but taxing wages at the household rather than the firm level. The X tax achieves much, but not all, of the simplicity of the VAT, because only wages are reported on household returns; for most households, the necessary information can be obtained from the W-2. The X tax also achieves much, but not all, of the progressivity of the PET, by taxing wages at graduated rates tied to annual wage income and imposing a high flat tax rate on business cash flow, which largely accrues to the well-off. To be sure, this progressivity is not as finely calibrated as that achieved by the PET, in which graduated rates are tied directly to annual consumer spending. On balance, the X tax offers an attractive combination of simplicity and progressivity.

The neutrality of consumption taxation with respect to the timing of consumption requires that the tax rate on consumption be constant over time. That gives the X tax a potential advantage over the PET. Under the PET's system of graduated tax rates, a household's movement between brackets across tax years could interfere with neutrality. Under the X tax, the tax rate that affects the timing of consumption is the flat tax rate on business cash flow. Of course, both taxes are vulnerable to tax rate changes arising from legislation. Also, the X tax applies graduated tax rates to wages, creating nonneutrality with respect to the timing of work.

On the other hand, welfare and social insurance programs would be easier to administer under the PET than under the X tax. The PET features household tax returns that provide detailed data on the household's well-being while the X tax features household tax returns that provide data only on the household's wages. Under the X tax, agencies administering transfer payments would need to gather information about potential recipients' non-wage incomes.

Aside from economics, the viability of a tax can also depend upon its "optics" (its appearance to the general public). The X tax and the PET each face challenges in this regard.

The optical challenge facing the X tax is that it is not readily understood to be a consumption tax and that it looks very odd if it is mistakenly viewed as an income tax. The problem is that the X tax lacks a visible tax on households consuming out of capital income. Of course, no consumption tax system imposes a marginal tax on capital income from new saving; that is done only by income tax systems. But consumption taxes do impose taxes on above-normal returns and preexisting capital, and it is politically appealing to make those taxes as visible as possible. Under the PET, households report capital income and deduct new saving on their tax returns, visibly taxing households that consume out of capital income. In contrast, the X tax imposes its tax on above-normal returns and preexisting capital less visibly, through the firm-level cash flow tax, while imposing a highly visible household-level tax on wages.

On the other hand, the PET faces two optical challenges. First, it appears to excuse business from "paying" taxes. This concern is economically nonsensical because firms cannot ultimately pay tax. Nevertheless, repealing the corporate income tax with no replacement firm-level tax may be a political drawback. Second, the PET, unlike the current income tax, taxes households on amounts that are borrowed. To be sure, the borrower deducts all subsequent payments on the loan, both principal and interest, which cancels out the initial tax in present discounted value, assuming that the household remains in the same tax bracket. Furthermore, the X tax and the VAT also tax consumption by borrowers, albeit less visibly at the firm level. Even so, the PET's treatment of borrowing may be perceived as unfamiliar or unfair.

The X tax has several potential drawbacks relative to the PET. The PET encounters no difficulties with international trade rules because it does not directly tax trade flows. The X tax encounters problems, however, because it taxes trade flows, but does so in a manner that deviates from the VAT framework around which the international trade rules were written. Another potential drawback of the X tax is its distinction between wages, which are taxed at graduated rates, and business cash flow, which is taxed at a high flat rate. Because many sole proprietors and partners provide both labor and capital to firms, there is no simple way to classify their payments from the firms. In contrast, the PET does not distinguish between wages and business cash flow, which are reported together and summed on household tax returns.

Negative tax liabilities also pose a challenge for the X tax. Under the PET, households are taxed on consumption, which must be positive, and there is no tax on firms. Under the X tax, firms are taxed on business cash flow, sales minus purchases minus wages, which can easily be negative for a given firm in a given year. The neutrality of the X tax depends on firms being able to immediately expense their investment purchases, which requires that firms with negative cash flow receive immediate tax savings based on their negative tax liability (or some other treatment that is equally good in present value). If, as is likely, Congress is unwilling to provide such generous treatment, then the neutrality of the X tax is impaired. A final problem concerns the tax treatment of financial institutions, whose activities often involve real production that is labeled as financial transactions. Because the X tax is real based, it may fail to properly tax these transactions. The PET avoids this difficulty because it is a real-plus-financial tax.

Given the X tax's attractive combination of simplicity and progressivity, it is likely to be the best approach, if the aforementioned challenges can be satisfactorily addressed. Robert Carroll and I are writing a book discussing ways to address the challenges facing the X tax.

The income tax can be completely replaced by a progressive consumption tax, but doing so will require the use of a relatively unfamiliar tax, either the Bradford X tax or the PET. Neither of these taxes has attracted much political support. In 1995, the Nunn-Domenici Unlimited Savings Allowance plan, which featured a PET, drew some attention, but it never gained traction in Congress and tax policy analysts concluded that the plan's specification of the PET was unworkable. One of the two tax plans recommended by the tax reform panel in 2005 featured an X tax, but retained a 15 percent flat-rate tax on capital income, thereby stopping short of a full movement to consumption taxation. The panel considered, but did not definitively recommend, an alternative plan that would have replaced the income tax system completely with an X tax. In any case, none of the panel's plans attracted political support. If the income tax system is to be replaced with a progressive consumption tax, public support for this approach must be built.

IMPROVING THE RESEARCH TAX CREDIT

Moving toward consumption taxation could help promote innovation as well as capital accumulation. A number of other tax policies may affect the spread of innovation through the establishment of new firms, including the treatment of start-up expenditures and net operating losses. Due to space constraints, I do not discuss these issues, focusing instead on the research tax credit, which has the most direct effect on innovation.

Some types of research may generate spillover or external benefits that are not captured by the firm doing the research. Bronwyn Hall (1996) concludes that there is "overwhelming evidence that some positive externalities exist for some types of R&D," but notes the difficulty of measuring the external benefits and determining which types of R&D generate them.[8] In the presence of positive externalities, efficiency calls for more generous treatment than even the zero marginal tax that consumption taxation provides for new investment, as there should be a subsidy to reflect the external benefit. Hall discusses whether the subsidy should take the form of direct government sponsorship of research or tax incentives for private research or a combination of both. In keeping with the focus of this chapter, I discuss tax incentives.

Although some observers have questioned whether research is sensitive to tax incentives, a number of empirical studies indicate that taxes have some effect. In her study of Compustat data Hall (1993) found particularly strong effects of the research tax credit.[9] Subsequent studies have also found an impact from tax incentives, although generally smaller than the effects estimated by Hall. Prominent examples include the study of state research tax credits by Wilson (2009)[10] and the cross-country study by Bloom, Griffith, and Van Reenen (2002).[11] The studies typically find that the responsiveness of research spending to incentives is significantly greater in the long run than in the short run.

As discussed below, the research tax credit expired on December 31, 2009, but is likely to be retroactively reinstated and extended. As further explained below, firms may claim either a 20 percent credit on qualified research spending in excess of a base amount linked to their 1984–88 research spending or a 14 percent credit on spending in excess of a base amount linked to more recent spending. I discuss three possible reforms of the credit.

---

[8] Bronwyn H. Hall, "The Private and Social Returns to Research and Development," in *Technology, R&D, and the Economy*, ed. Bruce L.R. Smith and Claude E. Barfield (Washington, D.C.: The Brookings Institution and the American Enterprise Institute, 1996), 160.

[9] ———. "R&D Tax policy During the Eighties: Success or Failure?" *Tax Policy and the Economy* 7, ed. James M. Poterba (Cambridge, MA: MIT Press, 1993), 1–35.

[10] Daniel J. Wilson, "Beggar Thy Neighbor? The In-State, Out-of-State, and Aggregate Effects of R&D Tax Credits," *Review of Economics and Statistics* 91 (2009): 431–36.

[11] Nick Bloom, Rachel Griffith, and John Van Reenen, "Do R&D Tax Credits Work? Evidence From a Panel of Countries, 1979–1997," *Journal of Public Economics* 85 (2002): 1–31.

Make the Credit Permanent

The research tax credit was enacted on August 13, 1981, effective retroactively to July 1, 1981, with an expiration date of December 31, 1985. A sequence of repeated expirations and extensions has followed, with most of the extensions being for only one or two years. As shown in table 1, the credit has faced fourteen scheduled expirations. In four instances, all of them early in the credit's history, Congress extended the credit before its scheduled expiration. In the other ten instances, Congress failed to act before expiration. In nine of the ten cases, Congress retroactively reinstated the credit to the date of its expiration, but waited between 66 and 408 days (237 days, on average) to do so. In one other instance, after the June 30, 1995, expiration, Congress waited until August 20, 1996, a lag of 417 days, to act and then reinstated the credit only back though July 1, 1996. As a result, no credit was provided for research spending in the second half of 1995 and the first half of 1996. The credit will face its fifteenth scheduled expiration on December 31, 2011.

Many observers have noted that the uncertainty surrounding the credit's temporary nature makes it difficult for firms to rely on the credit. In view of the 1996 experience, firms cannot be absolutely certain, in any given instance, that the credit will be retroactively reinstated back to its expiration. Consideration should therefore be given to permanent extension of the credit. Throughout the credit's history, presidential budget proposals have consistently recommended that it be made permanent. President Obama reiterated his support for permanence in the economic plan he announced on September 8, 2010.

Permanence faces significant political obstacles. Members of the tax-writing committees are able to use each extension of the credit (and other temporary tax provisions) as a way to obtain additional campaign contributions. Also, the February 2010 PAYGO budget law would require the ten-year revenue loss from permanent extension to be offset with tax increases or entitlement spending cuts, unless the requirement was waived by a three-fifths vote in the Senate. But there is a favorable precedent; the low-income housing tax credit was enacted on a temporary basis in 1986 and extended several times before being made permanent in 1993.

Yin (2009) argues that making tax incentives permanent hampers congressional oversight and impedes fiscal responsibility as budgetary offsets are not adopted for each year's extension.[12] These points would seem to be outweighed, however, by the advantages of a permanent credit. If full permanence is not desired, a middle ground would be to extend the credit for five to ten years.

Move to a Flat Credit

One other feature of the credit has led to instability and inefficiency. From the outset, the credit has been structured as an incremental incentive, with firms receiving credit only on their research spending above a base amount. The incremental structure is intended to provide a stronger incentive for research spending per dollar of revenue loss, or "more bang for the buck," but has led to some harmful consequences.

Consider a firm that would spend $100 on research in the absence of a credit, but would increase its spending to $110 in response to a 20 percent flat credit. Presumably, each of the additional ten dollars of research has an expected payoff to the firm greater than eighty cents (making it worthwhile in the presence of the credit), but less than one dollar (making it unviable without the credit). The flat 20 percent credit has a $22 revenue loss.

But suppose that the firm is instead given a 20 percent credit on its spending in excess of an $80 base amount. (For the moment, ignore the process by which this base amount is set.) According to stylized economic theory, the firm still spends $110 on research, because it has the same 20 percent marginal incentive. Yet this

[12] George Yin, "Temporary-Effect Legislation, Political Accountability, and Fiscal Restraint," *New York University Law Review* 84 (2009): 174–257.

incremental credit has a revenue loss of only $6, because only the last $30 of research spending receives the credit. The incremental credit gets the same bang for fewer bucks.

The success of this strategy depends, however, on three conditions holding. As discussed below, designing a credit that satisfies these three conditions is a formidable challenge.

First, the base value must be equal to, or less than, what the firm would have spent on research with a flat credit. If this firm is assigned a $120 base amount, for example, there is no incentive for additional research, because the firm's credit remains fixed at zero unless and until it reaches the base amount. In short, if the base amount is higher than what the firm would spend with a flat credit, there is no bang, although there also are no bucks.

Second, the base amount should not be too far below what the firm would spend under a flat credit, because a small base amount does little to limit the revenue loss. In combination, these two requirements mean that each firm's base amount should be set as close as possible to, but not above, what the firm would spend under a flat credit.

Third, each firm's base amount must be set in a way that does not have undesirable incentive effects. If a firm's base amount is linked to its other economic activity, for example, then the incremental credit effectively taxes that activity. The advantage of stronger research incentives per dollar of revenue loss may be offset by the disincentives for the other activities. Or, if the base amount is linked to past research spending, that linkage can itself undermine research incentives.

This last issue arose under the approach that Congress initially adopted on August 13, 1981. Firms received a 20 percent credit for research spending in excess of their average spending over the previous three years (a three-year rolling base). One problem was that a firm could easily spend somewhat less than its previous three-year average in a given year, meaning that it would receive no marginal incentive from the credit. More important, the credit offered little net incentive, even for firms that exceeded their base amounts each year. Under the rolling-base credit design, spending $100 more today provided a $20 initial credit. But in each of the next three years, the extra spending raised the base amount by $33.33, lowering the credit by $6.67. The $20 of initial tax savings was fully paid back over three years, albeit at a zero nominal interest rate; with a 5 percent market nominal interest rate, the $100 of research yielded only $1.85 of present-value tax savings. The rolling-base approach dramatically reduced the bucks, but also greatly reduced the bang.

In response to these problems, Congress switched to a fixed-base approach on December 19, 1989. Effective January 1, 1990, each firm's base amount was set equal to its average annual research spending in the fixed base period of 1984 through 1988, with certain adjustments discussed below. If a firm remained above its base amount, the credit provided a full 20 percent incentive, because there was no future payback. At first glance, the fixed-base design seemed to offer the desired increase in bang for the buck.

The fixed-base design imposed a large retroactive tax on 1984–88 research spending. With the benefit of hindsight, firms would have been well advised to sharply reduce research spending in those five years; each extra $100 spent per year increased the fixed base amount by $100, and lowered the credit by $20, in each year from 1990 onward, ignoring the special rules discussed below. If firms had foreseen Congress's action, there would have been no net gain in bang for the buck, because the increased incentive for research in 1990 and thereafter would have been offset by a massive disincentive for research in 1984–88.

Of course, firms did not foresee Congress's action. Congress obtained more bang for the buck by unexpectedly taxing something firms had already done. Such a "capital levy" is a way to raise revenue (in this case, to limit the credit's revenue loss) without disincentives, provided that taxpayers do not expect something similar to be done again. The fairness of punishing firms for their 1984–88 research in this way can be questioned. And it is unclear why a Congress that did this once would not do it again.

Even setting those issues aside, the fixed-base approach poses problems. Congress has responded to these problems in ways that diminish the bang of the credit, with many firms receiving less than a 20 percent marginal research incentive or facing disincentives in other areas. Seeking to set each firm's base amount as close as possible to, but no larger than, what it would otherwise spend on research, Congress made two adjustments to the base amount.

First, it provided that a firm's base amount in each year was its 1984–88 average research spending, adjusted by the subsequent proportional change in the firm's gross receipts. The idea was that a firm's desired level of research spending would change over time in proportion to its gross receipts, although a close link between receipts and research seems implausible. In any case, making the base amount proportional to gross receipts effectively placed a tax on gross receipts, similar to a turnover tax, which has its own disincentive effects.

Second, Congress provided that no firm could claim the credit on more than half of its research spending. In other words, a firm could not use a base amount smaller than one-half of its research spending. When this constraint binds, the firm effectively faces a 10 percent flat credit and its marginal research incentive is 10 percent rather than 20 percent.

As 1984–88 receded further into the past, the fixed base amount became more problematic. Some firms complained that their research spending in that period had been unusually high, for various reasons, and that they could never exceed their base amounts. On August 20, 1996, Congress responded to these concerns by giving firms an alternative to the fixed-base credit, allowing firms to choose an Alternative Incremental Research Credit (AIRC), effective July 1, 1996. Congress expanded the AIRC on December 17, 1999, effective July 1, 1999, and again on

December 20, 2006, effective January 1, 2007. This alternative credit was essentially a flat credit, with no link to past research spending. However, the credit rates were only about 3 to 5 percent, providing relatively small research incentives.

On December 20, 2006, Congress adopted a third option, the Alternative Simplified Credit (ASC), effective January 1, 2007. On October 3, 2008, Congress expanded the ASC and, in an abrupt change of course, repealed the recently expanded AIRC, effective January 1, 2009.

The design of the ASC resembles the rolling-base design used in 1981 through 1989, but is less flawed. Each firm's base amount is *half* of its average research spending over the three preceding years, making it less likely that firms will fall short of their base amounts. The credit rate was initially 12 percent, but was increased to 14 percent by the 2008 legislation. An extra $100 of research yields $14 of initial tax savings, while raising the base amount by $16.67, and reducing the credit by $2.33, in each of the following three years. In effect, half of the $14 is repaid over three years at a zero nominal interest rate. With a 5 percent market nominal interest rate, the present value of the net tax savings is $7.65.

Congress also has adopted special start-up rules that prescribe fixed base amounts for firms established after the 1984–88 base period. (Like older firms, new firms are allowed to use the ASC, and were allowed to use the AIRC before its repeal, in place of the fixed-base credit.) These start-up rules are ill designed because they link firms' permanent base amounts to their research spending in the sixth through tenth years of their existence. Newly established firms that increase their research spending during those years are penalized in much the same way as older firms that increased their 1984–88 research spending, with the conspicuous difference that the penalties are foreseeable for newly established firms.

In its current form, the credit provides uneven marginal incentives for research. The fixed-base credit provides a 20 percent incentive to some firms and a 10 percent incentive to other firms (those with base amounts fixed at half of current spending) while the ASC provides a 7.65 percent incentive and the start-up rules provide new firms with different incentives (or disincentives) in various years. Before it was repealed, the AIRC provided incentives of 3 to 5 percent. Other incentive rates can arise if firms move between the fixed-base credit and the ASC across different years.

The incremental credit has added other complexity. Rules have been adopted to allocate base amounts during mergers and spin-offs. Congress also has tinkered with the definition of gross receipts in an effort to make it a better scaling variable for the fixed base amount. Also, research spending must be defined consistently between the current tax year and the base period; for firms using the fixed-base credit, if the definition of qualified research is changed, the firm must recalculate its base amount by reclassifying its 1984–88 research spending in accordance with the modified definition.

In view of these difficulties, moving to a flat credit should be considered. Holding revenue loss fixed, a flat credit will provide a somewhat smaller research incentive, in the aggregate. But, the incentive will be uniform across firms, presumably producing a more efficient allocation of research spending. The complexity and instability of the current credit will be removed. The implicit turnover tax embedded in the fixed-base credit will be eliminated.

As 1984–88 continues to recede into the past, the problems of the incremental credit can only become severe. One ominous possibility is that Congress may replace 1984–88 with a new "fixed" base period. Any anticipation of such a development would create severe research disincentives of the kind that were avoided in 1984–88 only because the adoption of the fixed-base credit was not anticipated.

The quest for more "bang for the buck" has generally not led Congress to adopt an incremental design for other tax incentives.

For example, Congress has not limited taxpayers to deducting only the excess of charitable contributions over a base amount linked to past giving. Because there are no obvious features of research spending that make it more suited to the incremental approach than charitable giving or other tax-preferred activities, it may be time to bring the research tax credit into line with other tax incentives.

If a full movement to a flat credit is not desired, more modest steps could be taken. For example, a flat credit could be adopted for new firms. Another possibility is to expand the ASC, luring firms away from the much more deeply flawed fixed-base credit. President Obama's September 8, 2010, economic plan adopts just this approach, raising the ASC credit rate from 14 to 17 percent. With a 5 percent nominal interest rate, the research incentive is 9.28 percent for a typical firm. In the fact sheet justifying the proposal, the White House criticized the fixed-base credit formula as "complex" and "outdated." Nevertheless, President Obama did not propose abolishing the fixed-base credit.

Refine the Definition of Qualified Research

The final issue concerns the definition of research that receives the credit. As noted above, the goal of the credit is to subsidize research with spillover benefits not captured by the firm doing the research.

Congress has required that the research be "undertaken for the purpose of discovering information (i) which is technological in nature, and (ii) the application of which is intended to be useful in the development of a new or improved business component of the taxpayer, and (iii) substantially all of the activities of which constitute elements of a process of experimentation for a purpose … [related] to (i) a new or improved business function, (ii) performance, or (iii) reliability or quality." Congress also has disqualified research related to style, taste, cosmetic, or seasonal design factors; research in the social sciences, arts, and humanities; research performed after commercial production of the business component has begun; research that adapts a component to a particular customer's requirements; research that duplicates an existing component; and certain surveys and studies. Congress also has imposed restrictions on the availability of the credit for the development of internal-use software. Applying these rules has proven to be a difficult task.

While Congress required that the research be undertaken for the purpose of "discovering information," it did not specify whether the information must be new to society or only to the firm. On December 2, 1998, the IRS proposed regulations requiring that research be "undertaken to obtain knowledge that exceeds, expands, or refines the common knowledge of skilled professionals in a particular field of science or engineering." The IRS emphasized that Congress intended the credit to encourage research that increased the innovative qualities and efficiency of the U.S. economy. The IRS finalized the regulations, with only modest changes, on January 3, 2001, effective for research performed on or after that date.

The final regulations drew intense criticism as providing an unduly restrictive definition of research and imposing unduly burdensome documentation requirements. The regulations required that a firm document early in its research, or before it began, the questions the research sought to answer and the information that was sought. Also, any firm that wished to invoke a rebuttable presumption that its research satisfied the new definition was required to document that it had conducted an investigation early in the research, or before it began, confirming that the result sought by the research was not part of common knowledge. Eberle (2001) noted the concerns expressed about the research definition and the documentation requirement.[13]

The January 3, 2001, regulations proved to be short-lived, particularly because a new President took office seventeen days later. In the March 5, 2001, Internal Revenue Bulletin, the IRS announced

---

[13] James Eberle, "Analysis of the Final Research Tax Credit Regulations," *Tax Notes* 90 (2001); 1533-40.

that the regulations would be reconsidered and that firms would be allowed to rely on the pre-2001 regulations until the changes were finalized. On December 26, 2001, the IRS published proposed regulations that dropped the requirement that research seek to obtain information that expands, exceeds, or refines commonly held knowledge. On January 2, 2004, the IRS finalized the proposed regulations with little change. These regulations define creditable research as follows:

> Research is undertaken for the purpose of discovering information if it is intended to eliminate uncertainty concerning the development or improvement of a business component. Uncertainty exists if the information *available to the taxpayer* does not establish the capacity or method for developing or improving the business component, or the appropriate design of the component ... [creditability] does *not* require the taxpayer be seeking to obtain information that exceeds, expands, or refines the common knowledge of skilled professionals. (emphasis added)

There has been little further consideration of the issue since 2004.

Although research that adapts existing technology to business use may have some external benefits, the strongest benefits are likely to arise from research that discovers new information not previously known to society. It may be desirable, therefore, to narrow the definition of qualified research along the lines set forth in the January 2001 regulations.

If a narrower definition is adopted, onerous documentation requirements should be avoided and care should be taken not to exclude socially beneficial activities. The complexity and disruption of moving to a new definition would also have to be considered.

Conclusion

Tax policy can have significant effects on capital accumulation and innovation, the two key forces driving long-run economic growth. A move to consumption taxation could help promote capital accumulation. Some gains would arise if the income tax system could be partially replaced by a VAT, but larger gains could be achieved by replacing the entire income tax system with a progressive consumption tax, such as the Bradford X tax or a personal expenditures tax. Each of these taxes poses certain complications. On a smaller scale, the research tax credit could be modified to make it a more effective tool in promoting innovation.

Table 1: Scheduled Expirations of Research Tax Credit

Scheduled Expiration	Date Extended	Days Late	Extension (months)
Dec. 31, 1985	Oct. 22, 1986	295	36
Dec. 31, 1988	Nov. 10, 1988	N/A	12
Dec. 31, 1989	Dec. 19, 1989	N/A	12
Dec. 31, 1990	Nov. 5, 1990	N/A	12
Dec. 31, 1991	Dec. 11, 1991	N/A	6
June 30, 1992	Aug. 10, 1993	408	36
June 30, 1995	Aug. 20, 1996	417	11*
May 31, 1997	Aug. 5, 1997	66	13
June 30, 1998	Oct. 21, 1998	113	12
June 30, 1999	Dec. 17, 1999	170	60
June 30, 2004	Oct. 4, 2004	96	18
Dec. 31, 2005	Dec. 20, 2006	354	24
Dec. 31, 2007	Oct. 3, 2008	277	24
Dec. 31, 2009	Dec. 17, 2010	351	24

*From July 1, 1996.

8 ■ Advancing Antitrust Law to Promote ■ Innovation and Economic Growth

George L. Priest*

The effective implementation of antitrust law is central to the promotion of innovation and to the achievement of economic growth. Antitrust law defines the guidelines of a competitive private market that, in all economies, is the principal source of innovation and economic growth.

Put conversely, in the absence of a competitive private economy, innovation and economic growth are greatly retarded. State-(political-) controlled economies can generate innovation and economic growth over some range. But the experience of the past century shows that the range is limited, as evidenced, among endless examples, in the collapse of the Soviet Union in 1989 and the experience of China and India, where economic growth was retarded before and has been greatly expanded after the introduction of (some level of) private market operations.

Chiefly for political reasons, the principles of antitrust law in the United States have not generally been allowed to define the range of state-controlled versus private- (market-) controlled enterprise

* George L. Priest is the Edward J. Phelps Professor of Law and Economics and Kauffman Distinguished Research Scholar in Law, Economics and Entrepreneurship, Yale Law School. I am grateful to Peter Schuck and to participants at the Third Kauffman Summer Legal Institute for comments on an earlier draft.

that would maximize economic growth (see the Parker v. Brown line of cases restricting the application of antitrust law from areas under state political control [1]). From the standpoint of economic growth, this is a source of regret and an important subject worthy of further study. Nevertheless, putting aside, for the moment, the extent of state control of enterprise, an effective antitrust law will maximize economic growth within the private sector.

The relationship between antitrust law and innovation is somewhat more complicated. There is an interesting theoretical issue as to whether monopolies or cartels will invest as much in innovation as firms in competitive industries. There is a long popular tradition that believes that monopolies retard or, at the least, possess reduced interests in innovation because they are sheltered from competition. This idea is as old as the Case of Monopolies (1603),[2] and is reflected more modernly in Hicks' famous aphorism that the greatest monopoly return is a quiet life.

There are good economic reasons to question this belief. (See the Arrow-Demsetz debate on this issue.) If monopolists seek to maximize profits (which is typically the point of securing a monopoly), they will benefit from expanding demand—monopoly profits become greater—and thus will invest in innovation. Further, the antitrust laws are importantly amended by copyright and patent statutes whose principal idea is to hold out the prospect of monopoly in order to encourage innovation.

The debate over this issue, however, as is typical of much of modern antitrust analysis, largely ignores and, thus, obscures the dynamic character of innovation. The relationship between antitrust law and the copyright and patent regimes in encouraging innovation will be addressed later in this chapter. With

---

[1] *Parker v. Brown,* 317 U.S. 341, 63 S.Ct. 307, 87 L.Ed. 315 (1943). See, e.g., *City of Columbia v. Omni Outdoor Advertising, Inc.,* 499 U.S. 365, 111 S.Ct. 1344, 113 L.Ed.2d 382 (1991).

[2] "The 2d incident to a monopoly is, that after the monopoly [is] granted, the commodity is not so good and merchantable as it was before: for the patentee having the sole trade, regards only his private benefit, and not the common wealth." Trin. 44 Eliz., 11 Co. Rep. 84b, 77 Eng. Rep. 1260 (King's Bench 1603).

respect to the more typical objects of antitrust law—cartels and mergers to monopoly—the economic effects and the effects on innovation and economic growth are clear; neither need be debated. Monopolies and cartels have chiefly redistributive goals and effects: They take money from buyers and pocket it to sellers. The *redistribution* of wealth is generally antagonistic to the *creation* of wealth through innovation.[3]

As will be explained, much of the development of antitrust law in the United States—from the 1940s through the mid-1970s—focused on supposed redistributive effects of industrial practices and directed law and policy to reverse that redistribution in ways that most likely inhibited economic growth. That definition of antitrust law could not be defended and has been overturned in succeeding years. This is an admirable achievement and has contributed to economic growth.

Nevertheless, modern antitrust law, however liberated from rules inhibiting economic growth, still falls short of the broader affirmative effects that antitrust law might achieve. This paper will attempt to describe how antitrust law might be advanced more dynamically to promote innovation and economic growth.

Part I describes briefly the development of antitrust law in the United States from enactment of the Sherman Act in 1890 through, roughly, 1975 and explains how that development inhibited innovation and economic growth. Part I also outlines the change in antitrust law that began after 1975 and continues today, and explains how that change has (partially) enhanced economic growth. Part II describes how antitrust law might be redirected for the future to advance innovation and economic growth more successfully.

---

[3] An exception, as mentioned, is the grant of monopoly rights to patentees.

PART I: THE DEVELOPMENT OF ANTITRUST LAW IN THE UNITED STATES

Antitrust Law, 1890–1975

The Sherman Act was enacted in 1890, prohibiting "every contract, combination...or conspiracy, in restraint of trade" (Section 1) and monopolization (Section 2). For the first two decades of Sherman Act enforcement, the act was directed against unions and against companies that had merged to monopoly or formed cartels, often in the form of trusts, holding shares (and thus controlling the operations) of formerly competing companies. Antitrust jurisprudence at the Supreme Court paid no attention to questions of industrial organization. The principal legal issue was whether the act should be read literally: as a prohibition of "every" contract that could be construed to have restrained trade, or whether there was some mediating principle that limited the application of the act. In 1912, in the *Standard Oil* decision,[4] the Supreme Court decided that the Sherman Act must be interpreted by the "Rule of Reason": an invented legal proposition that means that only unreasonable restraints of trade are prohibited, in contrast to "reasonable" restraints of trade, the most common example of which is a partnership of two individuals, obviously possessing no market power.

Although there were many interesting prosecutions and debates following the *Standard Oil* decision, the next principal change in antitrust doctrine occurred during the Second New Deal in 1940, in which a Roosevelt-dominated Supreme Court expanded the reach of the antitrust laws by announcing the "per se" prohibition of price fixing—an absolute prohibition—in the important *Socony-Vacuum Oil* case.[5] No economist or student of public policy can support price fixing among competitors. There was not then, nor has there been since, any substantial critique of the Supreme Court's ruling in the case. The conception, however, of

---

[4] *United States v. Standard Oil Co. of New Jersey*, 221 U.S. 1, 31 S.Ct. 502, 55 L.Ed. 619 (1911).

[5] *United States v. Socony-Vacuum Oil Co.*, 310 U.S. 150, 60 S.Ct. 811, 84 L.Ed. 1129 (1940).

a per se prohibition of a particular industrial practice (i.e., that the practice was prohibited regardless of the analysis of economic effect, in direct contrast to a determination of whether a claimed restraint was "reasonable") was new and had an important impact on future Supreme Court antitrust jurisprudence.

Over succeeding years, until the mid-1970s, the Supreme Court, confident upon the acceptance of the *Socony-Vacuum Oil* approach, and largely hostile to nontypical business arrangements, progressively expanded the number of practices subject to per se antitrust prohibitions. Per se prohibitions were announced against all forms of price control starting, as indicated, with the per se prohibition of horizontal price fixing (*Socony-Vacuum*), but extended to include resale price maintenance (reinterpreting the 1918 *Dr. Miles* opinion) and maximum price limitations (*Albrecht*); vertical territorial restrictions (*Schwinn*); tying arrangements (*Northern Pacific*); group boycotts (*Fashion Originators' Guild*); and predatory pricing (*Utah Pie*); among others.[6] The Supreme Court also sanctioned what by any modern eye would be regarded as extreme limitations on mergers. In the 1966 *Von's Grocery* case,[7] the Supreme Court approved the prohibition of a merger of non-competing retail grocery companies in Los Angeles, each possessing less than 4 percent of the retail grocery market. This opinion signaled that the Court would sustain any challenge that the Justice Department brought against a proposed merger, leading the department in 1968 to promulgate draconian Merger Guidelines that outlined its policy toward merger challenges, stifling future merger activity.

Although I know of no studies exactly making this point, there is every reason to believe that this definition of antitrust law imped-

---

[6] *Dr. Miles Medical Co. v. John D. Park & Sons Co.*, 220 U.S. 373, 31 S.Ct. 376, 55 L.Ed. 502 (1911); *Albrecht v. Herald Co.*, 390 U.S. 145, 88 S.Ct. 869, 19 L.Ed.2d 998 (1968); *United States v. Arnold, Schwinn & Co.*, 388 U.S. 365, 87 S.Ct. 1856, 18 L.Ed.2d 1249 (1967); *United States v. Northern Pac. Ry. Co.*, 356 U.S. 1, 78 S.Ct., 514, 2 L.Ed.2d 545 (1958); *Fashion Originators' Guild of America v. F.T.C.*, 312 U.S. 457, 61 S.Ct. 703, 85 L.Ed. 949 (1941); *Utah Pie Co. v. Continental Baking Co.*, 386 U.S. 685, 87 S.Ct. 1326, 18 L.Ed.2d 406 (1967).

[7] *United States v. Von's Grocery Co.*, 384 U.S. 270, 86 S.Ct. 1478, 16 L.Ed.2d 555 (1966).

ed economic growth by the prohibitions it imposed on industrial enterprise. Certainly, the spirit of the law was hostile to economic growth. That spirit was basically redistributionist: halting the effort of successful firms to advance their operations; preventing potentially wealth-enhancing mergers; indeed, overtly redistributionist in protecting small business from large, especially in the context of retail dealers (the dealer liberty theory: *Klors*,[8] *Brown Shoe*).[9] The antigrowth effects were particularly pronounced with respect to vertical practices—tying arrangements; territorial allocations; vertical price restraints; vertical integration generally—based upon economically indefensible theories of market foreclosure.

Antitrust Law 1976–2010

In the middle of the 1970s, the Supreme Court began a dramatic change in its approach to interpretation of the Sherman Act. In succeeding years, the Court essentially adopted (though not perfectly) the analysis of antitrust law that Aaron Director had defined at the University of Chicago in the 1940s and 1950s. The progressive adoption of this approach (though with some fits and starts) continues today.

I have separately attributed as the principal catalyst of this change the appointment of John Paul Stevens to the Court in 1976. Though this fact has only been discovered recently, Stevens had taught the antitrust course at the University of Chicago Law School with Director, an opportunity he has described as "the most important intellectual experience of [his] life."[10] Whether or not it was Stevens who changed the Court's view on antitrust law is unimportant to this paper. Relevant to the subject of economic growth is that the Supreme Court, beginning in 1977, substantially changed its interpretation of the Sherman Act to largely

---

[8] *Klor's, Inc. v. Broadway-Hale Stores*, 359 U.S. 207, 79 S.Ct. 705, 3 L.Ed.2d 741 (1959).

[9] *United States v. Brown Shoe Co.*, 370 U.S. 294, 82 S.Ct. 1502, 8 L.Ed.2d 510 (1962).

[10] For a fuller discussion of Stevens's relationship with Director, see Priest, *Modern Antitrust Law: The Triumph of Aaron Director*, forthcoming 2011.

remove the impediments to economic growth that had been introduced in the preceding forty years.

- In an important case decided in 1977, *Pueblo Bowl-O-Mat*,[11] the Court vastly restricted the ability of competitors to file antitrust suits seeking redress from harms caused by market-expanding activities. The conceptual origins of the case are not fully understood, but its impact is significant because it reduced substantially the redistributive aims of antitrust law by curtailing antitrust suits brought by inferior against superior competitors.

- Over succeeding years, the Court progressively reduced the previously adopted per se prohibitions of various industrial practices. The effect of these many cases is to charge courts to investigate the economic impact of alleged offenses under the Rule of Reason, allowing firms the opportunity to explain how the practices under attack might enhance economic productivity.

- The change in antitrust law allowed firms to engage in practices with other firms in order to enhance output that had previously been prohibited. An example is the Court's adoption of a more nuanced understanding of what are categorized as group boycotts (*Northwest Wholesale Stationers*).[12]

- The Court's change in view—Director's direct legacy—led to a different understanding and treatment of vertical arrangements, including tying arrangements (*Fortner II, Jefferson Parish Hospital*), and predatory pricing (*Matsushita, Brooke Group*), among other vertical practices.[13]

---

[11] *Brunswick Corp. v. Pueblo Bowl-O-Mat, Inc.*, 429 U.S. 477, 97 S. Ct. 690, 50 L.Ed.2d 701 (1977).

[12] *Northwest Wholesale Stationers, Inc. v. Pacific Stationery & Printing Company*, 472 U.S. 284, 105 S.Ct. 2613, 86 L.Ed.2d 202 (1985).

[13] *United States Steel Corp. v. Fortner Enterprises, Inc.*, 429 U.S. 610, 97 S.Ct. 861, 51 L.Ed.2d 80 (1977); *Jefferson Parish Hosp. Dist. No. 2 v. Hyde*, 466 U.S. 2, 104 S.Ct. 1551, 80 L.Ed.2d 2 (1984); *Matsushita Elec. Indus. Co., Ltd. v. Zenith Radio Corp.*, 475 U.S. 574, 106 S.Ct. 1348, 89 L.Ed.2d 538 (1986); *Brooke Group Ltd. v. Brown & Williamson Tobacco Corp.*, 509 U.S. 209, 113 S.Ct. 2578, 125 L.Ed.2d 168 (1993).

- Though not initiated by the Court, yet entirely consistent with the Court's new approach, under another acolyte of Director, William Baxter, as chief of the antitrust division, the Justice Department's Merger Guidelines were amended in 1982 to define markets more dynamically, by including potential future production into product and market definitions, and vastly expanding the definition of markets, thus reducing the apparent effect of any potential merger in terms of market power.

These multiple changes in antitrust law following 1977 had the effect of removing the obstacles to economic growth characteristic of the earlier era. The changes substantially contributed to economic growth.

Still, with the exception of the revised Merger Guidelines, modern antitrust law contributes to economic growth only, as explained in Chapter 1, in a static manner: smoothing the path of industrial enterprise by eliminating obstacles to growth. Modern antitrust law, like modern private law, even if sensitive to economic considerations, applies the economic understanding statically, not dynamically. Antitrust law facilitates economic growth for existing enterprises, but it does not directly encourage growth for new enterprise.

The next section outlines ways that modern antitrust law might be defined to more dynamically promote economic growth.

Part II: Advancing Antitrust Law to More Robustly Promote Innovation and Economic Growth

The transformation of antitrust law since the mid-1970s was successful in reducing the impediments to economic growth imbedded in the earlier antitrust regime. Nevertheless, the transformation has been inadequate in many ways. As discussed, modern antitrust law has (at best) adopted a static conception of law and economic growth, the principal objective of which is to enhance *current* production. This conception is not unimportant, but it fails to adopt a dynamic conception of law and economic growth: creating a legal structure that promotes and encourages new innovation and future economic growth. This section discusses the possibilities of advancing antitrust law to enhance economic growth into the future.

There are several ways in which modern antitrust law could more fully recognize the opportunities of innovation to achieve the potential of enhancing economic growth:

- First, all antitrust authorities should acknowledge and build into their policy decisions the fact that, in our modern fluid economy, antitrust law is a very crude mechanism for controlling industrial practices. Serious antitrust prosecutions extend over many years, often over a decade. Given rapid changes in competitive markets, antitrust law should be viewed as serving, at best, as a last resort mechanism for affecting changes in industrial practices. The recognition of the limitations of slow-moving antitrust law in comparison to dynamic market competition also should inform courts facing antitrust suits brought by less successful against more successful competitors. Those suits should be presumptively disfavored.

- Toward the same point, modern antitrust law has ignored the significant effects of increased global competition. Antitrust law in the United States remains domestic law. The interpretation of the law has failed to consider the extraordinary modern effects of actual and potential global competition.

  – The existence of increased global competition should result in a diminution of antitrust prosecution, not an increase. Markets should be defined to include the prospect of global, not simply internal U.S., competition.

  – The United States should be aggressive, not passive, in opposing the application of the antitrust laws of other countries—most centrally, the European Union (EU)—that have different and economically less-informed antitrust regimes. Allowing the EU to block the GE-Honeywell merger is a prime example in which both the U.S. Justice Department and the EU competition authority concluded that the merger would dramatically reduce costs and improve product quality. This conclusion led the Justice Department to approve the merger, but the EU to prohibit it under its standard of prohibiting increased market dominance.

– Recognizing the force of increased global competition, the United States should expand the antitrust laws to prohibit protectionism and industry subsidies wherever they appear. Protectionism waxes and wanes at the federal level, where even seeming pro-market administrations embrace protectionist policies for political reasons. A broader definition of the scope of antitrust policy might harness such policies.

• This point is also relevant with respect to state-level regulation. As described earlier, under the *Parker v. Brown* line of cases, state protection of industry (favorable taxation or direct subsidization) is immunized from antitrust scrutiny. From the standpoint of economic growth, policies of this nature are hugely harmful. This is especially true in the context of increased global competition. State competition against other states for new companies through reduced taxes or subsidies—dynamic competition—is entirely appropriate. State subsidization of entrenched local production, however—deriving from political influence—should be prohibited. *Parker v. Brown* could be easily overruled on Commerce Clause authority. As explained in the Hadfield chapter in this volume, state "regulation" of the professions—in effect, immunization from regulation—is particularly harmful.

• Although the Aaron Director/Chicago School view of antitrust law has been extended over much of the field, it has not been seriously applied to the intersection of antitrust law and patent and copyright law. This is a great regret, since patent and copyright law remain mired in the understanding of vertical arrangements typical of the 1950s and 1960s. Another Director acolyte, Ward Bowman, wrote an important book on this subject,[14] though his basic point was simply that patent exploitation ought to be maximized. There is important study to be done analyzing how patent and copyright law should be reformed in order to advance dynamic innovation.

• Modern antitrust law has not successfully been applied to network industries that are perhaps the greatest source of innovation and economic growth in our modern society. I have remarked on this failing elsewhere.[15] Over the past decade, a considerable literature on the economics of network industries has developed. Much of this writing has focused on the most novel of network topics, such as first-mover effects, tipping, lock-in, and the like. These subjects are of substantial conceptual interest, but they are essentially esoteric and do not address the practical understanding of how networks are organized and how they operate. To date, the literature on network industries in both economics and law has failed to develop practical grounds for understanding what legal interventions will serve to enhance network benefits for consumers.

Because in simple terms a network industry is one in which, over some large and relevant range, the benefit of the industry's product or service to consumers increases as the network expands, the most basic antitrust question is this: What network configuration or operational characteristics best expand these benefits to consumers? This question resembles, but is not exactly equivalent to, an inquiry about achieving appropriate economies of scale.

Nevertheless, there are many examples of network competition in industries possible because the benefits of expanding networks diminish over some range or because of heterogeneous demand supporting competing networks.

These issues are important for modern antitrust law because of the increasing role of network industries in our expanded and increasingly connected society. Practices that may appear anti-

---

[14] Ward S. Bowman, Jr., *Patent and Antitrust Law: A Legal and Economic Appraisal* (Chicago: University of Chicago Press, 1973).

[15] Priest, "Flawed Efforts to Apply Modern Antitrust Law to Network Industries" in *High Stakes Antitrust*, ed. Robert Hahn (Washington, DC: AEI-Brookings Joint Center for Regulatory Studies, 2003).

competitive when adopted in the context of multifirm industries or even anticompetitive when adopted by a monopolist may take on an entirely different cast where the objective is to expand consumer benefits by expanding networks.

Again, the most direct standard for evaluating network-related practices for purposes of enhancing economic growth is whether a questioned practice enhances or diminishes network benefits to consumers.

To date, none of our courts, and surely not the Justice Department, has adequately considered how antitrust law must be redefined in the context of networks. In the important *Microsoft* case,[16] the Washington, DC Circuit Court of Appeals (in a ruling that effectively possesses Supreme Court significance), wisely overruled the more harmful features of the lower court's rulings against Microsoft, but without establishing new principles for addressing network industry practices more generally.

Network-related practices surely will be the subject of an increasing number of antitrust lawsuits, in particular greater claims of monopolization where one competitor succeeds in creating network benefits over others. In our increasingly connected economy, the adoption by standard-setting organizations of protocols that advance interconnection are inevitable. One or more firms that have developed a dominant protocol will gain; those rejected will lose. Because the antitrust treatment of this issue at the Supreme Court is not developed—the most "recent" Supreme Court precedent is *Radiant Burners*,[17] a case whose resolution preceded the development of the economic understanding of network effects—there will be substantial litigation over the standard-setting process, as we have already witnessed. To date, these issues have been addressed in Courts of Appeals' decisions—some quite sensitive to the network effects issues[18]—but many

---

[16] *United States v. Microsoft Corp.*, 56 F.3d 1448 (D.C. Cir. 1995).

[17] *Radiant Burners, Inc. v. Peoples Gas Light & Coke Co.*, 364 U.S. 656, 81 S.Ct. 365, 5 L.Ed.2d 358 (1961).

different variations of the question are likely to be raised until the Supreme Court addresses carefully the standardization question.

Finally, although treated glancingly in the *Microsoft* decision, the issue of how to employ the antitrust laws to encourage platform competition needs substantial development. The conditions under which platform technologies can exist as competitors versus domination by a single platform are not well worked out in economics, not to mention in antitrust law. Much further work is necessary to understand these conditions.

CONCLUSION

The antitrust laws can provide an important contribution to economic growth. Cartels among competing companies or monopolies acquired by artificial means (such as the merger of competitors in U.S. Steel),[19] inhibit economic growth. The purpose of the antitrust laws is to prohibit these forms of economic organization to enhance growth.

During the early years of antitrust enforcement in the United States (the first eighty-five years), the application of the antitrust laws partially achieved these ends, though surely not entirely, as the Supreme Court raised obstacles to economic enterprise through general hostility to business and through efforts to achieve redistributional ends. Since the mid-1970s, however, many of these impediments to industry have been removed.

Nevertheless, the modern interpretation of the antitrust laws remains dominated by a static, not a dynamic, conception of economic growth. For the future there are many ways in which the antitrust laws can be reinterpreted to dynamically enhance economic growth, in particular through a recognition of the limits of the effects of prolonged antitrust prosecutions in the context of a

---

[18] See, e.g., *Rambus Inc. v. F.T.C.*, 522 F.3d 456 (D.C. Cir. 2008); *Golden Bridge Technology, Inc. v. Motorola, Inc.*, 547 F.3d 266 (5th Cir. 2008).

[19] *United States v. U.S. Steel Corp.*, 251 U.S. 417, 40 S.Ct. 293. 64 L.Ed. 343 (1920).

dynamic economy; through an explicit redirection of policy given the increased significance of global competition; through the elimination of growth-retarding subsidies and protections at the federal and state levels; through a reanalysis of the intersection of antitrust law and patent/copyright law; and through an enhanced understanding of the operation of network industries.

9: Contract, Uncertainty, and Innovation

Ronald J. Gilson, Charles F. Sabel, and Robert E. Scott*

ontract today increasingly links entrepreneurial innovations to the efforts and finance necessary to transform ideas into value. In this chapter, we describe the match between a form of contract that "braids"[1] formal and informal contractual elements in novel ways and the process by which innovation is pursued.

It is hardly surprising that these innovative forms of contract have emerged first in markets, and that the common law, and the theory of contract, then play catch-up. Between the time contracting practice adapts to the demands of innovation and the time contract doctrine adapts to the demands of practice, law acts as a

* Ronald J. Gilson is the Marc and Eva Stern Professor of Law and Business, Columbia University; Charles J. Meyers Professor of Law and Business, Stanford University; European Corporate Governance Institute. Charles F. Sabel is the Maurice T. Moore Professor of Law, Columbia University. Robert E. Scott is the Alfred McCormack Professor of Law and Director, Center for Contract and Economic Organization, Columbia University.

[1] Ronald J. Gilson, Charles F. Sabel, and Robert E. Scott, "Braiding: The Interaction of Formal and Informal Contracting in Theory, Practice and Doctrine," *Columbia Law Review 110* (forthcoming 2010), http://ssrn.com/abstract=1535574. We draw here on this article, as well as on Ronald J. Gilson, Charles F. Sabel, and Robert E. Scott, "Contracting for Innovation: Vertical Disintegration and Interfirm Collaboration," *Columbia Law Review* 109 (2009): 431. We are grateful to the Kauffman Foundation for research support.

friction on the innovation process rather than a lubricant to it. Our goal here is to reduce that lag by providing a theory that can guide courts in developing case law that addresses current forms of innovation. Put differently, we seek to provide courts the logic necessary to order the experience that Holmes, as a pragmatist, thought so central to the life of the common law.[2]

This chapter provides an overview of our ongoing work. The starting point is the Knightian distinction between risk and uncertainty.[3] In our view, traditional contracting techniques and traditional contract law address problems of risk. Braiding, or contracting for innovation, addresses conditions of uncertainty. We illustrate the relevance of this distinction by describing the shift in the organizational location of innovation[4]—in particular a fundamental shift from vertical integration to contract as the organizing mechanism for cutting-edge innovation. We then describe the braiding of formal and informal contracting that has developed to organize collaboration across organizational boundaries where the desired outcome can, at best, be anticipated only very approximately. Next, we reexamine the interaction between formal and informal contracting to understand why braiding was not envisaged as a theoretical possibility before it became a salient reality, and to make theoretical sense of braiding now that it has. Finally, we look to recent case law to argue that the domain of braiding now includes contexts where uncertainty is not generated by technological development, and we examine the failure of courts to recognize the difference between and consequences of

---

[2] Oliver Wendell Holmes, *The Common Law* (1881), 3. When Holmes wrote that "The life of the law has not been logic: it has been experience," he was not referring to passive process. Rather, the pattern was one in which experience driven litigation gave rise to logic—the predicative value of the court's decision. This notion that law follows from, rather than developing internally independent of, experience reflected Holmes's strongly held view, driven by his battlefield experience in the Civil War, that logic isolated from experience was ideology, from which came the carnage of the war. Louis Menand, *The Metaphysical Club* (New York: Flamingo, 2001), 3–4, 61.

[3] Frank H. Knight, *Risk, Uncertainty and Profit* (1921), 197–232.

[4] See Ronald J. Gilson, "Locating Innovation: Technology, Organizational Structure and Financial Contracting," *Columbia Law Review* 109 (2009): 885.

low-powered and high-powered enforcement in addressing braided contracts.

In particular, our analysis gives courts concrete guidance in the area of preliminary agreements, where courts for the first time are undertaking to enforce formal agreements—whether in the context of a preliminary agreement, letter of intent, or corporate acquisition agreement—that establish a process by which the parties will determine whether an innovation is possible, but do not obligate the parties to go forward with the substance of the innovation.[5] In contrast to the unpredictability currently associated with judicial accounts of how these agreements will be enforced, our development of a theory of braided contracts gives the court clear guidance: enforce the process established by the formal element of the contract through low-powered reliance damages, but *never* enforce, through high-powered (expectation) damages, the informal substantive element of the braid. This rule prevents the formal element of the braided contract from "crowding out" the informal element, and thereby preventing the innovative activity from going forward at all.

INNOVATION, UNCERTAINTY, AND INDUSTRIAL ORGANIZATION

Knight's distinction between risk and uncertainty is central to understanding the role of contract in the innovative process. Risk exists when future states of the world can be estimated probabilistically. Given such estimates, a contract, through a series of "if X, then Y" clauses, can more or less specify what will occur in each realized state. Alternatively, markets can be used to hedge against particular realizations, such as the future prices of commodities, or interest or currency exchange rates.

Under uncertainty, in contrast, future states of the world cannot be expressed probabilistically. *Ex ante*, we cannot usefully specify

---

[5] For discussion, see Alan Schwartz & Robert E. Scott, "Precontractual Liability and Preliminary Agreements," *Harvard Law Review* 120 (2007).

the desired outcome(s), or assign an option providing protection to one or another party *ex post*. In our analysis, innovation is inherently uncertain: an innovation is defined in the same process that ultimately leads to its achievement. From this perspective, the term "linear innovation," sometimes used to describe the next step in a predictable sequence,[6] is an oxymoron.

The increasing importance of innovation in this sense can be seen in the tendency to vertical disintegration of industry. Conventional industrial organization theory predicts that when parties in the supply chain must make transaction-specific investments, the risk of opportunism will drive them away from contracts and toward vertical integration.[7] This pressure toward sole ownership will be especially powerful in innovative industries where rapid techno-logical change produces high levels of uncertainty in supply rela-tionships. Contemporary contract theory concurs. In the presence of uncertainty, it offers no general solution to the problem of assur-ing both efficient levels of transaction-specific investment *ex ante* and adjustment to an efficient outcome *ex post* after uncertainty is resolved. So from this perspective too, firms should dominate mar-kets as a means to organize supply relationships.

For much of the twentieth century, the organization of large industry tracked this account. The dominant firms in industries such as steel, automobiles, electric machinery, and food process-ing—both in the United States and worldwide—used the tech-nologies of the Second Industrial Revolution[8] to achieve dramat-ic economies of scale through the mass production of standard goods with single-purpose or dedicated machinery. The most

---

[6] Masahiko Aoki, "Toward an Economic Model of the Japanese Firm," *Journal of Economic Literature* 28 (1990): 1, and Peter A. Hall and David Soskice, "An Introduction to Varieties of Capitalism," in *Varieties of Capitalism: The Institutional Foundations of Comparative Advantage*, ed. Peter A. Hall and David Soskice (New York: Oxford University Press, 2001), 50-54, distinguish between forms of national capitalism that support linear innovation (for example, Germany and Japan) and those that support non-linear innovation (for example, the United States).

[7] Much of this transactions cost literature is an extension of the work of Oliver Williamson. See e.g., Oliver E. Williamson, *The Economic Institutions of Capitalism* (New York: The Free Press, 1985); and Oliver E. Williamson, *Markets And Hierarchies: Analysis And Antitrust Implications* (New York: The Free Press, 1975).

conspicuous organizational feature of firms in these industries was vertical integration.

More recently, however, contemporary practice is moving away from this solution. Companies recognize that the escalating rate of change and resulting uncertainty means that they cannot themselves maintain cutting-edge technology in every field necessary for an innovative product. Accordingly, companies are increasingly electing to acquire by contract inputs that in the past they had made themselves. Instead of vertical integration, we observe vertical disintegration of firms, the expansion of collaborative research and development across firm boundaries, and at the intersection of these, the rise of platform production (where the "operating system" and the "applications" it integrates are code-veloped by independent producers). In diverse industries ranging from contract manufacturing to pharmaceutical collaborations, these changes are accompanied by an increase in interfirm relations with both parties expecting to innovate jointly.

In previous work,[9] we explored three exemplars of this pattern that ranged from contracts that imposed a formal governance structure but no formally enforceable substantive obligations,[10] to collaborative research agreements that look to the development of a continuing stream of products,[11] to similar agreements limited to developing a particular product and a consequent end game.[12] None of the familiar mechanisms for coping with the problem of contractual incompleteness adequately respond to the challenge posed by structuring transactions in the face of continuous uncertainty. But these exemplars demonstrate that transactional lawyers in a number of industries apparently began

[8] Michael J. Piore and Charles F. Sabel, *The Second Industrial Divide: Possibilities For Prosperity* (New York: Basic Books, 1984).

[9] Gilson, Sabel, and Scott, "Contracting for Innovation."

[10] For an example, see the Deere-Standyne agreement, ibid.

[11] For an example, see the Apple-SCI agreement, ibid.

[12] For an example, see the Warner-Lambert–Ligand agreement, ibid.

responding to their clients' need to structure new relationships in light of the constraints imposed by uncertainty.

We term the novel result "contracting for innovation." In the next section we describe the components of this form of contracting and provide a theoretical account of why the contractual innovations that work in practice also work in theory.

CONTRACTING FOR INNOVATION

Taking innovation as we have defined it, the contracting problem is to craft a structure that (a) induces efficient, transaction-specific investment by both parties, (b) establishes a framework for iterative collaboration and adjustment of the parties' obligations under conditions of *continuing* uncertainty—circumstances when the resolution of one element of uncertainty merely gives rise to another, and (c) limits the risk of opportunism that could undermine the incentive to make relation-specific investments in the first place.

The common challenges facing parties contracting for innovation across organizational boundaries give rise to solutions with common elements. In each case, a process of collaboration substitutes functionally for *ex ante* specification of the desired product—the process defines the specification, not the other way around. In each case, the parties make relation-specific investments in learning about their collaborators' capabilities that raise the costs of switching to new partners, and so restrain either party from taking advantage of their mutual dependency.

Review of actual efforts of contracting for innovation informs our understanding of how braiding is used to achieve these outcomes, by relying on formal contracting to establish processes that make behavior observable enough to support informal contracting over the substance of the (uncertain) collaboration.[13] Braiding uses *formal* contracts to create governance processes that

---

[13] Gilson, Sabel, and Scott, "Contracting for Innovation," 476–89.

support iterative joint effort through low-powered enforcement techniques that specify only the commitment to collaborate, without controlling the course or the outcome of the collaboration. This formal governance arrangement has two closely linked components.

The first is a commitment to an ongoing mutual exchange of information designed to determine if a project is feasible, and if so, how best to implement the parties' joint objectives. The second component is a procedure for resolving disputes arising from the first. Its key feature—the "contract referee mechanism"[14]—is a requirement that the collaborators reach unanimous (or near-unanimous) agreement on crucial decisions, with persistent disagreement resolved (or not) by unanimous agreement at higher levels of management from each firm. Together these two mechanisms render observable, and forestall misunderstandings about, the character traits and substantive capabilities that support the *informal* contracting upon which the parties rely as, working under uncertainty, they encounter unanticipated problems that can only be solved jointly. At the same time, the parties' increasing knowledge of their counterparty's capacities and problem-solving type, a direct result of the processes specified in the formal contract, creates switching costs—the costs to each party of replacing its counterparty with another—that constrain subsequent opportunistic behavior.

The formal element of a braided contract is thus sharply and distinctively limited in what it aims to accomplish. It functions to allow both parties to learn about each other's skills and capabilities for collaborative innovation and to develop jointly the routines necessary to working together. The formal contract does not, however, commit either party to develop, supply, or purchase any product. That commitment emerges from the informal contract, where the barrier to *ex post* opportunism results not from formal enforcement of obligations created by explicit contract, but from

---

[14] Ibid., 479–81.

increased switching costs generated by the collaboration process itself.[15]

BRAIDING AND THE THREAT OF CROWDING OUT

The conceptual difficulty at this point in the analysis is with our premise—that formal and informal contracting in fact can be combined. The academic literature has long recognized the two components making up a braided contract: one strand that is formal and legally enforceable and one strand that is informal and subject only to self-enforcement. However, the literature largely has either ignored the possibility of combining formal and informal contracting, or largely treated the two techniques as mutually inconsistent substitutes. Contemporary contract theory typically assumes that formal and informal methods are separate responses to the problem of motivating relation-specific investments in a collective enterprise. If the threat of opportunism can be addressed explicitly either by specifying state contingent outcomes or by assigning decision rights among the parties, then we observe formal contracting; if not, we observe either self-enforcing informal contracts supported relationally or, when these cannot protect specific investment, vertical integration.[16] Work in experimental economics does in contrast address the possibility of formal–informal interaction, but focuses mainly on circum-

---

[15] Only where the subject of the braided contract is a discrete project do we see formal contracting over the output of the process. In the discrete project setting, switching costs discourage opportunism during the collaborative period, but the parties have to fear opportunistic renegotiation once the cooperative stage of the project is completed and switching costs no longer provide protection. The only issue then remaining is division of the gains from prior cooperation. As a result, an explicit constraint on opportunism must be employed; but at this stage, the uncertainty having been resolved, the contract theory solution of allocating rights to decision making is feasible.

[16] See e.g., Sanford J. Grossman and Oliver Hart, *The Costs and Benefits of Ownership: A Theory of Vertical and Lateral Integration,* Journal of Political Economy 94 (1986): 691, 697–700; Oliver Hart and John Moore, *Property Rights and the Nature of the Firm,* Journal of Political Economics 98 (1990): 1119, 1151; Oliver Williamson, *Assessing Contract,* Journal of Law, Economics, & Organization 1 (1985): 177; Benjamin Klein and Keith B. Leffler, *The Role of Market Forces in Assuring Contractual Performance,* Journal of Political Economy 89 615; L.G. Telser, *A Theory of Self-Enforcing Agreements,* Journal of Business 53 (1980): 27.

stances when the introduction of formal contracting degrades the effectiveness of, or "crowds out," informal contracting.

What is broadly lacking in both literatures is a theory of when and why the parties can make use of both techniques. In this section, we provide a first step toward developing a theory of the complementary interaction of formal and informal contracting that allows braiding.

THE LIMITS OF FORMAL AND INFORMAL CONTRACTING

Formal Enforcement: The Verifiability Problem

The capacity to compel disclosure of private information is the defining feature of formal enforcement. When a formal contract breaks down due to the opacity of the interactions or the guile of one or more of the parties, courts (or arbitrators[17]) function by assessing responsibility. To do this, courts must have better information than was available to the parties. But a judge, unlike, say, a basketball referee, cannot directly observe complex interactions on the field of play and then declare fouls. A legal referee must obtain information indirectly, from the very parties who dispute the facts of their "play." This requires that the court have the power to impose sanctions in order to force the disputants to provide essential information known only to them. The court then can *verify* outcomes through information each party may lack individually. Without a judicial sanction both for nonproduction and for misleading production favorable to a party's own position, a party would be motivated to conceal evidence known only to it: the court then would lack the ability to secure information even as good as the parties themselves possess. Breach by a party would not be verifiable.

Verification, however, is costly. As a result, formal enforcement can break down, particularly where the optimal actions for each

---

[17] Arbitration remains a formal enforcement strategy. While arbitration displaces some of the legal rules associated with litigation, it still requires the intervention of the state to enforce the arbitration award.

party depend on the future state that materializes, but the future is uncertain. In that circumstance, it is prohibitively costly or impossible to specify most future states, let alone the appropriate action that is to be taken if they occur. Under these conditions, parties relying on formal enforcement are confronted with two choices: the Scylla of "hard" terms (precise rules) and the Charybdis of "soft" terms (vague standards). Rule-based contracts will require renegotiation after the uncertainty is resolved, because their *ex ante* allocation of rights will frequently turn out to be wrong *ex post*. This will allow the party favored by fate to renegotiate from strength, and thus undermine incentives to invest. Similarly, the costs of verifying standards-based contracts and the corresponding risk of the court choosing the wrong proxy—the designation of what range of observable outcomes should dictate whether unobservable behavior would be "reasonable"—are high. To be sure, parties writing more complex contracts can ameliorate this problem by using combinations of standards and rules; but as uncertainty increases—precisely the circumstances of innovation—the performance of both standards and rules deteriorate.[18]

Informal Enforcement: The Observability Problem

Where formal enforcement depends on court verification, informal enforcement depends entirely on private behavior—one party's ability to observe directly the other's actions, and the capacity to sanction misbehavior when observed. For example, parties to an agreement often can observe whether one of them has exercised "best efforts" and can punish a slacker, even though it would be quite costly to convince a court to impose an equivalent punishment. The private, nonstate sanctions that comprise informal enforcement are generally thought to take three forms, which are mutually supportive at low-to-intermediate levels of uncertainty, increasing the actors' capacity to enforce contracts where behavior is directly observable to them, but outcomes are

---

[18] Robert E. Scott and George G. Triantis, "Anticipating Litigation in Contract Design," *Yale Law Journal* 115 (2006): 814.

hard to verify. However, as we will see, informal enforcement also breaks down at high levels of uncertainty, making it no substitute for formal enforcement when the actors are in significant ways ignorant of the future they intend to create. Put differently, collaborative innovation confronts the barrier that both familiar contracting strategies break down in just the circumstance that defines the environment of innovation.

A first type of informal enforcement is the threat that one party to an informal contract will respond to its counterparty's breach by reducing or terminating future dealings. This tit-for-tat strategy imposes losses on the defector that, in prospect, create disincentives to breach in the first place.[19]

A second type of informal enforcement is normative, supported either by the morality or tastes of the contracting parties rather than their calculations of individual gain. Much experimental evidence shows that approximately half of the test subjects do not behave opportunistically even when it is in their economic interest to do so and they are not under threat of punishment or retaliation.[20] Similarly, experimental evidence also indicates a widespread, but not universal, taste for reciprocity—an inclination to reward cooperators and punish opportunists even when the subjects derive no direct and particular benefits from doing so.[21] Like character, a preference for reciprocity provides one explanation for how (and why) this informal sanctioning works. Absent a taste for reciprocity, it may be irrational for individuals to absorb the costs of shaming, boycotting, and ostracizing.

---

[19] Even where the particular parties do not expect to deal with each other in the future, the tit-for-tat enforcement structure will still work if one party will trade with others in the future—that is, if trade will be multilateral rather than bilateral—so long as the repeat play party's reputation, the collective experience of parties who have previously dealt with a person or firm, becomes known to future counterparties. The action of future counterparties then serves to discipline the misbehaving party.

[20] For a review of the literature, see Ernst Fehr and Klaus Schmidt, "Theories of Fairness and Reciprocity: Evidence and Economic Applications" (working paper no. 75, University of Zurich, Institute for Empirical Research in Economics, 2001), 2–3.

A third type of informal enforcement is normative or disposition-al informal sanctions, which can operate at the level of social groups rather than among individuals. In compact and homoge-nous communities, for instance, the community as a whole can sanction the breach of one member's obligation to another by ostracizing the malefactor, cutting off not just business ties but all the benefits of belonging to the group.

The different supports for informal contracting generally comple-ment each other, at least as the uncertainty—and with it the com-plexity—of transactions remains at low-to-moderate levels. But informal enforcement depends on clear observation of counter-party's actions: the simpler a party's action, the easier it is for the counterparty to observe and characterize. Thus increasing com-plexity interferes with all three types of informal enforcement. The probability of a mistake in playing tit-for-tat increases with the difficulty of assessing the counterparty's actions. And by the same token, the capacity to assess whether one's counterparty has a taste for reciprocity, or is of a character to forgo opportunism, or is observing community norms, also degrades in a complex envi-ronment: the match between a party's actual behavior and the character of that party becomes more difficult to assess.

In a mistake-prone or "noisy" tit-for-tat environment, misreading a counterparty's actions as opportunistic first leads to retaliation, which in turn leads to responsive retaliation and a cycle of oppor-tunistic behavior that continues until another mistake resets the

---

[21] The experimental evidence on individuals' propensity to reciprocate yields two key findings. First, many people respond cooperatively to generous acts and, conversely, punish noncoopera-tive behavior. Second, the observed preference for reciprocity is heterogeneous. Some people exhibit reciprocal behavior and others are selfish. Taking all the experiments together, the fraction of reciprocally fair subjects ranges from 40 to 60 percent, as does the fraction of subjects who are selfish. For discussion, see e.g., Ernst Fehr et al., "Reciprocity as a Contract Enforcement Device: Experimental Evidence," *Econometrica* 65 (1997): 833, 850 (finding roughly half of subjects punish-ing shirkers, and roughly half rewarding nonshirkers); Ernst Fehr and Simon Gatcher, "Fairness and Retaliation: The Economics of Reciprocity," *Journal of Economic Perspectives* 14 (2000): 159, 162 ("Many studies have carried out detailed analyses of individual decisions and found that the frac-tion of subjects exhibiting reciprocal choices is between forty and sixty-six percent."). For applica-tions of this experimental evidence to contract theory, see Robert E. Scott, "A Theory of Self-Enforcing Indefinite Agreements," *Columbia Law Review* 103 (2003): 1641, 1661–75.

cooperative equilibrium. In such a setting, tit-for-tat is no longer the most effective strategy because it risks triggering a retaliatory cycle. The dominant strategy is more forgiving: it allows some percentage of the other party's defections to go unpunished.[22] This is where the complementarity of the supports for informal contracting becomes relevant. A significant probability that a counterparty has a taste for reciprocity, or is of a character that dictates forgoing opportunism, makes it less threatening to be more forgiving of an apparent defection. An independent reason to trust the counterparty results in a corresponding higher probability that the apparent defection was really a misunderstanding.

Moreover, just as the normative modes of informal enforcement can support tit-for-tat calculations of the value of ongoing relations when counterparty's actual behavior becomes less observable, so too can the existence of ongoing relations increase the effectiveness of normative enforcement. The presence of an ongoing relationship that allows for retaliation in the event of counterparty opportunism makes it less risky for a party to act on the probability that the counterparty values reciprocity or forgoes opportunism. In this sense, the existence of the continuing relationship allows the parties to learn about each other's tastes and character. Thus we see a virtuous cycle, in which each of the mechanisms that support informal contracting reinforces the others by making the conduct of the counterparties more observable—less subject to mistaken assessment—to each other. Indeed, given the mutually supportive relation among the types of informal enforcement, we can think of them (at least at low-to-moderate levels of uncertainty) as aspects of a single informal enforcement mechanism, one rooted in ongoing relations among parties supported by a (normative) disposition to reciprocity.

---

[22] The literature is well developed and uncontroversial: Generous tit-for-tat strategies outperform simple tit-for-tat strategies in noisy environments. See e.g., M. Nowack and K. Sigmund, "Tit for Tat in Heterogeneous Populations," *Nature* 364 (1992): 56–58; H.C.J. Godfray, "The Evolution of Forgiveness," *Nature* 255 (1992): 206; J. Bendor, R.M. Kramer, and S. Stout, "When in Doubt ...: Cooperation in a Noisy Prisoner's Dilemma," *Journal of Conflict Resolution* 35 (1991): 691; Robert Axelrod and D. Dion, "The Further Evolution of Cooperation," *Science* 242 (1988): 1385.

The experimental evidence suggests, moreover, that informal enforcement, when it is effective, is both cheaper and better than formal enforcement. Informal enforcement is cheaper because a party only incurs the costs of observing the other's behavior, while formal enforcement requires the parties to expend additional resources (attorney's fees, court costs, etc.) in verifying that behavior to a court. Moreover, when informal enforcement works, it is also better. It permits parties to make credible promises regarding observable (and perhaps only observable with repetition) but nonverifiable measures of performance, thus allowing parties to avoid the risk of opportunism arising from formal enforcement of a precise rule or the moral hazard associated with the *ex post* application of a broad standard. These advantages explain why, in commercial contracting, parties often rely on informal enforcement even when formal sanctions are available.[23]

These mechanisms of informal enforcement, however, are subject to inherent limitations. Informal contracting, even that supported by taste and character, works best with repeat play in the narrowest sense: the same actors doing the same things with each other again and again makes conduct more observable, an indispensable element of informal contracting. The more actors undertake novel things with strangers—precisely the conditions of collaborative innovation in the face of uncertainty—the greater their chances either of mischaracterizing each other's acts and intentions, or lacking the ability to characterize what the others are doing at all. When changing sequences of novel performances among unfamiliar actors dissipate the transparency necessary for informal contracting, a switch to forgiving strategies no longer interrupts the vicious cycles of mistake, retaliation, and counter-response, as can occur at lower levels of uncertainty. Instead, retaliations escalate and destroy the relation.

---

[23] This insight was first explored in Stewart Macaulay's classic account of how commercial contractual relationships rely on informal enforcement even when the parties previously have entered into to a formal, legally enforceable contract. Stewart Macaulay, "Non-Contractual Relations in Business: A Preliminary Study," *American Sociological Review* 28 (1963): 55.

In sum, formal contracting has an advantage where performance is verifiable *ex post* but not necessarily observable *ex ante*. Informal contracting has an advantage where performance is observable but costly to verify. But both can break down in the highly uncertain environments that are the domain of innovation. Can contract planners address such circumstances by combining the two strategies in a fashion that is more effective than either standing alone?

COMPLEMENTS OR SUBSTITUTES? EXPLAINING THE RIVALRY BETWEEN FORMAL AND INFORMAL ENFORCEMENT

The preceding discussion suggests that contracting parties should be motivated to capture the benefits of both formal and informal enforcement, by relying on formal enforcement to solve complex problems with noisy interactions and on informal mechanisms to enforce contingencies that are difficult to verify but clear enough to be observable. A mixed strategy is feasible if formal and informal enforcement mechanisms can be complements, but not if they are substitutes in that recourse to formal contracting "crowds out" the operation of informal contracting. Here the existing theory and evidence offer limited guidance. Predicting when the crowding out effect dominates requires an understanding of the mechanism through which formal enforcement degrades the operation of informal contracting.

Consistent with our analysis that informal contracting depends on the observability of a counterparty's actions, we argue that crowding out occurs when the presence of a formal contract and the potential for high-powered legal sanctions *degrade* the information about the nature of the counterparties and the nature of their interactions.[24] In other words, we see crowding out when formal contracting makes the parties' actions and performance less observable. This occurs because of the effects of two interrelated factors: (a) formal enforcement changes the way a party *perceives* the observed behavior of the counterparty and (b) formal enforcement reduces the number of observations of the very behavior that signals an intention to cooperate.

First, there is evidence that the parties' behavior will change depending on whether they believe they are engaged in norm-based or arm's-length arrangements.[25] The most familiar example is the experiment of using formal sanctions to cause parents to be timely in picking up their children from nursery school. In an effort to improve punctuality, a fine was imposed to encourage compliance. But rather than increasing compliance, imposing a fine caused late pickups to increase. The formal fine "crowded out" the reputation-based norm by changing the parents' perception of each others' obligation from a commitment to the community to a price for additional day care.[26]

---

[24] The distinction between high-powered legal sanctions that drive out informal enforcement and low-powered sanctions that, we argue below, do not result in crowding out is critical to our theory of how braiding works. High-powered enforcement consists of the imposition of standard breach of contract remedies for a failure to perform specified contractual obligations. High-powered enforcement, then, is tied to outcome variables and provides incentives that induce parties to take specified substantive actions designed to maximize expected surplus.

[25] We acknowledge that our argument could be cast entirely in terms of the conditions under which a more forgiving form of the self-interested strategy of tit-for-tat displaces a less forgiving one, without reference to the conditions under which intrinsic or moral motives are crowded out by extrinsic, gain-oriented ones. For two reasons, we choose instead to combine the two forms of argument, and, as in the preceding discussion, even to underscore their complementarity. First, we are convinced by the experimental evidence that intrinsic motivation—particularly a propensity to reciprocity—is a fact of (some) human behavior. To be sure, we are a long way from understanding the operation and implications of such intrinsic motivation; but it seems odd to transcribe what we do know of it into a rational-choice vocabulary that denies, or least questions, its existence. Second, to acknowledge the existence of intrinsic motivation is hardly to abandon the postulate of rational action in economic exchanges of the kind under consideration here. Rational actors are perfectly capable of making rational—calculating—decisions about when, and in relation to whom, to rely on intrinsic motivation. Indeed, a central claim in our braiding argument is that under uncertainty it is rational for actors to design institutions that allow them to develop a counterparty's propensity to reciprocity, along with her capacities. For an earlier effort to reconcile rational-choice and intrinsic approaches to trust, see Charles Sabel, "Studied Trust: Building New Forms of Cooperation in a Volatile Economy," in *Explorations in Economic Sociology*, ed. Richard Swedberg (New York: Russell Sage Foundation Publications, 1993), 104–44. For a review of the persistent tension between rational choice and intrinsic perspectives, see Christos J. Paraskevopoulos, Social Capital," *Comparative Politics* (July 2010): 475–494. We are grateful to Yochai Benkler for reminding us of just how far we are from a full understanding of intrinsic motivation and its relation to institutional rather than individual behavior.

Similar results are reported in more commercial settings.[27] Studies indicate that when offered a contract whose performance is based only on trust, a substantial number of individuals will both pay higher prices and extend higher levels of effort than narrow self-interest would dictate. But when offered the same choices *plus* the possibility of having a third party impose a monetary sanction if the promisor fails to perform, the average price offered and the average effort given declines significantly. The introduction of the formal enforcement option causes shirking to increase and trust vanishes almost completely.[28] In effect, the introduction of a formal sanction that governs all of the parties' actions under the contract results in a "cognitive shift that crowds out norm-based social behavior and increases the likelihood of income maximizing behavior."[29]

Moreover, when the introduction of formal penalties changes the parties' perception of their interaction, that change also may change the signal indicating the taste or character of the party who proposed the formal penalty. A party's willingness to expend resources to create a threat of significant damages for failure to perform the formal contract may indicate that the party is less likely to be a reciprocator. Once a counterparty's character becomes less observable and (correctly or not) the party is identified as potentially opportunistic, only fully formal contacts will be chosen.

---

[26] Uri Gneezy and Aldo Rustichini, "A Fine is a Price," *Journal of Legal Studies* 29 (2000): 1. An extensive literature in social psychology also considers the crowding out of intrinsic motivations. See Edward L. Deci, R. Koestner, and Richard M. Ryan, "A Meta-Analytic Review of Experiments Examining the Effects of Extrinsic Rewards on Intrinsic Motivations," *Psychological Bulletin* 125 (1999): 627.

[27] See e.g., Iris Bohnet, Bruno S. Frey, and Steffen Huck, "More Order with Less Law: On Contract Enforcement, Trust and Crowding," *American Political Science Review* 95 (2001): 131.

[28] Ernst Fehr and Simon Gachter, "Do Incentive Contracts Crowd Out Voluntary Cooperation?" (working paper no. 34, University of Zurich, Institute for Empirical Research in Economics, April 2002), available at http://ssrn.com/abstract=313028. A similar result is reported by Daniel Houser, Erte Xiao, Kevin McCabe, and Vernon Smith, "When Punishment Fails: Research on Sanctions, Intentions and Non-Cooperation," *Games and Economic Behavior* 62 (2008): 509.

[29] Houser et al., "When Punishment Fails."

Second, "high-powered" formal enforcement contributes to crowding out by suppressing information that supports reciprocity. For example, one party's request for an adjustment of contractual duties subsequently may be found to justify the other party's declaring an anticipatory repudiation of the contract, thereby exposing the requesting party to substantial damages. A single misstep can transform a surplus-generating cooperative enterprise into a zero-sum game.[30] This threat, in turn, deters actions—such as requests for mid-course adjustment of the contract—that invite a counterparty to reciprocate proportionally and informally and that can confirm a party's tastes or character. In short, high-powered penalties dramatically raise the stakes associated with observability-based informal contracting, leaving the parties to rely on verifiable formal rules.

BRAIDING IN THE COURTS: PRELIMINARY AGREEMENTS

Ideally, courts would respond to the need for the parties to initially address a project's feasibility by enforcing the chosen methods of mutual cooperation on terms consistent with the arrangements themselves. Low-powered sanctions designed to encourage compliance with the information exchange regime (and the informal relations it supports) would be imposed while avoiding high-powered sanctions that crowd out informality, and destroy the braid, would be avoided. And indeed, this is what we are beginning to see: courts in leading cases are sanctioning overtly selfish abuse of information-exchange regimes. But because the sanction relates only to the commitment to collaborate, damages are limited in principle to the reliance costs incurred in the collaboration

---

[30] In addition to the notion that only one party can breach and that material breach results in compensatory damages as well as loss of accrued contract rights, rules governing insecurity and anticipatory breach permit one party to threaten these consequences whenever the other discloses anticipated difficulties in performance. In addition, the mitigation doctrine only operates once a party forfeits all rights by breaching. Until there is a breach, the counterparty can ignore requests for adjustments that might reduce the consequences of nonperformance. The threat of the ultimate sanction thus deters parties from voluntarily revealing the information needed for the counterparty to adjust informally. Charles J. Goetz and Robert E. Scott, "The Mitigation Principle: Toward a General Theory of Contractual Obligation," *Virginia Law Review* 69 (1983): 967, 1011–1018.

rather than lost profits from not going forward with the project. In this way, the collaboration commitment can achieve its intended purpose of generating information and trust precisely; low-powered formal enforcement does not drive out informal enforcement.[31]

As might be anticipated in an emergent area of law, the decisions of courts called on to enforce braided contracts are not uniformly consistent with the enforcement theory we have developed here. Some decisions invite the award of damages for parties who participate faithfully in the information exchange regime but then decide that it is not profitable for them to pursue the joint project. Other decisions contemplate (or at least invite the possibility of) the award of full expectation damages—that is, high-powered enforcement—for breach of the information-exchange obligation. In both instances, courts fail to appreciate the importance of limiting formal enforcement to low-powered sanctions focused on willful violations of the collaboration agreement itself and thereby create the kind of incentives that undo braiding by inducing strategic crowding out of informal enforcement.

In this section, we review judicial decisions that address the contract doctrine applicable to contracting for innovation. Although pertinent cases have arisen in the context of contractual and antitrust disputes over joint development of technology,[32] we extend the reach of our analysis by focusing on the area of preliminary agreements or letters of intent, as they are termed in the context of corporate acquisitions. In these settings as well, parties realize that the feasibility of many projects can only be established by joint investment in the production of information necessary to make that very determination, and consequently distinguish agreement on the process of disciplined coevaluation from final agreement on the actual project.

---

[31] See Gilson, Sabel, and Scott, *Braiding*.

[32] See Gilson, Sabel, and Scott, *Braiding*.

We see cases in these domains in which courts get it right by applying low-powered enforcement to commitments to collaboratively determine the feasibility of a potential project, and declining to enforce at all claims that a party wrongfully refused to actually pursue the project. But we also see cases where the court gets it wrong by holding out the possibility either of imposing damages on parties who participate faithfully in the information exchange regime but then decide not to pursue the joint project, or the award of full expectation damages for breach of the information exchange obligation. The divergent approaches to formal enforcement reveal that the courts lack a sound theoretical construct that informs their treatment of braided contracts. We show here that a better understanding of theory can help courts to frame the proper contract doctrine, and thereby facilitate innovation.

Braiding in Preliminary Agreements

Assume two commercial parties agree to collaborate in investigating the prospects for what they hope to be a profitable commercial project.[33] The parties agree on the nature of the initial investment that each is to make to evaluate the project, but the terms of the ultimate project cannot be determined without that initial investment. Consequently, the parties agree to proceed with their initial investments and also agree to negotiate the remaining terms of the contract once they can observe the fruits of their efforts. These two parties have reached what the law now recognizes as a "preliminary agreement." Only by each party investing and sharing the information that their investment reveals can they determine collaboratively whether their project can succeed. The increased knowledge about the project revealed by the initial investments will then permit the parties to determine whether to finalize the deal with a fully enforceable contract and on what terms.

---

[33] The discussion in this section draws on Alan Schwartz and Robert E. Scott, "Precontractual Liability and Preliminary Agreements," *Harvard Law Review* 120 (2007): 661.

The legal question is to what extent a preliminary agreement that looks to the future exchange of private information is formally enforceable. The question is important because the parties meet as strangers with no necessary prospect of an ongoing relationship (and so with no basis for trust). Thus the risk of opportunism is significant. This is particularly the case where the parties undertake to make preliminary investments concurrently and then to share the information that the investments yield. Suppose one party then elects instead to wait and see what comes of her counterparty's investment—in effect reneging on the mutual commitment to collaborate. Delaying a promised investment under these conditions offers several strategic advantages. First, the passage of time and her partner's investment is likely to reveal whether the project will be profitable. If so, the opportunistic party—having yet to make any investment in the project—can exploit the counterparty in a negotiation over the terms of the ultimate contract. Second, if the project proves unsuccessful, delay permits the opportunistic party to avoid what otherwise would have been sunk costs. Those savings will likely be larger than any offsetting losses from delay if the project instead proves profitable.

Historically, such preliminary agreements were unenforceable under the indefiniteness doctrine of the common law of contracts. Recently, however, courts have affected a major shift in doctrine by relaxing the common law rule under which parties are either fully bound or not bound at all. Instead, a new enforcement rule is emerging to govern cases where the parties contemplate further negotiations.[34] This new rule responds to the increasing importance to successful collaborations of the search for new partners in an uncertain environment. The new rule starts with the presumption that preliminary agreements typically do not create fully binding contracts.[35] This presumption rests on the traditional common law view that courts should not hold parties to contracts unless the parties intended to make them. The shift comes from courts now recognizing that welfare gains can result from attaching some level of formal enforcement to agreements to collaborate that were intended to bind despite the need for further negotiation. The new default rule thus enforces "a mutual commitment to negotiate together in good faith in an effort to reach final agreement."[36] Neither party, however, has a right to demand performance of the contemplated transaction. If the parties cannot ultimately agree on a final contract, they may abandon the deal. Both parties thus enter into an option on the ultimate deal, which is exercisable after the parties learn the information produced through the preliminary investments and whose price is the cost of the preliminary investment.

This new rule governing preliminary agreements to collaborate—creating a legal duty to bargain in good faith but not requiring the parties to agree—is an appropriate first step in solving the parties' contracting problem. As we argued above, it is helpful to attach some formal support to agreements that depend on initial learning to achieve innovation, particularly when the imposition of low-powered enforcement stimulates the mechanisms that build trust. The contemporary judicial approach to preliminary agreements of this sort appropriately opens the door to judicial support of mutual learning in contracts for innovation. Nevertheless, the courts' experience so far provides little normative guidance concerning the breadth of the enforceable obligation, or the consequences of its breach. This is an important short-

---

[34] The rule originated with the opinion of Judge Pierre Leval in *Teachers Insurance and Annuity Association of America v. Tribune Co.*, 670 F. Supp. 481, 488 (S.D. N.Y. 1987). Judge Leval identified two separate types of "preliminary agreements." He labeled as "Type I" those cases where the parties have agreed on all material terms but have also agreed to memorialize their agreement in a more formal document. Disputes arise primarily because parties have failed to express clearly their intention as to *when* their arrangement would be legally enforceable. Here the question is solely one of timing—when have the parties manifested an intention to be legally bound? In contrast, "Type II" agreements concern binding preliminary commitments, the preliminary agreements we analyze here. In this latter case, the parties agree on certain terms but leave possibly important terms open to further negotiation. This requires courts to determine *whether* such an agreement had been made, *what* the duty to bargain in good faith entails, and *which* remedy should be awarded for breach of that duty. This framework has been followed in at least thirteen states, sixteen federal district courts and seven federal circuits. See Schwarz and Scott, "Precontractual Liability," 76–80.

[35] See *R.G. Group Inc. v. Horn & Hardart Co.*, 751 F.2d 69, 74 (2d Cir. 1984).

[36] *TIAA v. Tribune*, 670 F. Supp. 498.

coming when, as we have seen, the breadth of judicial enforcement is critical to whether crowding out is the unintended consequence of formal enforcement.

Our analysis of the function of the braiding mechanism suggests that the parties to this agreement should be legally required to comply with their initial commitments to pursue promised preliminary investments (typically investments in information) that are necessary to reveal whether or not the proposed project is feasible. But formal enforcement should play no role in determining whether or not the project should go forward and on what terms. After all, rational parties will pursue efficient projects and abandon inefficient projects. The parties already have strong incentives to negotiate faithfully over the conditions for achieving success. Rather, the challenge is to discourage parties from defecting early in the relationship before a robust pattern of cooperation has developed. The threat of a legal sanction, therefore, should only be designed to give the parties sufficient opportunity to develop patterns of cooperation supported by switching costs.

Then, how well does the new legal framework governing preliminary agreements support the braiding mechanism? In our analysis, the complementary braiding of formal and informal enforcement will be successful if and only if the following condition is satisfied: The courts only deploy low-powered incentives; that is, courts only sanction cheating on the parties' mutual commitment to iterative collaboration but do not attempt to regulate the course or the outcome of the collaboration. Put differently, if the preliminary agreement is breached, the court should require a party to repay the price the counterparty paid for the option—the amount spent on the preliminary investment. It should not require even a breaching party to exercise the option, whether by completing the transaction or by imposing expectation damages. An examination of litigated preliminary agreements suggests that courts are divided in their understanding of the breadth of their role.[37] We illustrate the lack of clarity in two manifestations of the

[37] For an analysis of the litigated cases, see Schwartz and Scott, "Precontractual Liability," 691–702.

preliminary agreement issue. The first is its application in a general commercial setting. The second is its application in a specialized form of preliminary agreement—a letter of intent in a corporate acquisition.

The Commercial Setting

Consider first *In re Matterhorn Group, Inc.*[38] There, Swatch wanted to sell more watches in the United States by expanding its franchise operations. Matterhorn and Swatch agreed to collaborate on pursuing the possibility of a long-term relationship: the parties signed a letter of intent granting Matterhorn the exclusive franchise for thirty possible sites. Under the agreement, Matterhorn undertook to invest in finding appropriate locations for retailing Swatch watches from among the list of possible locations. Swatch undertook to process diligently the applications for franchises at potentially profitable locations as Matterhorn filed them, and then to seek financing and approval of franchises at chosen locations from its parent firm. Thus, in our framework, the parties agreed to collaborate by making concurrent investments in pursuit of an entrepreneurial innovation: Swatch would incur opportunity costs (by granting exclusive rights to Matterhorn) and invest the human capital needed to evaluate Matterhorn's applications and to become familiar with the American business climate; Matterhorn would invest the search and information costs necessary to identifying profitable locations. The project contemplated an iterative exchange of information focused on finding profitable retail sites for selling Swatch watches in shopping malls, but precisely which locations, if any, would be mutually profitable could not be determined without the initial investments by both parties.

In this case, the parties had no prior history, they did not share membership in a homogeneous community, and they could not depend on the discipline of repeated exchange to constrain opportunism. As a consequence, informal sanctions were weak at

---

[38] 2002 WL 31528396 (Bk. S.D.N.Y. 2002).

the outset of the relationship and the parties were each at risk of exploitation. And, indeed, Swatch engaged in just the strategic behavior that our framework predicts: it delayed processing several applications and failed to secure the necessary approvals.[39] The court found Swatch to be in breach of a preliminary agreement to bargain in good faith and awarded Matterhorn reliance damages based on its investment expenditures in investigating the locations in question. Importantly, however, the court denied Matterhorn's claim for expectation damages based on lost profits, holding that "there is no guarantee that it would have opened a store in [that location]."[40] Thus the court compensated Matterhorn for the price it paid for the option, but did not protect it from Swatch's decision not to exercise it.

The result in *Matterhorn* is consistent with the hypothesis that narrowly defined duties of good faith will complement a regime that depends primarily on informal enforcement. A properly configured braiding mechanism, such as the one that appears to have been adopted by the court in *Matterhorn*, likely will not crowd out the informal mechanisms that build trust but rather will offer a low-powered complement during the early stages of collaboration, thereby giving reciprocity and trust the opportunity to evolve.

Preliminary Agreements in Corporate Acquisitions: Letters of Intent and the Duty to Negotiate in Good Faith

The pattern of preliminary agreements that contemplate concurrent preliminary investments can also be seen in the context of

---

[39] The court held: The rejection of the Vail application violated the Letter of Intent. The Letter of Intent granted Matterhorn the exclusive right to negotiate a lease in Vail despite Vail's geographical distance from Matterhorn's base of operation in the Northeast. Furthermore, it required Swatch to review the Vail application in good faith, and in a manner consistent with the criteria discussed above.... [Swatch] unilaterally rescinded the exclusivity that the Letter of Intent had granted, and Swatch's [decision] to reject the Vail application was improper. In addition, Matterhorn sent the Vail letter of intent in late April 1996.... Swatch took four months to complete its processing of the application.... Accordingly, Swatch breached the Letter of Intent by rejecting the Vail application for improper reasons. Ibid., 16–17.

[40] Ibid.

corporate acquisitions. We turn now to several cases that illustrate this pattern. They also illustrate the adverse consequences when courts fail to understand the interaction of formal and informal enforcement.

Tan v. Allwaste, Inc.

Tan v. Allwaste, Inc., involved a claim by shareholders of Geotrack that Allwaste had breached an obligation to negotiate in good faith Geotrak's acquisition. Discussions between Allwaste and Geotrack had led to the parties executing a letter of intent that stated Allwaste's intention to make the acquisition subject to satisfactory due diligence. The letter of intent also stated that it "does not constitute a binding agreement among the parties" and further stated that, according to the court, "the parties do not have a deal until a formal agreement was executed." However, the letter did contain some binding obligations. It bound the parties to pursue a deal in good faith and contained a "no-shop" clause by which Geotrack promised not to shop Allwaste's stock offer to other potential buyers. During the due diligence investigation, Allwaste discovered that Geotrack had not remitted payroll and withholding taxes to the Internal Revenue Service for some time. Allwaste withdrew from further negotiations and was unwilling to buy Geotrack even after it offered to lower the price.

This preliminary acquisition agreement can be fairly characterized as an innovative effort to secure the synergies that might arise from combining the Allwaste and Geotrack businesses, whose assessment and ultimate success depends on both parties making preliminary investments in the proposed project concurrently. Here the buyer invests in information (due diligence) to determine the actual condition of Geotrack's business and to develop the information necessary to assess the potential for synergy and the difficulty in actually achieving it. In turn, this investment is protected by a no-shop clause: the seller cannot use the fact of Allwaste's interest to induce other buyers to enter a competing bid and thereby devalue Allwaste's investment in information. Thus Geotrack makes an opportunity cost investment and incurs the potential costs of running the business without change and subject to its competitors' actions while Allwaste undertakes its investigation.[41] Concurrent investment and the passage of time together will show whether a profitable project exists, at which time the parties would be free to write a contract to complete the acquisition if the underlying innovation was feasible.

In this case, the court correctly held that the letter agreement was a preliminary agreement obligating Allwaste to negotiate further in good faith with Geotrack: in our terms, this was a low-powered formal obligation that supported the concurrent investment that was necessary to get the parties to the point where they could assess whether synergy gains could be captured and then decide whether to complete a transaction. However, the court went a step further by also concluding that there was sufficient evidence for a reasonable jury to conclude that although the target had failed to disclose that it had not paid its payroll and withholding taxes for some time, Allwaste had declined to go forward with the deal for reasons that were unrelated to Geotrack's actions, omissions, or financial status.[42] On this basis, the court concluded that the case would go to a jury to determine whether Allwaste had breached its obligation to negotiate in good faith because it may have declined to go forward with the transactions for reasons unrelated to the target's misbehavior.[43]

---

[41] Sellers in these acquisition agreements may also invest in the synergies that result from integration. See Gilson and Schwartz, "Understanding MACs," *Journal of Law, Economics, & Organization* 33 (2005): 330.

[42] In particular, plaintiffs noted the acquisition of Geotrack was to be debt free, so Geotrack's tax liability should not have affected Allwaste's analysis of the deal. Plaintiffs also provided evidence that Allwaste simply decided not to conduct any more acquisitions. 1997 WL 337207 at 4. However, Allwaste might well have concluded that a counterparty that lied about its liabilities may have been lying about other matters, such as the condition of its assets or the nondebt aspects of its financial condition that a debt-free acquisition would not protect against.

[43] The court appears to have concluded that if Allwaste declined to go forward with the acquisition because it "simply decided not to conduct any more acquisitions" (ibid. at 4), a jury could conclude that it breached its preliminary agreement. In other words, the court construed the obligation as prohibiting a change in one party's strategy.

Under these circumstances, exposing Allwaste to the threat of a jury finding a bad faith failure to negotiate transforms the preliminary agreement from a low-powered formal enforcement tool that supports the diligence process necessary to assessing the potential for innovation, to a high-powered sanction that exposes Allwaste to large damages from not making the acquisition.[44] There was no allegation that Allwaste had not made its preliminary investment in assessing the potential of the acquisition; it had paid the price for its option. Rather, Geotrack alleged that Allwaste had merely concluded that the acquisition was no longer advantageous, which the court concluded would be a breach. So expansive an interpretation of the good faith obligation and the expansion of the role of formal enforcement goes much further than the low-powered enforcement associated with a braiding strategy, which contemplates only that each party is held to making the preliminary investments necessary to assess the acquisition, but neither is obligated to close the transaction. More concretely, a braiding strategy does not envision that a letter of intent shifts the risk of changes in general economic conditions or the potential buyer's circumstances or strategy to the buyer. Such an expansion of formal enforcement is precisely the shift in the relative importance of formal and informal enforcement that is associated with crowding out the development of informal patterns of cooperation necessary to exploit the potential for innovation in the first place. The court in *Tan v. Allwaste* unwisely departed from the kind of low-powered enforcement necessary to support effective braiding, and thereby restricted the range of contractual techniques available to parties seeking to innovate.

VS & A Communications and Venture Associates

The potentially dysfunctional reasoning and result in *Tan v. Allwaste* is not simply an example of a single judge getting it wrong. The absence of a theoretically sound principle to guide

---

[44] The court did not limit potential damages to Geotrack's reliance costs, thus leaving open the possibility that Allwaste could be held to benefit of the bargain damages.

judicial enforcement of a letter of intent can be seen by comparing the efforts of two distinguished jurists confronting this problem—then-Delaware Chancellor William T. Allen, and then-Chief Judge Richard Posner of the United States Court of Appeals for the Seventh Circuit. Both reach the right result in the end, but Chancellor Allen inflicted on the defendant a costly trial that he later acknowledged was unnecessary,[45] and Judge Posner, albeit *in dicta*, held out the possibility that the damages for breach of an obligation to negotiate in good faith contained in a letter of intent might extend to expectation damages.[46]

In *VS & A Communications*, Chancellor Allen considered the claim that an obligation to negotiate in good faith, contained in a letter of intent concerning an acquisition, in effect required the seller to close the transaction on terms that the buyer alleges the seller could not in good faith have rejected.[47] While the facts that give the buyer's position at least surface plausibility are complicated, Chancellor Allen's framing of the issue is not:

> In my opinion [the letter of intent] does create an implied obligation to keep the Stations off the market and not to offer to sell or negotiate with others concerning the sale. In addition, [the buyer] was obligated to continue to assist the negotiation process in specific ways: to afford information, for example. These obligations are real and they would have value to one negotiating to buy the Stations. But the obligation ... does not go so far as to constitute a concession from the seller of its right as a property owner to change its mind ... prior to the time it agrees to bind itself legally to a sale. . . . Markets change. Negotiating a complex transaction is always subject to the risk that a material change in a relevant market will suddenly make a proposed deal

---

[45] *VS&A Communications Partners, L.P. v. Palmer Broadcasting Limited Partnership*, 1992 WL 339377 (Del.Ch. 1992).

[46] *Venture Associates Corporation v. Zenith Data Systems Corporation*, 96 F.3d 275 (7th Cir. 1996).

[47] The case is unusual in that typically it is the buyer who elects not to go forward.

uneconomic from one side of the transaction or the other. That risk inevitably exists until a party is legally bound.[48]

Thus Chancellor Allen reaches a conclusion that is consistent with low-powered formal enforcement of a braiding strategy and the avoidance of a crowding out. However, it is important to keep in mind that Chancellor Allen was writing a post-trial opinion. As he said, "It may be that, taking the view of this case that I now do, it would have been permissible to grant summary judgment of dismissal to defendants. That course would have saved the substantial effort and expense entailed in the trial that has now been completed."[49]

The risk of trial, especially trial to a jury as opposed to the bench trial found in the Delaware Chancery Court, becomes especially significant if the potential damage remedy extends not just to reliance damages (the amount of one party's preliminary investment), but also to benefit of the bargain damages (the profits the party would have earned had the acquisition actually been completed). And here is where Judge Posner's opinion in *Venture Associates Corporation*[50] becomes relevant.

Judge Posner correctly concludes, as did Chancellor Allen, that an obligation to negotiate in good faith contained in a letter of intent does not constrain a party from changing its view of the desirability of an acquisition in light of a change in conditions:

> Since [the seller] had not agreed on the sale price, it remained free to demand a higher price in order to reflect the market value of the company at the time of the actual sale. ... [The seller] was free to demand as high a price as it thought the market would bear, provided that it was not trying to scuttle the deal ... If the

---

[48] 1992 WL 339377 at 8.

[49] Ibid. at 2.

[50] *Venture Associates Corporation*, 96 F.3d 275 (7th Cir. 1996).

market value ... rose ... say to $25 million, [the seller] would not be acting in bad faith to demand that amount from [the buyer] even if it knew that [the buyer] would not go that high. [The seller] would be acting in bad faith only if its purpose in charging more than [the buyer] would pay was to induce [the buyer] to back out of the deal.[51]

Consistent with proper judicial enforcement of a braiding strategy, a party is not committed to exercising the option to close the transaction.

However, the risk of trial becomes a serious threat to crowd out informal contracting, even if the charge to the jury is correct, if the potential damages are calculated in terms of a breach of an obligation to pursue the ultimate deal. And here Judge Posner expresses the view that the threat is real: "[D]amages for breach of an agreement to negotiate may be, although they are unlikely to be, the same as the damages for breach of the final contract that the parties would have signed had it not been for the defendant's bad faith."[52] The difficulty with Judge Posner's invitation to courts to award expectation damages is that it blurs the separation between the formal portion of the braided contract and the informal portion, thereby increasing the risk of crowding out.

The conclusion in *Tan v. Allwaste* that a party who has made the contemplated preliminary investment cannot simply decline to close the transaction, together with Chancellor Allen's subjecting such a party to trial and Judge Posner's holding out the possibility that the party might be subject to expectation damages premised on a breach of the final contract, illustrates the importance of a theory to explain the underlying commercial behavior and prescribe the appropriate facilitative role for courts. No

---

[51] *Venture Associates Corporation,* 96 F. 3d at 279–80. Judge Posner does not address the broader point made by Chancellor Allen that the changed conditions that have affected the price would allow the seller in good faith simply to decline to complete the transaction.

[52] Ibid. at 278.

matter how sharp the intuitions of experienced judges, courts unguided by a theoretical framework are prone to err. Thus in both cases, the court failed to embrace fully the notion that an enforceable preliminary agreement only requires a party to pay the option price by undertaking a promised investment in acquiring and sharing information. Framing the obligation in this way should permit a party to properly obtain a summary judgment even though it walks away from the transaction for reasons wholly unrelated to the actions of the counterparty. And even if the promised investment is not made, the defendant's liability is properly limited to the investment cost and not to the expectancy that might result from a concluded deal.

How Courts Can Know Braiding When They See It

An important theme emerges from the preceding discussion of some of the evolving case law governing braided contracts. It is clear that the duty to negotiate in good faith in preliminary agreements and letters of intent provides a useful doctrinal placeholder permitting courts to imply a governance structure to support agreements that rely principally on iterative investments in information. However, the new obligation to negotiate in good faith is unmoored because the cases do not indicate what the parties are supposed to bargain over, or when the refusal to agree constitutes bad faith, or just what should be the remedy for bad faith. Under contemporary legal doctrine, for example, the question of when preliminary agreements should be enforced requires a multifactor analysis that invokes the language of the agreement, the existence and number of open terms, the extent of any reliance investments, and the customary practice regarding formalities. The court, in addition, is required to consider the context of the negotiations resulting in the preliminary agreement.[53] Such a laundry list of relevant factors leaves the decision process largely obscure. That is particularly the case when, as is typical, courts fail to

---

[53] See *TIAA*, 670 F. Supp. at 500–02.

attach weights to the factors or specify the relationship among them.[54] In the absence of a theory, the courts are left to interpret criteria for imposing liability that are unconnected to the operative facts that might justify formal enforcement.

Our theory of how courts can best support the braiding of formal and informal contracting provides a coherent way to think about the domain and limits of the obligation to negotiate in good faith: courts best respond to the proliferation of preliminary agreements induced by innovation under uncertainty by imposing low-powered sanctions designed to encourage compliance with the information-exchange regime while avoiding high-powered sanctions that crowd out informal enforcement and destroy the braid. In short, the duty to negotiate in good faith means that parties should be held to their commitment to make initial investments in collaboration and nothing else.[55] Thereafter, each party faces a choice whether or not to proceed to a fully enforceable, formal obligation. The key to understanding the nature of low-powered sanctions, therefore, is to recognize that an obligation to collaborate is not an obligation to bargain. Whenever a court holds, to the contrary, that the dissenting party has an obligation to bargain in good faith, it follows that there must be a state of the world in which failing to reach agreement is a breach. It is precisely that trap that led the court in *Tan v. Allwaste* and Judge Posner in *Venture Associates* to err.

---

[54] Schwartz and Scott, "Precontractual Liability," 675–6.

[55] Our principal concern has been the question of what it means to formally enforce these preliminary obligations. But, as noted above, the criteria for determining *when* parties have reached such an agreement are also needlessly vague. See ibid. Since parties are always free to indicate their desire to be completely free from formal enforcement, courts should hold all commercial parties to an obligation to invest as promised whenever they agree to invest collaboratively in a letter of intent or other similar form of transaction.

10: Torts, Innovation, and Growth

Gideon Parchomovsky and Alex Stein*

Our torts system aims at minimizing the total cost of accidents and accident avoidance.[1] To this end, it sets up rules that try to reduce the sum of the following social costs:

1) Primary costs that aggregate the cost of accidents and accident-avoidance expenses;[2]

2) Secondary costs that represent the distributional effects of the primary-cost bearing upon those who bear those costs under applicable legal rules;[3] and

---

* Gideon Parchomovsky is a Professor of Law at the University of Pennsylvania Law School and specializes in intellectual property, property law, and cyber law. Alex Stein is a Professor of Law at the Benjamin N. Cardozo School of Law, Yeshiva University. Formerly a Professor of Law at the Hebrew University of Jerusalem, Professor Stein has been widely published in the United States and abroad on evidence, torts, procedure, and criminal law. His writings combine law with moral philosophy and economic theories.

[1] See Guido Calabresi, *The Costs of Accidents: A Legal and Economic Analysis* (New Haven, CT: Yale University Press, 1970), 225-26, 250-59.

[2] Ibid., 26-27.

[3] Ibid., 27-28.

3) Tertiary costs that encompass the costs of adjudicating disputes over the allocation of primary and secondary costs.[4]

The conventional economic understanding of the torts system focuses on how to minimize the erosion of society's welfare that results from accidents and from the application of the rules allocating the primary, secondary, and tertiary costs. This welfare erosion aggregates the harm from the accidents that could not be prevented, the resources expended on accident prevention, the detraction from the wealth of the individuals forced to pay for the damages they caused, the suffering of the accident victims who still remain uncompensated, and the expenditures on adjudication and other law-enforcement mechanisms.

This understanding of the torts system pays no attention to the system's collateral benefits and costs. As Jennifer Arlen has recently demonstrated, our torts system does not merely reduce negative externalities.[5] Rather, it forces out standardization of care as well as production of collective goods, network externalities, and economies of scale in the form of improved precautions against harm.[6] As for the system's collateral costs, we have recently shown that the existing tort liability rules are unintentionally, but systematically, biased against innovation.[7] This bias is an unintended consequence of the custom criterion by which courts adjudicate medical malpractice, defective-product allegations, and negligence claims in general. This criterion animates the evidentiary requirements that courts use in determining negligence and product defects, and it also sets the substantive benchmark for determining doctors' malpractice.[8] As we show below, the custom criterion taxes innovators and subsidizes repli-

---

[4] Ibid., 28.

[5] See Jennifer Arlen, "Contracting Over Liability: Medical Malpractice and the Cost of Choice," *University of Pennsylvania Law Review* 159 (2011): 957.

[6] Ibid.

[7] Gideon Parchomovsky and Alex Stein, "Torts and Innovation," *Michigan Law Review* 107 (2008): 285.

[8] See Part I.

cators of conventional technologies; and by doing so, it chills innovation and distorts its path. This distortion, again, is unintended, but its economic consequence—the chilling effect on innovation—is significant. Lawmakers therefore should fix this problem, and in what follows, we make a number of proposals on how to do so.

The chilling effect on innovation is engendered not only by the custom rules as such, but rather by all governmentally determined liability criteria that apply in the area of torts. By allowing courts and administrative agencies (such as the Food and Drug Administration) to set up safety standards for torts, the legal system makes liability depend on whether the technologies that cause damage (both by themselves and in combination with other factors) align with the conventional knowledge that state agents have approved. Alignment with this knowledge insulates individuals and firms from liability in torts, regardless of damages they cause. On the other hand, failure to align with the prevalent conventions and customs makes the firm and the individual liable for damages resulting from that failure.

These rules deviate from the straightforward "result criterion" that rejects custom-driven proxies and calls for a direct assessment of the technologies' risks and benefits. Under this criterion, the technology's compliance or failure to comply with custom should play no role in determining its users' liability for tort damages. That is, defendants who comply with custom should receive no preferential treatment from the torts system. Each defendant's liability should be determined by the extent of the damage it actually caused, not by his compliance with custom or a governmentally imposed safety standard.

The torts system's deviation from the result criterion can hardly be justified by the saving of adjudicative expenses that the custom rules (and other decision-making proxies) bring about. Tort adjudication can be cost-effective without imposing a socially unnecessary tax upon innovators and without giving an anomalous subsidy to the replicators of conventional technologies.

To achieve this socially beneficial effect, the torts system can do a number of things. First, it can abolish the custom benchmark. This abolition will do away with the decisional shortcut that courts and agencies presently use. Courts and agencies will consequently have to carry out a risk-benefit analysis on a case-by-case (or category-by-category) basis, which will increase the overall cost of their decision-making processes. We believe that this increase will be offset by the value of innovations that the proposed reform will unlock,[9] but not everyone will share this belief.[10] We therefore have made another proposal: a proposal to set up special tribunals (with rotating experts) that will speed up the process of evaluating the safety of innovative technologies.[11] Under this system, a new technology that received the seal of approval from the relevant tribunal will be deemed to be as safe as a parallel customary technology. The special tribunals will accelerate the recognition of new technologies as satisfying (or not satisfying) the requisite criterion for tort liability. This proposal is not immune from skeptical challenge either. Arguably, streamlining the recognition of a new technology's safety is not necessarily a good thing because experience—the ultimate judge of whether the technology is safe enough—can only be acquired over time. The law's recognition of a technology's safety—so goes the argument—should therefore be synchronized with the formation of custom that was purposefully designed to be slow rather than fast.

We believe that this challenge isn't serious: if the tribunal adjudicating an innovation's safety does not have enough information for making a dependable decision, it will—presumably—say so. Some innovations' safety can be tested fairly fast. Their recognition as safe consequently should not depend on whether they became customary. More fundamentally, custom formation is not

---

[9] Ibid.

[10] See, e.g., Kenneth S. Abraham, "Custom, Noncustomary Practice, and Negligence," *Columbia Law Review* 109 (2009): 1784, 1813-15.

[11] Parchomovsky and Stein, "Torts and Innovation."

a purely epistemic process—one that involves knowledge-based persuasion, deliberation, and decision. Customs are also consequences of the incumbent power, and incumbents on the technologies' (and other) markets have a strong incentive to block newcomers instead of competing with them on equal terms. Contrary to what the law presently does, the incumbents' standards therefore should not be used as benchmarks for imposing liability in torts.

This paper explores yet another innovation-promoting reform: requiring tort plaintiffs to prove by a preponderance of the evidence that the innovative technology allegedly responsible for the damage in question is inferior to the customary technology as far as safety is concerned; and, moreover, that the defendant's adoption of the customary technology would have averted the damage. This change in the law of evidence would create the desired equalization between conventional and customary technologies. Correspondingly, it would level the tort-liability playground for innovators and replicators.

We unfold this proposal in three parts. Part I will specify the anti-innovation effects of the custom rules. Part II will state the disadvantages of the widespread recourse to agencies' determinations of safety as a benchmark for identifying "negligence" and product "defects." Part III will set forth our evidentiary proposal. A short conclusion follows.

PART I. THE CUSTOM RULES

Three main doctrines that make up tort law—general negligence, product liability, and medical malpractice—are founded upon custom.[12]

Begin with negligence. In assessing a defendant's conduct, courts generally presume that a defendant who failed to comply with safety-related customs prevalent in her industry acted

---

[12] This part is based on Parchomovsky and Stein, "Torts and Innovation."

negligently. The defendant consequently needs to rebut this presumption, which may in many cases be very difficult to do. Likewise, in product liability, courts turn to custom in determining whether the defendant's product design was defective. Deviation from industry customs, therefore, runs a greater risk of a ruling that the product is unsafe. Finally, in the area of medical malpractice, courts hold doctors to the "customary care" standard. Failure on the part of a physician to comply with this standard exposes her to a high prospect of liability. Custom thus constitutes the benchmark against which defendants' conduct is evaluated.

In the product liability area, custom plays a crucial role as well.[13] Under the prevalent regime, a manufacturer's conformity with the relevant industrial custom is admissible as evidence, tending to prove that its product was safe and not defectively designed.[14] Conversely, a manufacturer's failure to conform to custom is evidence of—once again, inconclusively—the presence of a defect in its product.[15] These factors go into determination of design defects under both "risk-utility"[16] and "consumer expectation"[17] criteria. Under those criteria, a product classifies as defective when it falls far below a reasonable consumer's expectation or creates a risk of harm that exceeds its benefits.

The effect of those custom rules is substantial. A product that conforms to the customary design will normally classify as more beneficial than risky and as satisfying a reasonable consumer's expectation. The product consequently will be held safe and nondefective, despite the damage that consumers may have suffered from using it. Conversely, a product that fails to align with the

[13] See David G. Owen, "Proof of Product Defect," *Kentucky Law Journal* 93 (2004-5): 1, 5-10 (documenting massive use of industry customs as a benchmark for determining design defects in product liability actions).

[14] Ibid., 8.

[15] Ibid., 7.

[16] See David G. Owen, *Products Liability Law* (Eagan, MN: West Publishing, 1995), § 5.7, at 303-4.

[17] Ibid. § 5.6, 295.

customary design will almost certainly fail both "risk-utility" and "consumer expectation" tests.[18] This failure will identify the product as unsafe and defective.[19]

The law of medical malpractice provides that a doctor must treat her patients with customary medical care.[20] This rule differs from the general negligence and product-liability rules in one important respect. Under the medical malpractice rule, a doctor's compliance with the relevant custom, practice or "school of thought" does not merely evidence the delivery of adequate care. Such compliance *is* adequate care as a matter of substantive law.[21] By proving her compliance with the relevant customary norm, the doctor therefore does more than simply increase her chances of winning the case; she guarantees herself this result.[22]

The law of torts relies on customs not only directly, by associating custom with precautions against harm that a reasonable person ought to take, but also indirectly, through evidentiary rules and presumptions that bolster the centrality of custom to adjudicative determinations of fault.[23] Chief among those is the *res ipsa loquitur* presumption that creates a strong evidential association between safety and conventional precautions against harm. Under this presumption, an unusual occurrence featuring an infliction of harm by an instrumentality over which the defendant exercised exclusive control prompts an inference that the defendant was

---

[18] Ibid. §§ 5.6, 5.7, 295, 306-7.

[19] Ibid.

[20] See Dan B. Dobbs, *The Law of Torts* (Stamford, CT: Gale Cengage, 2000), § 242, 633.

[21] Ibid.; *Jones v. Chidester*, 610 A.2d 964 (Pa. 1992) (articulating the "school of thought" rule as a complete defense against medical malpractice allegations). Courts, however, sometimes scrutinize doctors' customs that determine the level of risk of injury or death to which a doctor may and may not expose her patient: see *Helling v. Carey*, 519 P.2d 981 (Wash. 1974).

[22] See Dobbs, *The Law of Torts*, § 242, at 633.

[23] Courts' decisions about negligence routinely rely on proxies and evidentiary devices that include custom, the *res ipsa* rule and accepted expert opinion. See, e.g., *Twyman v. Twyman*, 855 S.W.2d 619, 633 (Texas 1993) (observing that "The issue of negligence is seldom decided without guidance from some external source: custom, relevant statutes and regulations, evidentiary doctrines such as res ipsa loquitur, or expert testimony on alternatives.").

negligent.[24] Taking conventional precautions against harm removes the occurrence from the "unusual" category.[25] Failure to take conventional precautions, in contrast, indicates negligence on the part of the defendant not only when she takes no precautions whatsoever, but also when she elects to employ a novel— i.e., "unusual"—technology.[26] When *res ipsa* applies, the case goes to trial automatically and the plaintiff is entitled to a jury decision as to whether the defendant acted negligently even when she cannot point to any specific negligent act. The ensuing prospect of losing the case puts the defendant under a serious pressure to settle.

Another rule inimical to innovation is the *Frye* doctrine[27] that controls the admissibility of expert evidence in many state jurisdictions.[28] Under *Frye*, expert testimony that falls outside of scientific or technological consensus is inadmissible as evidence and cannot be presented to fact finders. This evidential incapacitation works against innovators and in favor of users and producers of conventional technologies. The *Daubert* doctrine[29]—an alternative to *Frye*, used by federal and a number of state courts—has a similar effect. *Daubert*'s multifactor screening of expert testimony[30] includes four criteria that might keep the company's expert away from court. One of those criteria is the expert's alignment with the conventional technological wisdom.[31] This criterion is

---

[24] See W. Page Keeton et al., *Prosser and Keeton on Torts* 5th edition (Eagan, MN: West Publishing, 1984), § 39, 244-48 (explaining that the *res ipsa* rule applies predominantly to unusual events).

[25] See, e.g., *Aderhold v. Lowe's Home Centers, Inc.*, 643 S.E.2d 811, 812-14 (Ga. App. 2007) (denying *res ipsa* to a shopper struck by a box that fell from a shelf at Lowe's among other things because "the manner in which the boxes were stacked...did not appear to be unusual or dangerous").

[26] See, e.g., *Hailey v. Otis Elevator Co.*, 636 A.2d 426, 428 (D.C. 1994) ("Given the power of *res ipsa loquitur* to satisfy without further proof the element of negligence and the consequent caution with which it should be applied, we think that where the plaintiff relies upon "common knowledge" to invoke the doctrine, the fact that such events do not "ordinarily" occur "without negligence" must be based upon a widespread consensus of a common understanding." (emphasis added)).

[27] See *Frye v. United States*, 293 F. 1013 (App. D.C. 1923) (conditioning the admissibility of expert evidence upon "standing and scientific recognition" of its underlying methodology).

[28] See David E. Bernstein & Jeffrey D. Jackson, "The Daubert Trilogy in the States," *Jurimetrics Journal* 44 (2004): 351 (most states follow Frye in one form or another).

discretionary, rather than mandatory (as it was under *Frye*), but failure to satisfy it increases the testimony's chances of being excluded. Another criterion is a peer-reviewed publication of the expert's methodology.[32] This criterion is particularly hostile to technological innovations that are kept secret—away from imitators' eyes—for business reasons. Apart from that, peer review is often a wall erected by old-timers, and innovators will find this wall difficult to penetrate.[33] A similar timing problem arises in connection with two additional criteria set by *Daubert*: replicability of the new methodology[34] and ascertainment of its error rate.[35] For these criteria to be met, the new technology usually needs to undergo a long series of tests that will determine its dependability.

All these rules subsidize producers and users of conventional technologies while taxing innovators. This effect may well be unintended, but it is both prevalent and detrimental to society in that it slows down innovation and growth.

---

[29] See *Daubert v. Merrell Dow Pharm., Inc.*, 509 U.S. 579 (1993); *General Electric Co. v. Joiner*, 522 U.S. 136 (1997); and *Kumho Tire Co. v. Carmichael*, 526 U.S. 137 (1999). *Daubert* substituted the Frye standard by a multifactor balancing test requires the trial judge to make sure that the methodology underlying the expert's testimony is falsifiable by experiments that other experts can run; to consider whether this methodology underwent peer review and was published in the academic or professional literature after undergoing examination for possible flaws; to take into account the error rate, actual or potential, that accompanies the expert's testimony and methodology; to see whether this methodology attains acceptance in the relevant scientific or professional community; to examine the expert's inferences from methodology to conclusions for the presence of analytical gaps; and finally, to look into the testimony's capacity to mislead or prejudice the jury. For informative discussion of this test, see Kenneth S. Broun, ed., *McCormick on Evidence* 6th edition 1 (Eagan, MN: West Publishing, 2006), § 203, at 831-33..

[30] *Daubert*, 509 U.S., 591-95.

[31] Ibid., 594.

[32] Ibid., 593-94.

[33] See David F. Horrobin, "The Philosophical Basis of Peer Review and the Suppression of Innovation," *JAMA* 263 (1990): 1438 (arguing that peer review generally favors conventional wisdom and tends to suppress innovation).

[34] *Daubert*, 509 U.S., 592-93.

[35] Ibid. at 594.

Innovation entails three distinct activities: coming up with a viable idea for a new invention, research and development (R&D), and commercialization or marketing the invention to the public. Naturally, innovators critically depend on the reaction of the market to their innovation; the market success of new technologies determines the innovators' reward. Failure in the marketplace implies that investments in R&D (and the innovator's opportunity costs) will not be recuperated. As we will show, however, the market's reaction to innovations is a function not only of the innovations' quality but also of the innovator's expected liability in torts. When an innovator cannot reduce this liability by improving the quality of her innovation, the effect of the law of torts on the incentive to innovate is perverse. This effect, of course, does not stop *all* innovators dead in their tracks. Many remarkable innovations are produced under the current regime. Yet, the heightened risk of liability puts a drag on innovation and diverts its path.

In addition to exerting this chilling effect on innovation, the custom rules skew the direction of technological progress. The heightened risk of tort liability induces innovators to limit their R&D endeavors to the conventional technological frameworks. Instead of focusing upon genuine technological breakthroughs, innovators will strive to produce incremental improvements of customary and conventional technologies. The custom rules effectively tell firms: "If you want to minimize your prospect of paying for damages that your activities may cause, go conventional, align yourself with the custom, and never stand out."

PART 2. BUREAUCRATIZATION OF SAFETY STANDARDS

Federal agencies—the Food and Drug Administration (FDA), the Consumer Product Safety Commission (CPSC), the National Highway Traffic Safety Administration (NHTSA) and others—issue rules and regulations with regard to the safety of food, drugs, medical devices, motor vehicles, and other consumer products.[36] These rules and regulations are subsequently used as shields and swords in tort litigation. Violation of those rules and regulations constitutes negligence in virtually every single case.[37] A consumer product that fails to comply with those rules and regulations is considered defective.[38] By the same token, compliance with those rules is generally identified with adequate care.[39] Moreover, those rules and regulations often establish a preemption system that prevents the imposition of tort liability upon firms under applicable state law.[40] In some cases, tort actions are blocked completely.[41] In other cases, tort actions can be filed, but state courts cannot make decisions that conflict with the federal safety standard.[42]

The rule that imposes tort liability for failure to comply with a federal safety standard makes perfect sense. A firm violates a safety standard that a federal agency had devised to fend off the risk of damage. The firm's action causes damage that the federal standard aimed to prevent. If compliance with the standard was cheaper than the expected damage, the firm acted suboptimally and should pay for the damage it caused. This payment obligation will induce firms to prefer cheaper precautions to a costly damage. Absent such obligation, firms will externalize risks of damage even when they avoid this externalization at a relatively low cost. On the other hand, if compliance with the federal standard costs more than the expected damage, then the firm should go ahead and externalize the risk. Under this scenario, the firm will be paying for the damages it will cause but it will be making

---

[36] See Samuel Issacharoff and Catherine M. Sharkey, "Backdoor Federalization," *UCLA Law Review* 53 (2006): 1353; Catherine M. Sharkey, "Products Liability Preemption: An Institutional Approach," *George Washington Law Review* 76 (2008): 449; Catherine M. Sharkey, "Federalism Accountability: 'Agency-Forcing' Measures," *Duke Law Journal* 58 (2009): 2125.

[37] See Issacharoff and Sharkey, ibid.

[38] Ibid.

[39] Ibid.

[40] Ibid.

[41] Ibid.

[42] Ibid.

a greater saving on precautions. Because firms are always best positioned to determine the economically best course of action with regard to their products, federal regulation in this area reinforces Calabresi's "cheapest cost avoider" criterion for liability in torts, while taking advantage of standardization and other economies of scale. From an efficiency perspective, therefore, a federal agency only needs to set up precautions that generally cost less than the expected damage.

The compliance rule, on the other hand, makes no economic sense. To induce firms to comply with federal safety standards, the lawmaker only needs to impose tort liability upon those who fail to comply. Since the "stick" achieves the desired result, why give firms a "carrot" as well? This "carrot" produces a serious anomaly. Under the compliance rule, a firm complying with the requisite safety standard can cause as much damage to consumers as it pleases and go scot-free. This rule creates an incentive for firms not to innovate in the products' safety area. Instead of trying to improve the safety of its products, a firm will virtually always be better off complying with the federal checklist.

For both good and bad reasons, this checklist will often mirror the prevalent custom. As a practical matter, an agency would normally find it hard to require firms to adopt nonstandard technology. Any such requirement would be risky to make and costly to enforce. The requirement would also face resistance from firms that use conventional technology and are not interested in investing in innovation. Basing the requisite safety requirements on existing customs thus saves the agency's time and effort. Moreover, old-timer firms that dominate the market would exert pressures to convince the agency to stick to the old standards that those firms follow. Some of those pressures (such as lobbying) would be legitimate. Others (e.g., bribes) would not. In either scenario, the agency's adoption of the prevalent customs will be perceived as a totally appropriate form of regulatory conservativism. The agency—or, more accurately, those who run it—thus have every reason to align regulation with the prevalent customs and protocols.

This regulatory strategy would subsidize replicators of conventional technologies, who would receive complete immunity against liability for damages they cause. This immunity would perversely discourage innovation in the product safety area. Instead of trying to improve their products' safety, firms would prefer to stay in the safe harbor of the agency-approved customary safety measures. This preference would likely be the prevalent mode across many firms. As such, it would further entrench the custom-based compliance rule.

To illustrate the perverse effect of this rule, consider the following scenario.[43] Innovator N develops a new technology for maintaining electric hoists. The new technology is as safe as, but more cost-effective than, the dominant technology on the market. Absent liability for accidents, N can provide the new maintenance service at $80 per hoist.

N is not the only provider on the market for hoist-maintenance services, however. Its competitor is O, who provides a similar service using the old and conventional technology. Absent liability for accidents, O can provide the maintenance service at a price of $100 per hoist.

Under a no-liability assumption, over time N will drive O out of the market and the new technology will replace the old. This, of course, is the socially efficient outcome.

The compliance rule, however, changes the analysis dramatically. Assume that the agency regulating construction equipment safety issued a custom-based safety standard similar to the one used by O. This regulation might forestall N's innovation completely, as the agency may decide to enjoin N from providing services not aligning with the customary protocol. At the very least, the custom-based regulation will make N responsible for any damage caused by its new technology, should N go ahead and use it. O, in contrast, will be completely exempted from liability in torts under the compliance rule. The old and the new technology are equally

---

[43] This example is adapted from Parchomovsky and Stein, "Torts and Innovation."

prone to accidents. But the compliance rule subsidizes O and taxes N, who may consequently decide to abandon its new development. This consequence is plainly anomalous.

PART 3. USING EVIDENCE LAW TO LEVEL THE TORT LIABILITY PLAYGROUND FOR INNOVATORS AND REPLICATORS

The lawmaker can use evidence law to equalize the conditions under which innovators compete with replicators of conventional technologies in the domain of torts. To achieve this effect, the lawmaker can require tort plaintiffs to prove that innovative technologies are inferior to customary ones in terms of their safety. Specifically, in order to succeed in a suit for negligence, a defective product, or medical malpractice, a plaintiff will need to establish two additional elements. First, any such plaintiff would have to prove by a preponderance of the evidence that if a conventional technology or a customary procedure were implemented by the defendant, her injury would have been avoided. Second, the plaintiff would also have to establish that overall, across the relevant range of all possible accidents, the innovative technology is less safe than the customary alternative. Only upon making *both* showings will the plaintiff be allowed to recover damages for her injury.

The proposed evidentiary mechanism will eliminate much of the disincentive to adopt innovative technologies. Although this proposal puts the burden of comparing conventional and innovative technologies on the plaintiff, it is reasonable to expect that defendants, too, will conduct similar comparisons on their own accord. Not investigating *ex ante* would expose businesses to the risk of losing a particular case in court, as well as the broader risk of being stuck with a substandard precaution. Businesses that failed to make the optimal decision would therefore face a Hobson's choice between paying multiple future plaintiffs and replacing the inferior technology. Both options are costly.

We are cognizant of the fact that our proposal raises a fairness concern. It is possible to argue that it is unfair to impose additional evidentiary requirements upon plaintiffs, especially plaintiffs with meager financial means. This concern may be partially addressed by allowing successful plaintiffs to recover the full cost of litigating the case or, alternatively, the cost of making the additional showings.

CONCLUSION

America's torts system should become more welcoming of innovations. To achieve this effect, the system can eliminate courts' reliance on custom in making liability determinations. Alternatively, it can set up a rule instructing courts to give innovations whose safety was verified by independent industry experts the same deference they give custom. This paper proposes another plausible reform: the legal system can impose a special proof burden on the plaintiffs who challenge the safety of an innovative technology and blame their damage on the defendant's preference of this technology over the conventional one.

Each of those reforms eliminates the anomalous tax that innovators presently pay and do away with the anomalous subsidy that replicators of conventional technologies presently receive. None of those solutions is cost free.[44] However, the costs of those solutions are likely to be outweighed by the benefits of unhindered innovation.

---

[44] Parchomovsky and Stein, "Torts and Innovation."

11 : The Effects of Modern Tort Law on Innovation and Economic Growth

George L. Priest*

his paper addresses how the expansion of tort liability in the United States since the mid-1960s has affected innovation and, as an inevitable consequence (as explained in Chapter 1), economic growth. The paper will attempt to explain how this expansion has operated as a tax—and not an inconsiderable tax—without commensurate benefit to consumers. The effect of expanded tort liability has been to suppress innovation and reduce U.S. economic growth.[1]

Part I presents a brief history of underlying conceptions of tort law and of the development of those conceptions following the mid-1960s, which describes the modern era. Part II discusses the economic effects of the expansion of modern tort liability. Part III briefly addresses the ideas of Parchomovsky and Stein, who argue in this volume that harm-causing practices qualifying as customary, or that comply with regulatory standards, should not

* George L. Priest is the Edward J. Phelps Professor of Law and Economics and Kauffman Distinguished Research Scholar in Law, Economics and Entrepreneurship, Yale Law School.

[1] There are many other undesirable effects of the tort law tax—such as its regressive distributional effect—that are beyond the scope of this paper. For a discussion of this issue, see Priest, "The Current Insurance Crisis and Modern Tort Law," *Yale Law Journal* 96 (1987): 1521.

be treated in tort law advantageously relative to novel practices. This section explains that their argument, though attractive as an ideal, addresses only a minor feature of modern tort law. More seriously, their focus misestimates the effects of modern law described in Part II. As a consequence, their analysis of the custom defense and of the effect of presumptions regarding federal regulatory standards confuses the effects of modern law on innovation and economic growth.

PART I. A BRIEF DISCUSSION OF HISTORICAL CONCEPTIONS OF TORT LAW AND THEIR CHANGES OVER TIME

For the first centuries of the common law, private law—tort law, contract, and property law—was viewed as serving chiefly a redistributive end.[2] According to this conception, private law and the system of private law damages operate to compel redistribution in a defined set of circumstances: Where a first party has imposed a loss on a second party through an alleged tort or property violation or through breach of contract, the first party is compelled to compensate the second party to the extent of the second party's loss as long as the alleged violation meets the legal standard for recovery. In tort, the legal standard was the "fault" of the injurer or "negligence" where the injurer had failed to act with "due care;" in contract, the standard was breach of the express promise of one of the parties. The damages payment imposed by law serves a compensatory—i.e., redistributive—purpose. From this light, compensation, as reflected in the dominant legal remedy of compensatory damages, seeks no more than to restore the victim to its pre-loss position.

Though of ancient vintage, this view of the role of private law has been supported in recent times by philosophical theories of corrective justice that attempt to justify this form of redistribu-

---

[2] To be fair, the distinction between the production of new resources versus the redistribution of existing resources has not been generally discussed in the analysis of law.

tion. These theories do not ignore the effects of legal decisions and rules on future behavior, but the role of private law viewed as a system of corrective justice, at best, is to prevent the need for future redistributive decisions; more typically, simply to restore the injured party (as much as can be done through money damages) to its pre-injury position, thus reinstating, except for the injury, the earlier status quo.

The corrective justice conception of private law ignores the effect of law on economic growth. As it has been defined, corrective justice is a deontological, in contrast to an instrumental, approach to law. In essence, the role of the law is to square off on equal terms what in essence (shifting to instrumental terms) is a zero-sum game of life's interactions or worse, a negative-sum game, in the sense that—especially in the context of torts—any gain to the injurer from engaging in a risk-generating activity is typically substantially less than the loss to the victim.

The modern—quasi-economic and purely instrumental— approach to the role of tort law was initiated in the 1940s, but became widely embraced in the 1960s, and expanded thereafter.[3] Supported somewhat by academic literature, the first iteration of what would become the modern view was the concurring opinion of Justice Roger Traynor of the California Supreme Court in the now-famous case, *Escola v. Coca-Cola*.[4] The case was simple: A waitress in a restaurant was cut when a Coca-Cola bottle exploded. The court's majority opinion resolved the case on *res ipsa loquitur* grounds, a doctrine that presumes negligence from the facts of the case alone.[5] Justice Traynor, however, in a concurring opinion, argued that the manufacturer should be held absolutely liable for the injury, without regard to a showing of fault or negligence or even of a presumption of negligence through the *res ipsa loquitur* doctrine. He justified the position

[3] For a more detailed discussion of this history, see Priest, "The Invention of Enterprise Liability: A Critical History of the Intellectual Foundations of Modern Tort Law," *Journal of Legal Studies* 14 (1985): 461.

[4] *Escola v. Coca-Cola*, 24 Cal. 2d 453, 461, 150 P.2d 436, 440 (1944).

giving two reasons, both of which have something of an economic cast. First, the manufacturer is in a superior position to reduce the risk of injury:

> Even if there is no negligence, public policy demands that responsibility be fixed wherever it will most effectively reduce the hazards to life and health inherent in defective products that reach the market. It is evident that the manufacturer can anticipate some hazards and guard against the recurrence of others, as the public cannot.[6]

Second, even if the accident cannot effectively be prevented, the manufacturer can provide a form of insurance, passed on to the product's consumers in the product price:

> The cost of an injury and the loss of time or health may be an overwhelming misfortune to the person injured, and a needless one, for the risk of injury can be insured by the manufacturer and distributed among the public as a cost of doing business.[7]

These two quasi-economic goals—reducing the incidence of loss (improving safety) and, for losses that cannot be prevented, providing insurance through tort law damages—constitute the cornerstone of modern tort law. These goals were adopted as central to products liability law during the mid-1960s with the general adoption of the doctrine of strict products liability, first by the

---

[5] The case appears so simple to the modern eye that one wonders why the jury verdict in favor of the waitress was appealed to the California Supreme Court. In historical context, the case raised an interesting issue regarding the *res ipsa* doctrine since the manufacturer had delivered the bottle to the restaurant some substantial time (thirty-six hours) prior to the accident. At the time, a defense to a *res ipsa* claim was that the manufacturer had relinquished control of the product and thus should not be responsible for any subsequent event, which was attributed to the user or consumer. Conceptually, strict liability excuses consumers from most efforts to prevent accidents.

[6] *Escola*, 150 P.2d at 440. Note the presumption in Traynor's explanation that only manufacturers, and not consumers, can take measures that have the effect of reducing accidents from product use. That presumption is characteristic of the modern regime, though there is no empirical foundation for it.

[7] *Escola*, 150 P.2d at 440–441.

California Supreme Court;[8] then in the American Law Institute's *Second Restatement of Torts*;[9] and ultimately, by courts or legislatures in all of the states.[10] The goals have been extended to other areas of tort law, beyond products, over the succeeding years.

The goals of employing the law to reduce the frequency of accidents and to provide insurance do not directly address economic growth. As quasi-economic goals, they are not entirely unrelated to growth. The resources of a society will be greater if the number of injuries that can be cost-effectively prevented is reduced. As explained in Chapter 1, this represents a static, not a dynamic, conception of efficiency.

Providing accident insurance in the price of a product or service as compelled by law is more problematic. As a general proposition, a society wants to maximize the cost-effective provision of insurance for losses that cannot be prevented. The existence of insurance allows citizens to engage in a wider range of productive, though risk-causing, activities and, thus, will spur innovation and economic growth, a subject worthy of further study. As Justice Traynor formulated the idea as indicated in the quotation above, however—and as most modern courts have viewed the matter—providing accident insurance through liability judgments serves chiefly a redistributional welfare goal. As explained in Part II, the actual effect of using private law to provide insurance is to reduce net welfare and hamper economic growth.

More recently, these goals of employing the law to improve safety and provide insurance have been subsumed in the more general economic concept of "internalizing" the costs of injury to the injury-causing entity. The concept of internalizing costs is more centrally economic. The idea is to affect the productive decisions of all entities in the society by compelling them—through private

---

[8] *Greenman v. Yuba Power Prods., Inc.,* 59 Cal 2d 57, 377 P.2d 897, 27 Cal. Rptr. 697 (1963) (Traynor, C.J.).

[9] *Restatement (Second) of Torts,* §402(A) (1964).

[10] For a fuller discussion of these events, see Priest, "The Invention of Enterprise Liability: A Critical History of the Intellectual Foundations of Modern Tort Law."

law—to take accident costs into account in each of their productive decisions. Thus, the law serves to perfect the pricing system by requiring risk-generating entities to include in decision making the price of accidents that result from their production. At a very general level, the concept is plausible. The concept becomes difficult when the issue of causation is carefully addressed. As Ronald Coase showed many years ago, in the context of an interaction between a person injured and the entity whose production was involved in the injury, unless it is clear that one of the parties could have cost-effectively prevented the accident at a cost less than the other, one cannot from an economic standpoint confidently attribute causation of the accident to either single party.[11]

The internalizing costs concept is especially unhelpful with respect to the allocation of the burden of insuring losses that cannot be cost-effectively prevented. Again, the Traynor and modern law formulation is entirely redistributive and welfare oriented. It does not derive from a careful study of the most effective means of providing insurance.

Nevertheless, the goal of internalizing costs in order to create incentives to reduce the accident rate and to provide accident insurance commands private law today. This goal has provided the justification for courts to expand substantive tort liability standards and to restrict legal defenses in a broad range of areas, from occupational safety to job-site discrimination. The goal—in particular, the internalizing costs concept—also has provided the basis for the expansion of recovery of noneconomic damages, such as pain and suffering and loss of the value of life on the argument that, if costs are to be internalized, damages should equal the full costs of the accident, measured as completely as possible.

Together, these concepts have led to a vast expansion of tort liability over the past fifty years. Whether measured in terms of

---

[11]Ronald H. Coase, "The Problem of Social Cost," *Journal of Law & Economics* 3 (1960): 1.

actual private law judgments or, more fully, judgments plus settlements, or more fully yet, judgments plus settlements plus attorneys' costs and fees, the amount of money transferred through the legal system has increased by many multiples and perhaps exponentially since the mid-1960s.[12] The next part discusses the economic effects of this development and, in particular, its effect on economic growth.

PART II. THE ECONOMIC EFFECTS OF THE EXPANSION OF TORT LIABILITY

What have been the effects of the extraordinary expansion of tort liability since the mid-1960s? Measuring the effects of tort law is particularly difficult since no adequate statistics exist recording either the benefits of tort judgments and settlements or their costs at any particular point or over time.

There exists, however, less systematic evidence from which inferences can be drawn as to the effects of the expansion of tort liability. As examples, at various points in time when the continuous increase in liability judgments has appeared to spike, various products and services have been withdrawn from the market. In the mid-1980s, for example, many pharmaceutical products were withdrawn; day care centers closed; many doctors shifted from obstetric and specialized surgery practices to less litigation-prone practices; and manufacturers of private aircraft went out of business, all allegedly attributable to the increase in liability judgments.[13] There were similar withdrawals of service—especially of medical services such as obstetrics—during periods of the 1990s and early 2000s.

---

[12] For some mid-term evidence of this trend, see Priest, "Products Liability Law and the Accident Rate," in *Liability: Perspectives and Policy*, ed. Robert E. Litan and Clifford Winston (New York: Brookings Institution Press, 1988); Priest, "How to Control Liability Costs," *Fortune*, April 24, 1989, 323.

[13] For a discussion of this period, see Priest, "The Current Insurance Crisis and Modern Tort Law."

One of the ambitions of the expansion of tort liability is to create incentives for the withdrawal of products or services that are excessively dangerous, in the sense that their costs of production, including resulting injury costs, exceed the benefits from use of the product. In some cases, the law may have that effect. It is difficult to believe, however, that medical services such as obstetrics or specialized surgery are too dangerous to provide in any form. Moreover, there is evidence that, where legislatures have adopted measures limiting the expansion of liability, previously withdrawn products and services have been restored, such as general aviation manufacture after the enactment of federal tort reform.

Why would products that are not inherently excessively dangerous be withdrawn from markets with the expansion of tort liability? The quasi-economic goals of increasing safety and providing insurance themselves provide no obvious answer. It is well established as an economic proposition that enhanced liability will lead manufacturers and service providers to make investments in increasing safety, up to the point at which the marginal benefit and marginal cost of further investments are equated.[14] Additional liability will not increase investments in precaution beyond the point of maximum cost-effectiveness; it will only shift the burden of insuring losses that cannot be prevented from the victim to the injurer.

If the insurance provided through the tort system levied on manufacturers were superior to the insurance that could be obtained by potential victims—which Justice Traynor presumed—then the expansion of liability would increase the availability of risky products by reducing total product costs (manufacturing costs plus insurance). If the insurance provided through the tort system were the equivalent of private victim insurance, there would be no general effect on production. In contrast, where insurance provided by the injurer through tort law is more costly than the

---

[14] E.g., William M. Landes and Richard A. Posner, *The Economic Structure of Tort Law* (Cambridge, MA: Harvard University Press, 1986), 54–80.

insurance that could be obtained by potential victims, and the difference in insurance costs exceeds the net benefit of the product to consumers, products and services that are not excessively dangerous will be withdrawn from markets on account of the expansion of liability because consumers are not willing to pay the increased insurance costs.

There are strong reasons to believe that tort law insurance is substantially more costly than private insurance available to consumers. Damages as measured by tort law differ dramatically from accident insurance benefits typically purchased directly by consumers or indirectly, when provided by their employers. Third-party tort law insurance provides full recovery of medical expenses and lost income; private first-party insurance never provides full recovery, but is uniformly attended by deductibles and forms of coinsurance. Tort law insurance, in addition, provides full recovery of pain and suffering loss; in contrast, there is no private first-party market for pain and suffering insurance because pain and suffering is largely unmeasurable (making it uninsurable) and does not implicate financial well-being, the equalization of which over time is the economic function of insurance.[15] Moreover, private first-party insurance is structured in order to constrain loss in ways impossible for third-party tort insurance.[16] Finally, the costs of providing third-party tort law insurance—including attorneys' costs and fees in the judgment and settlement process—are vastly greater than the administrative costs of providing and delivering first-party accident insurance.

These systematic differences between the magnitude and structure of third-party tort law insurance and first-party insurance explain why the expansion of tort liability is not universally beneficial to consumers or other potential victims. Products and services that are not excessively dangerous will be withdrawn

[15] For a further discussion of these points, see Priest, "The Current Insurance Crisis and Modern Tort Law."

[16] See Priest, "How Insurance Reduces Risk," mimeo. (1996).

from markets where the differential insurance costs are greater than the net benefits of the product or service to the dominant set of users.

This analysis also suggests the broader effect of the expansion of tort liability on innovation and economic growth. The withdrawal of products and services that are not excessively dangerous from the market on account of expanded liability reduces economic welfare. Such withdrawals, of course, only can occur when the affected product or service already has been introduced. The harm from expanded liability, however, is greater. The prospect of having to include expected liability costs in the product or service price will affect the introduction of new products and services. Products and services never introduced because of a judgment that expected liability costs would make them unmarketable constitute losses to innovation and economic growth that can never be observed. For these potential innovations, tort law insurance serves as a deadweight loss like a redistributive tax, impairing economic growth.

The next part addresses the analysis of custom as a defense by Parchomovsky and Stein and the effects on economic growth of their proposal to subject customary and agency-approved practices to the liability standards imposed on novel practices.

PART III. PARCHOMOVSKY AND STEIN ON CUSTOM AS A DEFENSE AND REGULATORY COMPLIANCE

Parchomovsky and Stein, in Chapter 10 in this volume, criticize the legal doctrine providing that, in certain circumstances, a product or service that is held to comply with customary standards of a field or with government regulations can invoke that compliance as a defense to a liability claim.[17] Their criticism, in brief, is that compliance with custom or federal regulations as a defense unfairly advantages old (customary) products and serv-

[17] Gideon Parchomovsky and Alex Stein, *Torts, Innovation, and Growth*, this volume, chapter 10. See also, Parchomovsky and Stein, "Torts and Innovation," *Michigan Law Review* 107 (2008): 285.

ices in comparison to new products and services and, thus, retards innovation. In order to offset the advantage, they propose (1) abrogating the defenses; (2) the creation of special committees of industry experts to advise courts on the safety of innovative technologies; and (3) that tort plaintiffs bear the burden of proving the inferiority of innovative products or services. For reasons presented below, I believe that their analysis is seriously misdirected and that their proposals would do little to repair the harm to innovation and economic growth from the expansion of liability over the past five decades, described above.

First, I believe that Parchomovsky and Stein exaggerate the importance of the custom as a defense doctrine. It is well-known that the strong trend of modern tort law is to restrict all tort law defenses, including the custom defense. The doctrine is strictly limited in the *Third Restatement of Torts*,[18] and many analogous rules, such as the state-of-the-art defense in products liability law, have been generally repudiated by courts. Parchomovsky and Stein do not estimate the number or percentage of tort cases effectively invoking the doctrine, but it is unlikely to be substantial.

Second, Parchomovsky and Stein overestimate the current significance of federal agency approval—such as approval by the Food and Drug Administration or the National Highway Traffic Safety Administration—of safety-related features of products. They argue that agency approval "insulates" complying products from liability. In fact, except for those few areas in which courts have ruled that federal regulation preempts state tort law, agency approval may be introduced as evidence, but is never controlling and, in much modern litigation, is often counterproductive where plaintiff attorneys use the introduction of the evidence to enable their demonstration of various forms of regulatory misconduct.

---

[18] For a thorough discussion, see Kenneth S. Abraham, "Custom, Noncustomary Practice, and Negligence," *Columbia Law Review* 109 (2009): 1784.

Third, and more generally, the Parchomovsky-Stein analysis of custom as a defense does not carefully define what practices the doctrine will find as complying with custom and how those practices differ from practices regarded as noncustomary,[19] which may or may not mean more innovative. Finding a product or service liable because it failed to comply with custom—which Parchomovsky and Stein claim "taxes" innovation—may not relate at all to innovative products and services, but to outdated ones. Parchomovsky and Stein do not put forward a theory or explanation of how the accumulation of knowledge leads to the generation of a "custom." Their analysis treats "custom" as if it meant "status quo." But compliance with the status quo is not a defense in tort law. Without a careful definition of what types of practices are held to constitute "custom" and which do not, the operative effect of the doctrine is largely hypothetical.

Fourth, the attempt to put on equal footing for liability purposes the consideration of older versus newer practices is probably unrealistic. By definition, there will always be greater information available concerning older versus newer products or services. As a consequence, any fact finder will have greater confidence with respect to the old than to the new. To the opposite effect, though equally suggestive of the restricted relevance of the doctrine, if one of the characteristics of a novel product or service is enhanced safety, the custom defense will never be successful, and should not be.

Fifth, Parchomovsky and Stein give no careful consideration to the issue of institutional competence to evaluate safety-related technologies. They propose to equally subject customary and novel technologies to liability, presumably by lay jury decision making, though they propose to convene independent industry experts to advise courts on safety. They do not explain why these industry expert committees are superior to or even different from expert trial testimony, also presented to juries. Nor do they

---

[19] Ken Abraham is somewhat better on this point, though still not precise. See, ibid., 1788 (defining custom as "a widespread and, for some courts, nearly universal practice").

284

justify the superiority of industry-expert committees to federal regulators, compliance with whose safety-related standards they criticize. Their proposal to require tort plaintiffs to prove the inferiority of a novel design is a burden that tort plaintiffs already bear.

Finally, and most seriously, Parchomovsky and Stein ignore the deleterious effects of modern tort law. Their proposal to equalize old and new by rejecting the custom defense, as well as all presumptions deriving from compliance with governmental regulations, neglects entirely the harm to innovation and economic growth resulting from the expansion of liability since the mid-1960s, with its mandated substitution of third-party tort law insurance for first-party insurance. Given that harm, available defenses, including compliance with custom or federal regulations (the importance of which, again, they overstate) are advances. Economic growth and innovation would benefit if these defenses were strengthened, even if that left innovative practices subjected to higher standards of safety. By eliminating these defenses, the Parchomovsky and Stein proposals would further expand modern tort liability. Parchomovsky and Stein do not discuss the insurance implications of their proposal, though the implications are significant. Their proposals, regrettably, would further dampen innovation and economic growth.

CONCLUSION

There are strong reasons to believe that the expansion of tort liability since the mid-1960s has hampered innovation and economic growth. There is little doubt that the effect of the expansion has been to shift an insurance burden to manufacturers and service providers. There is no doubt that the provision of third-party tort law insurance is substantially more costly in many dimensions than the provision of first-party accident insurance. This shift in the insurance burden provides no benefit to consumers; to the contrary, it causes harm. The prospect of paying damages on account of the expansion of liability impairs innovation and economic growth because the increased insurance burden acts as a deadweight tax on innovation. Innovation and economic growth could be enhanced if tort liability were shorn of its insurance features and liability attached only where a party failed to make a cost-effective investment in prevention of the loss. Proposals, such as those of Parchomovsky and Stein of expanded liability, fail to consider these insurance effects and thus, if adopted, would further impair innovation and growth.

12: Land Use Regulation, Innovation, and Growth

Nicole Garnett*

We live in an era when the dominant land use regulation question about growth is not how to promote it, but rather how to curtail it. Concerns about global warming, sustainability, environmental stewardship, suburban sprawl, and urban disinvestment take center stage in discussions of land use and environmental-law policies. For example, in 2007, California Attorney General Jerry Brown sued San Bernardino, California, for failing to adopt a comprehensive plan that adequately addressed global warming by limiting new growth. The suit, which settled out of court, is but one example of growth-phobia.[1] Each year, communities across the country enact hundreds, if not thousands, of regulatory restrictions on growth—ranging from anti-"big box" retail ballot initiatives to total moratoria on new development. Motivations for these efforts range from elite snobbery about dominant American

---

* Nicole Garnett is a Professor of Law at the University of Notre Dame Law School. Her teaching and research focus is on property, land use, urban development, local government law, and education.

[1] Margot Roosevelt, "State Reaches Settlement on Gas Emissions: San Bernardino County Officials Agree to Measure How Much the Region Contributes to Global Warming and Sets Goals to Cut Pollution." *L.A. Times*, August 22, 2007, B1.

consumption preferences—as Robert Brueggman has observed, the very word "sprawl ... has always conveyed a not-so-subtle accusation against the way that other people choose to live their lives"[2]—to genuine concern about environmental degradation and urban disinvestment. *Sprawl* has come to be seen as a modern plague on our culture. In some circles, the spread of the foreclosure crisis to suburban communities was welcomed with a kind of voyeuristic glee, with opinion leaders penning doomsday articles declaring that the collapse of the housing bubble, combined with the decline in fossil fuels and global warming crisis, portend "The End of Suburbia."[3]

Suburban growth is, to be sure, not costless. Global warming and environmental degradation are serious concerns—although suburban growth is but one cause of both. And urban disinvestment and concentrated urban poverty are serious problems—although the causal link between current urban woes and current suburbanites' housing choices is attenuated at best. Moreover, *geographic* growth—that is, an expansion of the urban footprint—should not necessarily be equated with *economic* growth. There is no reason to believe that dense land use patterns are inconsistent with economic growth and innovation. On the contrary, it is conceivable that urban density might, in fact, promote both by concentrating their necessary inputs—human and economic capital—in relative proximity to one another. In the United States, however, for better or worse, it is extremely difficult to disentangle economic growth and innovation from the explosion in suburban growth that began during the last decades of the nineteenth century. For better or worse, we are a suburban nation, where economic growth has long been linked with urban expansion. By the 1960s, more Americans lived in suburbs than in central cities; the employment balance shifted to the suburbs by the 1980s. By 1990, a solid majority of all Americans were suburbanites.

---

[2] Robert Brueggman, *Sprawl: A Compact History* (Chicago: University of Chicago Press, 2005).

[3] Christopher B. Leinberger, "The Next Slum? The Subprime Crisis is Just the Tip of the Iceberg. Fundamental Changes in American Life may Turn Today's McMansions into Tomorrow's Tenements," *The Atlantic*, March 2008.

The importance of suburban growth to economic growth is suggested by a number of factors. The first is the dramatic decline in the traditional radial commuting patterns—that is, commutes between suburban homes and urban jobs—a reality that plagues proponents of public transportation. Today, the number of Americans who "reverse commute" (between city homes and suburban jobs) or "cross commute" (between two suburbs) outnumber traditional suburb-to-center-city commuters by a two-to-one margin. The second factor is that, while some major cities continue to act as important centers of finance and information—hence, commuters to city jobs tend to have higher wages than suburban employees, suburban locales (for example, Silicon Valley; Redmond, Washington; and Route 128 in Massachusetts) have become the most important incubators of innovation. In fact, during the recent economic downturn, the majority of new high technology jobs have been located in southern states (Texas, Georgia, North Carolina, and Virginia), characterized by suburban land use densities.[4] The third factor is that suburban growth also has long acted as an important economic and social safety valve. That is, suburban expansion has enabled and responded to upward mobility and fueled the housing filtering process, by which a wealthier individual moving to a larger house sets off a "chain of successive housing moves" that increases the availability of quality housing for poor and moderate-income individuals—and opens up the suburbs, with their economic and educational opportunities, to them as well.

Many academics and policy leaders endorse three, intersecting, legal reforms to address the "problem" of growth—(1) comprehensive growth restrictions, (2) new regional government institutions, and, (3) most recently, "new urbanist"-inspired regulatory alternatives to traditional zoning practices. Versions of these reforms have been enacted in a number of states—perhaps most comprehensively in Oregon, where all three have become firmly entrenched. Comprehensive, statewide growth management

---

[4] Jeffry Bartash, "High Tech Sector Seen 'Weathering' Downturn," *Market Watch*, March 31, 2009, http://www.marketwatch.com/story/high-tech-sector-seen-weathering-downturn.

regimes also are in place in Florida, Hawaii, Maryland, New Jersey, Tennessee, Rhode Island, Vermont, and Washington. Additionally, regional government institutions now control some aspects of growth in a number of metropolitan areas, either through regional government institutions, as in the Portland, Oregon and the Minneapolis-St. Paul, Minnesota regions, or through city-county consolidations, as in Indianapolis, Louisville, Miami, and Kansas City, Kansas. Many cities are also experimenting with form-based land use regulation, especially, although not exclusively, for redevelopment and urban "infill" efforts. Pressure to implement versions of all three of these reforms remains intense in many states where they have not yet been adopted. Where enacted, each has its intended effect—to slow the pace, and alter the landscape, of suburban growth. And each raises the same concerns about the consequences of these intended effects— an increase in housing prices, a reduction in the efficiencies generated by interjurisdictional competition for development, and transitional fairness concerns raised by curtailing growth at a time when minorities have begun to account for the bulk of suburban population gains.

The regulatory reforms outlined in the previous paragraph also may negatively affect economic growth and innovation for at least three reasons. First, and perhaps most importantly, the centralization of control over land use regulation—either through comprehensive growth management or regionalization—limits interjurisdictional competition within metropolitan areas and may prevent local governments from responding flexibly and invitingly to the development of new pockets of innovation. Second, growth restrictions impose additional costs on entrepreneurs seeking to start new businesses, a particular problem in light of evidence that startups, which all agree are the engine of economic growth, are particularly sensitive to regulatory costs, including the costs of land use regulations. Third, by limiting interjurisdictional mobility within metropolitan areas, growth restrictions may restrict access to high-quality elementary and secondary schools, and thus the educational opportunities necessary for economic success, especially among the less fortunate.

This chapter will focus on three major alternatives to the standard antigrowth toolkit that address legitimate concerns about urban expansion without stifling economic growth and innovation. Each of these reforms can be implemented through wise regulatory reform (and, in some cases, the rejection of unwise ones):

Price growth, don't prohibit it. Although growth restrictions come in many forms, most adhere to a traditional "command-and-control" model of regulation. These regulations are justified as a means of "rationalizing" growth, but, in practice, they tend to increase housing prices, exacerbate the exclusionary effects of existing land use regulations, and promote sprawl. They also may impede the spontaneous development of agglomeration economies by preventing local governments from promoting (and responding to) the development of pockets of innovation. In contrast, properly calibrated exactions can enable efficient growth by pricing growth, thereby forcing developers and consumers to internalize the costs of new development.

Promote interjurisdictional competition, don't stifle it. There are many policies and proposals designed to mute interjurisdictional competition within U.S. metropolitan areas—by, *inter alia*, transferring local government authority over land use regulation to new regional government institutions or mandating fiscal sharing between local jurisdictions. "Regional government" proponents argue that these policies will promote growth by increasing the overall health of metropolitan regions. The difficulty is that, as Charles Tiebout influentially predicted, interjurisdictional competition generates many benefits by subjecting local governments to some approximation of market competition. Importantly, interjurisdictional competition may spur regulatory innovations that themselves promote growth and innovation. Regional government proponents have failed to demonstrate that the benefits of centralized control will outweigh the efficiencies lost by reduced intrajurisdictional competition.

Develop alternatives to traditional zoning regulations. Zoning, the standard template for development in the United States, negatively impacts growth and innovation by, *inter alia*, preventing the development of rational work-life arrangements; prohibiting the mixed land use environments that promote the social connections needed to generate economic and social innovation and collaboration; and enabling the exclusion of less-affluent residents from wealthier suburban jurisdictions. While numerous proposals for zoning innovation are worthy of serious consideration, care must be exercised when implementing new forms of land use regulation. There is a risk that the predominate alternative to use-based zoning today—"form-based" aesthetic codes promoted by "new urbanist" architects and planners—might backfire and unnecessarily stifle growth and innovation by dramatically driving up development costs. This chapter explores an alternative to new urbanist codes—a system of regulatory prices that could address the limitations of zoning without unnecessarily escalating development costs.

Price Growth, Don't Prohibit It

As discussed above, state and local governments rely on a variety of regulatory devices to control suburban growth. Examples include:

- "Urban growth boundaries," which seek to channel new development into built-up areas and exclude it from undeveloped ones
- Development moratoria
- Restrictions on the rate of new development (often called "phased growth" requirements)
- "Adequacy of public facilities" or "concurrency" regulations that link new development to a guarantee of sufficient infrastructure and public services
- Minimum lot and square-footage requirements
- Restrictions on chain or "big box" retail outlets

Additionally, regulators, by design or effect, restrict the pace and scale of growth through innumerable other requirements imbedded in the land use regulation process. These include the subdivision approval process, environmental permitting requirements, "inclusionary zoning" and "housing linkage" set-asides for affordable housing, a host of exactions, historical preservation and other aesthetic controls, "development agreements," and "community benefit agreements."

Growth Management: The Problems

Proponents argue that growth restrictions are needed to prevent urban disinvestment and environmental harm, and to rationalize suburban growth. Suburban growth, to be sure, is not costless, but neither are the tools that are commonly implemented to control it. A full explication of the debate over growth restrictions is the subject of a voluminous literature and far beyond the scope of this discussion, which instead focuses on three negative consequences of standard growth management policy. The first is the risk that growth management will, perversely, exacerbate the problem of suburban sprawl. The second is the likelihood that growth management will limit the supply of affordable housing and restrict access to suburbs (and their public amenities, including high-quality public schools) to those of limited means. The third is the possibility that growth management will impede the natural development of agglomeration economies, and the network effects that flow from them, by seeking to force economic activity into existing urban centers and by increasing the costs of entrepreneurship. The latter two risks are particularly problematic to those concerned about promoting *economic* growth, since both education and agglomeration economies are critical, albeit for different reasons, to future growth and innovation.

1) Growth Restrictions and Suburban Sprawl

Most growth management efforts are implemented at the local government level. Many are the result of "ballot box" zoning initiatives motivated by resident frustration over the pace of growth in their community. And these public expressions of official opposition to growth are dwarfed by the thousands of actions taken by local officials each year to slow growth—such as intentional delays in the subdivision approval and permitting processes— which are essentially invisible to the public's eye. There is little question that local growth controls are effective at doing the work that they are designed to do—that is, limit growth within a local jurisdiction.[5] There also is, however, significant evidence that local growth controls may, in fact, encourage suburban sprawl.

To understand why, it is necessary to view local governments as in competition, as Charles Tiebout influentially predicted, for residents (or Tiebout's "consumer voters").[6] Land use regulations provide an important means of competing because they enable local governments to design built environments that appeal to would-be residents. Logically, local governments located on the suburban fringe initially will welcome growth and invite it by enacting relatively lax land use regulations. Over time, however, as suburbs develop and political pressure for growth limits increase, local governments begin to restrict growth. But excluding growth from one jurisdiction naturally generates pressure to accommodate it elsewhere—and exurban, underdeveloped jurisdictions are naturally more likely to be inviting. Thus suburban governments within a metropolitan area may become locked in a pattern of exclusion and invitation, with more sprawl its natural consequence. As William Fischel has observed, growth controls "probably cause metropolitan areas to be too spread out…[L]ocal ordinances cause developers to go to other communities. The most likely alternative sites are in exurban and rural communities, where the political climate, at least initially, is more favorable to development."[7] The available empirical evidence tends to sup-

---

[5] Some economists question whether adequacy of public facilities requirements may actually enable, rather than restrict, new growth. The same can be said of exactions policies that essentially "lowball" the price of new development.

[6] Charles M. Tiebout, "A Pure Theory of Local Expenditures," *Journal of Political Economics* 64 (1956): 416.

[7] William A. Fischel, *Do Growth Controls Matter?* (Cambridge, MA: Lincoln Institute of Land Policy, 1990).

port Fischel's hypothesis. For example, one well-known study of the San Francisco Bay region found development was disproportionately concentrated in municipalities without growth restrictions, leading the author to conclude that growth controls exacerbated sprawl in the Bay Area.[8] Anecdotal visual evidence of this phenomenon can be found by viewing Boulder, Colorado on Google Earth. Boulder, which has implemented extremely restrictive growth controls, including an urban growth boundary and severe rate of growth restrictions, appears surrounded by an undeveloped greenbelt. Suburban development in outlying jurisdictions, however, is easily visible beyond the city's boundary and outside of the reach of city regulators.

2) Growth Management, Affordable Housing, and Economic Mobility

Moreover, while demographic change and economic growth are not synonymous, they are related because geographic mobility is a primary way that Americans of limited means secure access to the tools they need to contribute to our economy and, ideally, to become engines of economic growth and innovation. Therefore, it is important to acknowledge that growth limits enacted at the local level are often little more than exclusionary zoning in disguise—that is, a way that wealthier jurisdictions exclude poorer residents. Many common local growth management tools—for example, large-lot zoning—are essentially indistinguishable from exclusionary zoning devices. Moreover, growth restrictions drive up the price of existing houses, thus making them less affordable to those of modest means. As Robert Ellickson has observed, "Antigrowth measures have one premier class of beneficiaries: those who already own residential structures in the municipality doing the excluding."[9] All exclusionary land use policies, including those packaged as "growth management," tend to deprive poorer residents of access to the economic opportunities and,

[8] Q Shen, "Spatial Impacts of Locally Enacted Growth Controls: The San Francisco Bay Region in the 1980s," *Environment & Planning B: Planning and Design* 23 (1996): 61.

[9] Robert C. Ellickson, "Suburban Growth Controls: An Economic and Legal Analysis," *Yale Law Journal* 86 (1977): 385.

importantly, high-quality public schools found in wealthier locations. They therefore have serious consequences for the overall rate of economic growth and innovation, because without access to these economic and educational opportunities many poorer Americans simply will not enter the mainstream economy at all, let alone generate growth.

In part to prevent local parochialism and mute its negative effects, most academics favor comprehensive growth management enacted and enforced at the state or regional, rather than local, level. A favorite model is Oregon's statewide growth model, which requires the establishment of "urban growth boundaries" for each metropolitan area in the state and channels all new development to the areas inside these boundaries. In contrast to the Boulder example described above, Portland's urban growth boundary is administered by an elected regional government institution known as "Metro." Growth management proponents argue that by wresting control of growth policy from local governments, comprehensive growth management actually will curb exclusionary zoning and prevent tragedy-of-the-commons scenarios from replaying themselves throughout our metropolitan regions.

Unfortunately, statewide or regional growth management regimes likely exacerbate, rather than ameliorate, the price effects of growth controls. Economists generally agree that suburbanization has helped generate a stable supply of affordable housing in the United States. Not only are the kinds of homes that Americans prefer (that is, single-family detached homes) more affordable in far-flung suburbs, but suburbs increasingly feature a wider variety of housing choices—including townhomes and multifamily apartments. Moreover, new suburban growth promotes the housing filtering process, by which a wealthier individual moving to a larger house sets off a "chain of successive housing moves" that increases the availability of quality housing for poor and moderate-income individuals. It is reasonable to expect, therefore, that comprehensive growth management will be more effective than local controls in increasing overall regional housing prices, by dramatically reducing the supply of property available for housing. And while some proponents argue that properly structured growth management policy need not necessarily increase housing prices, their assertion that the law of supply and demand may be suspended in the growth-management context depends upon the implementation of a host of other regulatory devices (such as "inclusionary zoning" laws requiring developers to sell or lease some new units at "affordable"/below-market prices). Public-choice realities, however, suggest that there is a significant risk that policymakers may lack the political will to implement affordability promotion tools on a large enough scale to counter the regressive effects of growth management.

Moreover, even if a regional development strategy succeeded in holding constant the overall cost of housing, most affordable housing will likely continue to be found in center cities and older suburbs. Regional growth-management strategies aim to channel new development into built-up areas. Yet suburbs still represent the urban poor's hope for a better life, as suburbs have throughout the modern industrial age. The reality is that suburbs offer the good schools, economic opportunities, and environmental amenities that wealthy urban dwellers can afford to purchase and poorer ones cannot—and that social science evidence continues to demonstrate are key to harnessing the intellectual and economic potential of the disadvantaged. Finally, there is something slightly unseemly about dramatically curtailing suburban growth at a time when racial minorities are responsible for most new suburban population gains. It is difficult to avoid concluding that changing the rules of the development game at this time is tantamount to pulling the suburban ladder out from under those who previously were excluded from suburban life by economic circumstance, exclusionary zoning, and intentional discrimination.

3) Growth Management and Agglomeration Economies

Growth management proponents argue that the law should channel new development "where it belongs"—that is, into built-up areas, preferably the urban core. There is certainly no *a priori* reason to believe that urban density and innovation are inconsistent. As the literature on "agglomeration economies" suggest, economic and social connections tend to fuel innovation—and density might be expected to promote the economic and social connections. That said, economic history suggests that economic growth and innovation sometimes flourish in unexpected places—including, especially in the United States, in the suburbs. And, while the reasons for the geographic locations of centers of innovation—such as Silicon Valley, or Austin, Texas, or Boston's Route 128—remain somewhat opaque, legal rules are not irrelevant to the emergence of agglomeration economies.[10] Moreover, there is little question that economic growth is highly correlated with an abundance of small entrepreneurial firms or that innovators thrive when they work in proximity to one another. Growth management may impede the network effects necessary for the next wave of innovation by limiting local governments' ability to flexibly and invitingly respond as these concentrations began to emerge. This might occur if regulators miscalculated in their assumptions about where development "belonged" or if the innovators simply rejected the lifestyle and working conditions required by a growth management policy. Moreover, as Edward Glaeser's work suggests, entrepreneurs—who are the engines of economic growth—are sensitive to start-up costs, including the costs imposed by new land use regulations.[11]

Pricing Growth: An (Imperfect) Alternative

Many of these concerns would be addressed if lawmakers, in place of regulatory restrictions on new development, instead priced growth through a rational exactions policy. Exactions— that is, concessions demanded as a condition of regulatory

---

[10] Ronald J. Gilson, "The Legal Infrastructure of High Technology Districts: Silicon Valley, Route 128, and Covenants Not To Compete," *New York University Law Review* 74 (1999): 575.

[11] Edward L. Glaeser, *et al.*, "Clusters of Entrepreneurship" (working paper 15377, National Bureau of Economic Research, September 2009), http://www.economics.harvard.edu/faculty/glaeser/files/Clusters.pdf; Edward L. Glaeser, *et al.*, "Urban Economics and Entrepreneurship" (working paper 15536, National Bureau of Economic Research, November 2009), http://www.economics.harvard.edu/faculty/glaeser/files/Urban%20Economics.pdf.

approval for new development—are a ubiquitous feature of the land use regulation landscape. Exactions are nothing new. The Standard State Zoning Enabling Act, adopted in many states in the 1920s, authorizes local governments to require developers to construct streets, water mains, and sewers in new developments. Many local governments have, since that time, required developers to construct and dedicate facilities to the community. Over time, communities began to expand their demand for such dedications beyond basic infrastructure such as sewers, streets, and sidewalks.[12]

While the nature and extent of local government exactions is not well understood, it is clear that current practices depart dramatically from earlier antecedents. Importantly, a majority of cities now impose monetary exactions, or "impact fees," in lieu of—or in addition to—traditional in-kind exactions. A 2004 U.S. Department of Housing and Urban Development report characterized "the increasingly widespread adoption of impact fees" as a "dramatic change in the regulatory environment" and asserted that "communities are asking developers to bear a larger share of the front end burden of supplying new infrastructure and added services as a means of paying for continued growth."[13] Moreover, cities increasingly are expanding the types of development subject to impact fees to include nonresidential land uses and even renovations of existing properties. Exactions and impact fees are also being used to fund a much wider range of services and facilities. As recently as 1985, the vast majority of impact fees funded water lines, sewers, and roads. More recent studies suggest that increasing numbers of local governments rely on impact fees for other public services, including schools, low-income housing, fire and emergency services, traffic mitigation, public transportation, and open space. A growing minority of communities rely upon

---

[12] Alan Altschuler and Jose Gómez-Ibanez, *Regulation for Revenue: The Political Economy of Land Use Exactions* (Washington, DC: Brookings Institution Press, 1993).

[13] United States Department of Housing and Urban Development, "Why Not in Our Community? Removing Barriers to Affordable Housing," 2004.

exactions for the provision of affordable housing as well, through "linkage" and "inclusionary zoning" requirements.[14]

Exactions are theoretically preferable to command-and-control restrictions on development because, ideally, they price growth rather than prohibiting it. A properly structured exactions policy ought to enable efficient—and curb inefficient—growth. Impact fees, in particular, have generally been championed as a way to internalize the full cost of new development. As Vicki Been observes, "by requiring the developer and its customers to mitigate the negative effects a development may have on a neighborhood…impact fees may encourage efficiency by making the developer and its customers internalize the full cost of harms that the development causes."[15] This view is generally shared across the political spectrum. For example, in the conservative Heritage Foundation's *Guide to Smart Growth*, Samuel Staley asserts that, "[p]roperty owners and developers should bear the full cost of property development."[16]

Indeed, the idea that developers and their customers should shoulder the cost of new development is rarely challenged, although both judges and economists have questioned the ability of government to accurately calibrate those costs. Objections to exactions generally focus on policy design questions about the level and extent of exactions. There is a significant concern that local governments may dramatically overcharge developers— that is, that impact fees do not simply force newcomers to internalize the cost of new developments, but rather act as a plan of

---

[14] Linkage programs require developers, especially commercial developers in central cities, to agree to "offset" the anticipated costs of the proposed development. Inclusionary zoning programs impose similar requirements on residential developers. Usually, inclusionary zoning rules require developers to set aside a certain percentage of new residential units for "moderate income" residents and to sell or lease these units to the targeted residents at "affordable" (i.e., below market) prices.

[15] Vicki Been, "Impact Fees and Housing Affordability," *Cityscape: A Journal of Policy Development and Research* 8 (2005): 139.

[16] Samuel R. Staley, "Reforming the Zoning Laws," in *A Guide to Smart Growth: Shattering Myths, Providing Solutions*, ed. Jane S. Shaw and Ronald D. Utt (Washington, DC: The Heritage Foundation, 2000).

extortion by cash-strapped local governments desperate for a new source of funds. This is a particular concern today, in light of the fiscal crises facing many cities, which are desperate for new revenues and eager to find a way around state-law debt and tax limits. Staley, for example, asserts that "fees are often abused and become a source of general revenue for local governments."[17] His concerns are echoed in a recent report by the Department of Housing and Urban Development, which warns that many impact fees are "disproportionate to the actual development costs" and unreasonably drive up the cost of housing as a result.[18] If development is overpriced, exactions may have the same growth-restrictive effects as explicit growth controls, with the same consequences. There is some limited evidence that localities intentionally use exactions policy to limit growth, although most local jurisdictions reporting that they use exactions policies in this way also report that other growth restrictions are both in place and more effective. Vicki Been's comprehensive survey of impact-fee practices, conducted in 2004, found that impact fees did increase housing prices, although she also found that the price effects of impact fees varied dramatically by jurisdiction. Finally, it is worth noting that policies that seek to force new owners to internalize the cost of their mobility also raise transitional fairness concerns. If impact fees are excessive, and the overcharge is used as a supplementary revenue source, then existing homeowners in established suburbs will have succeeded in extracting rents from new homeowners in fringe suburbs. And even perfectly calibrated fees may signal to suburban newcomers that they are being required to "pay twice"—first to fund their own improvements directly and again through tax revenues for services provided to older homes. These transitional fairness problems have both a generational and a racial component, since older, white Americans are more likely to own their homes.

---

[17] Staley, "Reforming the Zoning Laws"; William A. Fischel, *The Homevoter Hypothesis: How Home Values Influence Local Government Taxation, School Finance, and Land Use Policies* (Cambridge, MA: Harvard University Press, 2001).

[18] HUD, "Why Not in Our Community?"

These concerns make careful regulatory design of exactions policy an imperative, but they do not negate the case for pricing, rather than restricting, growth for at least three reasons. First, impact fees may in fact enable economic growth that would not otherwise occur, especially where land use regulators would otherwise impose moratoria or other restrictions on development. Impact fees, for this reason, are most attractive if they come to supplant, rather than supplement, growth controls. In jurisdictions imposing multiple forms of growth restrictions (as many do), impact fees may actually impede, rather than enable, economic growth. Second, competition for growth among local governments (discussed in more detail below) provides a check on exactions because jurisdictions that overprice growth will "lose" the competition for economic growth. This competitive effect will, however, be muted or negated if municipalities primarily use exactions as subterfuge growth restrictions or if a regional government, rather than multiple local governments, was charged with calibrating fee levels. Third, in contrast to other regulatory arenas, the U.S. Constitution places outer limits on exactions policy, since the Supreme Court has interpreted the Fifth Amendment's Takings Clause to require rough parity between the exaction demanded and the development effect that the local government seeks to mitigate.[19]

PROMOTE INTERJURISDICTIONAL COMPETITION, DON'T STIFLE IT

Calls for new "regional" governments, vested with authority to regulate development (among other things), are closely linked with the demand for comprehensive growth restrictions. Regional government proponents object to the current structure of local government law, which vests local government authority in multiple, overlapping governmental institutions. They argue that this system—known as "metropolitan fragmentation" in the

---

[19] The question of whether this "rough proportionality" rule, adopted in *Dolan v. City of Tigard*, 512 U.S. 374 (1994), applies to monetary exactions remains open.

local government literature—makes little sense in an era characterized by political, economic, and social membership within metropolitan regions, rather than individual municipalities. Metropolitan fragmentation emerged in the early twentieth century, as state legislatures began to enact general municipal incorporation laws that enabled suburban locales to protect themselves from annexation by their urban neighbors.[20] Zoning laws, which emerged during the same time period, may have, as William Fischel has argued, accelerated the pace of metropolitan fragmentation by enabling suburbs to legally exclude industrial land uses that required the infrastructure previously offered by large cities as an incentive to accept annexation.[21] Since most state laws now immunize incorporated municipalities from annexation—a legal norm that also emerged during the early twentieth century—many large cities find themselves "landlocked" (surrounded by multiple incorporated suburbs and lacking any room for geographic expansion). Metropolitan fragmentation also is characterized by the proliferation of multiple special purpose local governments—water districts, school districts, sewer districts, parks districts, transportation authorities, etc.—which also began to emerge in large numbers in the early twentieth century. The result is that local authority over important government functions within our metropolitan areas is distributed among hundreds of local governments with overlapping boundaries. For example, a single school district might serve residents of several municipalities.

Regional government proponents argue that metropolitan fragmentation is both inefficient and unjust. The system is inefficient because within American metropolitan regions, local governments—with close to absolute autonomy over development and, in some states, education and taxation policy—compete for residents. This competition results in suburban sprawl and exclu-

---

[20] In the nineteenth century, municipal incorporation generally required an act of the state legislatures.

[21] Fischel, *The Homevoter Hypothesis*.

sionary zoning, and the overinvestment in infrastructure improvements. The system is unjust, in this view, because metropolitan fragmentation also results in a stark maldistribution of fiscal resources among the local governments within a metropolitan area. Since all municipalities are viewed as coequal in the eyes of state law, wealthier local jurisdictions are able to effectively turn their backs on their poorer neighbors; and since all municipalities are vested with land use authority, they are also able to exclude poorer newcomers by using land use regulations to set what are essentially high entrance fees.[22] By doing so, the wealthier jurisdiction is able to maintain a high level of services at a relatively low tax rate. But the exclusion deprives poorer residents of access to the amenities that it uses to attract wealthier ones—good schools, low crime rates, employment opportunities, etc.—thereby, for the reasons discussed above, dramatically curtailing the possibility that the excluded will become engines of economic growth and innovation.

There are many policies and proposals designed to mute the interjurisdictional competition within U.S. metropolitan areas, by either limiting local control over land use regulation or mandating fiscal sharing between local jurisdictions. Regional government proponents argue that these policies will not only minimize the unjust interjurisdictional disparities but will also rationalize infrastructure policy and, ultimately, promote economic growth by increasing the overall health of metropolitan regions. Comprehensive regional government reforms, which have been implemented in only a few U.S. metropolitan regions, take various forms. For example, in Minnesota, state law mandates fiscal sharing among municipalities within the Twin Cities metropolitan area and also vests a regional entity, the Metropolitan Council of the Twin Cities, or Met Council, with the authority over the infrastructure needed for new development. Portland's Metro controls the size and location of the urban growth boundary and

---

[22] A municipality may "price out" unwanted residents by, for example, enacting zoning laws that do not accommodate multifamily housing or that impose minimum lot/square-footage requirements on single-family homes.

operates a public transportation system. Thus far, calls for new, general-purpose regional governments, vested with the full panoply of local powers, have not come to fruition, although city-county consolidations in a number of states represent a step in that direction.

The difficulty with regional government proposals and reforms is, as Charles Tiebout influentially predicted, that interjurisdictional competition among the multiple local governments within our metropolitan areas subjects local governments to some approximation of market competition. Tiebout argued that local governments within a metropolitan region compete for "consumer voters" by structuring the package of local services, public goods, and taxation policy that will appeal to desired residents. And the available evidence strongly suggests that—even when Tiebout's assumptions (including, importantly, perfect information and costless mobility) are relaxed—Tiebout was right. That is, interjurisdictional competition works. For example, a number of scholars have found that the public school students' scores on standardized tests improve as the number of school districts within a metropolitan region increases. Other scholars have demonstrated that competition among local governments reduces local taxes. And while many social commentators bemoan the relative monotony of the suburban landscape, local governments clearly use their land use policies to design communities that appeal to new residents—with the growing diversity of land use patterns in suburbs suggesting that inter-jurisdictional competition may also spur regulatory innovation. Interjurisdictional competition also clearly spurs local governments to offer regulatory and tax concessions in an effort to generate economic growth, although some economists argue that interjurisdictional competition for economic development is essentially an irrational, zero-sum game.

Metropolitan fragmentation, however, is also the primary generator of the metropolitan inequalities bemoaned by proponents of regional governments. Wealthier suburbs, and the residents who can afford membership in them, generally fare better than center cities and some inner-ring suburbs (think Detroit compared with Gross Pointe, Michigan). Regional government proponents claim that the reforms they propose can address these inequalities without stifling "good" economic growth and innovation. In fact, pointing to evidence linking overall metropolitan economic health to the economic well-being of center cities, they argue that rationalizing the distribution of resources and the location of new development in our metropolitan regions will actually promote economic growth and innovation. The difficulty is that centralizing local government power in a metropolitan region will mute intergovernmental competition—that is, after all, the point of regional government reforms. And while some economies of scale may result from centralizing local government power, there is little evidence that these benefits will exceed the efficiencies generated by the competition that metropolitan fragmentation enables.

Moreover, there is evidence that center cities, in particular, are getting better at competing with their suburban neighbors, and that the competition itself may spur innovation and growth. Recent decades have witnessed an unexpected urban resurgence. While the reasons for that resurgence are complex and somewhat opaque, Edward Glaeser and Joshua Gottlieb plausibly argue, city fortunes may have improved in part by rising incomes, educational attainment, and an increased affinity among intellectual elites for city life, especially for the social interactions and consumer amenities enabled by dense, mixed-use urban environments.[23] If so, a plausible case can be made that by capitalizing on the amenities available to them (especially density and older, mixed-use urban neighborhoods), the traditional "losers" in the interjurisdictional competition game may be able to attract the residents who are most likely to promote innovation and growth—the group that Richard Florida has influentially termed the "creative class."[24] And they do not necessarily need the help

---

[23] Edward L. Glaeser and Joshua D. Gottlieb, "Urban Resurgence and the Consumer City," *Urban Studies* 43 (2006): 1275.

[24] Richard Florida, *The Rise of the Creative Class* (New York: Basic Books, 2002).

of coercive land use policies or a radical restructuring of local government authority to do so.

DEVELOP ALTERNATIVES TO USE-BASED ZONING

Regulatory reforms offering alternatives to traditional use-based zoning may prove to be one way to enable more effective competition among local jurisdictions—and to promote innovation and economic growth. Zoning, the standard template for development in the United States,[25] negatively impacts growth and innovation by preventing the development of rational work-life arrangements and prohibiting the mixed land use environments that may promote economic and social innovation and collaboration. Zoning is also a primary contributor to suburban sprawl (because it mandates relatively low-density "suburban" land use patterns) and to metropolitan inequality (because it enables the exclusion of less-affluent residents from wealthier suburban jurisdictions).

Zoning has been subject to criticism since it emerged nearly a century ago. Zoning reforms, however, have long foundered—in part because local governments are jealously protective of the authority provided to them by zoning laws and in part because homeowners view zoning as a form of property-value insurance. Although numerous proposals for regulatory innovation are worthy of serious consideration, a full explication of these proposals is beyond the scope of this discussion, which instead focuses on two zoning alternatives—Lee Anne Fennell's proposal to replace command-and-control land use restrictions with self-assessed regulatory prices and the new-urbanist promoted "transect zoning," which recommends that zoning controls be swapped for aesthetic "form-based" regulations of building design.

Entitlements Subject to Self-Made Options

The standard justification offered for zoning, from the time of its inception, has been that it prevents harmful land use spillovers.

---

[25] Every major city in the United States except Houston, Texas has a zoning law in place.

To be sure, zoning does serve this purpose, along with other, less-benign purposes (including, for example, class segregation). Since local governments (and private developers) can rarely calibrate the level of regulation to residents' true preferences, however, zoning prohibitions frequently impose excessive prevention costs. That is, the costs imposed by the regulations to prevent possible, future harms tend to exceed the benefits of actual harm prevention. But because property owners—especially, homeowners—are extremely risk averse, they accept (even demand) high prevention costs as a means of shielding their investment. In a recent book, Lee Anne Fennell proposes that in lieu of the standard prohibitory land use regulations, local governments or private developers could give property owners the right to buy or sell certain land use entitlements at prices set by the entitlement holders themselves.[26] That is, rather than prohibiting outright activities that might generate harmful spillovers, regulators could price the right to engage in, and to be free from, the potentially harm-producing activities. Fennell calls her proposed regulatory innovation "entitlements subject to self-made options," or "ESSMOs." Options provide the legal right, but not the obligation, to buy (a "call option") or sell (a "put option") a given commodity at a preset price. Traditional liability rules are, in a sense, "call options." That is, they give an actor the right, but not the obligation, to purchase an entitlement at a price set by a third party. Fennell's ESSMO system would rely on options by entitling owners to purchase the right to engage in a land use activity, or to enjoin neighbors from the same, and would be "self-made" because it would use self-valuation devices to price land use entitlements. Since the options employed to regulate land uses would be self-priced, the ESSMO proposal addresses the central difficulty of previous proposals to price land use entitlements—namely the risk of undercompensation presented by third-party valuation of entitlements.

---

[26] Lee Anne Fennell, *The Unbounded Home: Property Values Beyond Property Lines* (New Haven, CT: Yale University Press, 2009).

Fennell makes a strong case that self-priced options could better calibrate land use controls to residents' true preferences than zoning rules. But she arguably undersells the transformative power of this intriguing proposal by assuming that it primarily addresses intralocal regulatory spillovers and discounting the possibility that it might address regional inequalities as well. As discussed above, most proponents of regional government and growth control proceed on the assumption that poorer jurisdictions simply cannot compete with wealthier jurisdictions for the "right" kind of residents. But the relative status of poorer jurisdictions and their less-advantaged residents also would be improved if poorer jurisdictions *could* compete successfully with wealthier jurisdictions. Unfortunately, existing land use regulations frequently impose "suburban" land use patterns on city neighborhoods, arguably hamstringing urban officials' ability to capitalize on this advantage. Yet even city officials who recognize this as a problem—and many do not—find it difficult to use land use policy to promote density and vitality because urban residents often are only marginally less averse to spillover risk than the suburban homeowners. Fennell's ESSMO proposal, however, might well enable cities to achieve greater land use diversity while addressing property owners' risk aversion and thereby gain an edge vis-à-vis suburbs in the competition for residents with a taste for urban life. And by reducing homeowner anxieties, it also might serve to open up wealthier suburbs to less-advantaged residents. Moreover, jurisdictions experimenting with regulatory pricing might be well positioned to attract innovators—who, for example, wish to work from home, or closer to home than zoning laws permit—thereby promoting new geographic pockets of innovation.

Consider a hypothetical illustration of the proposal: Innovationville, a medium-sized Midwestern city, wishes to attract more start-up firms. In order to make Innovationville attractive to entrepreneurs, local elected officials need to streamline the process by which businesses can "repurpose" older homes along certain busier streets (zoning variance procedures tend to give neighbors a near veto over such conversions) and eliminate zoning rules that dramatically restrict the scope of home businesses (by, for example, prohibiting them from employing anyone who does not reside in the home). Innovationville leaders, however, know that homeowner anxieties about business-related spillovers pose a significant impediment to implementing these reforms. Fennell's insight is that Innovationville leaders could assuage homeowner anxieties—and minimize political opposition to needed reform—by monetizing the property-value/spillover protection provided by zoning laws' regulatory prohibitions. For example, instead of giving homeowners in "residential" zones an absolute entitlement to live in a business-free environment, Innovationville might permit a homeowner who wishes to start a home-based business the right to purchase her neighbors' "no businesses allowed" entitlements from them. Using various value-eliciting devices that Fennell explores in detail, Innovationville might even allow homeowners to set the price at which their entitlements would be waived. Over time, this regulatory innovation might give Innovationville an edge on attracting entrepreneurs over neighboring municipalities—leading to more technological innovation and ultimately more economic growth.

To be sure, Fennell's proposal raises a number of complex institutional design questions that are beyond the scope of this volume. For example, ESSMOs cannot govern every aspect of community life. Not only would the administrative costs of identifying and then pricing the entitlements to be protected likely overwhelm any regulatory systems, but normative considerations may weigh against pricing some entitlements. Even after the universe of ESSMO protection is determined, however, numerous questions remain—from the difficulty of eliciting truthful valuation information and avoiding strategic behavior to the need to enable regulatory evolution as individual and community preferences inevitably change. In the end, a second-best solution may be for local jurisdictions, through the subdivision approval process, to waive zoning restrictions if developers agree to impose covenants substituting options for standard regulatory prohibitions.

"Form-Based" or "Transect" Zoning

Currently, the dominant alternative to use-based zoning is a system of aesthetic controls promoted by new urbanist proponents of mixed-use urban neighborhoods. New urbanists argue that cities should regulate property based upon building form, not building type. Their regulatory alternative to zoning proceeds upon the assumption that development naturally progresses from urban (most intense) to rural (least intense). New urbanists call this progression the "transect" and urge cities to replace use zoning with the regulation of building form appropriate to the various "transect zones" along the progression. Theoretically, the concept is relatively simple: buildings appropriate for the city center should go in the city center (regardless of what they are used for); suburban buildings should look suburban. New urbanists promise that their system of regulation promotes careful planning that balances the need for city busyness with the concern about land use spillovers.

The new urbanists have made valuable contributions to thinking about urban development in recent decades. Nearly a century of single-use zoning has shaped our cities and suburbs—and our views about cities and suburbs—and new urbanists mount a serious challenge to these longstanding practices and assumptions. Indeed, even those who remain unconvinced by the new urbanists' grandiose claims that more "urban" community design will make us better, more complete people, cannot help but be moved by their nostalgia for the "old neighborhood" and their case, *qua* Jane Jacobs, for urban life. Unfortunately, as the saying goes, the devil is in the details. And the new urbanists' alternative to zoning is detailed indeed. The movement is dominated by architects, and new urbanist coding consequently relies heavily on detailed architectural design standards. Moreover, political resistance to scrapping traditional zoning usually guarantees that these standards tend to supplement, rather than supplant, traditional zoning tools when they are adopted. New urbanists have specific ideas about how buildings should look: ugly, unwelcoming buildings, in their view, can be just as detrimental to community life as is sterile, single-use planning. For example, the regulatory code for the Park East redevelopment district in Milwaukee—a project initiated by the city's former mayor, John Norquist, who is now president of the Congress for the New Urbanism—includes hundreds of pages of architectural renderings and photographs of "appropriate" building types. The project has stalled, in part because developers have balked at the complexity and cost of the regulations.

New urbanist coding promises to make some city projects— including infill efforts and mixed-income public housing developments—look very nice. It also may help attract some wealthy elites who prefer an urban aesthetic but remain concerned about the disorder and background noise associated with city life. Still, complying with these design standards may prove daunting and expensive, especially for those without financial means or formal education, and it may ultimately impede growth by increasing dramatically the cost of development.

CONCLUSION

Land use rules seek to direct the pace and scale of economic growth—and, in so doing, to discern between "good" growth that should be enabled and "bad" growth that should be curtailed. In recent decades, the prevailing system of land use regulation— characterized by command and control regulations, implemented by multiple local jurisdictions in competition with one another for residents and business—has come under considerable fire. Proponents of growth management, regional government, and, most recently, the new urbanism claim that most of the growth enabled by local regulations is bad—and propose a new model of comprehensive controls to guarantee that new development will be better. Proponents of these proposals raise questions worthy of serious consideration—but other legal rules can address the questions without raising the same risk of stifling economic growth and innovation.

13: Growth-Oriented Law for the Networked Information Economy: Emphasizing Freedom to Operate Over Power to Appropriate

Yochai Benkler*

From the "rough consensus and running code" approach of the Internet Engineering Task Force, through the World Wide Web's ascendance, to Skype's voice over Internet approach or YouTube, the rate of change, the complexity of interactions, and the practical, technical feasibility of rapid, informal, low-cost experimentation have driven growth and innovation on the Internet on an evolutionary model rather than an engineering model. Variation, selection, adaptation, and survival/replication through user adoption, rather than planning and high investment, have repeatedly offered the more robust approach in this new complex and chaotic environment. Rapid, low-cost experimentation and adaptation on a mass scale, underwritten by the ease of cheap, fast implementation and prototyping, and cheap widespread failure punctuated by a steady flow of unpredictable successes, have been more important to innovation and growth in the networked economy than models of innovation

* Yochai Benkler is the Jack N. and Lillian R. Berkman Professor of Entrepreneurial Legal Studies, Harvard Law School; Faculty co-Director, Berkman Center for Internet and Society, Harvard University. I am grateful to the detailed and thoughtful comments of the participants in the Kauffman Summer Legal Institute, and in particular to Robert Litan for detailed comments and thoughts.

based on higher-cost, more managed innovation aimed at planning for predictable, well-understood returns. Judges and legislators who want to increase growth over time by increasing technological innovation in this unusual space should therefore orient their efforts towards minimizing institutional barriers to experimentation and implementation. This is a very different emphasis than the baseline set of assumptions that has driven much of copyright and patent doctrine and legislation, which focused on assuring existing investors the ability to secure payments for the products of their investment. While this slower moving, higher investment focused approach may have been appropriate to slower moving fields with intrinsic high-capital requirements, like small molecule pharmaceuticals, jet airplanes, or Hollywood blockbusters, it leads to precisely the wrong results in the new technological context that typifies the networked information environment.

Freedom to operate is more important than power to appropriate. Appropriation of the benefits of one's investment is critical *ex post,* and there is no question that at root, its anticipation drives investment in commercialized applications, services, and cultural goods. But in a globally connected, networked world, the level of uncertainty and the rapid changes in modes of appropriation of the benefits of innovation are so great that agility and continuous updating for responses to actual practices and technical, social, or behavioral opportunities is more important than the ability to plan clearly for a release schedule and a well-specified model in advance, and then execute reliably in a predictable environment. The benefits of crisply defined and enforced appropriation models are outweighed by the fact that in order to secure that appropriability, the law has set up a set of rules that, in protecting yesterday's actors, limits to too great an extent the freedom of new innovators to operate today. In two studies from 2007 and 2010, the Computer and Communications Industry Association (CCIA) claimed that the "fair use industries," industries that depend on and benefit from *limitations* to copyright, rather than its extension, account for $4.7 trillion, with a value added of $2.7 trillion, or about one-sixth of U.S. GDP, employing about 17.5 million employees with a per-employee productivity that was over 25 percent higher than economy-wide average productivity.[1]

The CCIA studies, which like all studies produced by lobbies need to be taken with more than a grain of salt, are the mirror image of the much longer practice by the copyright industries themselves, which have often published studies touting their own contribution to the economy. They reflect a relatively new recognition in industries that depend on freedom to operate that the regulatory policies that broadly fall under the umbrella of "intellectual property" essentially regulate how they do business in order to secure the business model of other industries, whose business model is optimized to take advantage of these forms of government-granted exclusivity: mostly Hollywood and the recording industry for copyright, and the pharmaceutical industry and the patent bar for patents. This conflict of lobbying studies underscores a simple fact about intellectual property laws: while their total effect on innovation may be questionable, they unquestionably support some business models—those that rely on invoking these particular grants—at the expense of other businesses, which appropriate the benefits of their investments in research and innovation on other models—be they supply side improvements like know-how acquisition, demand side improvements like first-mover advantages and network effects, or noncommercial models, which play a larger role in innovation economies than in other, grain-and-steel based systems.[2] The most extensive effort to quantify the trade-offs found that the costs of patent litigation faced by public companies outweighed the benefits from patent-related revenues by a factor or three or four during the innovation boom of the late 1990s.[3]

---

[1] Computer & Communications Industry Association, *Fair Use in the U.S. Economy: Economic Contribution of Industries Relying on Fair Use* (Washington, DC: CCIA, 2007), http://www. ccianet.org/CCIA/files/ccLibraryFiles/Filename/000000000085/FairUseStudy-Sep12.pdf ; CCIA, *Fair Use in the U.S. Economy* (Washington, DC: CCIA 2010), http://www.ccianet.org/CCIA/files/ccLibraryFiles/Filename/000000000354/fair-use-study-final.pdf.

[2] Yochai Benkler, "Intellectual Property and the Organization of Information Production," *International Review of Law and Economics* 22 (2002): 81.

Another way of putting it is that for innovation, flow is more important than stock, but the owners of existing stocks of knowledge can afford to influence more votes in legislatures and hire more lawyers to make arguments in court. This means that we should expect the institutional interests of the owners of stocks of existing materials—the owners of copyrights in existing works, and the owners of patents in industries where single innovations yield high returns for sustained periods—to be more powerfully and explicitly defended in our institutions than the interests of future innovators, who may make connections between existing pieces of knowledge in ways that are harder to quantify now, and therefore harder to convert into paid advocacy. This feature of the political economy of both legislative and judicial development of the law systematically biases our institutions in favor of stocks to the detriment of flows. As a result the current baseline of law is tilted in favor of past industries, and against present industries. Any growth-oriented lawmaking body—courts, legislators, or administrative agencies—needs to compensate for this systematic bias in the information flow to it by adopting a thoroughgoing and systematic skepticism toward claims of the necessity of increasing protection over existing information, knowledge, culture, and platforms at the expense of new uses and users who are making creative or productive use of the existing body of human knowledge and creative expression.

Courts and legislatures should consistently try to limit the extent to which existing players who own elements of systems that new players are building on use law to extract value from the new players by:

- Emphasizing exemptions and narrow construction that create freedom to operate, such as narrow construction of copyright to exclude claims about linking or crawling, or expanding the definition of what use counts as *de minimis* in copyright. All are ways of creating zones of freedom to operate.

---

[3] James Bessen and Michael J. Meurer, "Do patents perform like property?" *Academy of Management Perspectives* 22 (2008): 3, 8–20.

- Emphasizing freedom to operate and revenue sharing over forcing *ex ante* negotiation or creating deterrence. In the classic terms of liability versus property rules, this emphasizes liability systems, but a certain limited liability type: more on the model of disgorging a share of the profits than the torts or contracts model.

- Capping risks of liability, tying it to revenue from the new use, and providing an anchor for negotiations in the shadow not of exclusion or massive crippling damages, but of upside sharing among successful operations that choose a revenue-generating or profit-making model. Charges imposed as liability for access to existing information, standards, or elements, should be minimized. Courts should adopt *ex post* upside-sharing rules as quasi-liability rules, rather than *either* (a) *ex ante* property rules, which create risks of hold ups and high transactions costs, or (b) liability rules that are not tied to revenue or profit of the innovator, such as strict damages based on high statutory levels or hypothetical lost sales or similar mechanisms that courts in the past have used when driven by a property-protection model that conceived of follow-on innovation without permission as a species of theft or injustice.

Change and complexity emphasize an evolutionary model of innovation. The critical characteristic of innovation and growth on the Internet has been its unpredictability. It has resulted from rapid, repeated innovation, at very low cost, over an open network, with massive rates of failure surrounding rare but regularly occurring success. This form of distributed, scrappy innovation outstripping well-ordered, planned innovation has typified the Internet, both commercial and noncommercial, both "deep" innovation in the network and "user facing." The World Wide Web is the classic example. When Lotus released Notes 1.0 in 1989, and had a team of developers working on it, and certainly by 1995 when IBM bought it, one would not have predicted that the actual architecture for document sharing and collaboration would come out of a scrappy, informal system, one of dozens then being developed by young computer scientists and users to solve the same set of problems. And yet, it was Tim Berners-Lee's World Wide Web, not IBM's Lotus Notes, that won the day. It was then Marc Andreessen and Eric Bina at University of Illinois at Urbana-Champaign who created Mosaic, the first graphical user interface to the Web, and who founded Netscape. It was Brian Behlendorf, from the same academic research group, whose Web server, Apache, won out against both Netscape's own Web server and Microsoft's server. Behlendorf's was open source software, developed by a distributed group, and has been adopted and employed by between 50 and 65 percent of the Web server market for over fifteen years, including many of its e-commerce giants like Amazon. The same was true of Jimmy Wales's Wikipedia over Microsoft's Encarta. Instant messaging came from the periphery—ICQ was created by four kids in their twenties from Israel. The first generation successes—Amazon and eBay, Yahoo and Google—all follow the path of small, peripheral experimenters trying something out, implementing at incredibly low costs, surrounded by dozens of others in the same space, trying their own experiments. Second-generation successes—from voice over IP like Skype, which itself was built on the architecture developed by its founders for KaZaa, the peer-to-peer music file-sharing system, to video like YouTube, to social networking like Facebook and Twitter—all have followed a similar trajectory. Almost none of the major innovations that underlie how the Internet is used have followed the path of efficient, orderly, investment in R&D by established industry players. Instead, they have been the result of entrepreneurial experimentation, both commercial and noncommercial, by edge players, outsiders who emerged from a field of thousands of similar experimenters who failed. Innovation on the Internet has been a lightning-speed evolutionary process, with diversity and variation, selective pressure, and local or global successes replicating and establishing themselves through continuous learning, experimentation, and adaptation. For those aspects of IT industries, like semiconductor design, where patents have been common, evidence suggests that the patent portfolios are amassed more for protection from strike suits by competitors or non-innovators than because they are themselves necessary to sustain innovation in markets that offer many other models of appropriation—first-mover advantages, know-how learning effects, etc.[4]

Three major reasons account for the importance of the edge-driven, rapid-evolution model of innovation.

First, the physical capital necessary to develop, prototype, pilot, implement, revise, and redeploy in real time is widely available at low cost. For the first time since the Industrial Revolution, the core physical capital goods, in the core economic activities, of the most advanced economies are widely distributed in large portions of the population. That leaves the primary cost associated with trying something the cost of human labor and human capital.

Second, the kinds of innovations that can be implemented in software, text, images, etc., do not generally require massive teams working for years before something usable can begin to run (although refinement over time is a different matter). The labor and human capital cost for initial experimentation, therefore, is also relatively low (again, by comparison to pharmaceuticals or jet airplanes, which formed the model cases of innovation in the physical industrial age).

Third, the innovations are incremental and can be deployed over a standards-based, open system. As a technical matter, no one's permission need be sought to implement and experiment. In many cases, depending on the particular application, no lawyers need be hired, no contracts signed. The technical and institutional system in which these innovations occurred provided nearly absolute freedom to operate, with high uncertainty about models of appropriation should the innovation succeed. Needless to say, this freedom to operate meant that a lot of nonsense happened, as well as harmful activity. But the nonsense came and went cheaply, without imposing too great a cost on most people around it.

---

[4] B. H. Hall and R. H. Ziedonis, "The patent paradox revisited: An empirical study of patenting in the U.S. semiconductor industry, 1979–95," *RAND Journal of Economics* 32 (2001): 101–128.

Failure was cheap and rapid. And the harm was, broadly speaking, less than the typical threats associated with living in a big, thriving city. Metaphorical hyperbole notwithstanding, the risks online are still, by and large, not as severe as the risks in the physical world. And "piracy" online still stands for potential, often hypothetical, lost sales, not for sunken ships, maimed sailors, and enslaved passengers. The first two reasons, then, had to do with low capital barriers to innovation. The third had to do with low institutional barriers.

As a result of these characteristics, innovation in the networked environment is characterized by rapid change, complexity, imperfection, and constant learning and experimentation. It is typified by:

- Change and complexity, rather than predictability and "well behaved" change
- Innovation and growth, rather than efficiency and optimization
- "Scruffy," adaptive learning systems with late-binding design that do better than tightly-coupled, slower-moving, optimized systems
- Open systems, which emphasize freedom to operate on standardized interfaces among different actors and components, that do better than closed systems that emphasize control and well-ordered development and interaction among components and actors

In such an environment, the critical challenge for law, lawmakers, and judges is to resist the temptation to impose order on this chaotic realm. Accepting that it is precisely the chaotic, complex, open nature of this system that has been so important to innovation and growth in the past two decades is extremely difficult for law as a cultural concept, and for lawyers and judges as people who are trained to think in terms of order, and to see their roles as constructing systems that increase predictability and order. That basic impulse is not entirely mistaken, but can easily lead to the introduction of counterproductive barriers to experimentation, innovation, and growth in the context of the networked information economy. It requires self-discipline for a judge to accept that sometimes not protecting claims that are framed as "rights" is a way to assure innovation and growth, because as lawyers we are trained to think that clear, strong rights enable markets, rather than create barriers. In this context, however, where the rights are intellectual property-type rights, or rights to control standards or other necessary facilities, the claims of right are often more of a hindrance to entrepreneurship than a help.

Assume that any given attempted innovation has a chance of 1:1,000 to succeed. Assume further that there is a threshold level of cost of innovation and experimentation that can be borne by a large number of potential innovators as part of their baseline existence. This can mean many different things. It might mean a couple of college roommates working at night, or a few twenty-somethings who decide to work, using some of their parents' or relatives' money, or day jobs, to cross-subsidize experiments that they are doing because they hope to be the next big entrepreneur or at least gain experience and a reputation. Or it might mean that it is a way for an existing big company to occupy some of its slack, or generate motivation and enthusiasm among its knowledge workers, working "off the clock" or using specially designated free "play" time. There are many strategies, by many different actors in society, able to sustain highly uncertain activities that are in some measure rewarding in their own right, and in some measure able to deliver very high returns at a vanishingly small probability. Above a given threshold, however, experimentation becomes something that requires a real source of financing—an investment from a venture capital firm, a loan from a bank, etc. That cost represents a "threshold," in the sense that it represents a dramatic drop-off in the number of actors and the diversity of the models they can use to sustain their innovative exploration. Say there is some number—$100,000 per year, or 2,000 engineering or artistic hours, or 100 billable hours by a lawyer—above which the range of actors able to persist is drastically reduced to those who can raise money in sufficient quantities: that is, those who can make a well-defined case for appropriation of the returns to investment to an investor who has alternative options in a more well-behaved market. If the increase in cost reflected a corresponding increase in likelihood of success, then in principle the level of innovation could be maintained. But as long as the number of experiments and experimenters declines more rapidly than the probability of success increases, we will get fewer successful innovations. Imagine that under cost condition one, below the threshold, we have 10,000 experiments with a 1:1,000 probability of success, and so ten are likely to succeed. On the other hand, imagine that above the threshold, we have only 500 experimenters, and let's imagine that their probability of success is ten times greater, not 1:1,000, but 1:100. In this case, we can expect five successful innovations. While these numbers are, of course, hypothetical, they illustrate the basic intuition: as long as the amount of experimentation that occurs above a threshold cost has decreased by more than the probability of any given experiment's success on average has increased for the new types of more carefully selected experiments, the level of innovation at a societal level has decreased.

The critical facts about a given ecosystem's rate of innovation, then, become: (a) the value of the threshold; (b) the rate at which experiments drop after the threshold is reached; (c) the success rate of all organizations/individuals capable of functioning at costs below the threshold rates; and (d) the success rate of the subset of organizations capable of continuing to experiment, at the number of feasible experiments, above the threshold rate.

There are no current measurements of this trade-off. What we have is the practical experience of the past twenty years in online innovation. Even the most innovative companies, like Google, find themselves buying innovations from outside sources, even where they tried to innovate in the same space internally. Google had its employees working on a video platform and created Google Video, but ended up buying YouTube as the more successful innovation in the same field. The fact that the experimenter was Google turned out not to predict who among the dozens or hundreds of experimenters working on online user-generated video platforms would end up winning. The point is that if there is a baseline level of innovative experimentation that can go on in a society as long as its costs are below a given threshold, and if there is an insufficiently tight correlation between being a present successful company with a stock of knowledge and being the entrepreneur and innovator who creates tomorrow's successful innovation, then keeping the cost of experimentation below that threshold becomes the critically important target. That state of the world indeed seems to describe the shape of experimentation and innovation online better than the alternative model, which depends on a more predictable rate of success, from larger investments made by a more predictable set of actors in a more well-behaved innovation system.

The implication of accepting this model of evolutionary innovation in the online environment is quite substantial. It means that assuring the costs of experimentation remain below the threshold that allows large numbers of low-cost, low-expected-return (given the discounted probability of success) experimenters is more important than emphasizing the predictability of appropriating the return should it happen, where doing so would raise the cost level in the first place. In the context of intellectual property, this means that the potential negative effects on follow-on innovation, always known to exist in any IP system, have a particularly acute effect in this more chaotic innovation system. Whatever the beneficial effects on the investment incentives of the platform or IP owner, they are likely to be swamped, in a dynamic, evolutionary analysis, by the decline in experimentation by everyone else.

Practical proposals to promote experimentation. Accepting a growth-oriented framework, particularly accepting that innovation and experimentation are characterized by a nonlinear, threshold effect whereby, once costs increase above a given threshold, the amount of experimentation lost swamps the amount of investment secured by the increased investments of the smaller set of players able to play above the threshold cost, has stark implications for copyright law and its neighboring rights online, like business methods patents. Here, I will describe and outline what these reforms would look like, although without working out the specific doctrinal moves for each or the detailed analysis of how each would directly affect innovation. They are all intended to present pathways for reform, and specific targets of reform, for a judge and a legislature concerned with innovation in this new, chaotic, and complex networked innovation system.

Narrow construction of scope and applicability of control points based on copyright or patents.

- Read the idea or fact/expression dichotomy broadly.
- Use preemption to limit application of licensing agreements that attempt to limit reverse engineering and similar efforts to promote interoperability.
- Expand *de minimis* freedom to operate.
- Revise *Grokster* back to *Sony*.
- Continue to expand the Digital Millennium Copyright Act (DMCA) exceptions through the Librarian of Congress.

Innovation and creative experimentation always represent a tension between the freedom to operate of today's innovators, and the ability of yesterday's innovators or owners of existing information resources to make money from last year's investments. This is not unique to the Internet, and is driven by two factors. First, one of the raw materials for tomorrow's innovation or creative expression is yesterday's universe of knowledge. This is particularly so in a networked information environment, where the raw materials, the transportation hubs, the machines, are largely made up of yesterday's knowledge base. Second, information, knowledge, and culture are strictly public goods in the economic sense. Once produced, even in the most well-behaved and simple model, their marginal cost is zero. That is, to the extent that they are available only for a positive price above their cost of distribution, they will be underutilized by future innovators. These two understandings have been at the core of the economic understanding of innovation and IP at least since Nobel Laureate economist Kenneth Arrow's pathbreaking work on the rate and direction of innovation almost fifty years ago. That tension is the underlying economic rationale, under the traditional approach, of various limitations of copyrights and patents, from the limited terms required by the Constitution, to the more-or-less high requirements of novelty and nonobviousness in patent, and through to the various exceptions and carve outs in copyright law.

This tension is heightened in the distributed, complex networked environment. Because major innovations come from peripheral players, both commercial and noncommercial, preserving the power of yesterday's innovator to appropriate does not provide revenue streams for tomorrow's innovations to the same extent that was true in the past. Because the cost of experimentation and innovation is so low, the expectation of appropriation need not be as great, and the "incentives" problem is solved by the tippy nature of networked markets—first-mover advantages are substantial, network effects lock in successful leads, and large numbers of users tend to provide sufficient levels of revenue to attract investment and effort in search of the next big thing even in an open, fluid environment. Much of the legal system's emphasis in the past twenty years on control and its exercise has been driven by law suits and policy drives by non-innovative industries—like the recording industry, Hollywood, and some of the older-line software companies—in an effort to leverage older investments to capture future rents at the expense of today's innovators.

Copyright law provides various doctrines with which to create substantial freedom to operate for next-generation innovators. One classic example that has been enormously important was the more-or-less categorical acceptance by courts of the position that copying a computer program for purposes of reverse engineering did not violate copyright, mostly by protecting it under the fair use doctrine. The case of reverse engineering is a classic instance of efforts to leverage earlier innovation to constrain later innovation: it is the classic image of freedom to operate trumping power to appropriate. Beginning in 1988,[5] and then throughout the

1990s, circuit courts throughout the country largely protected the privilege of software developers to act in ways that formally violate copyright, say, by making an unauthorized copy or derivative work, as long as this was done as part of the process of reverse engineering: that is, figuring out how the software works so as to make use of its functionality, usually in order to create software that interoperates with the software that is being reversed engineered.[6]

This widely adopted rule was, in turn, quite widely accepted within the industry, but came under pressure after the passage of the Digital Millennium Copyright Act of 1998 and the introduction of an increasing number of End User Licensing Agreements (EULAs) that prohibited reverse engineering. The DMCA's core provision constrained circumventing technological protection measures. The "anti-circumvention" provisions responded to a concern by copyright owners. They hoped to maintain, and indeed refine, their control over digitized information goods by wrapping them with encryption, so that they could avoid unauthorized copying but also enforce much more subtle techniques of price discrimination—for example, by making sure that a digital music file sold in the United States for $15 could not then be resold in Europe, where it is available for EUR 15; or to sell one-time viewings, or three-time viewings, etc., at different pricing. The fear to which the anti-circumvention provisions responded was that other software developers would be able to build devices that would get around—circumvent—the encryption. The DMCA made both the act of circumventing a copy-protection design, and the act of making or distributing the tools to do so, civil and potentially criminal offenses. Within a short period, these provisions began to be used by companies to prevent competitors from entering their markets. Typical of these cases was the *Lexmark* case. One printer company, Lexmark International,

---

[5] *Vault Corp. v. Quaid Software Ltd.*, 847 F.2d 255, 270 (5th Cir. 1988).

[6] For a review of the cases and problems associated with its extension to software patents see Julie Cohen and Mark Lemley, "Patent Scope and Innovation in the Software Industry," *California Law Review* 89 (2001): 1.

tried to use the DMCA to prevent competitors from making toner cartridges that could work with its own printers. It did so by including a microchip and piece of software with the cartridges, without which a competing cartridge would not be run by the printer. Another company, Static Control Components, created a compatible, unauthorized microchip that could be installed in the cartridges by other companies, which, in turn, could compete in the market for replacement toner for Lexmark printers. To do so, Static Control had to both make use of a Lexmark's Toner Loading Program, in ways that included copying it, and circumvent the protection measure provided by the chip.[7]

The Sixth Circuit decision provides a model for what a court concerned with freedom to operate to support growth should do. The first was to define the boundaries of copyrightability narrowly. Rather than relying on fair use, which involves substantial litigation risk, the court analyzed the program copied for its character as functional, within the classic idea/expression and merger framework. That is, copyright law specifically excludes from its coverage the idea embodied in an expression from coverage; anyone is free to express the same idea in different words. What is interesting about the way the Sixth Circuit applied this basic principle of copyright law to this case is that it created a broad categorical freedom to operate for access controls of the kind at stake, instead of subjecting each future effort to achieve interoperability to the vagaries of fair use. Note that fair use is a four-factor doctrine, is relatively uncertain, and presents a relatively high litigation risk for defendants. Second, the court construed the DMCA's provision narrowly to avoid the facts of the case, and emphasized the importance of the core function of Static Control's program— enabling interoperability. Together, these two components anchor an important part of the broader approach: assuring that where a later innovator uses the functions, ideas, or facts embedded in a copyrighted work, even when doing so technically requires using the work itself, that act is not itself infringing.

---

[7] *Lexmark International, Inc. v. Static Control*, 387 F.3d 522 (6th Cir. 2004).

By contrast, the Eighth Circuit in *Blizzard v. BnetD* took the opposite route. There, Blizzard, a major computer games company, used a code to limit play of its online, multiplayer game to players who used servers that it owns and controls. BnetD was an open source project that permitted the owners of copies of Blizzard games to direct their instances of the program to play on different servers not owned by Blizzard. (The servers are essentially databases that store all of the data about past "behaviors" of the players, and continuously update the data on who has manipulated his or her software in the past in ways that move a character, build a feature, etc. These games are essentially vast relational databases that the users manipulate through the interface of the richly rendered game environment.) Blizzard argued that enabling its players to use their games over other systems' servers violated the terms of its end user license agreement (EULA), which, among other things, prohibited reverse engineering. While the court agreed that reverse engineering was "necessary" in order for the BnetD software to be developed, it nonetheless sided with Blizzard, holding that enforcing a prohibition on doing something that was privileged under federal copyright law was not preempted by that law. To so hold, the court would have to assume that the freedom of software developers to reverse engineer under federal copyright law was not itself a core component of federal policy, and it did so explicitly rejecting the applicability of the reverse engineering cases, going back to *Vault*, which did in fact hold that federal law preempted terms of service or a EULA that prohibited reverse engineering. The court in *Blizzard* effectively made a choice: assuring that Blizzard was able to control use of its game software by having a secure, controlled playing environment was more important than assuring that new innovators and entrants had the freedom to operate they needed to create new systems that interoperated with the existing systems. It is a preference for defending stocks over enabling flows. While not a doctrinally implausible decision, it put the thumbs on the scale on the wrong side from the perspective of driving innovation and growth. This becomes even clearer in the case of Blizzard, because the game is a multiplayer online persistent environment—that is, it is a database service company, which sells access to a continuously updated database (which records and reports the "location" and "actions" of the game characters). As such, from the perspective of assuring appropriability, it is not at all clear that multiplayer online game makers like Blizzard require any more intellectual property protection than do other database producers: which is to say, none at all.

The point of the discussion here is not necessarily or specifically to criticize the *Blizzard* decision and support extension of *Lexmark*. It is to emphasize that courts and judges concerned with growth and focused on innovation in a complex, rapidly changing environment should model their analysis on the *Lexmark* case, and avoid the pitfall of imagining that what they are seeing is a pathway to piracy on the model of *Blizzard*. The particulars will change from one case to the next. In one, courts might be asked to treat crawling of images and reproduction of thumbnails by an image search engine as violations of the underlying copyright in the image;[8] in another, courts might be asked to hold that crawling the contents of news sites to develop an aggregate sense of what news is currently important violates a newly reinvigorated "hot news" doctrine on the model of *International News Service vs. Associated Press* (a mostly abandoned approach in which the Supreme Court created a property-like right in the factual contents of news reports; this allowed news media to sue competitors who copied the factual content of the news, which cannot be protected by copyright, for the period during which the news had commercial value).[9] The fundamental idea that a growth and innovation perspective underscores is that all of these types of cases include the same core structure, and should be treated as cases of constraints on freedom to operate in the face of pressure from yesterday's innovators and creators to slow innovation and growth down so as to stabilize their ability to appropriate the fruit of their own past investments. While it will not always be practical for a court to refuse to provide such a remedy, the basic

---

[8] *Kelly v. Arriba Soft Corporation*, 336 F.3d 811 (9th Cir. 2003); *Perfect 10, Inc. v. Amazon.com, Inc.*, 487 F.3d 701 (9th Cir. 2007).

stance we propose here is one of skepticism and minimalism, rather than of creative judicial extension of rights that might be recommended by a more static, efficiency- or security-centric analysis.

Specifically, *Lexmark* and the reverse engineering cases (prior to *Blizzard*) stand for the benefits of using two major doctrinal levers more powerfully in defense of freedom to operate for follow-on innovators and creators.

- *Idea/fact versus expression doctrine.* In particular, *Lexmark* used the fact that the copying was used to achieve interoperability to anchor its holding that however initially "creative" the Lexmark code was, once it is used to protect access, then using it and its unique features becomes a fact about interoperability. That is to say, the function merges with the expression based on the fact that using what might otherwise have been protected elements becomes necessary to interoperate with the earlier work.

- *Preemption of licenses that constrain follow-on uses.* Courts should treat elements of copyright law that preserve freedom to operate for follow-on uses as preempting the field, and preempt licenses that constrain follow-on uses beyond what a growth-sensitive, flow-protecting interpretation of copyright or patent would support.

A similar transformation can occur by a broad reading of the *de minimis* doctrine. Copyright law recognizes that minimal uses do not rise to the level of copyright violation. Yet courts have been highly circumspect in their use of the *de minimis* doctrine. In *Bridgeport Music*,[10] for example, the Sixth Circuit held that a three-note riff sampled and transformed was sufficient to invoke copyright, subject only to the fair use doctrine. But the fair use doctrine is uncertain and an invitation to litigate. Far more effective

[9] 246 U.S. 215 (1918). The idea of reviving this largely defunct doctrine was presented by news organizations in the context of Federal Trade Commission workshops on the future of journalism. E.g., Current Copyright Issues in Journalism panel, FTC Workshop, "How Will Journalism Survive the Internet Age?" Washington, DC, March 9, 2010.

would be to create safe harbors for creative reuse of existing materials. The critical frame of mind appropriate for such a determination is as follows: is this the kind of violation or revenue stream without which the original investment would not have been made? In the case of music and sampling, the basic question is whether there is any song recorded and distributed where, at the margin, the investment in creating, recording, and distributing the music would not have been made but for the expectation of sampling royalties. As long as the kind of use would not have made the marginal difference to incentive—that is, as long as there is a clear market absent royalties from this particular creative downstream use—then imposing liability creates a downstream blockage without obvious marginal contribution to investment in creative work.

Reinstitute the Sony *Doctrine by reversing* Grokster. The fear of rampant online music piracy led the Supreme Court to a split decision that unnecessarily increased the litigation risk for innovators and entrepreneurs that develop platforms for user creation, storage, and communication of cultural expression, thereby dampening and increasing the costs of entrepreneurship.[11] When Sony's Betamax technology was challenged in court, the Supreme Court ultimately held that even a relatively modest amount of substantial noninfringing use was sufficient to provide an innovator with a safe harbor against contributory liability for copyright infringements committed by users who use its product or platform (in that case, a video cassette recorder).[12] When the doctrine was revisited by the Supreme Court in the *Grokster* case,[13] the Court was faced with three options. First, advocated by the movie and music industry, was a doctrine that would have required innovators to show, with extensive evidence of actual usage patterns, that the uses that users made of the technology after it was deployed were largely legal. The risk posed by this standard would have been, of course, that innovators of relatively flexible platforms cannot in advance know what the uses will be, or how

---

[10] *Bridgeport Music, Inc. v. Dimension Films,* 410 F.3d 792 (6th Cir. 2005).

usage and adoption patterns would develop. Any platform capable of infringing uses alongside its noninfringing uses would represent enormous investment risk, particularly in light of massive damage awards discussed below. The second option was to keep the innovation-supporting *Sony* doctrine in place. This had the benefit of over two decades of practice, during which creativity by the copyright industries continued undiminished, and innovation in the electronics industries was widespread. The third option, which the Court chose, was to permit a more fact-based inquiry not into patterns of use after the fact, but into intentions of the platform provider at the time of the creation of the innovation—whether there is evidence that supporting piracy was intended as the major application. While not as restrictive as the position advocated by the copyright industries, this position certainly created new litigation risks for platform innovators, because the kind of fact-based inquiry required by the court makes these kinds of cases less susceptible to summary dismissal and therefore more likely to kill an entrepreneurial company if brought, irrespective of what the ultimate merits of the case might be were the innovator to have the wherewithal to litigate to

---

[11] Note that I use the terms "risk" and "uncertainty," and sometimes, as in the case of the innovation environment that drives experimentation, it has a positive valence; and in others, like litigation risk, a negative one. From a purely financial, options basis, "risk" is desirable. When we consider different sources of risk, however, we can see that some of them drive toward better applications or uses being established—these are risks associated with whether a technology will or will not work; with whether consumers will or will not adopt a technology—because the risk is associated with whether or not a desideratum of the platform will, or will not, turn out to be as valuable and adopted as its designers intend. To overcome such a risk, the person deploying the platform can aim to make whatever it is they are deploying more of what it is intended to be—useful, attractive, etc. Litigation risk, by contrast, has to do with the fact that uncertain doctrines like fair use, or the new *Grokster* doctrine, expose parties to risks of payment that are not correlated with how good or early or useful their application or service is. They also are not a reflection of how harmful their activity is to an earlier actor; or how useful that earlier actor is. Efforts to mitigate such risks cannot therefore be directed *ex ante* at avoiding harm to valuable incumbents, or improving one's service; they involve simply added insurance costs, in effect, against a risk that it not correlated to any desirable dimension of the innovation or development itself. Hence, while from the financial investment perspective one bet is as good as another, from the perspective of risks that drive to desirable investments (those that increase the probability of success, or decrease harm to valuable incumbent activities), the two kinds of risks are not parallel.

[12] *Sony Corp. of America v. Universal City Studios, Inc.*, 464 U.S. 417 (1984).

[13] *MGM Studios, Inc. v. Grokster, Ltd.* 545 U.S. 913 (2005).

conclusion. Given that there is no evidence that the original *Sony* doctrine was insufficient, either a legislative or judicial revisiting would help to lower the risk and cost of innovation in a broad range of online applications.

Continue to expand exemptions through the Librarian of Congress. The DMCA included a specific process through which the Librarian of Congress can identify classes of behavior that require circumvention of digital protection devices, but are privileged under copyright and therefore require an exemption from liability. In the first two or three reviews, the Librarian of Congress began to issue a very small set of exemptions. Most recently, the Librarian extended an exemption to iPhone "jailbreaking": the practice of overcoming the iPhone's internal security that allows Apple to control which applications run on the phone, so as to make those applications compatible with the iPhone platform. This is an enormously important decision, because it opens up for innovation a platform that, at least potentially, could come to replace the laptop as the primary mobile Internet device through the same kind of chaotic innovation model that typified the Internet. The Librarian also extended the exemption to circumvention of video protection measures if the use that is made of the video is noncommercial creative transformation—that is, mashup. Given that user-generated video is an important pathway for consumer product innovation, again, this likely is a mid-level intervention to increase freedom to operate at the expense of some reduction in power to appropriate.[14]

Create a new kind of injunctive relief in copyright cases that would tie damage-like payments to actual revenue of entrepreneurs that use existing copyrighted materials without permission. Injunctions and damages present important risks, particularly to early stage commercial, and noncommercial, efforts. The risk to innovation and entrepreneurship is not so much that a successfully commercialized platform will be required to pay a reasonable share of its

---

[14] Statement of the Librarian of Congress Relating to Section 1201 Rulemaking, July 23, 2010, http://www.copyright.gov/1201/2010/Librarian-of-Congress-1201-Statement.html.

profits and revenues to an enabling underlying innovation or creative cultural input. While clearly excessive damages or poorly thought-out injunctions can gum the works up even at those later stages of commercialization, the higher risk is that early stage experimentation will be stifled by potential liability irrespective of successful commercial establishment for (a) early stage commercially oriented experimentation and innovation and (b) noncommercial innovation and experimentation, which, as noted earlier in this chapter, have made unusually large contributions to innovation in the networked environment because of their particular pattern of distributed physical capital investment and relatively low cost of implementing innovation.

Both injunctions and damages that are not tied to actual revenues of the infringer can cause significant dampening of innovation that depends on use of existing knowledge, platforms, or cultural inputs. Because of the nonrivalry of information—that is, its nature as a public good—even a perfectly functioning set of property rights enforced by injunction would lead to underutilization of existing information inputs. Moreover, there are significant imperfections involved in identifying whose existing IP rights would potentially be implicated by a given new application or business model and in transacting over these rights, and there are many opportunities for strategic behavior and holdout where one party holds an exclusive right over inputs that are essential to the functioning of a dependent product. Particularly in an innovation environment where low-cost, high-risk innovation is the *modus operandi*, leaving the clearance of right to an injunction-enforced property-type system imposes relatively high costs and relatively high degrees of constraint on the freedom of innovators to operate in the networked economy.

A partial solution to this dampening effect is the one presented in *eBay v. MercExchange*.[15] There, the Supreme Court refused to follow the U.S. Court of Appeals for the Federal Circuit's practice of assuming that injunction was the normal remedy in patent cases, but rather decided that the issuance of an injunction even in patent cases was subject to the standard equitable analysis, requiring irreparable injury, inadequacy of damages, balance of hardships, and public interests. Lower court cases since then have indeed applied this standard and denied injunctions in a substantial minority of cases. The cost of this approach is increased uncertainty for the rights holders. The benefit is that this increased uncertainty decreases the expected value of the suits, and therefore likely decreases the number of suits, in particular suits against impecunious defendants, who are precisely the kinds of defendants that are most likely to be driven out of business by suits and that form the set of experimental entrepreneurs of particular concern to the networked innovation system. Within the traditional injunction model, levers like balance of hardships and public interest can be particularly productive in creating an early stage freedom to operate for early innovators and noncommercial players to generate the distributed innovations that have played an important role in the online environment.

Judicial discretion in granting injunctions provides the doctrinal pathway through which to implement some of the insights of the benefits of using liability-like regimes in these areas of extensive small- to mid-scale innovations with high mutual dependencies that are so typical of the online environment. The idea behind the long-standing drive of scholars like Jerome Reichman and others has been that a legal regime that emphasizes flows over stocks, assuring access and sorting out revenue sharing later, is particularly conducive in an innovation system that depends so heavily on radically distributed innovation, with high dependencies between incremental improvements made by disparate organizations and individuals. Here, the failures of a property system are strongest, and the benefits of a mechanism for settlement arrangements after it becomes known which innovations got commercialized, and their dependencies, emphasizes a "do first, distribute later" approach.

But a liability regime itself can create as much, if not more, of a drag on innovation and investment than a property/injunction

---

[15] *eBay v. MercExchange, L.L.C.*, 547 U.S. 388 (2006).

regime, if the expected damages are unmoored from the actual potential business models to which they apply. A classic example of this threat is the holding in *UMG v. MP3.com*.[16] There, MP3.com introduced a music distribution service that was much more manageable and plausibly legal than the peer-to-peer file-sharing services that emerged with its demise. Nonetheless, the company was not owned by the record labels, and was sued for providing a service that allowed users to listen to music anywhere, as long as they had once proven that they owned a copy of the music by inserting a CD of it into their computer while logged into the service. As a technical, practical matter, to offer the service MP3.com made copies of the music, and violated the copyrights of the record labels. As a practical business matter, MP3.com was an innovative firm that was able to create a market that could have provided a much more manageable online marketplace for recording companies than the chaos of the decade that followed. But the recording industry was not ready to give up the level of control it had enjoyed in the off-line world. In the suit, MP3.com was held liable for statutory damages of $25,000 per CD, which could have totaled over $160 million. The company settled for $53 million with UMG and another $110 million with the other firms. As a result, the company became too financially weak to operate, was initially bought out at a tiny fraction of its value in IPO by one of the recording labels, Vivendi Universal, and then broken up and sold in pieces.

The statutory damages created a set of crushing liabilities entirely divorced from either real damages caused to the labels or actual revenues captured by the innovative firm. The *in terrorem* force of such damages is hard to overstate. They exist irrespective of any showing of a single displaced sale. They exist and are available against any infringer. And where an injunction can shut off a pathway or line of business, the damages pose an immediate threat of wiping out investors in bankruptcy.

---

[16] *UMG Recordings, Inc. vs. MP3.com, Inc.*, 92 F.Supp. 2d 349 (2000).

What, then, is the solution? How do judges or legislators preserve the freedom to operate for innovators who depend on existing materials, without subjecting them to excessive strategic holdouts through injunctions and without creating unacceptable risks of very high damages that are independent of their revenues? One possible answer is to use the equitable powers that are implicit in the injunction remedy, expanding the approach introduced in *eBay v. MercExchange*. The driving idea is to give innovative models a space to explore and experiment, while preserving a framework to force payment should a given experiment succeed and become a significant source of revenue. A court could issue an injunction, subject to purchase by the infringer at a rate equivalent to an industry-standard royalty for the works used. An entrepreneur facing a decision whether to experiment with a platform or service that uses existing information, knowledge, or culture with possible proprietary claims will face neither the prospect of holdup nor the prospect of bankruptcy, but rather the prospect of paying a standardized royalty should the experiment succeed. That entrepreneur would still prefer to acquire a license so as to minimize uncertainty. But the bargaining posture is very different when the rights holder cannot stop the entrepreneur from operating, and cannot expect to win more than an industry-standard royalty, than when the rights holder can put the entrepreneur out of business through either injunction or overwhelming damages.

This proposal is far from trivial to implement. It has the virtue of creating extensive freedom to operate in experimentation with online business models, technical platforms, and services around existing cultural materials. It would represent a dramatic departure from the trend of the past twenty years, which has systematically emphasized the power of rights holders to appropriate the value of their existing cultural goods, rather than the freedom of entrepreneurs to innovate. An imperfect version of this approach could be implemented by judges by applying the discretion left to them in awarding damages and fashioning injunctions under the copyright act, although the constraints of statutory damages still leave rights holders the power to elect imposition of, at a minimum, a $750 per-violation damage award. Still, a systematic judicial practice of imposing only the bare minimum in statutory damages, to be credited against the value of the royalty from actual revenues, should limit the effects of the threat of damages. Of course, a more complete and refined reform could be adopted by Congress, although the political economy strongly favors protecting currently known rights holders at the expense of future and currently unknown innovators and entrepreneurs.

Eliminate business methods patents. Quite possibly the most misguided application of patent doctrine was its extension to business methods. It was a laughable idea that entrepreneurs need a government-granted twenty-year monopoly over a particular way they developed to serve customers or calculate payments among holders of syndicated credit notes, and that the returns in the market from such innovations is insufficient to support them. And it was laughable from the moment the Federal Circuit first decided to extend patent protection to business methods (in particular, an automated system for pooling the funds of mutual funds).[17] Business methods patents have been subject to extensive criticism since they were first introduced. Partly, this is because the very idea is so patently unnecessary. Partly, it is because the quality of patents granted has been so low. (As this manuscript was being prepared, Amazon was granted a patent on social networking, on a patent application filed four years after Facebook had been launched, whose abstract reads like a joke about how a patent attorney would describe Facebook's affordances; note too that Facebook itself was a latecomer, following Six Apart, Friendster, and later MySpace.)[18]

It took slightly over a decade for the Federal Circuit to begin to reverse course, and in its *en banc* hearing of *In re Bilski*, that court, without formally reversing *State Street Bank*, limited it extensively by tying the availability of patenting to the implementation of a business method under the historical "machine or transforma-

---

[17] *State Street Bank and Trust Company v. Signature Financial Group, Inc.*, 149 F.3d 1368 (Fed. Cir. 1998).

tion" test. As a practical matter, this would largely contain the use of business methods patents, without overturning their availability in principle. The Supreme Court granted *certiorari*, affirmed the result (the patent holder lost), but reversed the exclusive use of the "machine or transformation" test as too narrow and outdated a basis for patentability.[19] Four concurring justices would have categorically excluded business methods patents from patentability.[20] Justice Kennedy did not exclude the possibility that the Federal Circuit would find other, less textually cramped approaches to limiting patentability in ways consistent with enhancing innovation. Indeed, his opinion was very explicit in embracing the idea that it is precisely the widely distributed, open innovation ecology of the Internet that creates the new challenges for patent law:

> It is important to emphasize that the Court today is not commenting on the patentability of any particular invention, let alone holding that any of the above-mentioned technologies from the Information Age should or should not receive patent protection. This Age puts the possibility of innovation in the hands of more people and raises new difficulties for the patent law. With ever more people trying to innovate and thus seeking patent protections for their inventions, the patent law faces a great challenge in striking the balance between protecting inventors and not granting monopolies over

---

[18] Brian D. Robertson et al., Amazon Technologies, Inc., US Patent 7,739,139, social networking system, filed May 27, 2008, and issued June 15, 2010. The abstract reads: "A networked computer system provides various services for assisting users in locating, and establishing contact relationships with, other users. For example, in one embodiment, users can identify other users based on their affiliations with particular schools or other organizations. The system also provides a mechanism for a user to selectively establish contact relationships or connections with other users, and to grant permissions for such other users to view personal information of the user. The system may also include features for enabling users to identify contacts of their respective contacts. In addition, the system may automatically notify users of personal information updates made by their respective contacts."

[19] *Bilski v. Kappos*, 561 U.S. (June 28, 2010).

[20] Slip op at 33.

procedures that others would discover by independent, creative application of general principles. Nothing in this opinion should be read to take a position on where that balance ought to be struck.

For now, business methods patents are still available. The pathway that the Federal Circuit pointed to, that four justices would have adopted already, and that the majority certainly left open, is for their elimination.

Other policy areas involve trade-offs between control and freedom to operate. The basic problem identified here—a trade-off between law and policy positions that aim to stabilize and order an otherwise-chaotic system at the expense of raising the cost of innovation and entrepreneurship on the Internet—is repeated in other contexts as well. These other areas are too complex to be covered in detail in this short chapter. They raise distinct issues from those of IP, and there is no intention of resolving them here. Nevertheless, it is important to identify the fact that each of these areas, in addition to other aspects of the problems they present, also represent the problem of trading off control and the opportunities it provides for appropriation by the owners of a valuable resource, and freedom to operate for innovators who require access to and use of those resources to experiment, pilot, deploy, and innovate. The debate over net neutrality has a similar shape: opponents claim that carriers need the power to control flows over their networks in order to provide incentives for infrastructure investment, while proponents argue that freedom to operate over a set of open standards that treat all bits equally provides greater flexibility for innovation and avoids transactional barriers for entrepreneurs and innovators developing new applications online. Privacy concerns also have a similar shape. Here, the tension is not between security for large investment and freedom to experiment, but between security of individual context and the same freedom to experiment. Because the tension is between an economic, growth-oriented interest and a noneconomic interest, the trade-off is harder to settle along a common dimension. Nonetheless, it is important to understand that (a) the tension has the same impact on innovation and entrepreneurship, and (b) that solutions to concerns over privacy that depend on widely adopted technical standards, that then permit widespread innovation without imposing higher costs, have the benefit of serving the noneconomic interests implicated by privacy and the growth interests concerned with widespread freedom to operate for innovation. Internet security is another interest that, like privacy, is somewhat distinct from investment security. As Jonathan Zittrain has described in detail, precisely the wide-open characteristics of the Internet, what he called its generativity, are also the characteristics that made deployment of experiments so trivial. Approaches based on trusted systems that will refuse to run programs not authorized by a given party—say, Microsoft through the operating system, or Apple through its App Store—certainly offer greater control and security against viruses and malware, but only at the expense of creating a drag on experimentation and innovation. The Internet, in this regard, is like a city: a big, open space, where many diverse characters come and meet for their mutual benefit, but also a space that invites crime and abuse. The trick for modern cities has always been to manage the tension between openness and innovativeness, on the one hand, and insecurity on the other. That same tension underlies contemporary efforts to assure online security.

CONCLUSION

Growth depends on innovation. In the networked information economy, innovation and entrepreneurship seem to have depended more on freedom to operate in an environment that allows mass-scale experimentation by diverse and distributed innovators than on well-ordered investment by predictable innovators. This importance of edge innovation seems to be driven by the complexity of the network and its global reach, by the rapid rate of change, by the low capital cost barriers to experimentation, and by the technical and institutional openness of the Internet as a network for invention, rapid prototyping and experimentation, very rapid global adoption for successful stories, and more-or-less graceful, low-cost exit for the vast number of failures. The Internet therefore seems to have characteristics that mark it as the kind of system where very large amounts of low-cost experimentation are feasible and productive of growth, and that the potential constriction in the number and diversity of experiments caused by efforts to impose more orderly innovation systems, with higher costs, is likely to result in less, rather than more, innovation. The policy implications of this observation are many and diverse, but they share a common theme and a common focus. They argue that in a wide range of policy choices, judges, legislators, and regulators focus on preserving freedom to operate, even where doing so comes at the expense of power to appropriate.

14: Digital Firm Formation

Oliver R. Goodenough*

INTRODUCTION AND ACTION STEPS

F irm formation is a critical element in promoting and sustaining economic growth. Startups help drive economies forward. Increasing the ease of creating startups, and the universe of players with whom a startup can be formed, will necessarily contribute to economic progress. Digital communication is increasing the scope and ease of many forms of human interaction. We are using the Internet, cell phones, and such blended devices as the iPad to keep track of friends, date, make restaurant reservations, pursue education and commerce, and file our taxes. The boost in efficiency and reach resulting from the digitization of these activities is significant–sometimes even revolutionary.

The digital revolution is affecting law as well, and digital firm formation is now a possibility. As creating and operating a firm

_____

* Oliver R. Goodenough, a fellow at The Berkman Center for Internet and Society at Harvard Law School, a Professor of Law at the Vermont Law School, and an Adjuct Professor at Thayer School of Engineering at Dartmouth College, is an expert in the law of business, including corporations, entertainment law, intellectual property, securities law, and trademarks.

343

through a medium like the web becomes easier, more completely integrated, and more widely available, it too will create a significant boost in the possibilities for establishing start-up companies. We can accelerate this process and capture the benefits sooner by pushing forward on a series of action steps, working to:

- Recognize the potential for digitization to bring speed and efficiency to many realms of law and their application to human needs, with a particular focus on the law of company formation and operation;

- Pass legislation and reform regulations so as to authorize the formation and operation of digital companies and to recognize the character and treatment of algorithmic ownership interests;

- Develop platforms that integrate software, communication systems, and law so as to allow users to capture the potential created by these legal changes; and

- Educate entrepreneurs and their legal advisors in law about these changes and about how to use them to create reliable legal structures for business with greater efficiency, reduced friction, and increased client autonomy.

As we face a period of predicted slow economic growth following the sharp downturn of 2008-9, cultivating institutions that better support innovation and entrepreneurship is a priority for the United States and the world.

In laying out the case for digital firm formation, this chapter will first explore the importance of legal institutions for economic activity and the potential impact of digitization on the creation of such institutions. It will then describe more fully the four action steps set out above, reporting on progress to date and suggesting implementation strategies that will help to accelerate the acceptance and application of digital firms. Finally, it will return to a wider assessment of the benefits that will flow from digital company laws, benefits that go well beyond the immediate goals of reducing costs and boosting efficiency.

This chapter focuses largely on legal developments in the United States. This choice reflects limitations of scope and authorial expertise, and not any inherent lack of interest in laws and events outside the United States. That said, the digital corporation and LLC amendments passed in Vermont still stand out as leading steps in this field, and U.S. law is illustrative of the general points to be made. Any gains that might come from an extended comparative treatment would be limited for the purposes of the arguments set out here.

Background 1: Firm Formation Matters for Growth

Why is firm formation particularly important for sustained growth? Economic progress can be usefully differentiated between "catch-up" growth and innovation-led growth. Catch-up growth involves the adoption of existing models of technology, production, and distribution by less developed countries. As contemporary examples like China and India demonstrate, it is an important part of the story for increasing prosperity and well-being around the globe. But it is also essentially a finite part of that story. When everyone catches up, this kind of development levels off and stagnation can set in.

Innovation-led growth, by contrast, keeps expanding the frontier of the possibilities of prosperity. Innovation can come in new, more competent technological processes or in better institutions for organizing and financing economic activity. This type of growth is the hope of the current leaders in the world economy, such as the United States, who set the standards to which catch-up economies aspire, and in future years it will be the source of solutions to such challenges as sustaining and growing prosperity in a resource-constrained world.

Catch-up growth is essentially imitative. It does not need the spark of new discovery, just a good eye for what is working for somebody else and the willingness to move from locally established practice and adopt the observed improvements. These attributes can often be accommodated by existing firms, and so catch-up growth is less dependent on new firm formation. Innovative growth, on the other hand, is inherently a matter of finding new approaches to put new ideas to work. Existing firms can be a source of innovation, but the full vision of creative destruction in a growing economy requires a constant stream of new enterprises pushing the boundaries outward. The ease with which new startups can be established within an economy has a direct impact on its potential for growth.

Baumol et al. recognize this, putting firm formation among the first elements on their list of necessary factors for an innovative system: "[I]n the successful entrepreneurial economy, it must be relatively easy to form a business, without expensive and time-consuming bureaucratic red tape."[1] Summing up the problem succinctly, they declare, "If entrepreneurship is about starting and growing a commercial enterprise... then it must be easy and inexpensive to do."[2] The unspoken villain of the red-tape nightmare is the legal system. While firms can be—and often are—founded on handshakes, most advanced economies offer legally supported forms of expectation and commitment through which a more formal, explicit, and enforceable arrangement can be made. The availability of these private legal institutions is important for growth. The trick, of course, is to make the barriers to establishment low in terms of complication, time, and expense—goals the digital world can often help to accomplish.

Background 2: Legal Institutions Matter for Firms

The importance of legal institutions in economic growth is widely recognized. As Jones and Romer remark: "There is very broad

---

[1] William J. Baumol, Robert E. Litan, and Carl J. Schramm, *Good Capitalism, Bad Capitalism, and the Economics of Growth and Prosperity* (New Haven, CT: Yale University Press, 2007).

[2] Ibid.

agreement that differences in institutions must be the fundamental source of the wide differences in growth rates observed for countries at low levels of income and for the low income and TFP [total factor productivity] levels themselves."[3]

Similarly, when Baumol et al. (2007) describe the preconditions for a successful entrepreneurial economy, something they characterize as "a well oiled economic growth machine," they spell out four necessary elements, *all* of which involve institutions. The first two—firm formation and the law of contract and property—are private law spaces within which participants get to fashion their own collaborative structures. The second two—government policies and regulations—are public institutional domains.[4] Clearly, legal institutions matter for growth, and private legal institutions—and business organization laws in particular—can matter as much as the society-wide institutions of macroeconomic policy. How does meeting this need help innovation?

In the public imagination, new inventions are often the product of a lonely, innovative genius, toiling away in isolation. If the inventor is successful, and the critical light-bulb moment occurs, then the idea generator magically morphs into an expert manager of the processes of commercialization. While this is sometimes the case, the myth of the lone inventor/entrepreneur is more often just that—a myth. Innovations are seldom solitary achievements, and particularly not in these times of technological complexity, when mashing together a diversity of skills and knowledge is often the source of new knowledge. In *The Rational Optimist: How Prosperity Evolves*, Matt Ridley argues that innovation occurs when "ideas have sex," a process that is likely to require more than one mind as the source of those ideas.[5]

---

[3] Charles I. Jones and Paul M. Romer, "The New Kaldor Facts: Ideas, Institutions, Population, and Human Capital," *American Economic Journal: Macroeconomics* 2, no. 1 (2010): 224-45.

[4] Baumol et al., *Good Capitalism, Bad Capitalism.*

[5] Matt Ridley, *The Rational Optimist: How Prosperity Evolves* (New York: Harper Collins, 2010).

Collaboration is even more important for taking an idea into production and bringing it to market. Here again, the skill sets involved are likely to be only partially represented in any one person, and collaboration will increase the chances of success. Furthermore, skills alone are frequently not enough—capital is generally a requirement, and a requirement that must often be sought from sources beyond the coalition of idea and management providers so far assembled. As it labors to bring ideas to practice, entrepreneurship often creates a team, bringing together capital, technical expertise, management acumen, and expertise in dealing with legal and governmental requirements. Whether it is two people or ten, the team will generally only commit the required resources of time, talent and money against a reasonably reliable expectation of a share in the hoped-for gains that the innovative activity can produce.

The challenge of capturing and sharing the gains that arise from productive cooperation and collaboration is a general one, with application well beyond the context of human economic activity. The potential problems come in several variants, ranging from active deceit, defection, and predation to less aggressive but equally destructive free-riding. In their classic biological treatment, *The Major Transitions in Evolution*, John Maynard Smith and Eors Szathmary argue that solutions to just such problems of benefit capture and sharing underlie several of the significant changes of efficiency and scale that punctuate the path from primordial chemistry of early life to the complex biology and social structures of modern humanity.[6] Entrepreneurial collaboration can be viewed as a powerful next step in this story of transitions.

Game theory provides insights into many of these challenges (e.g. Gintis 2000).[7] The subdiscipline of mechanism design has as its project the creation of institutional mechanisms that match sacrifice and reward with enough reliability to enable collaboration to

---

[6] John Maynard Smith, and Eors Szathmary, *The Major Transitions in Evolution* (Oxford: Oxford University Press, 1995).

[7] Herbert Gintis, *Game Theory Evolving* (Princeton, NJ: Princeton University Press, 2000).

occur, particularly in the sphere of information disclosure (e.g. Parkes 2001; Goodenough 2008).[8] At the level of real-world application, we might call the process of redenominating the entrepreneurial game-form so as to provide good expectations for the players "institutional design." The rule of law enables many of the best solutions to the challenges of institutional design.

Law—particularly property law—starts by providing a bulwark against the expropriation of the benefit by those outside the team. Whether sneak thieves, protection artists, imitative competitors, or the law giver itself, there are many players who will happily take slices of the gains away from the team. Physical and intellectual property regimes can protect against these external predators, and property rights are widely recognized as an important predicate to growth (e.g. de Soto 2000; Baumol et al. 2007).[9] But what about the team itself? How are its players given assurance of future participation and reward among themselves as the entrepreneurial enterprise goes forward? Contracts play an important role, particularly if the contribution is limited in scope and the reward is relatively well defined.

When the contributions to the team and the expectations of reward are more open-ended, however, then the relationship is not easy to define in a one-off contract. The incompleteness of the contract with respect to specific outcomes can be managed by conceptualizing the arrangement as joint ownership of the project with other major, ongoing contributors, a more loosely defined arrangement through which the contingent flows of success and failure can be accounted and allocated. In the U.S. context, such approaches are structured through the law of business organizations. This area of law takes pieces from property,

---

[8] David C. Parkes, *Iterative Combinatorial Auctions: Achieving Economic and Computational Efficiency.* (PhD diss., University of Pennsylvania, 2001), accessed November 15, 2010, http://www.eecs.harvard.edu/~parkes/diss.html; Oliver R. Goodenough, "Values, Mechanism Design, and Fairness," in *Moral Markets: The Critical Role of Values in the Economy,* ed. Paul J. Zak (Princeton, NJ: Princeton University Press, 2008), 228-255.

[9] Hernando de Soto, *The Mystery of Capital: Why Capitalism Triumphs in the West and Fails Everywhere Else* (New York: Basic Books, 2000); Baumol et al., *Good Capitalism, Bad Capitalism.*

contract, fiduciary duties, even government, and while there have been determined efforts by some to restate it all in one or another of these categories, it is also worth thinking of the law of the firm as a separate category.

Part of the genius of business organization law, as it has evolved in most developed economies, is the way it provides solutions to a whole range of the dilemmas faced in a free-market, entrepreneurial economy. One set of much-studied attributes cluster around the relations of the firm, its assets, and its members to the outside world, and in particular around questions of legal personhood, limited liability, asset sequestration, and entity shielding (e.g., Hansmann et al. 2006).[10] Another cluster looks at the relations among firm participants, and in particular questions of governance in larger firms with widespread public participation (e.g., Anabtawi and Stout 2008).[11] A third cluster focuses on the increasing "contractualization" of business entity forms, in which there is a move from standardized legal requirements in governance rules to a world of permissive default settings with a wide range of acceptable variation established by contract among the participants (e.g. Hansmann et al. 2005; Hansmann and Kraakman 2010; but see Hansmann 2006).[12] Each of these identifies important issues, which affect firm governance and growth at various points over the life cycle of the business.

At the point of formation, establishing rights and duties among the team becomes particularly salient. We need to create reliable structures within which the collaborations of innovation and

---

[10] Henry Hansmann, Reinier Kraakman, and Richard Squire, "Law and the Rise of the Firm," *Harvard Law Review* 119, no. 5 (2006): 1333-1403.

[11] Iman Anabtawi and Lynn A. Stout, "Fiduciary Duties for Activist Shareholders," *Stanford Law Review* 60, no. 5 (2008): 1255-1308.

[12] Henry Hansmann, "The New Business Entities in Evolutionary Perspective." *University of Illinois Law Review*, 2005, no. 1 (2005): 5-14; Henry Hansmann and Reinier Kraakman, "The Contractualization of Organizational Law," in *Festschrift für Klaus J. Hopt zum 70. Geburtstag am 24. August 2010 Unternehmen, Markt und Verantwortung*, edited by Stefan Grundmann et al. (Berlin: De Gruyter, 2010), 747–764; Hansmann, "Corporation and Contract," *American Law and Economics Review* 8, no. 1 (2006): 1-19.

entrepreneurship can take place, structures that will motivate not just correct treatment but enthusiastic striving toward the common goal. In designing such structures, biology suggests that outcome interdependency plays an important role. Early in the development of terrestrial life, the loosely tied grouping of mutually beneficial catalytic chemistry called the "hypercycle" changed to a powerhouse of cooperative interaction and evolution called the "cell" once it was wrapped in a membrane. The membrane boundary contained the benefits of the interaction of the constituent parts and linked their outcome, for good or ill, in a mutual fate.[13] Tying people, and their outcomes, together in the legal structure of a firm has this same potential for driving productive collaboration.

By facilitating a made-for-the-purpose team to create new ideas and bring them to market, it is no surprise that the ability to form a legally grounded business organization is a key factor in promoting innovative growth. The development of successful, growth-oriented capitalism is at least partly a story of the development of better private business institutions within which firms can be structured. In the United States, we often take a well-developed business organization law for granted. But its significance was better recognized when the developments were new. In 1911, Nicholas Murray Butler, then president of Columbia University, gave a frequently quoted description of the importance of business organization law for growth:

> I weigh my words when I say that in my judgment the limited liability corporation is the greatest single discovery of modern times.... Even steam and electricity are far less important than the limited liability corporation, and they would be reduced to comparative impotence without it.[14]

---

[13] Smith and Szathmary, *The Major Transitions in Evolution.*

[14] Nicholas Murray Butler, "Address at the 143rd Annual Banquet of the Chamber of Commerce of the State of New York, November 16, 1911." Quoted in William Meade Fletcher, *Cyclopedia of the Law of Private Corporations* 1, s. 21 (Chicago: Callaghan and Company, 1917), 43.

The history of business organization law has been marked by several steps that have made formation easier and the resulting entity better tailored to the needs of entrepreneurial startups. In the nineteenth century, for instance, general incorporation laws, which require a simple filing to create a company, replaced the expensive and time-consuming requirement of a specific legislative act for the grant of a corporate charter. More recently, close corporation statutes, better partnership laws, and the development of the LLC (limited liability company) and the LLP (limited liability partnership) have extended the contractualization approach, mentioned above, so that by the late twentieth century the design of relations between participants in a firm was nearly wide open, at least as a matter of business organization law, and "private corporate law" became a possibility.[15] Each of these developments has coincided with burst of entrepreneurial activity.

But that old villain, "red tape," is still lurking here in the legal weeds. Whether in the area of firm formation or elsewhere, access to legal processes and assurances can be expensive and time-consuming. This is true both for large, established businesses and for shallow-pocketed graduate students with a killer idea. Part of the solution is the digitization of law.[16] Developments in software, the Internet, cloud computing, and mobile devices are revolutionizing many domains of commercial life, from production to sales, causing a cascade of disruptive progress. This cascade is beginning to affect the creation and operation of institutions in the financial and business worlds. We are at the early stages of an institutional change that has the potential to be equally empowering for innovative business: digital business laws that permit the formation and operation of "virtual companies." While the process is in some ways inevitable, we can improve the outcomes

[15] Gillian K. Hadfield and Eric Talley, "On Public versus Private Provision of Corporate Law," *Journal of Law, Economics and Organization* 22, no. 2 (2006): 414-441.

[16] Richard Susskind, *The End of Lawyers? Rethinking the Nature of Legal Services* (Oxford: Oxford University Press, 2008); Brock Rutter and Oliver Goodenough, "Digital Lawyering in the Law School Curriculum," (paper, in preparation, 2010).

and bring them forward in time by taking four action steps as a society.

ACTION STEP 1: RECOGNIZING THE POTENTIAL FOR DIGITIZED LEGAL ACCESS

Computing, the Internet, and related digital technologies are changing how we conduct our lives, and doing so at a rapidly increasing rate. Digital communication, via the Internet, cell phone text messaging, and other emerging technologies, is reshaping many aspects of life. In a few short years, the relatively simple medium of e-mail has become the primary avenue for text-based communication—a position already under challenge from texting on cell phones and other mobile devices and exchanges posted within Facebook.com or other sites of shared social contact.

Digital processes are making many economic activities cheaper and easier as well. In the commercial world, transactions as diverse as purchasing books, energy trading, and selling the contents of one's garage are safely and routinely handled via the web. Internet banking allows digital control over transactions with a high need for security—and it all works remarkably well. This revolution ranks with steam power, telegraph and telephone, rail transport, electricity, and the handful of other complete "game changers" in economic history.

Law is beginning to feel the winds of change. Many aspects of legal services will be affected—including the delivery of previously "bespoke" services in cheaper, and more democratically available, online forms.[17] Businesses like LegalZoom.com and MyCorporation.com have already sprung up, offering inexpensive—even free—chartering of corporations and LLCs via an Internet interface. The banner on MyCorporation.com reads

---

[17] Susskind, *The End of Lawyers?*; see generally Gillian K. Hadfield, "Law for a Flat World: Legal Infrastructure and the New Economy," (paper, 2010) in *The Selected Works of Gillian K Hadfield*, http://works.bepress.com/ghadfield/35, accessed November 15, 2010.

"entrepreneurs welcome," and so they are. But the end product of these twenty-first century marketing efforts is still a nineteenth century artifact—a paper-based corporate charter, in a paper-based minute book, with paper-based bylaws and operating agreements. These sites are nowhere near to capturing the full potential of digitization for enabling firm formation and operation. In a sense, MyCorporation.com, like e-mail, is already old news. We are on the edge of the next big step: fully digitized business organizations.

ACTION STEP 2: CHANGES TO LAWS AND REGULATIONS

In order for digital business organizations to come about, certain legal groundwork must first be laid. Under U.S. law, business organizations with limited liability and legal personification must receive a government charter of some kind and must fit within a set of enabling rules, typically granted under state law. While these rules have become increasingly flexible in recent years, most still contemplate a world of paper and in-person interaction, supplemented by the postal service, telephone, and fax. Changes in state law are then first steps in creating the necessary legal landscape for digital firm formation and operation.

The default context for deliberative actions by shareholders, boards of directors, and formal committees is a meeting, with due notice given and the opportunity for participation by all (e.g., for directors, Model Business Corporation Act § 8.20 and 8.22; Delaware General Corporation Law §141). Relaxing this model somewhat, most, and perhaps all, states allow attendance by telephone conference call (e.g., for directors, Model Business Corporation Act § 8.20(b); Delaware General Corporation Law §141 (i)). Most also offer the possibility of an action in writing in lieu of a meeting, although most require physical signatures and unanimity, at least for directors (e.g., Model Business Corporation Act § 8.21; Delaware General Corporation Law §141 (f)). Some, like Delaware, now authorize consent to be given to this kind of action through electronic transmission, and permit keeping board minutes in digital form (Delaware General Corporation Law §141 (f)).

On the formation step, some states have already gone beyond LegalZoom and MyCorporation.com. Rather than working through such an intermediary, these states allow the direct online formation of a corporation or limited liability company, using the government website to fill out the forms and charging the filing fees by credit card (e.g. Florida at https://efile.sunbiz.org/onl-menu.html). This relaxation is useful, but it is just the beginning. The full payoffs of convenience and new possibilities grow from allowing all of the formal, legally mandated relations among owners, managers, and their agents to be conducted through digital means as well. For instance, the text-based rules set out in bylaws can just as easily be set out in a computer program that would direct notices, host meetings, count votes, and authorize transactions with banks and other financial depositories. In addition to meetings held in person, via phone, or through written action, allowed by traditional corporate law, the statutes should be modified to expressly authorize meeting management software that would create a kind of super chat room through which corporate directors and LLC managers could discuss issues and arrive at decisions, all managed by the agreed bylaw software. What these steps need is statutory authorization.

In 2008, Vermont passed the first law explicitly designed to foster the development of fully digitized business organizations. The law established the opportunity for businesses to fully integrate their legal structure with the opportunities of the Internet and other forms of digital communication. The bill (H.888) containing these changes, as passed by into law, is available in full at: http://www.leg.state.vt.us/docs/legdoc.cfm?URL=/docs/2008/acts/ACT190.HTM.

The Vermont law aimed at three basic steps—steps that should be part of any enabling legislation in other jurisdictions looking to authorize digital business organizations. As a first step, it authorized a fully digital formation process for corporations and LLCs.

As mentioned above, Vermont is not alone in this—other states have authorized this as well, and LegalZoom and MyCorporation provide a mediated interface that gives the equivalent experience for the others. It is nonetheless a necessary part of the full package. (Ironically, implementation in the Vermont secretary of state's office has lagged a bit, and intermediation is, for the moment, still a useful resource.) The second step is the authorization of a wide range of digital communication as ways in which the formal actions of the corporation or LLC may be taken. While other states, such as Delaware, have made steps in this direction, the Vermont law broke new ground in the scope of its authorization. The final step is the authorization to use software as the original means for setting out the agreements and bylaws that govern the actions of the members and managers of LLCs and of the officers, shareholders, and directors of corporations.

This last authorization has two important effects. First, when coupled with the other steps, it means that the formalities associated with running a company can be completely migrated to a digital environment, thus allowing the formation of companies where digital communication is the only medium of interaction for its participants. Second, it allows the execution of the formalities to be fully integrated with the software that describes them. A single software package can describe the procedures for governing contributions, distributions, and voting, can supervise its implementation, and can keep a record of the process and its results.

Thanks to Vermont, the legal platform for digital corporations and LLCs has been established—and in 2010 Vermont added nonprofit corporations to the list as well. Other jurisdictions are likely to follow suit in due course.

In addition to these enabling statutes, there are constraints under other applicable laws, such as the securities regulations (e.g., Bradley 2007).[18] While small digital companies, with only a few

---

[18] Caroline Bradley, "Gaming the System: Virtual Worlds and the Securities Markets" (paper, 2007), accessed November 15, 2010, http://papers.ssrn.com/sol3/papers.cfm?abstract_id=1022441 and http://works.bepress.com/cgi/viewcontent.cgi?article=1000&context=caroline_bradley.

directly involved participants, are likely to fall easily into traditional SEC exemptions for active owners and private offerings (e.g. Regulation D under the Securities Act of 1933), realizing the full potential when the new forms involve many players may require rule changes. And some developments will challenge the very assumptions of existing regulation. Consider, for instance, the digital or algorithmic security, where the master description of the rights of sharing, voting, and other characteristics of equity participation are denominated and indeed calculated entirely through an algorithm embedded solely in software. Such a beast is possible under the new Vermont laws; as examples emerge, our regulatory structures will need to change to accommodate their characteristics.

ACTION STEP 3: DEVELOPING THE PLATFORM FOR DIGITAL ENTERPRISE

Law changes may permit digital firms, but they don't bring them into being. The other necessary ingredient for making virtual companies a real possibility is a technical platform that can allow the migration of a company's institutional rules and formal interactions into the digital domain. What is a "platform"? This much-used word can refer to (1) a type of processor and/or other hardware, (2) software with a wide range of applicability such as an operating system, or (3) the combination of hardware and software creating the potential for an expansive set of uses. (e.g. http://www.linfo.org/platform.html). The iPhone is usefully described as a platform, combing hardware and applications. The web itself can be considered a platform, as can sub-universes within the web such as Facebook.com. In the digital firm context, we are looking at an example of a digitized governance platform,[19] a technical combination tailored specifically to the institutional needs of business collaboration.

---

[19] See John H. Clippinger, "Digital Innovation in Governance: New Rules for Sharing and Protecting Private Information," this volume, chapter 16.

There are several design approaches that can be taken in building a platform for automating the formation and formalities of a business organization. These range from (1) a fully contained, "cradle to grave" software package that completely automates the formalities of forming, running, and winding up a targeted form of business organization through (2) purpose-designed software that performs only part of the process, such as a digital minute book, and on to (3) an assembly of "off the shelf" components from tool kits like Google Wave that performs some or all of the necessary tasks.

Developing a model "cradle to grave" package for a simple LLC under the Vermont statute has been a project at Harvard's Law Lab, where I am a codirector. A description of our process can provide guidance to others embarking on a similar project. The first step involved establishing goals for the scope, flexibility, and universality of the platform. Going straight for the development of a fully flexible, general-purpose governance platform was a possibility. Such a structure would require the modeling and programming of a significant number of processes and requirements that are common to business organizations generally. The Law Lab list includes such features as robust identity measures, contribution metrics, reputation systems, benefit assignment rules, work and information communication channels, decision-making algorithms, exclusivity and loyalty provisions, and transfer and expulsion rules.[20] Developing a platform that would permit "dial setting" flexibility across these many domains was initially attractive; it remains a targeted goal for the Law Lab and will be an important step in the enabling some of the more "exotic" entrepreneurial venture possibilities discussed below.

On reflection, however, a more narrow focus was chosen for the first effort, targeting the typical small founder group as the first use case. If the software was to be truly aimed at requiring little, if any, lawyer intervention as clients put it to use, it needed to be designed around widely applicable default approaches, rather

---

[20] Ibid.

than heavily tailorable flexibility. Thus, the initial platform becomes a web-based application that instantiates rules for a start-up LLC aimed at a small group of founding members, all of them active in the business. While flexibility is preserved on contributions and profit sharing, we made the decision to mandate unanimity as the basis for most decision making. In small, cooperative groups, unanimity provides protection against oppression by a majority and allows full psychological buy in.

The platform involves a purpose-built software package, allowing a high degree of control over the result and greater protection against malicious interference as it gets rolled out for commercial application in a sponsored environment. At this writing, our fully developed prototype is available for demonstration at digitalllc.org. The first phase of its commercial rollout is in active development. It will be a "white label" service, available for offer in a customized version by such interested companies as law firms, banks, and other service providers to start-up companies.

A less ambitious step is the purpose-built creation of tools for parts of the digital company's activities. Managing and keeping a record of meetings and other decision-making forums is a source of annoyance in almost all companies, and a source of low-quality work for lawyers cast in the role of corporate secretaries. Internet-savvy groups such as the World Wide Web Consortium (W3C) are creating their own solutions to these problems, and a commercial version is likely to emerge soon.

An alternative on the other end of the spectrum from the purpose-built approach is to make use of off-the-shelf functionalities developed by others. The emerging world of social interaction tools, such as Google Wave, has elements that can be incorporated into an institutional governance platform. Google tells you that, "A wave is a live, shared space on the web where people can discuss and work together using richly formatted text, photos, videos, maps, and more." Tools include voting possibilities—many of the elements are there, but not yet the whole package.

The development and proliferation of law-related software solutions like these will be accelerated by the establishment of an "app store" for legal software. As inventors and collaborative groups find their own solutions, an established marketplace for their advertisement and sale will help move the best of them from a local convenience to an industry changer. Such an app store would, of course, have an impact on the development of digitized legal services across a wide range of domains.

ACTION STEP 4: EDUCATING LAWYERS AND CLIENTS INTO A NEW MODE OF INTERACTION

Our final recommended action step grows out of a question with Shakespearian overtones: where will this leave all the lawyers? Why kill them all, as Dick the Butcher advocates in *Henry VI, Part 2*, when making them irrelevant, as Richard Susskind predicts in *The End of Lawyers*, will work just as well? As a professional teacher of lawyers, I do not think we are really at the end of lawyers in the formation process, but I do think we are likely to see the lawyer role redefined, and educating lawyers and clients into new, less dependent and less expensive modes of interaction is the final action step on our list.

What will lawyers do to help digitized firm formation? At the consultative level, the web will offer opportunities for quick and relatively inexpensive contact with lawyers who will help entrepreneurs to understand and customize largely prepackaged approaches. Phone calls and e-mails to "technical assistance" are part of the landscape for implementing all kinds of largely do-it-yourself computer applications, and legal-access applications for firm formation will be no exception. Financial yields per consultation may not be what most lawyers are used to in the current paradigm of customized service, but volume and the dependability of credit-card payment systems can provide a living wage.

There will also be a role for designers in this process: "knowledge engineers," who will set the initial templates, and develop standard forms around which entrepreneurial expectations can coalesce. Conceptualizing rules and approaches for legal service platforms is an expert task, and Susskind predicts that such designers will occupy a small but lucrative niche. Much as standardized creative commons licenses have streamlined certain kinds of deal making in the high-tech realm, so too will standard terms be developed and applied for digital business organizations, with the help of lawyers expert in both institutional design and computer programming.

Educating lawyers for these new relationships will require significant shifts in the curriculum at law schools and in continuing legal education to include these new skill sets. Developing such approaches for training good practitioners for both the design and helping stages will accelerate the realization by society of the gains from digital firm formation and other digital delivery of legal information and services. Courses such as Vermont Law School's "Digital Drafting" offer training at both of these levels of practice.[21]

The other side of the coin is educating entrepreneurs to be savvier about the choices they face in setting up companies. Classes on "Law for Entrepreneurs" too frequently focus on the impediments that law can pose for following up on business opportunities. Training in the institutional design principles that law helps make possible and in the software that will increasingly be available for their implementation should be a part of entrepreneurial studies everywhere. An early example of the approach can be seen in "Law, Technology, and Entrepreneurship," offered in the curriculum of Dartmouth's Thayer School of Engineering, as part of their Master of Engineering Management program. Its catalog description reads:

> Taking a good idea and turning it into a successful product and a profitable business poses a number of

---

[21] See http://www.vermontlaw.edu/x303.xml?faculty=x6606&category; see generally Brock and Goodenough, "Digital Lawyering in the Law School Curriculum."

technical, managerial, and financial challenges. The solutions to many of the challenges of entrepreneurship in general, and to those of starting up a technologically based business in particular, are provided by the law. A grounding in the law of intellectual property, contractual transactions, business structures, debt and equity finance, and securities regulation, both in the U.S. and in an international context, will help inventors and entrepreneurs to manage this part of the process intelligently and with a high likelihood of success.[22]

Providing clients with both the tools and the knowledge to take firm formation largely into their own hands, coupled with providing lawyers with the skills to design good platforms and to deliver short, targeted advice on specific concerns, will help maximize the benefits from digital firm formation both for the individuals directly involved and for the economy as a whole.

THE FINALE: OPPORTUNITIES FOR A NEW "CAMBRIAN EXPLOSION"

So just what *are* the benefits for entrepreneurship and growth that can be unleashed by digitizing firm creation and management? First of all, there is the simple goal described by Baumol et al. of making firm creation and management "easy and inexpensive to do."[23] Putting standard approaches onto the web, for little or no cost, is as good a way to accomplish this goal as we know about in 2010. But making traditional startups easier is only the starting point.

If the collaborative mashup of ideas and talents among a group of people is a frequently recurring pattern for entrepreneurial innovation, then migrating the process to the digital world can open up an exponentially larger set of innovative possibilities. As the

---

[22] "Graduate Course Descriptions," Thayer School of Engineering at Dartmouth, accessed November 15, 2010, http://engineering.dartmouth.edu/graduate/courses/details.html#ENGM188.

[23] Baumol et al., *Good Capitalism, Bad Capitalism.*

spread of "Web 2.0"-style social media amply demonstrates, physical proximity is no longer a requirement for frequent and even intensive interaction among people. The entrepreneurial stewpot can now easily include players from around the world, only interacting through the web; the institutional framework that gives them the outcome assurance they need to make commitments to each other needs to be equally web-based. Proximity has often been credited as part of the success story of Silicon Valley; digital means make virtual proximity a trivial matter.

Furthermore, making digital business organizations available via the web and via mobile devices more generally has the potential to deliver good institutions to parts of the world where they are sorely lacking. Paul Romer has argued that "charter cities" can help to create islands (perhaps literally) of good institutions—and particularly good legal institutions—in countries and regions where they are in short supply (www.chartercities.org). This good idea has so far run into practical roadblocks. The bad institutions often help enrich exactly the corrupt governing class that would have to agree to the establishment of the charter cities. It will be much easier to end-run the governing class and build these charter cities not in sovereign territory but in the digital "cloud." Institutions delivered through "cloud law" can be beneficial both in their own right and as goads to the development of better institutions in subpar physical jurisdictions.

Yet another benefit is in the kinds of collaborative initiatives that can be supported. David Johnson and Yochai Benkler have each argued that web-based peer production and other networks of cooperation can provide new avenues for innovation and growth.[24] Wikipedia, while nonprofit, is just the most noted example of this kind of new value creation. Digital institutions provide the only practical means for structuring an organization that would include a widely disbursed, web-communicating

---

[24] David R. Johnson, "Virtual Companies" (paper, 2008), accessed November 15, 2010, http://dotank.nyls.edu/june18virtualcorp.html; Benkler, Yochai. *The Wealth of Networks* (New Haven, CT: Yale University Press, 2006).

group of contributors. Nor is communication the only challenge. Complex problems of contribution assessment and benefit allocation can also be better solved algorithmically in a digital world than through word-based formulas and paper based agreements.

Coming full circle back to more traditional forms for startups, such digitized participation formulas also have the potential to improve the fairness—and performance—of small group innovative companies. Setting start-up participations among founders by bright-line fractions or other nearly arbitrary means when shares in a business are first allocated invites defection, slacking, resentment, and disputes as the work goes forward. An algorithmic ownership definition, incorporating a digitized adjustment process agreed to in advance and built into the code, can help to hold everyone to their promises and to reward actual contributions to the common cause, promoting both fairness and efficiency at the same time.[25]

While the focus of this chapter is on solutions to the challenges of participants in dealing with each other, digital organizations will offer innovative solutions to challenges businesses encounter in facing the outer world as well. For instance, even small digital firms will have expanded options in raising capital. Digital management of the sale and transfer of participant interests creates the possibility of continuous equity markets in small company equity and debt, providing improved liquidity and removing some of the blocking power of a single important investor, such as a venture capital firm, a power that allows it to extract potentially "unfair" concessions from founders in subsequent funding rounds.

---

[25] Clippinger, "Digital Innovation in Governance"; Gavin Clarkson and Marshall W. Van Alstyne, "The Social Efficiency of Fairness" (paper, 2009), accessed November 15, 2010, http://papers. ssrn.com/sol3/papers.cfm?abstract_id=1514137.

CONCLUSION

New laws in jurisdictions like Vermont are providing a legal basis for fully digitizing firm formation. And with the spread of software that can exploit these developments, one of the key elements of innovative growth will get significantly cheaper and easier. Looking a little further into the future, we can envision that "cloud law" will make good innovation-building institutions widely available for traditional startups, and that the power, reach, and scalability of digital interactions will enable entirely new combinations of people, ideas, and capital—with the potential to unleash new possibilities for innovation and growth. While movement in this direction is in some ways inevitable, with thought and intentional action we can create a better future faster, with concomitant benefits flowing in the United States and beyond.

If we get it right, soon, when a group of innovative entrepreneurs meet up in some virtual social-networking café, one of them can suggest something like: "Let's structure it on a Vermont equal-start model, adjustable based on earn-in algorithm B, with standard Google Wave majority voting. I'll tweak the software and send you the link for the company." The velocity of innovation and growth will have increased as a result.

15: Can the Patent Office Be Fixed?[*]

Mark A. Lemley[**]

THE PROBLEM OF BAD PATENTS

The Patent and Trademark Office (PTO) finds itself caught in a vise. On the one hand, it has been issuing a large number of dubious patents over the past twenty years, particularly in the software and electronic commerce space. It issues many more patents than its counterparts in Europe and Japan;[1] roughly three-fourths of applicants ultimately get one or more patents, a higher percentage than in other countries.[2] Complaints about those bad patents are legion,[3] and indeed when they make it to litigation they are quite often held invalid.[4] Even the ones

---

[*] © 2010 Mark A. Lemley.

[**] Mark A. Lemley is the William H. Neukom Professor, Stanford Law School, and partner, Durie Tangri LLP. Thanks to Rose Hagan and Stu Soffer for comments.

[1] Bruno Van Pottelsberghe de la Potterie, "The Quality Factor in Patent Systems" (working paper 2010-027, European Center for Advanced Research in Economics and Statistics, 2010).

[2] Mark A. Lemley and Bhaven Sampat, "Is the Patent Office a Rubber Stamp?" *Emory Law Review* 58 (2008): 181.

[3] Adam Jaffe and Josh Lerner, *Innovation and Its Discontents* (Princeton, NJ: Princeton University Press, 2004).

that turn out to be valid are often impossible to understand; in the information technology industries, there is no lawsuit filed in which the parties don't fight over the meaning of patent claim terms.[5] The natural reaction is to say that the PTO needs to do more than it does to make sure it is awarding patents only to those who deserve them.

On the other hand, it is not clear that we can or should weed out bad applications at the PTO. The vast majority of patents are never litigated or licensed; spending a lot of money to ensure their validity would be wasted.[6] And the structure of the patent prosecution process makes it very difficult for the PTO to do so. Patent examiners can never finally reject a patent application; applicants dissatisfied with the outcome can come back an unlimited number of times to try again through various mechanisms.[7] Efforts beginning in 2006 to change that rule upset patent lawyers a great deal, and were ultimately abandoned.[8] And because of the inability of the PTO to finally reject applications, when the PTO started making it harder to get patents several years ago, the result was to create an enormous backlog of patent applications as examiners would reject applications and applicants would try again (and again, and again) to get a patent. That backlog in turn created its own set of problems, delaying the issuance of good patents and reducing certainty for both applicants and third parties.

Some have suggested that those delays—and the use of continuation applications more generally—are the result of oddities in

---

[4] John R. Allison and Mark A. Lemley, "Empirical Evidence on the Validity of Litigated Patents," *AIPLA Quarterly Journal* 26 (1998): 185; John R. Allison et al., "Patent Quality and Settlement Among Repeat Patent Litigants," *Georgetown Law Journal* (forthcoming 2010).

[5] James Bessen and Michael Meurer, *Patent Failure: How Judges, Bureaucrats and Lawyers Put Innovation at Risk* (Princeton, NJ: Princeton University Press, 2008).

[6] Mark A. Lemley, "Rational Ignorance at the Patent Office," *Northwestern University Law Review* 95, no. 4 (2001).

[7] Mark A. Lemley and Kimberly A. Moore, "Ending Abuse of Patent Continuations," *Boston University Law Review* 84 (2004): 63.

[8] *Tafas v. Kappos*, 586 F.3d 1369 (Fed. Cir. 2009).

the system for evaluating and rewarding patent examiners. The so-called "count" system gave credit to examiners for certain acts; patent lawyers often complain that examiners "make" them file continuations in order to boost their counts. Whether or not that was true, however, it doesn't appear to be behind the growth of continuation applications. The PTO changed the count system in 2009 to try to address this problem. And it has been issuing record numbers of patents in recent months. But preliminary data from Dennis Crouch suggests that the number of continuation applications is still on the rise, up 27 percent from 2009 to 2010,[9] suggesting that the use of continuations is largely applicant rather than examiner driven.

The evaluation of patent applications in the PTO is further complicated by recent empirical evidence. One recent study shows that junior patent examiners are a lot more zealous in weeding out bad patents than senior examiners. The longer examiners spend in the PTO, the less searching they do, the more likely they are to grant patents, and the more likely they are to grant patents on applications that their counterparts in other countries have rejected.[10] A second study shows that whether senior or junior, examiners pay attention almost exclusively to prior art that they find themselves, and not to information submitted by patent applicants, even applicants who are passing on art found by patent examiners in other countries.[11] The implication of this evidence is that we need to pay attention not only to legal rules, but also to examiner behavior and reward systems.

---

[9] Dennis Crouch, "Requests for Continued Examination Continue to Rise," *Patently-O*, http://www.patentlyo.com/patent/2010/07/requests-for-continued-examination-continue-to-rise.html (2010).

[10] Mark A. Lemley and Bhaven Sampat, "Examiner Characteristics and Patent Office Outcomes," (working paper 2010).

[11] Christopher A. Cotropia et al., "Do Applicant Patent Citations Matter? Implications for the Presumption of Validity" (working paper, 2010).

CAN THE PROBLEM BE SOLVED?

How, then, can we fix the PTO, allowing examiners to effectively distinguish between patentable and unpatentable inventions, without slowing the process to a crawl or wasting a bunch of money?

What Won't Work

First, some things that likely won't work.

Preventing fee diversion. The PTO is funded through user fees imposed on applicants and owners of issued patents. For much of the last twenty years, some of that fee revenue (typically 10-20 percent of it) has been diverted by Congress to general federal revenue. It is a commonplace among patent lawyers that the way to solve the PTO's problems is to stop fee diversion, "fully funding" the PTO.

Stopping fee diversion is certainly a good idea. Whatever the merits of government user fees over taxes as a general matter, it seems particularly foolish social policy to tax innovators in particular to raise general revenue. But stopping fee diversion is hardly a panacea. In the last several years, the PTO has been fully funded—that is, Congress didn't divert fees. Nonetheless, the backlog grew. The addition of 10 to 20 percent of operating revenue wasn't enough even to enable the PTO to hold steady.

Fee-setting authority. In recent years the PTO's efforts have shifted to seeking permission from Congress to set their own fees.[12] This would allow the PTO to (presumably) raise fees on applicants and patentees, using the money to pay for a more intensive examination. There is some reason to believe that fee-setting authority, if nothing else, may result from the six-year patent reform effort in Congress.[13]

---

[12] Arti K. Rai, "Growing Pains in the Administrative State: The Patent Office's Troubled Quest For Managerial Control," *University of Pennsylvania Law Review* 157 (2009): 2051.

Giving the PTO the authority to set its own fees might or might not be a good idea, depending on the relative incentives the PTO and Congress have to set fees rationally. But as noted above, it is likely not a good idea simply to spend more money to weed out bad patents. Most of that money will be wasted on applications that are of no consequence to anyone. And because of the structure of the examination system, it might not even succeed in weeding out bad patent applications.

Even if it did, however, the current fee structure makes patent quality self-limiting. The PTO is paid by applicants to process their applications at each stage. But those payments are not enough even to sustain the limited examination that now occurs. The difference is made up by patent "maintenance fees"—periodic payments made by the owners of issued patents to keep those patents in force. Because the PTO's ability to examine new applications is dependent on revenue from previously granted ones, the PTO faces a problem: the more bad applications it rejects, the fewer patents will pay maintenance fees, and the less money it will have to conduct a detailed examination. The PTO ran into this problem in the late 2000s, when—as a result of a lowered grant rate coupled with companies abandoning patents during the recession—it found itself in a financial crisis. The broader lesson should be clear: the current system for funding the PTO works only if the PTO continues to issue patents on a large percentage of the applications it receives.

The PTO might begin to address this problem by changing the way it collects fees. At one extreme, it could abandon maintenance fees altogether, and pay for enhanced examination through higher application fees. That solves the self-limiting problem, but

---

[13] The issue is bound up with the larger question of the role of the PTO as a full-fledged administrative agency with rulemaking authority. For discussion of that issue, see, e.g., Stuart Minor Benjamin and Arti K. Rai, "Fixing Innovation Policy: A Structural Perspective," *George Washington Law Review* 77 (2008): 1; John R. Thomas, "The Responsibility of the Rulemaker: Comparative Approaches to Patent Administration Reform," *Berkeley Technology Law Journal* 17 (2002): 727; Liza Vertinsky, "Comparing Alternative Institutional Paths to Patent Reform," *Alabama Law Review* 61 (2010): 501.

it raises the cost to startups seeking patents at an early stage of development, which may not be ideal. Alternatively, the PTO could simply raise the maintenance fees significantly, to perhaps ten times their current rate. Doing so might make the weeding out of bad patents revenue neutral, though as more bad applications are rejected the tax on those who actually obtained patents would have to increase further to compensate. And as the PTO raises its maintenance fees, fewer people will choose to maintain their patents. Depending on the elasticity of demand, paying for examination out of higher maintenance fees may or may not work.

Some have suggested raising maintenance fees for a different reason—to prevent patent lawsuits by trolls who buy up patents in order to enforce them. But that is unlikely to work. According to a 2009 American Intellectual Property Law Association (AIPLA) report, the median cost of taking a major patent case to trial is $5.5 million per side in attorney's fees.[14] A maintenance fee of $40,000-$50,000—ten times the current fee—may weed out more patents that aren't being used, but it is unlikely to deter someone considering spending perhaps 100 times that much to litigate a patent. And the patents that aren't being used aren't really the problem.[15]

Retaining patent examiners. Another problem commonly cited by patent lawyers is the high rate of turnover at the PTO. Being an examiner is not an easy job, and it doesn't pay all that well. Not surprisingly, examiners often leave relatively quickly for jobs in engineering, jobs in law firms, or to go to law school. Indeed, one recent study found the median examiner had been at the PTO for just over three years.[16] The high rate of turnover means that the PTO needs to hire more than 1,000 examiners a year just to keep even with attrition. In recent years the PTO has found it virtually

---

[14] American Intellectual Property Law Association, *2009 Report of Economic Activity.*

[15] Raising maintenance fees would weed out patents that sit on a shelf now but might be sold in the future to a troll that will assert them against product companies. In that limited sense it might reduce the number of troll lawsuits.

[16] Lemley and Sampat, "Examiner Characteristics and Patent Office Outcomes," 2010.

impossible to grow the examining corps. And of course those new examiners must be trained. Perhaps the solution to the PTO's problems, then, is to find ways to keep those examiners from leaving.

There may well be benefits to reducing examiner attrition. But the evidence suggests that weeding out bad patents is not among them. Empirical research by Lemley and Sampat shows that the longer examiners spend at the PTO, the less searching they do, the less likely they are to issue initial rejections or demand claim amendments, and the more likely they are to ultimately grant a patent.[17] It is the most junior examiners who are most likely to reject applications. The reason is not precisely clear, but may have to do with increased workloads on senior examiners, or with acculturation into a corps whose ethos is to grant rather than deny patents. Either way, keeping examiners around longer may hurt rather than help the cause of weeding out bad patents.

Outsourcing search. Reacting both to workload and to a sense that examiners don't find the most important prior art, a number of initiatives both within and outside the PTO have tried to relieve examiners of the burden of searching for prior art. They have variously proposed to require the applicants to do their own search for prior art,[18] to invite the public to review applications and submit prior art,[19] or to share the burden of searching with patent examiners in other countries. These initiatives seem promising because they outsource a function examiners don't seem particularly good at—finding the most relevant information on the ground—to others who are positioned to do it better.

But recent empirical evidence suggests that it might not work. Cotropia et al. studied the behavior of patent examiners in responding to applications, and found that they rely almost

---

[17] Ibid.

[18] There is currently no such requirement.

[19] Beth Simone Noveck, "'Peer to Patent': Collective Intelligence, Open Review, and Patent Reform," *Harvard Journal of Law and Technology* 20 (2006): 123.

exclusively on art they find for themselves, not art submitted by applicants. And that doesn't appear to reflect either applicants drafting around the art they found or the weakness of that art; U.S. examiners largely ignored even art that was submitted because it was found important by a foreign patent examiner during examination of a counterpart application.[20] If examiners are psychologically primed to rely principally on things they find for themselves, it won't help to have others provide them with the best art. And it might even hurt, causing examiners not to focus on the best prior art.

What Might Work

The problems with the PTO are deep rooted. Increased funding won't solve the problem of bad patents, and a variety of other commonly suggested fixes for the PTO are unlikely to solve the problem, and indeed could even make it worse.

Other proposals have a greater chance of addressing the problem of bad patents, though they come with their own uncertainties.

Second pair of eyes. Shortly after the Federal Circuit held business methods patentable in 1998, the PTO was inundated with business method patent applications. Most of those applications went to Class 705, which refers to the collection of patent examiners who focus on business methods. Indeed, by 2001, Class 705 had the largest application volume. In response to this flood, the PTO initiated a specific "quality control" measure in this class in March 2000: the "second pair of eyes" review (SPER), under which applications are subjected to mandatory assessment by more than one examiner before being allowed.[21] Requiring two examiners to agree seems to have had a dramatic effect: a 2009 study found that class 705 has the lowest grant rate among high volume classes.[22] One possible explanation for the low grant rate

---

[20] Cotropia et al., "Do Applicant Patent Citations Matter?"

[21] John R. Allison and Starling D. Hunter, "On the Feasibility of Improving Patent Quality One Technology at a Time: The Case of Business Methods," *Berkeley Technology Law Journal* 21 (2006): 729.

in this class is that the second pair of eyes is working, and that the grant rate reflects better rigor during examinations, rather than application volume.

The fact that SPER leads to more rejections in Class 705 doesn't mean it is an unalloyed success, however. Allison and Hunter demonstrate that its adoption in Class 705 led applicants to try to characterize their business method patents in ways that got them out of Class 705. It is possible that the applications that were not so characterized were systematically weaker (or their lawyers systematically less skilled) than the ones that avoided Class 705. The differences Lemley and Sampat found were so striking, however—a 16.1 percent grant rate in Class 705, compared with 72 percent on average—that it seems unlikely this can explain the full difference.

Allison and Hunter's objection is significant. But it applies only to a class-specific use of SPER, and wouldn't condemn a broader application of the policy to all art units. Nonetheless, there are reasons to think carefully before expanding SPER to all patent applications. Doing so would roughly double the cost of patent prosecution across the board. It would also delay the prosecution process further; Class 705 applications are among the slowest to be processed. Further, at least as currently configured, SPER is asymmetric—it requires a second hurdle before allowing patents but not before rejecting applications.[23] As a result, it is likely to weed out bad patents, but also to catch some good ones within the net of rejected applications. Given the PTO's historic bias in the other direction, perhaps that is a risk worth taking, but it is still a social cost we should avoid if we can. If SPER or some other review process is to be adopted, it should apply evenhandedly to grants and rejections.

---

[22] Lemley and Sampat, "Is the Patent Office a Rubber Stamp?" 2008.

[23] There is a similar problem with the PTO's quality review mechanism, which reviews a random subset of grants. Examiners can be punished for mistaken grants if caught in the quality control process, but are not punished for mistaken rejections, which are never reviewed (Katznelson 2010). Effective October 1, 2010, the PTO changed its quality evaluation system to be more evenhanded.

Interestingly, the PTO recently shut down the SPER program in business methods. Too much success, it seems, carries its own risks.

Changing examiner incentives. Recent empirical evidence suggests that much of the problem with patent examination revolves around examiner incentives and human resource policies. Examiners do less well at policing bad patents the longer they stay at the PTO. The problem could be their distance from the technology, or a tenure effect, or their increased workload. In any case, changes in training, workload, or promotion rules could affect those incentives. Examiners pay attention to their own searches, and not prior art submitted by others. The problem could be overconfidence bias, or simply triage. Either way, human resource policies could be brought to bear, training examiners to search better, or giving them more time, or finding other ways to eliminate bias. And it seems obvious—though likely politically infeasible—that the rules should not treat allowances differently than rejections.[24]

These are good ideas, and they are worth exploring further. But implementation may be politically difficult. And some of the possible explanations point in different directions: should we give examiners more time to search, or less, for example?

Tiered review. The problem is not precisely that the Patent Office issues a large number of bad patents. Rather, it is that the Patent Office issues a small but worrisome number of economically significant bad patents and those patents enjoy a strong, but undeserved, presumption of validity.

Framed this way, the solution naturally follows: the Patent Office should focus its examination resources on important patents and pay little attention to the rest. But it is difficult for the government to know ahead of time which patents are likely to be important.

---

[24] Ron Katznelson, "Patent Examination Policy and the Social Costs of Examiner Allowance and Rejection Errors," *Stanford Technology Law Review* (2010).

There are two groups, however, that have better information about the likely technological and commercial value of inventions: patent applicants and competitors. To harness information in the hands of patent applicants, we could give applicants the option of earning a presumption of validity by paying for a thorough examination of their inventions. Put differently, applicants should be allowed to "gold plate" their patents by paying for the kind of searching review that would merit a presumption of validity.[25] An applicant who chooses not to pay could still get a patent. That patent, however, would be subject to serious— maybe even *de novo*—review in the event of litigation. Most likely, applicants would pay for serious review with respect to their most important patents but conserve resources on their more speculative entries.[26] That would allow the Patent Office to focus its resources, thus benefiting from the signal given by the applicant's own self-interested choice. The Obama campaign proposed this sort of tiered review, and the PTO has recently taken a step towards implementing a scaled-down version, in which applicants can choose the speed but not the intensity of review.[27]

Tiered review is only as good as the examination process that creates it, however, and if "gold-plated" patents are too easy to obtain, the point of the system will be lost. If they are too hard to obtain or too expensive, no one will use the system. Further, tiered review can at best be only a partial solution, because applicants do not always have accurate information about the future value of their applications. These are real objections, but they do not undermine the value of some sort of targeting in the use of PTO examination resources.

Oppositions and adversarial evaluations. Competitors also have useful information about which patents worry them and which do

---

[25] Mark A. Lemley et al., "What To Do About Bad Patents," *Regulation* Winter 2005-6 (2005): 10.

[26] For a more detailed working out of the tiered review proposal, see Douglas Lichtman and Mark A. Lemley, "Rethinking Patent Law's Presumption of Validity," *Stanford Law Review* 60 (2007): 45.

[27] Unfortunately, that proposal came with a bias against foreign applications that makes little sense as an economic matter, and may also render it suspect under U.S. treaty obligations.

not. A post-grant opposition system would seek to harness that information. Post-grant opposition is a process by which parties other than the applicant would have the opportunity to request and fund a thorough examination of a recently issued patent. A patent that survives collateral attack would earn a presumption of validity similar to the one available through tiered review. The core difference is that the post-grant opposition would be triggered by competitors—presumably competitors looking to invalidate a patent that threatens their industry.

Like tiered review, post-grant opposition is attractive because it harnesses private information; this time, information in the hands of competitors. It thus helps the Patent Office to identify patents that warrant serious review, and it also makes that review less expensive by creating a mechanism by which competitors can share critical information directly with the Patent Office.[28] A post-grant opposition system is part of proposed patent reform legislation, but at this writing it seems unlikely to pass.

The success of post-grant opposition depends on the willingness of third parties with good information about the validity of a patent to challenge that patent in a public forum, rather than settling privately. Some commentators are skeptical; pointing out that invalidating patents is a public good that the challenger would share with every other competitor.[29]

Patent law already has mechanisms that could be used to achieve the same goal. Some issued patents are returned to the PTO after issuance and are reevaluated through an adversarial process known as *inter partes* reexamination. This is an evaluation to which some deference is appropriate, though today the law gives complete deference to that determination. Even traditional *ex parte* reexamination, while not truly adversarial, allows the filer to

---

[28] Lemley et al., "What To Do About Bad Patents."

[29] Christopher A. Cotropia, "Modernizing Patent Law's Inequitable Conduct Doctrine," *Berkeley Technology Law Journal* 24 (2009): 723; Joseph Farrell and Robert P. Merges, "Incentives to Challenge and Defend Patents: Why Litigation Won't Reliably Fix Patent Office Errors and Why Administrative Patent Review Might Help," *Berkeley Technology Law Journal* 19 (2004): 943.

submit an initial explanation of the reasons for reexamination, and the result has been that in recent years patents fare worse in reexamination than applications do in initial examination.

The biggest risk with post-grant opposition and related systems is that we give challengers too many bites at the apple, allowing them to inundate patentees with an endless set of challenges. To solve that problem, it is appropriate to place some limits on the number and perhaps the timing of challenges, and to imbue patents that survive those challenges with a strong presumption of validity.

Living with Imperfection

The reform proposals identified in the last section are a start. They likely will improve the prosecution process and help to weed out bad patents, and most will do so at an acceptable cost. But none of them will solve the problem of bad patents, or even come especially close to doing so. Part of the process of patent reform must involve acknowledging the inherent imperfections in the patent examination process, and adapting to those imperfections.

In particular, we will continue to rely on litigation for the foreseeable future as a primary means for weeding out bad patents. That is as it should be. Litigation elicits information from both patentees and competitors through the adversarial process, which is far superior to even the best-intentioned government bureaucracy as a mechanism for finding truth.[30] More important, litigation is focused on the very few patents (1-2 percent) that turn out to be important and about which parties cannot agree in a business transaction.

Litigation can be abused, and examples of patent litigation abuse have been rampant in the last two decades. But a variety of reforms have started to bring that problem under control, and the courts have the means to continue that process.[31]

---

[30] Lichtman and Lemley, "Rethinking Patent Law's Presumption of Validity."

Part of the process must include a realistic recognition of the shortcomings of the patent prosecution system. In particular, courts should weaken the presumption of validity for issued patents. A presumption like that embraced by the current "clear and convincing" standard must be earned, and under current rules patent applicants do not earn it. We should replace that high hurdle with a more appropriate level of deference such as the "preponderance of the evidence" presumption currently given trademarks and copyrights, in recognition of the fact that the scrutiny given patents doesn't warrant more. And we should apply the presumption with some eye toward reality. The current presumption is so wooden that courts today assume a patent is valid even against evidence that the patent examiner never saw, much less considered, a rule that makes no sense.[32]

But the presumption of validity should be dynamic, not static. Improvements to the patent prosecution process might justify a stronger presumption. In particular, surviving more extensive scrutiny, whether by opting into tiered review, being subject to an opposition proceeding, or perhaps even getting approval from two examiners rather than one, should justify a stronger presumption. A dynamic presumption will allow the courts to play their proper role as the guardians of the public interest while encouraging applicants and the PTO to shoulder their burden as well.

---

[31] Dan L. Burk and Mark A. Lemley, *The Patent Crisis and How the Courts Can Solve It* (Chicago: University of Chicago Press, 2009).

[32] Lemley et al., "What To Do About Bad Patents," Lichtman and Lemley.

16: Digital Innovation in Governance: New Rules for Sharing and Protecting Private Information

John Henry Clippinger*

INTRODUCTION

et us begin with a prediction: Within the next five years, the movements, locations, communications, relationships, health status, behaviors, finances, interests, purchases, and civic status of more than two billion people will be monitored, captured, and analyzed on a daily basis. By 2014, 3.6 exabytes (one billion gigabytes) of data will be generated monthly on mobile networks alone.[1] This does not include the exabytes of data generated by wireline broadband networks and corporate and government networks or cloud computing consortia. The capture of data from multiple forms of surveillance—satellite, sensor networks, mobile networks, e-mail, voice, social networks, corporate networks, intelligence/security RFIP, GPS, video, data mining—will not just be pervasive, but essential for the functioning of networked public and private enterprises. With these trends, the Internet becomes not just a global infrastructure, but a

* John Henry Clippinger is Co-Director of The Law Lab, Berkman Center for Internet and Society at Harvard University.

[1] Stacey Higginbotham, *Cisco: The Mobilpocalypse Is Coming*, www.gigaom.com, February 9, 2010.

collection of many Internets, each with their own policies and practices for protecting and sharing private information.

The risk of Balkanization is clear and with it the undermining of those very principles of openness and interoperability that made the Internet such a global engine of innovation and productivity. Traditional notions of territorial sovereignty are now asserting themselves as countries and regions try to exercise control over digital resources and domestic freedoms in the name of the nation state. The mounting of the Great Firewall of China, for instance, is replaying an ancient reflex to have a wholly controlled and homogeneous—"harmonious"—Chinese Internet. Arab and Middle Eastern countries are following suit under the banner of protecting their cultural and religious values. In truth, all countries as well as companies are struggling to discover the boundaries of their autonomy and how to assert effective control over what they consider their legitimate resources. In both cases, they are coming up against unresolved issues about how to protect the privacy of their networks, users, and citizenry while providing the flexibility and freedoms needed to participate in a rapidly evolving and increasingly digital global economy.

The goal of this chapter is to propose new forms of governance and rule making that combine digital and physical means— frameworks, policies, contracts, and mechanisms—to enable the protection and sharing of private information. In Western societies, especially the United States and European Union countries, there are very strong provisions for the protection of the privacy of citizens and consumers. While the United States and the European Union have different legal standards and approaches for protecting, they both, nonetheless, have adopted an approach of prohibitions that limit the collection and transmission of certain kinds of personal identifying information without proper consent and oversight. In the European Union, there are prohibitions for the collection of certain types of data and its transfer across national borders—creating enormous obstacles and costs to global coordination and integration of financial and health care information. As digital globalization increases, it is not clear whether the harms of failed protections exceed those engendered by a lack of information sharing and flows. In short, the weaknesses of imposing a uniform privacy standard upon a rapidly changing field are becoming all too apparent. Even though such regulations can be written with the intent of anticipating future innovations and circumstances, they often fall short and impose costs and impediments without providing the intended benefits of protections and sharing.

Harms of Too Much and Too Little Privacy

Two of the most pervasive means for achieving privacy protections are explicit prohibitions against the uses of certain kinds of data, and the requirement of informed consent for opting in or out of a privacy policy. While such practices are pervasive and the cornerstones of most online privacy practices, they are not only ineffective, but they also can provide a false sense of privacy protection while in effect providing none in practice. In many cases, the *potential* harms that such notifications are intended to protect consumers or patients from are often not nearly as severe as the *actual* harms resulting from the failure to share critical health and consumer information.

A prime illustration of this point is the Health Insurance Portability Accountability Act of 1996 (HIPAA), which was intended to protect the privacy of medical information for consumers and encourage the adoption of electronic data transfer standards for more effective and efficient health services and payment systems.[2] This is a complex form of legislation with many provisions, but of relevance here is Title II, known as the Administrative Simplification (AS) provisions, which required the formation of national standards for electronic health care transactions and national identifiers for providers, health insurance plans, and employers. What were conceived as administrative simplifications proved to be anything but, and, while well

---

[2] For more information on HIPAA see http://www.hhs.gov/ocr/privacy/.

intended, were grounded in technologies and processes that have become outdated and alien to the ways in which health care practitioners and consumers actually behave. When combined with stiff enforcement penalties and extensive paperwork compliance, many HIPAA requirements have become synonymous with overreaching and counterproductive regulations. Rather than acting as an incentive for innovation and effectiveness, it has discouraged research collaboration and the sharing of data among parties with legitimate needs and interests to do so. Requiring written and authorized consent from a fixed and pre-identified category of stakeholders has discouraged the legitimate sharing of medical information for research and clinical use. By creating real and perceived barriers to the exchange and sharing of different types of medical information, the costs for treatment have ballooned and undermined incentives to act in the best interests of the patient. In the case of evidence-based medicine, for instance, where data on outcomes are used to identify new treatments and best practices, the fear of litigation and the requirement to sequester patient information have made it very difficult for the medical profession to learn from its mistakes. Yet with new encryption and "zero knowledge proof" technologies, it is technologically feasible to share private data without compromising anonymity. Again, in this case, protections against potential harms of a "breach" are given greater consideration than actual harms resulting from not being able to share and analyze data on the success of different treatments.

Another example of an inappropriate weighting of harms for the sharing of data is in the area of intelligence and national security. This is a well-documented failing and is attributed as one of the causes of the September 11 terrorist attacks.[3] Laws written to prevent the inappropriate sharing of data between the FBI and intelligence agencies were so poorly drafted that agencies were unable to pool and collaborate data to identify and intercept terrorists. Yet even within the Department of Defense (DoD), the

---

[3] The Markle Foundation Task Force on National Security in the Information Age, *Nation at Risk,* March 2009, www.markle.org.

Department of Homeland Security (DHS), and the National Security Agency (NSA), bureaucratic and statutory prohibitions against the sharing of classified data and the inability to achieve interoperability of credentials and access privileges have not only created a huge and unnecessary security risks, but severely inhibited the DoD from working more efficiently with fellow agencies, contractors, and allies. This issue has become especially acute when partnering with allies such as the United Kingdom in the joint development of the F-22 fighter. In this case, it became virtually impossible to share some classified data because of the absence of equivalent credentials between the United States and the United Kingdom agencies. As in the HIPAA example, the harms were weighted toward protecting the status quo. In the case of the DoD, no senior official wants to be charged with sharing secret information with a potential terrorist or allowing a breach of highly secret information; so the risk calculation is made to do nothing, even though the harms of doing nothing could be far greater than those of a security breach. The iconic image of a senior official being responsible for a security leak or breach that resulted in the explosion of a nuclear bomb in a major city is so strong that there is a "zero risk tolerance" mentality in the DoD and DHS. Yet in all likelihood, the failure to collaborate and share information up and down the command chain and across agencies is far more likely to result in that outcome than a failure to secure a particular piece of information.

In both the medical and the security scenarios, the probable harms are more likely due to a failure to share and collaborate than to secure a particular datum. Yet all the incentives and penalties are weighted toward protecting the status quo, not identifying problems or seeking remedies and implementing them. In all the examples cited, there are technologies that could both protect and share sensitive information. Yet they were not and are not being used. One reason for this is that there are no "risk absorption mechanisms" (like underwriting) for making it possible to undertake new approaches and for an organization to learn from its mistakes and improve its processes. Today there are negative incentives to innovate. On the other hand, if there were positive incentives to learn from one's mistakes, such as safe harbor provisions to reward rapid accountability, finding effective remedies, and resolving costly disputes over liability and responsibility, then both national security and national health care would be far better served.

REVEAL AND CONCEAL: THE DISCOVERY OF PRIVACY

In a world where competitive success will increasingly depend upon countries' and enterprises' abilities to share and protect valuable information, the old privacy and security regulatory frameworks of uniform standards, top-down policies, and practices that rely upon prohibitions, penalties, and consent notifications simply will not cut it.

To examine an alternative approach for balancing the protection and sharing of private information, this chapter will discuss how the notion of "privacy" has evolved over time from oral traditions to digital surveillance, and then how rule making and regulatory practices necessarily need to reflect the same level of institutional and technological innovation to effectively protect individual freedoms and to enable economic growth. The chapter will propose a new governance framework for "trusted member networks" that is being developed in conjunction with the White House National Strategy for Trusted Identities in Cyberspace (NSTIC), the Federal Trade Commission, the Open Identity Exchange (OIX), and the World Economic Forum that is potentially applicable not only in the United States but also in the countries of the European Union and elsewhere.

Privacy as it is understood and practiced in developed countries today is largely an artifact of Western, especially Anglo-Saxon, cultural experience. In densely populated countries such as India and China, expectations of privacy are markedly different than they are in the West, reflecting different cultural experiences and roles of the individual and the group.

The first inkling of Western privacy awareness manifested itself nearly one thousand years ago with the issuance of the *Doomsday Book* (so named after the Anglo-Saxon term "doom," for reckoning, accounting, judgment) by the Norman king, William the Conqueror, in 1086. For the first time in the West, a ruler had a written record in Latin of the major property holdings of his subjects. For non-Normans, it was a greatly feared and resented registry, because it gave the Norman king unprecedented powers to tax properties and assemble armies. Here is an account of it roughly one hundred years later: "That is why we have called the book 'the Book of Judgment' ... because its decisions, like those of the Last Judgment, are unalterable."[4]

Given that majority of the Anglo-Saxon populace lived within an oral tradition, and could not read Latin, this registry gave the king privileged powers of surveillance and social control that he never had before. What was once was private was now public, visible, and an instrument of the king. "This change in the method of obtaining information—from hearing the testimony of reliable local men to looking up a book kept by the Exchequer— is one indicator of the transition from memory to written record."[5]

A by-product of this appropriation of oral communications by written texts, however, was that the Anglo-Saxon subjects became aware of a natural right that they once had, but now had lost— that of privacy. Only by having it appropriated by a new kind of technology did they then become aware of its importance as something natural, distinct, and alienable.

---

[4] C. Johnson, ed., *Dialogus de Scaccario, the Course of the Exchequer, and Constitutio Domus Regis, the King's Household* (London: 1950), 64.

[5] M.T. Clanchy, *From Memory to Written Record: England, 1066-1307* (Cambridge, MA: Harvard University Press, 1979), 20.

PRIVACY AND INDIVIDUAL RIGHTS

To appreciate how critical the notion of privacy is to Western societies, it is important to consider the origin of the term and its role in shaping the identity and rights of the individual. The term "privacy" is derived from the Latin term, *privatus*, meaning separated from the rest. The right to separate from the rest and not be subject to the gaze and judgment of the group, be it a clan, tribe, or secular or religious authority, is foundational to the notion of the modern individual and democratic state. With the expectation not to be overheard or seen by others comes the evolution of a "private" identity that is separate from a public or group identity. Such a notion is foundational in Western societies as it gives individuals the expectation that they can legitimately have private and separate spaces, personhoods, and rights that are not wholly subject to the powers and surveillance of the public or government. By separating out an individual's right for private information from that of a group, public, or government, the right of privacy forms the basis for a broad base of individual rights such as dignity, speech, worship, and happiness. Hence, under certain conditions, such as in one's home, a confidential communication, or in the company of friends, in a secluded setting, there is the expectation of privacy where one's communications and activities are trusted to be protected and not shared outside the confines of a trusted group or context. The *Doomsday Book* is an early example of a Western government being given the explicit powers to break down informal barriers of expected privacy to collect information to enhance its powers of taxation, conscription, confiscation, surveillance, and control. What was once implicitly private and protected by the inherent limitations of oral tradition and custom was suddenly exposed and made markedly less private. The written word in this case, a Latin census, created an awareness of privacy by exposing the weakness of informal, oral protections.

The Physical Conditions of Privacy

Before the current digital era, the collection of data about someone depended upon the physical acquisition of documents and artifacts containing expressions of people's activities, opinions, and interests. It required a physical intrusion, a physical breach of a barrier such as a door, and a physical search, such as the movement and opening of objects and artifacts, and the physical collection and movement of objects such as the seizure of documents, tapes, or a computer. Hence, Fourth Amendment prohibitions against unreasonable search and seizure would be tied to rules that prohibited physical actions of surveillance, search, and seizure. Even as the digital technology advanced, the legal rule making still tried to adhere to a model of privacy that was essentially grounded in the physical world. However, by relying upon this physical typing of the problem, legal and regulatory frameworks have become progressively strained and less effective as privacy issues became more and more digital. Still, the prevalent means for resolving privacy issues continue to be based upon physical objects, equating data with the physical artifacts they were stored in or used by. The boundaries of private spaces continue to be defined in terms of physical boundaries and devices. Privacy statutes, policies, and regulations continue to be quite literal, conflating types of technologies with specific technologies. For example, the Federal Communications Commission has had different regulatory rules for voice, data, text, and video, although they all are now processed digitally. Similarly, for many online transactions, handwritten signatures are required, although there are more effective digital means for authenticating a document or individual. Another example is the National Institute of Standards and Technology (NIST) standards for four "levels of assurance" (LOA) for increasing levels of security that require digital security certificates and tokens, although less expensive and potentially more effective methods for achieving assurance are now available. Here the drafters of the standards assumed that the only way of achieving assurance was to have different types of security tokens and digital certificates.

THE DIGITAL TYPING OF PRIVACY

Where the physical typing of privacy totally breaks down is around physical boundaries—that is, jurisdictions based on sovereignty that are tied to a specific physical border. As is well known, the Internet is a virtual global network whose boundaries are defined by transient data packet routes. In this world of cyberspace, what does location really mean? Certainly not physical location. (Perhaps IP addresses or persistent, power law networks?) As more and more computing and software services move to the "cloud," the failures of physical metaphors become all the more acute. For instance, the definition and enforcement of property rights for data cannot be tied to where data is located because data can be dynamically generated, shifted, and stored arbitrarily around the world. The physical privacy typing problem becomes especially strained when trying to define the actors and actions around unreasonable search and seizure, when the actors can be automatically generated "bots" that can number in the millions, "live" and "die" with impunity around the world, and be totally anonymous in their origin and purpose. Moreover, the difference between a malevolent and benevolent "bot" or "actor" can just be a matter of circumstances and context. A piece of data in one context may not be personally identifying or damaging, though in another context, or when combined or correlated with another datum, it could be highly damaging. Such circumstances cannot be predicted as data mining algorithms discover novel correlations to expose private data. Unlike physical artifacts, digital and virtual artifacts can be replicated and distributed at no cost. Hence, once privacy-violating data are released or "escape," they may never be returned. Data that is defamatory, inaccurate, security breaching, and even life threatening, can travel globally and hide and live indefinitely with impunity. Data also can be altered—video, pictures, and documents—to fraudulently assert facts, events, quotations, and claims that are dangerously false. The near absence of friction or cost in the generation, replication, modification, storage, and distribution of digital media of all sorts—this includes video, computer programs, bots, and active forms of digital media—is not to be found in the physical world, and hence, privacy laws, rules, and remedies based upon these analogues will invariably fail to appreciate the consequences of the mutability and frictionless nature of digital media.

THE DARK SIDE OF BEING DIGITAL

As we noted at the beginning of this chapter, more and more of everyday life is becoming enveloped by data, from something as simple as Google's Street View service to ubiquitous surveillance video cameras to military surveillance satellites. This trend will only increase. The technology exists today for recognizing people's faces on three-dollar video cameras, using that image to create a trackable, unique identifier, and then tracking those people over time. That was done by the Dubai government to the Mossad-sponsored assassins of the Hamas leader, Mahmoud al-Mabhouh, in his hotel room in Dubai. Such a tracking capability could become routine and inexpensive within the next decade. Similarly, the ability to deploy dust-sized, self-organizing sensing networks (called "smart dust" or mote networks) that communicate with satellite and drone surveillance systems is another technology that not only significantly alters privacy expectations, but could give state and nonstate actors alarmingly pervasive and lethal powers. This again is technology that exists today in its introductory form and has proven to be successful against a difficult and astute adversary, such as the Taliban and Al-Qaeda in Pakistan. Imagine what such technology will do to our expectations of privacy, sovereignty, and individual autonomy in ten years. The point is a simple one. One can no longer think of the expectation of privacy as a natural state, something that can simply mimic conventions in the physical world. In the virtual world, which will increasingly overlay and interact with the physical world, there needs to be a conscious and explicit effort to design physical and virtual "spaces" or contexts where the expectations of privacy and security are met and enforced. Statutes and regulations can no longer be seen as piecemeal, passive "safeguards" to new technologies; rather, they must encourage—

incentivizing the innovative use of those technologies to create whole *private* contexts where the expectations of privacy can be met and enforced. This is a very different way of thinking about "privacy" statutes or regulations since the fundamental purpose of the rule making is not prohibition, notification, and consent per se, but to effectively encourage rule-making innovations that enforce general principles of protection *and* sharing. Rather than have rules that identify and punish specific privacy violations, the goal is to encourage the *generation* of private contexts and technologies that define and protect privacy-preserving spaces. Implicit in the design of such generative rules is recognition that it is impossible *ab initio* to pre-identify best privacy practices and threats, as these will change as technology and circumstances change.

One of the difficulties in moving to dynamic and holistic regulatory frameworks of privacy and sharing is that some of the fundamental principles still in use today for framing and enforcing of privacy policies are technologically and organizationally woefully out of date. The notion of Fair Information Practice Principles (FIPP) was first developed in 1973 and is the core of the Privacy Act of 1974, and they still represent the dominant principles for the current privacy practices for the Federal Trade Commission, the Department of Homeland Security's National Strategy for Trusted Identities in Cyberspace, many U.S. state laws, and many countries around the world. The FIPP are, in effect, the "motherhood and apple pie" of privacy principles. Yet despite their widespread use, they make certain assumptions about technological functionality and practices that are dated, simplistic, and limiting, and thereby have limited innovation in privacy practices.

To see why this is the case, and why subsequent privacy principles should not be based upon FIPP, the eight basic FIPP principles are listed below and are followed by a brief critique that explains why they should not be relied upon.

FAIR INFORMATION PRACTICE PRINCIPLES (FIPP)

Transparency: *Organizations should be transparent and provide notice to the individual regarding collection, use, dissemination, and maintenance of personally identifiable information (PII).*

At first glance, this requirement would seem straightforward, but in practice it makes a number of assumptions about notice and consent that are simply impractical and ineffective. For instance, given the volumes of data that will be swirling about on every person in the very near future, consumers would have to spend an inordinate amount of time reviewing consent agreements they simply do not understand. This is one of the complaints about HIPAA and, increasingly, about privacy notices for websites and security tokens. These practices really do not achieve transparency, because only a rare few can understand the agreements and fewer still are interested in reading them every time they are brought to their attention. Transparency is something much more subtle than notification and consent. It entails seeing and understanding the consequences of different practices and having the information presented in such a manner that it does not hinder effective operations by the organization in question, and at the same time, achieves accountability and encourages self-correction and improvement.

Individual Participation: *Organizations should involve the individual in the process of using PII and, to the extent practicable, seek individual consent for the collection, use, dissemination, and maintenance of PII. Organizations should also provide mechanisms for appropriate access, correction, and redress regarding use of PII.*

Under the principle of "individual participation," many complex and competing requirements are included. People have neither the time nor the interest in participating in all the decisions required for consent and methods for redress. Moreover, Personal Identifying Information (PII) has changed over time from the obvious candidates of Social Security number, address, and age, to virtually any combination of sufficient data attributes to identify someone. With new data mining techniques, it is now very hard to find any combination of data that are not personally identifying. So full compliance with this principle would be both impractical and impossible. Given the fear of severe penalties as in the case of the breach of HIPAA rules, it is no wonder that hardly any information is released without an impossible pile of excessive paperwork.

Purpose Specification: *Organizations should specifically articulate the authority that permits the collection of PII and specifically articulate the purpose or purposes for which the PII is intended to be used.*

This is much more easily said than done. Again, with the volume of data being collected and innovations in methods of mining and analyzing data—as well as the number of potentially different parties involved—compliance could be crippling. Also, as noted before, it will never be clear as to what PII is since it could change by context and application. From a compliance and self-interested adversity to risk perspective, it would make more sense to do nothing. The presumption here, as in the other cases, is that data have to be collected, held, and stored. This is no longer the case, as they can be encrypted and used to "ping" against some value and not retained by any third party, who would not even have to know, much less store, the "physical" data. That was not the implied technological model the framers of these principles had in 1976.

Data Minimization: *Organizations should only collect PII that is directly relevant and necessary to accomplish the specified purpose(s) and only retain PII for as long as is necessary to fulfill the specified purpose(s).*

This is a good principle, but again, purposes change and emerge out of myriads of processes and interchanges, especially if there are multiple parties involved. Hence, the full enforcement of this principle could limit sharing since all purposes could not be identified *a priori*. Since data can be used for authentication, access approval, and validation without being stored, there may not be a need to retain it, and hence, little actual harm.

Use Limitation: Organizations should use PII solely for the purpose(s) specified in the notice. Sharing PII should be for a purpose compatible with the purpose for which the PII was collected.

Again, there is a lot of wiggle room for good and ill in defining a purpose, and it is not clear what "compatible with the purposes" for which the PII was collected means and whether it can or should have a precise meaning. Technology could reframe the issue and provide a solution that was never considered by the principle but would be precluded by it.

Data Quality and Integrity: Organizations should, to the extent practicable, ensure that PII is accurate, relevant, timely, and complete.

A laudable aspiration, but how does one ensure and independently verify that the data are relevant (an especially murky notion), timely, and complete? Each of these criteria needs a replicable, evolvable, and independent test. And as before, the very notion of PII itself is flawed, and hence it is a misleading notion upon which to rely.

Security: Organizations should protect PII (in all media) through appropriate security safeguards against risks such as loss, unauthorized access or use, destruction, modification, or unintended or inappropriate disclosure.

The challenge here is to determine a standard of risk and loss appropriate to the type of data under consideration. NIST notions of four Levels of Assurance (LOA) or other notions of Levels of Protection (LOP) are appropriate here as to considering the security versus privacy harms of a breach. Once again, the notion of PII is problematic, as data that are not by themselves personally identifying can become so when combined with other "innocuous" data. Does that mean that all such data need to be appropriately protected? This becomes one of those open-ended requirements that is impossible to comply with. Where security becomes a real issue is around the integrity of the system so that it becomes impossible to know—or to verify—that data are not being copied, modified, or destroyed by an unauthorized third party (such as the case of a "rogue bot" or an organized "army of bot mercenaries" without an identifiable human actor or beneficiary).

Accountability and Auditing: Organizations should be accountable for complying with these principles, providing training to all employees and contractors who use PII, and auditing the actual use of PII to demonstrate compliance with these principles and all applicable privacy protection requirements.

These ideas are another example of impossible requirements to comply with, primarily because of the generous use of the quantifier "all" being applied to employees, contractors, and "applicable privacy protection requirements." Since audits by themselves do not necessarily create accountability, there is also a need for consequences, enforcements, and remedies to be part of the requirement. Likewise, audits need to be wholly independent, and in intervals and with metrics that effectively regulate and correct the behavior of the organization.

A PROPOSED FRAMEWORK FOR PROTECTING AND SHARING PRIVATE DATA

Within the United States and the members of the European Union, there is widespread recognition of the need for new privacy and security laws and regulations. Of special concern to the United States, especially the DoD and DHS, is the scale and constancy of cybersecurity attacks that are not only hemorrhaging DoD of vital intelligence data, but creating the opportunity for cyberespionage to threaten America's critical infrastructure, especially the financial system and the national grid. The integration of the physical and the digital in banking, intelligence, and the power grid is happening at an accelerating pace and, unless protected, poses a genuine physical threat to national security.

Some have argued for a laissez-faire, market solution to achieving a secure cyberinfrastructure by letting market "forces" discover how to resolve the trade-offs between privacy and sharing, and appropriately price the risks for levels of investment in a secure cyberinfrastructure. Although markets can be highly efficient resource allocators when there are reliable price signals, cyberinfrastructure investments, such as identity and authentication platforms, are public goods, for which there are no simple price signals. There are a variety of requirements—constitutional, shared access, resiliency, interoperability—that preclude a market solution. Once established, however, as in the case of open software and services platforms, private actors can compete, innovate, and differentiate themselves by the price and quality of their services within a secure and trusted cyberinfrastructure platform. There is no inherent requirement that the government by itself should necessarily manage or even own an open-identity platform, but rather it can establish the ground rules, goals, and principles by which such platforms should be governed. The government should act as an independent referee, arbitrator, and enforcer of open-platform rules. Rather than attempting to prescribe or design in advance what the specific rules, technologies, harms, and remedies should be, the regulatory goal should be to create the conditions whereby new rules, mechanisms, and policies can naturally emerge.[6]

OPEN GOVERNANCE PLATFORM: NEW ECOSYSTEMS OF TRUST

In many industries where new technologies and services are involved, there is growing recognition that different players need to cooperate to build a common and open infrastructure that no one party dominates. If any one party tries to dominate a nascent market, it will stifle the overall revenue potential and limit inno-

---

[6] See the literature on complexity sciences and emergent organization: John Henry Clippinger, *Biology of Business, Decoding the Natural Laws of Enterprise* (San Francisco, CA: Jossey-Bass, 1998); Clippinger, *A Crowd of One: The Future of Individual Identity* (New York: Perseus, 2007); Stuart Kauffman, *Origin of Order; Self-Organization and Selection in Evolution* (New York: Oxford University Press USA, 1993); Kauffman, *Reinventing the Sacred: A New View of Science, Reason and Religion* (New York: Basic Books, 2008); John Holland, *Hidden Order: How Adaptation Builds Complexity* (Reading, MA: Addison-Wesley, 1996); Steven Wolfram, *A New Kind of Science* (Champaign, IL: Wolfram Media, 2002); and Brian Arthur, *The Nature of Technology: What it is and How it Evolves* (New York: Free Press, 2009).

vation. This was the case with operating system (OS) software, which Microsoft once dominated. But with the advent of Linux and new open-source software licensing agreements (GPL, Eclipse), not only was there increased competition among OS software, but new markets for applications software and services flourished. With the success of open source, OS software has become open-source software in server, database, browser, desktop applications, and cloud computing—and virtually all aspects of computer software. Instead of there being a closed market dominated by a few dominant suppliers, a diverse and rapidly evolving software ecosystem came into being. This model is now being adopted in synthetic biology, mobile communications, computer hardware, energy, transportation, media, and other industries. Rather than turn to the government to determine the rule sets for new business ecosystems and be the sole arbiter and enforcer of the public interest and welfare, we have seen companies, activists, customers, and various stakeholders come together using an open-source methodology to develop their own rule sets to make it possible for all stakeholders to effectively leverage a common infrastructure. As Parker and Van Alstyne (2009) have argued in their research on platform strategies, there are clear business models for creating open, multiparty platforms that have been the source of considerable innovation in diverse industries.[7]

The identity and privacy arena has been one area where private-sector, academic, and NGO initiatives have been successful in coming up with a user-centric, interoperable open platform identity. Starting in 2004 at the Berkman Center at Harvard University and initially supported by Microsoft, IBM, Novell, and Best Buy, a series of workshops and conferences were undertaken helping to spawn a variety of initiatives—Project Higgins,[8] Open ID Foundation, Identity Commons, Identity Gang, Internet Identity

---

[7] Geoffrey Parker and Marshall Van Alstyne, "Six Challenges in Platform Licensing and Open Innovation," *Communications & Strategies* no. 74 (2nd quarter 2009): 17.

[8] For more information on Project Higgins, see www.eclipse.org/projecthiggins.

Workshop, Information Card Foundation,[9] and Project VRM. As open-source software was developed for user-centric identity management through Project Higgins, I-Card Foundation, and Open ID Foundation, companies such as Equifax, Google, Bank of America, PayPal, Microsoft, Verizon, Oracle, and Facebook started to develop products and services leveraging this new open-source identity software. Involved in these discussions also were advocacy groups such as EPIC (Electronic Privacy Information Center), EFF (Electronic Frontier Foundation), and CDT (Center for Democratic Technology). In 2010, the I-Card Foundation and Open Identity Foundation jointly formed the Open Identity Exchange (OIX),[10] which became an independent nonprofit vehicle for certifying different identity "trust frameworks" that identity providers such as Google, Citi, PayPal, or Equifax would be offering.

The General Services Administration, a federal agency, took an important step in forming a government-sanctioned trust framework (ICAM) for identity services for the U.S. government. An important feature of this approach is that the government is not a provider of identity services, but rather sets standards for private vendors who are in turn certified by the Open Identity Exchange. The challenge, however, is to provide a legal framework that is supportive of this new approach to privacy and identity and can encourage innovation and adaptation while "reinventing" the notion of privacy in the context of rapid and fundamental technological innovations. Without strong governing principles, a willingness to let market acceptance alone define norms or expectations of privacy could fundamentally undermine democratic principles. If people could be enticed to relinquish their privacy rights in exchange for financial and other incentives, and if governments and corporations could form their own surveillance and behavior monitoring networks at will, then the citizenry would over time be relinquishing their autonomy and democrat-

---

[9] For more information on the I-Card Foundation, see www.informationcard.net.

[10] For more information on OIX, see www.openidentityexchange.org.

ic powers to the government or other entities. Hence, a viable notion of digital privacy requires a digital form of effective democratic governance whereby not only public institutions but private ones as well are accountable to principles of fairness, choice, dignity, transparency, and public welfare.

Fortunately, there is a growing recognition among significant policymakers in the United States and the European Union to develop new approaches to protecting and sharing private information that embodies a more open platform and ecological approach. The differences between the more holistic and evolutionary approaches and the more classic mechanistic models of the past are significant and have broad implications on how to frame, oversee, and implement complex regulatory policies.

The newly emerging trust framework being developed by NSTIC, and which is scheduled to have presidential backing in January 2011, provides a set of principles that are clearly informed by new software design methods, such as open source, as well as ecological principles that emphasize self-organization, resilience, interoperability, and emergence. In its "vision statement" of June 2010, NSTIC emphasized principles such as "easy-to-use," "confidence," "choice," and "innovation," which stand in contrast to the FFIP principles of thirty-four years ago. Given the importance of this new perspective and its contrast with prior regulatory principles for privacy, it is worth referencing the NSTIC vision and principles in their entirety.[11]

NSTIC VISION

Individuals and organizations utilize secure, efficient, easy-to-use, and interoperable identity solutions to access online services in a manner that promotes confidence, privacy, choice, and innovation.

---

[11] National Strategy for Trusted Identities in Cyberspace, *Draft National Strategy for Trusted Identities in Cyberspace*, June 2010, www.nstic.ideascale.com.

More specifically, the Strategy defines and promotes an Identity Ecosystem that supports trusted online environments. The Identity Ecosystem is an online environment where individuals, organizations, services, and devices can trust each other because authoritative sources establish and authenticate their digital identities.

The Identity Ecosystem Enables:

Security, *by making it more difficult for adversaries to compromise online transactions;*

Efficiency *based on convenience for individuals who may choose to manage fewer passwords or accounts than they do today, and for the private sector, which stands to benefit from a reduction in paper-based and account management processes;*

Ease-of-use *by automating identity solutions whenever possible and basing them on technology that is easy to operate with minimal training;*

Confidence *that digital identities are adequately protected, thereby increasing the use of the Internet for various types of online transactions;*

Increased privacy *for individuals, who rely on their data being handled responsibly and who are routinely informed about those who are collecting their data and the purposes for which it is being used;*

Greater choice, *as identity credentials and devices are offered by providers using interoperable platforms;*

Opportunities for innovation, *as service providers develop or expand the services offered online, particularly those services that are inherently higher in risk.*

Note that these principles presume there will not be some independent regulatory body and responsible entity alone, but that much of the regulatory success will depend upon the quality of the user experience as shaped by continuous technological and legal evolution, innovation, and improvement. Also note that there is no use of the quantifier "all" or even mention of PII. The

NSTIC strategy also makes use of "use cases" to illustrate how such an ecosystem might work and what the benefits would be for the different stakeholders.

What is important is that such principles can be embedded and tested in different kinds of trust frameworks that can in turn be branded by different vendors who experiment with and develop new technologies and services for their markets. How such values and principles are implemented will be left to private innovations in mechanisms of protection, sharing, visualization, and contract law. But the application of such principles to preserve, adapt, and further democratic principles should be the province of government, and it is important that governments understand how different combinations of policies, mechanisms, and technologies can advance or erode democratic principles. The point of government in this capacity is to be the innovator in digital governance principles, as these principles will have to be reinvented to keep pace with the technology. This is a tall order and probably best done through government support of research on open-source governance platforms and activities. Although within the United States there is a general consensus that new forms of privacy legislation may be needed, there is still considerable uncertainty about the scope and nature of what such legislation should cover.

COMPUTABLE TRUST FRAMEWORKS FOR PRIVACY AND SHARING

With the integration of the physical and the digital over the coming years, pervasive technological change will be a constant shaper of what is possible. Consequently, it will be impossible to predict (1) what kinds of technological and policy changes will either impede or further privacy, and (2) the appropriate information flows to advance new kinds of commercial, personal, health, educational, and civic services. It must be remembered that we are using technologies and policies to construct new kinds of privacy, governance, and commercial norms and institutions, and hence, continuous innovation is absolutely required, not only at the service level but at the governance and policy levels as well. Therefore, there will need to be an open, evolving governance platform for privacy and security that encourages and enables an ongoing series of real-world market experiments. Those who are providing identity and security services should be encouraged through safe harbor protections to develop competing trust networks to provide branded "rules and tools" that implement different approaches to protecting privacy while providing new models for sharing and monetizing information. It will be the role of government agencies to facilitate this process through funding, research, standards setting, procurement practices, independent auditing and oversight, and the development of guidelines and principles for building and hosting identity and security services. Every effort should be made to prevent the capture of key processes and technologies by special interests. As in the case of open software, such as in Linux or the LAMP stack, the core common identity technology should be kept open and subject to an Eclipse or LGPL license. We would propose having an *open identity kernel* that would include the software for registering and authenticating claims about a person's different "personas," such as those associated with health, financial, professional, purchasing, or social activities and information. The identity kernel would include a "dashboard" for individual and third-party auditing of how one's personal information was being used. Relevant personal data would be "kept" in or accessed through a Personal Data Store (PDS) where it would be encrypted to all but the individual and trusted third parties. There also should be different damages and auditing schemes for different types of information—personal, professional, financial, commercial, health care, and civic. Data would be auditable and traceable so that there would full transparency on the actions of all parties participating as members of a trust network.

MEMBER TRUST NETWORK

A key element to making this approach work is the notion of a "member network," which is a kind of social network in which all members are authenticated and identifiable (by a variety of innovative means) and agree to abide by the policies, mechanisms, contracts, and agreements of the member network. The Member Trust Network is a kind of member network that uses a combination of governance mechanisms—identity authentication, dispute resolution, reputation systems, auditing, credit assignment, voting, and enforcement—to provide a variety of competitive solutions to privacy, security, and information solutions. There are technologies such as I-card technologies, zero knowledge proof technologies, reputation currencies, digital contracting, and auditing technologies that make it possible to implement trust member technologies that embody different policy frameworks. The role of regulatory agencies such as the FTC and DHS would be to establish policy baselines and safeguards that act as guidelines to direct new forms of innovation in services and governance.

CONCLUSIONS AND RECOMMENDATIONS

This paper began with a prediction about the future, saying that in just five years the digital lives of more than two billion people would be actively monitored, recorded, and analyzed. Data measured in the exabytes will become the new fuel for a global economy increasingly shaped by digital technologies. The traditional approach to protecting and sharing private data over the years has been weighted toward protecting against harms resulting from the exposure of PII. As the amount of data collected on people around the world has grown exponentially, traditional protective measures such as prohibition, notification, and consent are no longer adequate or even appropriate. In the case of medicine and national security, it can be argued that the harms from not sharing critical information in many cases exceed the harms resulting from not protecting private information. The challenge is to develop governance frameworks for protecting and sharing private information that are incentivized to create new policies, rules, private contracts, governance mechanisms, and software services that are highly adaptive. It is argued that the FIPP principles are grounded in dated technology and are no longer adequate, and that newer principles drawing from an ecosystem approach are required.

This new approach to rule making was then applied to the area of digital privacy and security regulation. The argument has been made that most current privacy protections policies and statutes are conceived as remedies for preserving privacy in a physical world. The digital sphere is so radically different in terms of what is possible from the vantage point of privacy and security that there are but very few useful precedents in the physical world. Rather than grounding expectation of privacy upon precedents in the physical world, it was argued that the point of digital privacy policy is to encourage the construction of new concepts of privacy that reflect the possibilities of the technology. The rise of cloud computing, virtual worlds, total surveillance, data mining, and unforeseen technologies for anonymizing, de-anonymizing, encrypting, de-encrypting data, and faking authentication make it impossible for citizens and regulators to predict future events. Rule sets and regulations, therefore, will need to evolve with the technologies and services and business models in a principled basis. The challenge for government is to understand how to translate democratic governance principles into this fast-changing digital world. In this instance, there has to be genuine exploration and innovation in forms of governance. It was argued that the best method for doing this has been the development of open platforms whereby different stakeholders develop a common infrastructure that supports the emergence of new business ecosystems. Currently, there is an open-source effort in identity and security that is being embraced by many major companies in the private sector as well as by academics, NGOs, the United States government, and the intelligence and defense agencies. This effort is in its infancy, but nonetheless represents a major shift in how such complex policy issues are being conceptualized and addressed.

A key challenge for the coming decade for governments will be how to develop trusted institutions and relationships in a progressively digital and interconnected world. How this challenge is dealt with will be determinative of growing free, vital, and innovative networked societies. In light of these challenges the following near-term recommendations are made.

- **Revise FFIP and devise *digital* fairness principles and practices:** These should avoid notions of PII, be technology agnostic, and encourage interoperability with European Union and other privacy and identity frameworks.

- **Develop identity ecosystems using open platform methodologies and technologies:** Recognize that solutions need to be holistic and self-organizing and self-correcting, combining innovations in governance mechanisms as well as contracts and policies.

- **Conduct large-scale experiments for trust frameworks**: Encourage discovery and innovation in the marketplace that generate new value and financial incentives.

- **Provide safe harbor protections to innovators:** Provide protections to those innovators who take legitimate risks to improve the protection and sharing of private information.

- **Encourage the underwriting of authentication risks:** Make a business case and opportunity for absorbing risks in much the same way that enabled the growth of the credit card industry.

- **Encourage the adoption of independent digital auditing and rating mechanisms**: Without full independent audit and rating systems there cannot be trust in the Identity Ecosystem. Hence, new approaches and technologies should be encouraged.

Taken together and acted upon, these recommendations might help reframe current policy perspectives toward privacy and help move them in a direction that combines technology and rule making in a manner and at a pace that meets the challenges of global digital societies and economies.[12]

---

[12] Additional resources used in the development of this chapter include John Henry Clippinger, "An Inquiry into Effective Reputation and Rating Systems," in *The Reputation Society: How Online Opinions are Reshaping the Offline World,* ed. Mark Tovey and Hassan Masum (Cambridge, MA: MIT Press, 2011); and John Henry Clippinger and David Bollier, "The Renaissance of the Commons," in *Code: Collaborative Ownership in the Digital Economy,* ed. Rishab Ghosh (Cambridge, MA: MIT Press, 2005).

17 : Innovation and Growth through Open Access to Scientific Research: Three Ideas for High-Impact Rule Changes

Victoria Stodden*

O ur stock of scientific knowledge is now accumulating in digital form. Our DNA is now encoded as genome sequence data, scans of brain activity exist in functional magnetic resonance image datasets, and records of our climate are stored in myriad time series datasets—to name a few examples. Equally as important, our reasoning about these data is recorded in software, in the scripts and code that analyze the digitally recorded world. The result is a deep digitization of scientific knowledge, spreading across fields and generating new ways of understanding our surroundings. With the parallel development of the Internet as a pervasive communication mechanism for digital data, an unprecedented opportunity for access to society's scientific understanding is at hand.

At present, the notion of unmitigated access to scientific knowledge largely remains an unrealized opportunity. This paper pro-

---

* Victoria Stodden is Assistant Professor of Statistics at Columbia University, completing both her PhD in statistics in 2006 and her law degree in 2007 at Stanford University. Her current research focuses on how pervasive and large-scale computation is changing our practice of the scientific method; reproducibility of computational results; understanding factors underlying code and data sharing among researchers; and the role of legal framing for scientific advancement.

poses three changes to our current regulatory system designed to take into account the new reality of scientific innovation in a digital world and thereby promote innovation and economic growth. Our current intellectual property framework developed with a view to protecting original expressions of ideas in established media, such as literature, film, and sound recordings. Scientific innovations, such as code written to implement a new algorithm or an image produced for academic journal publication, now fall within a copyright structure that was developed for an entirely different normative environment, and the result is the creation of barriers to scientific innovation.

Part I of this essay explores the mismatch of intellectual property laws with scientific norms regarding the treatment of ideas, and proposes an alternative structure designed to facilitate deep sharing of scientific innovation through open code and data, thereby realigning the legal environment with long-standing scientific norms.

Part II addresses the role of federal agency policy in funding scientific research. Federal funding agencies create incentives for openness through their grant guidelines and enforcement. Changes to both accommodate the impact of computation on reproducibility, and therefore openness, are suggested.

Part III proposes ideas for the facilitation of code and data sharing through a process of disentanglement of ownership rights and the establishment of sharing protocols. Scientific research is becoming increasingly collaborative, particularly with industry researchers, and without a clear understanding of ownership rights in data and code, open sharing is hampered, if not obstructed completely. Methods for streamlining this process at the university level to permit the disclosure of the underlying code and data at the time of publication are presented.

The case for openness in science is not a new one. Scientific research is predicated on an understanding of scientific knowledge as a public good—this is the rationale underlying today's multibillion-dollar subsidies of scientific research through various federal and state agencies. The scientific view is not one of adding nuggets of truth to our collective understanding, but instead one of weighing evidence and assigning likelihoods to a finding's probability of being true. This creates a normative structure of skepticism among scientists: the burden is on the discovering scientist to convince others that what he or she has found is more likely to be correct than our previous understanding. The scientific method's central motivation is therefore the *ubiquity of error*—the awareness that mistakes and self-delusion can creep in absolutely anywhere and that the scientist's effort is primarily expended in recognizing and rooting out error. As a result, standards of scientific communication evolved to incorporate full disclosure of the methods and reasoning used to arrive at the result. Since the 1660s, the gold standard for scientific communication has been reproducibility, to create both the greatest chance of the accurate transmission of the new discoveries and also to maximize the likelihood that any errors in the reasoning would be identified.

Today, massive computation is transforming science, as researchers from numerous fields, even historically nontechnical ones, launch ambitious projects involving large-scale computations. A rapid transition is under way—visible particularly over the past two decades—that will finish with computation as absolutely central to scientific enterprise. From the newcomer's struggle to make even the simplest computer program run, to the seasoned professional's frustration when a server crashes in the middle of a large job, all is struggle against error. The understanding necessary for reproducibility is typically not transmitted, as computational results are frequently of a complexity that makes the effective explanation of the methodology all but impossible in a typical scientific publication today. To affect reproducibility, and the transfer of the knowledge embodied in the scientific finding, the code and data on which the result is derived must be communicated such that the result can be independently replicated and verified.

As a contribution to society's stock of knowledge, a scientific finding has the potential to be both developed and extended into commercial settings and to become the foundation for further scientific discoveries. Acceleration of innovation is facilitated by the incorporation of the open release of code and data in today's computational science practice. A number of changes are essential to catalyze both scientific advancement and the development of applications and discoveries outside academia.

PART I. THE LEGAL FRAMEWORK FOR SCIENTIFIC INNOVATION AND DISSEMINATION: COPYRIGHT IS A BARRIER

The Intellectual Property Clause of the Constitution has been interpreted to confer two distinct powers: the first power provides the basis for copyright law—securing for a limited time a creator's exclusive right to their original work;[1] the second power provides the basis for patent law—giving inventors a limited-term exclusive right to their discoveries in exchange for disclosure of the invention. Authors do not have to apply for copyright protection, as it adheres automatically when the original expression of the idea is rendered in fixed form. Many perfectly standard scientific activities, such as writing a script to filter a dataset or fit a statistical model, will produce a copyrighted output, in this case the code written to implement these tasks. Building a new dataset through the original selection and arrangement of data will generate ownership rights through copyright for the dataset creator, to give another example.[2]

The default nature of copyright confers an intellectual property framework for scientific ideas at odds with long-standing scientific norms in two key ways.[3] First, by preventing copying of

---

[1] For a discussion of the Copyright Act of 1976 see e.g. Pam Samuelson, "Preliminary Thoughts on Copyright Reform Project," *Utah Law Review* 3 (2007): 551, accessed March 7, 2009, http://people.ischool.berkeley.edu/~pam/papers.html.

[2] See *Feist Publications Inc. v. Rural Telephone Services* Co., 499 U.S. 340 (1991), 363-364.

the research work, it creates a barrier to the possibility of legally reproducing and verifying another scientist's results without the need to obtain prior permission from the authoring scientist.[4] Second, copyright also establishes rights for the owner over the creation of derivative works. Scientific norms guide scientists to build on previous discoveries—using copyrighted work in derivative research typically requires obtaining the permission of the copyright holder, thus creating a block to the generation of new scientific discoveries. Particularly as computation becomes increasingly central to the scientific method, copyright on code and the potential for copyright in data are barriers to the advancement of science and economic growth. When scientists share their research on the Web, for example, the original expression of their ideas automatically falls under copyright.

Copyright law is often understood as a trade-off between providing incentives for the production of creative works by granting the author certain limited-term exclusive rights over their work, and the public's desire to access the work. By blocking the ability of others to copy and reuse research, copyright law acts counter to the prevailing scientific norms that encourage scientists to openly release their work to the community in exchange for citation.

An exception is made in our federal copyright code under fair use for "teaching (including multiple copies for classroom use), scholarship, or research,"[5] but this does not extend to the full research project. A relatively straightforward solution to the barrier copyright imposes would be to broaden the fair use exception to include scientific research that takes place in research institutions such as universities or via federal research grants.[6]

---

[3] For a detailed discussion of copyright law and its impact on scientific innovation, see Victoria Stodden, "Enabling Reproducible Research: Licensing for Scientific Innovation," *International Journal for Communications Law and Policy* 13 (Winter 2008-9), http://www.ijclp.net/issue_13.html.

[4] See Victoria Stodden, "The Legal Framework for Reproducible Scientific Research: Licensing and Copyright," *Computing in Science and Engineering* 11, no. 1 (January/February 2009): 35.

[5] U.S. 17 § 107.

Distinguishing legal fair use is not a clear exercise, and an extension to research more broadly may still not sufficiently clarify rights. A preferable step would be to include academic research, identified perhaps by federal funding, directly in the fair use exception.

Another mechanism for realigning intellectual property rights with scientific norms is the Reproducible Research Standard (RRS). The first component of this standard is the application of an appropriate license to remove restrictions on copying and reusing the scientific work, as well as adding an attribution requirement to elements of the research compendium.

Components of the research compendium have different features that necessitate different licensing approaches. Licensing is given strength through rights created by the underlying copyright law: if these licenses are found invalid by a court, the work will still be considered under copyright. Effectively, this means that even if a license fails to be recognized as a valid contract by a court, use of the work will remain subject to injunction and other remedies associated with copyright violation.[7]

With myriad options for licensing copyright-protected work, a principle for scientific licensing can guide choices:

Principle of Scientific Licensing: *Legal encumbrances to the dissemination, sharing, use, and re-use of scientific research compendia should be minimized, and require a strong and compelling rationale before application.*[8]

The goal of an intellectual property legal framework for scientific research must be to increase what Benkler terms "that most precious of all public domains—our knowledge of the world that

---

[6] This idea was suggested in Paul A. David, "The Economic Logic of 'Open Science' and the Balance between Private Property Rights and the Public Domain in Scientific Data and Information: A Primer," Accessed January 12, 2009, http://ideas.repec.org/p/wpa/wuwpdc/0502006.html.

[7] This recourse to copyright for enforcement may not be necessary: a recent case (*Jacobsen v. Katzer*, 535 F.3d 1373 (Fed. Cir. 2008)) found a software license to be enforceable like a copyright condition for which courts can apply the remedy of injunction.

surrounds us."[9] This effort involves an alignment of the private incentives faced by a scientific researcher and the societal benefit of increasing our stock of public knowledge. Scientific norms have arisen to align these interests in practice, and an associated intellectual property structure should reflect these norms to allow scientific research to flourish.[10]

The Paper, Figures, and Other Media Files

For media components of scientific work, alignment with scientific norms is most readily and simply achievable through use of the Creative Commons attribution license (CC BY), which frees the work for replication and re-use, with the condition that attribution must accompany any downstream use of the work.

The Code

A plethora of licenses exist that allow authors to set conditions of use for their code. In scientific research, code can consist of scripts that are essentially stylized text files (such as MATLAB or R scripts) or the code can have both a compiled binary form and a source representation (such as code written in C). Use of the CC BY license for code is actively discouraged by Creative Commons.[11]

---

[8] A research *compendium* refers to the triple of research paper, and the code and data that underlies its results. See Robert Gentleman and Duncan Temple Lang, "Statistical Analyses and Reproducible Research" *Journal of Computational and Graphical Statistics* 16, no. 1 (2007): 1-23, http://www.bepress.com/bioconductor/paper2/.

[9] Yochai Benkler, "Constitutional Bounds of Database Protection: The Role of Judicial Review in the Creation and Definition of Private Rights in Information," *Berkeley Technology Law Journal* 15 (Fall 1999): 3, http://ssrn.com/abstract=214973.

[10] See Robert K. Merton, *The Sociology of Science* (Chicago: University of Chicago Press, 1973), for a description of the four scientific norms. Of particular interest to us is the "Communitarian" norm: that scientists relinquish ownership rights over their work in exchange for acknowledgement through citation or perhaps the naming of discoveries. This, in conjunction with the norm of "Skepticism" that establishes the close inspection and review of research work by the community, implies open access to scientific research, satisfying the interests of the larger community in the openness and availability of scientific research work. Paul David has made this observation in "The Economic Logic of 'Open Science'," 5.

The (Modified) Berkeley Software Distribution (BSD) license permits the downstream use, copying, and distribution of either unmodified or modified source code, as long as the license accompanies any distributed code and the previous authors' names are not used to promote modified downstream code.[12] The Modified BSD license is very similar to the MIT license, with the exception that the MIT license does not include a clause forbidding endorsement.[13]

The Apache 2.0 license is another common method for developers to specify terms of use of their work.[14] Like the Modified BSD and MIT licenses, the Apache license requires attribution. It differs from the previously discussed licenses in that it permits the exercise of patent rights that otherwise would extend only to the original licensor, meaning that a patent license is granted for those patents needed for use of the code. The license further stipulates that the right to use the work without patent infringement will be lost if the downstream user of the code sues the licensor for patent infringement. Attribution under Apache 2.0 requires that derivative works carry a copy of the license, with notice of any files modified. All copyright, trademark, and patent notices that pertain to the work must be included. Attribution can also be done in such a notice file.

Scientific Data

Collecting, cleaning, and otherwise preparing data for analysis is often a significant component of scientific research. Copyright law in the United States does not permit the copyrighting of "raw facts," but original products derived from those facts are copy-

[11] "[W]e do not recommend that you apply a Creative Commons license to software code," "FAQ." accessed January 5, 2009, http://wiki.creativecommons.org/FAQ.

[12] "Open Source Initiative OSI—The BDS License," accessed January 2, 2009, http://www.open-source.org/licenses/bsd-license.php.

[13] "Open Source Initiative OSI—The MIT License," accessed March 5, 2009, http://www.open-source.org/licenses/mit-license.php.

[14] "Apache License, Version 2.0," accessed January 1, 2009, http://www.apache.org/licenses/LICENSE-2.0.

rightable. In *Feist Publications, Inc. v. Rural Telephone Service*, the Supreme Court found that the white pages from telephone directories are not themselves directly copyrightable, since copyrightable works must have creative originality:[15]

> ...the copyright in a factual compilation is thin. Notwithstanding a valid copyright, a subsequent compiler remains free to use the facts contained in another's publication to aid in preparing a competing work, so long as the competing work does not feature the same selection and arrangement.[16]

Currently, the Court holds *original* "selection and arrangement" of databases protectable:[17] the component falling under copyright must be original in that "copyright# protection extends only to those components of the work that are original to the author, not to the facts themselves...."[18] The extraction of facts from a database does not violate copyright. Attaching an attribution license to the original "selection and arrangement" of a database can encourage scientists to release the datasets they have created by providing a legal framework for attribution and re-use of the original selection and arrangement aspect of their work.[19] Since

---

[15] *Feist Publications Inc. v. Rural Telephone Service Co.*, 363-364.

[16] Ibid., 349. See also Miriam Bitton, "A New Outlook on the Economic Dimension of the Database Protection Debate" and Hongwei Zhu and Stuart E. Madnick, "One Size does not Fit All: Legal Protection for Non-Copyrightable Data" (working paper CISL# 2007-04), accessed January 4, 2009, http://web.mit.edu/smadnick/www/wp/2007-04.pdf.

[17] Miriam Bitton, "A New Outlook," 4.

[18] *Feist Publications, Inc. v. Rural Telephone Services Co.*, 340. The full quote reads "Although a compilation of facts may possess the requisite originality because the author typically chooses which facts to include, in what order to place them, and how to arrange the data so that readers may use them effectively, copyright protection extends only to those components of the work that are original to the author, not to the facts themselves... As a constitutional matter, copyright protects only those elements of a work that possess more than *de minimis* quantum of creativity. Rural's white pages, limited to basic subscriber information and arranged alphabetically, fall short of the mark. As a statutory matter, 17 U.S.C. sec. 101 does not afford protection from copying to a collection of facts that are selected, coordinated, and arranged in a way that utterly lacks originality. Given that some works must fail, we cannot imagine a more likely candidate. Indeed, were we to hold that Rural's white pages pass muster, it is hard to believe that any collection of facts could fail." For a discussion of the Constitutional limits on Congress's ability to create property rights in facts see Yochai Benkler, "Constitutional Bounds of Database Protection."

the raw facts themselves are not copyrightable, it does not make sense to apply such a license to the data themselves. The selection and arrangement may be implemented in code or described in a text file accompanying the dataset, either of which can be appropriately licensed.

Since the components of research compendia are varied, licenses should be applied as appropriate to each component in accordance with the Principle of Scientific Licensing. Using CC BY on the media components of the research, such as text and figures, permits other scientists to freely use and reuse this work provided the original author is attributed. The same result is obtained by using a software license that provides an attribution component for the code components, such as the Apache License 2.0, the Modified BSD License,[20] or the MIT License. The original selection and arrangement of data can be similarly licensed depending on whether it takes a code or text format. Since an attribution license cannot be attached to raw facts, data can be released to the public domain by marking with the CC0 standard.[21] A licensing structure that makes media, code, data, and data arrangements— the research compendium—available for re-use, in the public domain or with attribution, is termed the Reproducible Research Standard.

PART II. GOVERNMENT FUNDING AGENCY POLICY SHOULD REQUIRE OPENNESS

Government funding agencies such as the National Institutes of Health (NIH), the National Science Foundation (NSF), and the

---

[19] See Anselm Kamperman Sanders, "Limits to database protection: Fair use and scientific research exemptions," *Research Policy* 35, no. 6 (July 2006): 854-874 (859 for a discussion of the international and WIPO statements of the legal status of databases).

[20] Creative Commons provides the BSD as a CC license, accessed March 5, 2009, See http://creativecommons.org/licenses/BSD/.

[21] For details on the CC0 protocol, see Creative Commons, "Creative Commons Launches CC0 and CC+ Programs," news release, December 17, 2007, http://creativecommons.org/press-releases/entry/7919 (accessed February 12, 2009).

Department of Energy (DOE) support an overwhelmingly large percentage of academic research in the United States. They often have policies that recommend and even require open release of funded research, including data and code, yet there is very little implementation or enforcement of these policies.[22] Washington is currently considering the extension of the open access implementation for manuscripts policies enacted by the NIH to other agencies,[23] but two things need to occur. Data and code must be included in the discussion of open access, and these policies of open access must be extended to agencies beyond the NIH. Each agency addresses very different bodies of research and thus implementation of open research may vary by agency, permitting each to face issues such as privacy, confidentiality, scientific norms including versioning and citation, and legal issues such as appropriate licensing of manuscripts, code, and data, as appropriate to the research communities involved. To aid in this effort, a number of research projects could be selected as pilots for the implementation of reproducible research thus providing an experiment in the full release of the code and data. Such carefully chosen pilot projects could help map out needs for open research, and then support could be given for these projects to facilitate their production of really reproducible research. This would create a scenario where it would be possible to learn what

---

[22] On May 10, 2010, the NSF announced that it would require the submission of a two-page data management plan along with grant applications for funding, beginning in October 2010. The impetus for the requirement is the need for open shared data: "Science is becoming data-intensive and collaborative," noted Ed Seidel, acting assistant director for NSF's Mathematical and Physical Sciences directorate. "Researchers from numerous disciplines need to work together to attack complex problems; openly sharing data will pave the way for researchers to communicate and collaborate more effectively." "This is the first step in what will be a more comprehensive approach to data policy," added Cora Marrett, NSF acting deputy director. "It will address the need for data from publicly funded research to be made public." See National Science Foundation, "Scientists Seeking NSF Funding Will Soon Be Required to Submit Data Management Plans," news release, May 10, 2010, http://www.nsf.gov/news/news_summ.jsp?cntn_id=116928&org=NSF.

[23] On April 15, 2010, Rep. Doyle reintroduced the Federal Research Public Access Act (H.R. 5037), seeking to make published papers from federally funded research publicly available over the Internet. See http://thomas.loc.gov/cgi-bin/bdquery/z?d111:HR05037:@@@P for the full text of the bill. A similar bill was introduced in the Senate on June 25, 2009 (S. 1373), by Senators Lieberman and Cornyn.

support, in terms of repositories, funding, or infrastructure, is needed and at what expense.[24]

To give an example, the National Science Foundation (NSF), through its role as a funding agency, makes a key contribution to the research incentives faced by many computational scientists and is in a unique position to address issues regarding verification of results, both through its research funding activities and policy leadership. There are five interlocking barriers to code and data release within funding agency purview: crafting appropriate release guidelines; collaborative tool development; intellectual property issues; facilitating access to research compendia;[25] and provision of "best practices" statements.

Issue 1: Enforcement of Existing Grant Guidelines

The NSF, for example, requires data and other supporting materials for any research it funds to be made available to other researchers at no more than incremental cost (with a provision for safeguards the right of individuals and subjects). The following passage is from the January 2009 NSF Grant General Conditions:

> **38. Sharing of Findings, Data, and Other Research Products**
>
> a. NSF expects significant findings from research and education activities it supports to be promptly submitted for publication, with authorship that accurately reflects the contributions of those involved. It expects investigators to share with other researchers, at no more than incremental cost and within a reasonable time, the data, samples, physical collections and other support-

---

[24] On January 18, 2011 the National Science Foundation will require the submission of a two-page *Data Management Plan* with every grant, thereby creating a complementary experiment that also will reveal research needs and the costs associated with supporting reproducible research. See http://www.nsf.gov/bfa/dias/policy/dmp.jsp.

[25] The term research "compendium" was coined by Robert Gentleman and Duncan Temple Lang to refer to "both a container for the different elements that make up the document and its computations (i.e. text, code, data...), and as a means for distributing, managing and updating the collection." See Gentleman and Lang, "Statistical Analyses and Reproducible Research."

ing materials created or gathered in the course of the work. It also encourages grantees to share software and inventions or otherwise act to make the innovations they embody widely useful and usable.[26]

This passage requires the release of data collected through NSF-funded activities, and recommends the release of accompanying software.

Recommendation 1.1: NSF Policy Expression

An important step would be to open the discussion of rewording the General Conditions to include the release of software, just as data are required to be released. Section 38 could be modified in the spirit of the following:

> **38. Sharing of Findings, Data, and Other Research Products**
>
> a. NSF expects significant findings from research and education activities it supports to be promptly submitted for publication, with authorship that accurately reflects the contributions of those involved. It expects investigators to share with other researchers, at no more than incremental cost and within a reasonable time, the data, samples, physical collections and other supporting materials, *such as software and inventions, created or* gathered in the course of the work. *Data and software should be made available in such a way that they are easily reusable by someone knowledgeable in the field.* (emphasis added)

Often the steps taken to generate computational results are embodied in software scripts or code. Computational research can includes a large number of small decisions—from data collation and filters, to software invocation sequences and parameter settings used in algorithms—that are impossible to capture com-

---

[26] National Science Foundation, *Grant General Conditions (GC-1)*, January 5, 2009, http://www.nsf.gov/pubs/gc1/jan09.pdf (accessed Sept. 26, 2009).

pletely in the final published paper, simply due to their multiplicity. A potentially fruitful way of communicating research methodology in these cases is to release the underlying code for inspection. Release of the accompanying data is the second necessary step for reproducibility of published computational findings.

Recommendation 1.2: Grantee-developed Release Plans

A blanket requirement of code and data release indicates funding agency intent but is not sufficient to create a regulatory environment in which researchers share easily reusable code and data, due to the difficulty in preparing code and data for release and widespread use. The use of computational tools is appearing in an increasing number of aspects of modern scientific research, making the myriad research settings in which these tools are used very complex, highly differentiated, and granular. One size does not fit all research problems, and a heavy-handed release requirement could result in *de jure* compliance—release of code and data—without the extra effort necessary to create usable code and data that facilitates the verification of the results. A solution partially under way (see footnote 28) would be to require grant applicants to formulate plans for release of the code and data generated through their research proposal, if funded. This creates a natural experiment where grantees, who know their research environments best, contribute complete strategies for release. This experiment would allow the funding agency to gather data on needs for release (repositories, further support); understand which research problem characteristics engender what particular solutions; identify what solutions are most appropriate in what settings; and uncover as yet unrecognized problems particular researchers may encounter. These findings would permit the funding agency to craft code and data release requirements that are more sensitive to barriers researchers face and the demands of their particular research problems, and implements strategies for enforcement of these requirements. This approach also permits researchers to address confidentiality and privacy issues associated with their research. This would not be the first implementation of this approach to policy crafting. The Wellcome Trust in the

United Kingdom began requiring grant applicants to submit comprehensive data release plans more than two years ago, and they are on the cusp of enforcing and observing these plans in action as grantees are now beginning to generate datasets from their funded research.[27]

Issue 2: Tools for Collaboration and Work Sharing

In the world of computing in general, not just scientific computing, the ubiquity of error has led to many responses, including special programming languages, error-tracking systems, disciplined programming efforts, and organized program-testing schemes. These efforts are key in developing a system of code and data release that does not create an overwhelming burden on the part of the computational scientist.

Recommendation 2.1: Funding of Software and Tool Development

Researchers use computational resources in very different ways. Examples range from short MATLAB scripts to the millions of lines of code, perhaps spanning several languages, that can underlie a complex simulation. The underlying software was typically not designed with scientific needs in mind and is generally a dialog with a single user, who would like to implement an algorithm or other innovation. It is up to the user to take extra steps to save the coding efforts and decisions taken, to record program invocation sequences and parameter settings, and otherwise track provenance of their research. These are exactly the steps it is important to share for verifiability, yet they are often not recorded as a natural part of the computational research process. In the heat of a computational project, researchers store many things in short-term memory that are needed at that moment to use the code productively. Facilitating the burden of code and data release means avoiding reliance on this soft, transient knowledge

---

[27] Nicole Perrin, Senior Policy Advisor, Wellcome Trust Limited, UK, "Data Matters: A Research Funder's Perspective" (keynote speech at COMMUNIA, Torino, June 29, 2009). See also "Wellcome Trust, policy on data management and sharing," last modified August 2010, http://www. wellcome.ac.uk/About-us/Policy/Policy-and-position-statements/WTX035043.htm.

and, more specifically, codifying that knowledge objectively and reproducibly. An analogy could be drawn to the lab notebook kept by experimentalists. Its purpose is to record experimental methodology precisely, and is standard practice for all experimental sciences.

Tools for provenance are emerging but need to be developed at a much faster rate and for a much wider number of research problems, at a wider range of scales.[28] Even the solo researcher running software on his or her laptop can benefit from a system designed with the understanding that elements of the work that produce published results will be shared. Version control systems for code exist but are not routinely used by all computational scientists. Provenance tools must be easy to use since many researchers who use computational methods are not computer specialists. Aspects such as unit testing and standardized test beds (as is typical in open source code development) should be emphasized and even required for scientific code.

The scope of this problem is broad enough to warrant a discussion of targeted funding from the NSF and other agencies that fund computational work, particularly as research begins to move into the cloud and increasingly takes place in shared virtual spaces. Many computational scientists will require retraining in the use of software that tracks provenance and allows for such workflow sharing.

In a recent survey of computational scientists, the incremental amount of work involved in preparing code and data for release was the primary barrier to open code and data sharing.[29] Routinely used software tools typically lack a system of incorpo-

---

[28] See http://twiki.ipaw.info/bin/view/Challenge/FirstProvenanceChallenge; the UK-funded Taverna software package, http://www.mygrid.org.uk/; the Sumatra package for reproducible simulations, http://neuralensemble.org/trac/sumatra; the Pegasus system developed at the University of Southern California, http://pegasus.isi.edu/; and Galaxy software developed at Penn State University, http://galaxy.psu.edu/. See Microsoft's Trident Workbench for an oceanography example, http://research.microsoft.com/en-us/collaboration/tools/trident.aspx.

[29] See Victoria Stodden, "The Scientific Method and Computation: Reproducibility in the Computational Sciences" (forthcoming).

rating the preparation of code as data for release, as the research is progressing. Recreating steps previously taken is difficult for any scientist when working in a programming environment designed for running code, but not for sharing or working collaboratively. Such tools will not only facilitate the release of coherent and reusable code and data, but ease research collaboration and facilitate communication of work in progress between coauthors. A challenge for scientific research is developing software environments to enable collaborative research, and facilitating reproducibility of computational results is a key step in this process.

Recommendation 2.2: Funding of Statistical Methods for Simulation-Based Modeling

An increasingly pervasive methodological tool is the use of massive simulations of a physical system's complete evolution, repeated numerous times while varying simulation parameters systematically. Such models in climate research provide the foundation for some of our most crucial public policy decisions and are beginning to represent scientific research in the public dialogue. Statistical machinery analogous to such long-standing tools in conventional modeling as error bounds on prediction, parameter estimation, and overall model fit must be developed in the case of computer simulation. An important step is the development of workflow-tracking software environments to facilitate tracing of error sources as mentioned previously, but further research is needed to understand how to evaluate the output of simulations. Since this is a new area of research, framing of the uncertainty quantification problem should be carefully undertaken as a preliminary step to a broader research agenda.

Issue 3: The Intellectual Property Framework for Code and Data Release

Even though scientists produce public goods, their work is not immune to intellectual property strictures, as elaborated in Part I.

Recommendation 3.1: Adopting the Reproducible Research Standard

As discussed in the previous section, the Reproducible Research Standard (RRS) realigns the intellectual property framework faced by computational researchers with longstanding scientific norms.[30] The RRS suggests a licensing structure for research compendia, including code and data, which permits others to use and reuse code and data without having to obtain prior permission or assume a fair use exception to copyright, so long as attribution is given.[31] Using the RRS on all components of computational scholarship will encourage reproducible scientific investigation, facilitate greater collaboration, and promote engagement of the larger community in scientific learning and discovery.

Issue 4: Access to Published Research Papers and Supporting Materials

Asking computational scientists to embrace reproducibility poses questions with regard to location of research compendia on the Internet and access to published results.

Recommendation 4.1: Funding Agency Public Access Policy

Reproducibility requires not only access to underlying code and data, but access to the original published article. Funding agencies such as the NSF and DOE could create a digital archive, analogous to the National Institutes of Health's PubMed Central, and require the deposit of their funded final manuscripts. The NIH

---

[30] For a full discussion of the Reproducible Research Standard, see Victoria Stodden, "Enabling Reproducible Research."

[31] Fair use is how the U.S. copyright law provides for the use of copyrighted works without the need to obtain the copyright holder's permission, in order to provide flexibility in balancing the interests of copyright holders and the public's desire to make use of copyrighted works. The copyright statute states that "...the fair use of a copyrighted work, including such use by reproduction in copies or phonorecords or by any other means specified by that section, for purposes such as criticism, comment, news reporting, teaching (including multiple copies for classroom use), scholarship, or research, is not an infringement of copyright." (17 U.S.C. § 107). Whether or not use of copyrighted material can be deemed fair use is fact specific and subject to a four-factor test. How far the scholarship exception extends is unclear, and scientists may not feel comfortable relying on it when building on another scientist's research through, for example, reusing code.

requires that papers that arise from NIH funds comply with their public access to policy: final peer-reviewed journal manuscripts must be submitted to PubMed Central upon acceptance for publication, and become accessible to the public no longer than twelve months after publication.[32]

The NIH further requires that copyright be addressed. If publicly funded research falls under the Reproducible Research Standard as described in Section 3, articles will be licensed using the Creative Commons attribution license, therefore removing copyright barriers from the paper. Many journals, however, require authors to assign copyright to the journal as a condition of publication, but will allow an earlier version to be posted publicly. The NIH has made publication in journals that permit the article, or a version thereof, to be posted in PubMed Central a requirement of funding—this strategy is an option for other funding agencies as well.

The final requirement the NIH makes of grant recipients is to use the PubMed Central identifier at the end of citations. Encouraging the use of unique identifiers of papers, as well as code and data, can encourage the release and hence citation of all forms of computational research.[33] Such a unique identifier would indicate compliance with funder agency open-access policies.

It is important that these requirements be tied to grant funding and a mechanism established that allows compliance to be reflected in future grant determinations. Strategies for release of code and data arising from a particular grant should be subject to peer review in the grant evaluation process.

---

[32] The twelve-month post-publication grace period could be applied to code and data release, upon researcher request. This strategy was advocated for genome data in "Prepublication data sharing," *Nature* 461, (10 September 2009): 168-170, http://www.nature.com/nature/journal/v461/n7261/full/461168a.html.

[33] See e.g. Altman and King's Uniform Numerical Identifier proposal for data citation, http://thedata.org/citation/standard. This also can ensure that an unmodified version of a dataset is used in different research studies, when confidentiality or other concerns prohibit open release of the dataset.

Recommendation 4.2: Funding Agencies Support Digital Archiving for Data and Code

For papers whose results can be replicated from short scripts and small datasets, many computational scientists who do engage in reproducible research are able to host their research compendia on their institutional web pages or using hosting resources their institution is willing to provide.[34] Not all computation research involves small amounts of supplemental code and data; hosting very large datasets or complex bodies of code may be necessary and home institutional support may not be available to the researcher. A funding agency could create code and data repositories as for papers (perhaps even jointly among agencies), or seek to increase support of the growing set of data repositories emerging at institutions.[35] Data is necessary for reproducibility of computational research, but an equal amount of concern should be directed at code sharing. As yet, code sharing repositories are not established to the extent that data repositories are.

Tagging of research compendia is an important issue for communicating work, facilitating topical web searches, and aggregating a researcher's contributions, including their code and dataset building activities. Development of a standard RDFa vocabulary for HTML tags for publicly funded research would enable searches for code, data, and research as well as facilitating the transmission of licensing information, authorship, and sources. That such a standard would enable searches by author would allow a more granular understanding of a scientist's research contributions, beyond citations. This would provide an incentive to release code and data, and give groups, such as funders, award committees, and university hiring and promotion committees, access to a more accurate representation of the researcher's work. Such a tagging vocabulary could include unique identifiers for code and data, ideally the same as those required for repository deposit as

---

[34] See e.g. http://sparselab.stanford.edu and http://www-stat.stanford.edu/~wavelab.

[35] See e.g. The Stanford Microarray Database, http://smd.stanford.edu/.

discussed in the previous section, and thus facilitate and encourage their citation.

Issue 5: Reproducible Research "Best Practice" Recommendations

Computational scientists may be unaware of the need to work reproducibly, researchers may be unaware of what it means to do so, and funding agencies and journals may find it useful to have a clear explanation of the issue and its implementation at the funding agency.

Recommendation 5.1: Release of Funding Agency "Best Practice" Recommendations

Such a document would be publicly available at a stable URL, updated with versions, and intended to provide clarity on all relevant issues. It would be framed to suggest ideal recommendations, rather than list a series of requirements. Some points that such a list may wish to touch on follow below.

Reproducibility is a goal of computational science, and practicing reproducible research means:

- Uploading the final peer-reviewed journal manuscripts that arise from agency-funded research to a digital archive upon acceptance for publication;
- Making the code and data required to reproduce results in agency-funded works publicly available online within twelve months of publication (or less);
- Utilizing appropriate licensing structures for agency-funded research, such as the Reproducible Research Standard; and
- Utilizing tagging structures for agency-funded compendia release, as part of inclusion in repositories or posting on institutional repositories.

The Necessity of a Multifaceted Approach

This discussion is intended to frame issues that arise with the implementation of reproducibility in computational science.

These recommendations reflect a set of interlocking issues, and progress from one recommendation will be facilitated by implementation of other recommendations.

Part III. Untangling Ownership Issues for Scientific Collaboration and Open Dissemination: A New Vision for University Leadership

With the advent of large-scale data and the pervasiveness of computing in scientific research, ownership issues for code and data have yet to be fully addressed. Data often are generated in collaboration with co-researchers, who may be in academia, government, or the private sector, and funding sources can be equally as varied. Copyright endows authors of code with exclusive rights, contracts with universities often give home institutions a claim, and evidence suggests that journals are turning their publishing models for articles toward hosting and releasing the associated code and data. To make matters more complex, repositories for both code and data are coming online with their own ownership and licensing schemes for scientific products.

When data and code are widely shared, such ownership issues come sharply to the fore. What is missing today is clarity regarding ownership rights, which can vary by case, and one ownership model may not transfer from one research setting to the next. To accelerate the wide dissemination of newly discovered scientific knowledge, an ombudsman position needs to be created at the university level, perhaps within the Copyright Office or Provost's Office, to streamline the process of rights ascertainment and negotiate agreements for sharing of collaboratively created code and data. This position would be regarded as temporary, perhaps lasting a decade, during which a set of typical sharing arrangements would emerge. In the longer term, negotiation over ownership and sharing rights would be shifted to the beginning of the project, when collaborators could typically adopt one of the small number of established emergent ownership models.

There are a limited number of possible claims in data and code ownership. The scientists themselves, their university, or funding bodies (public and private) are principal stakeholders. Ownership rights vested in the scientist present the least complex case, in that norms of openness in methods and in reproducible research exist, even if they are not always carefully implemented. In my recent survey of computational scientists, there emerged a clear tension between open science and code patenting.[36] Some respondents noted that a reason not to share their code even after publication was the possibility of patents (and the possibility of forming a company around the patented technology). A perhaps unexpected result of the Bayh-Dole Act of 1980, passed on the eve of the computer revolution in scientific research, was the creation of incentives for universities and academic researchers to lock scientific knowledge in patents. With the intention of providing an impetus for universities to transfer innovations outside academia and thus facilitate commercial and industrial development, the result has been the creation of a barrier to both scientific integrity and openness in the communication of scientific discovery, insofar as innovations are not shared openly.[37] For scientific findings to be reproducible, code and data must be open and verifiable, and to accelerate scientific innovation the code and data must be modifiable, reusable, and able to be applied to novel research problems. Patented code inserts the university's Office of Technology Licensing into this process, disrupting the open flow of downstream scientific research. A second recommendation is an automatic exception from patent use restrictions on code used for academic research purposes, still permitting commercial development of new technologies. This could be achieved through an open licensing structure that distinguishes between commercial and noncommercial downstream use of the scientific output.

---

[36] Victoria Stodden, "The Scientific Method in Practice: Reproducibility in the Computational Sciences" (MIT Sloan Research Paper no. 4773-10), http://papers.ssrn.com/sol3/papers.cfm?abstract_id=1550193.

[37] For a further description, see Joseph Stiglitz and John Sulston, "The Manchester Manifesto" (November 2009), Available at http://www.isei.manchester.ac.uk/TheManchesterManifesto.pdf.

Open code is emerging as a requirement for publication and is a clear component of reproducible computational research. A clash is emerging between the requirements for scientific integrity in the computer age—open code and data—and the incentives of the university to extract licensing fees from patented code written by university researchers. Without the creation of an exemption for code re-use in the academic setting, including the verification of published results and the application to new research problems, scientific integrity will suffer, deepening the current credibility crisis in computational science.[38] The university is uniquely positioned to play a key leadership role in establishing standard protocols and sharing agreements among scientific collaborators that facilitate the wide dissemination of discoveries and knowledge, thereby accelerating innovation and growth.

---

[38] An analogous proposal has been made by Paul David, when he suggested expanding the Fair Use provision in copyright law to encompass all academic research output. See Paul David, "The Economic Logic of 'Open Science.'"

18: Innovating Our Way to Disasters? Incentivizing Secure Platforms for Growth's Future

Benjamin Wittes*

INTRODUCTION

Imagine for a moment that the Gulf oil spill had taken place as a consequence of a premeditated attack, rather than an accident. Perhaps a terrorist group hit the Deepwater Horizon. Or, if you like, choose your favorite rogue state as the malefactor. The damage is the same; the oil flowed in the same volume. The only difference between this dark fantasy and the reality that unfolded in the summer of 2010 is volition: in the fantasy, someone meant to do it.

A few conclusions and insights would follow ineluctably from this counterfactual scenario. We would, first, immediately recognize the event not merely as a disaster but as an event of national security magnitude. Indeed, we would understand it as the most successful assault on the United States since September 11, 2001. We would notice something else as well: the United States

* Benjamin Wittes is a senior fellow in Governance Studies at The Brookings Institution. He is the author of *Detention and Denial: The Case for Candor After Guantánamo*, forthcoming from the Brookings Institution Press, and *Law and the Long War: The Future of Justice in the Age of Terror*, published in June 2008 by The Penguin Press.

government—despite its ability to project military force anywhere in the world—lacked the capacity to defend the country effectively and swiftly against this particular attack. The government had no capacity to stanch the flow of oil or to plug the well. That capacity, rather, lay in the hands of a private corporation, one of a select group of corporations that have proven enormously innovative in offshore oil drilling. These corporations have proven so innovative, in fact, that only they, and not the U.S. federal government, have the technological and logistical capacity to defend the country against the national security events their very innovations can now bring about. In the BP disaster, the role of the federal government was largely that of coordinator of private-sector response. Add the element of volition and it becomes obvious that there exists a class of attack using innovation as a platform against which the federal government is no longer capable of defending the country.

This rather startling conclusion represents a profound challenge to a country whose constitution vests the power to defend the nation in a unitary presidency. Indeed, it presents a challenge to any state that assumes that its government can protect it against external attack and preserve some measure of internal order. Over the past several decades—in a trend that is sure to accelerate rapidly with continued innovation—we have developed a category of nonmilitary technologies outside of government hands and control that, when misused, can threaten extreme harms of various types, harms which government lacks clear power, authority, or even simple capability to prevent. BP's recent disaster is far from the most extreme example of this trend. Though usefully vivid in our minds now, oil drilling actually exhibits only some of the features of the innovations that most directly pose this challenge.

The trend is not futuristic. It already is well under way across a number of technological platforms—most prominently the life sciences and networked computer technology. The technologies in question are widely proliferated. They are getting cheaper by the day. They are classic innovations of the best, most growth-inducing sort. As a global community, we are becoming ever more dependent upon them not just for growth, jobs, and development but for health, agriculture, communications, even culture.

Yet these same technologies—and these same dependencies—make us enormously vulnerable. Whereas once only states could contemplate killing huge numbers of civilians with a devastating drug-resistant illness or taking down another country's power grids, we must now contemplate the possibility of ever-smaller groupings of people undertaking what are traditionally understood as acts of war. The latter part of the twentieth century and the first few years of the new one saw the migration of the destructive power of states to global nonstate actors, particularly Al-Qaeda. The twenty-first century seems likely to continue that migration, ultimately giving to every individual with modest education and a certain level of technical proficiency the power—if he is innovative enough—to bring about catastrophic damage.[1]

This development obviously raises a serious problem for anyone interested in fostering long-term growth and innovation. Growth, after all, does not take place in the absence of some basic conditions of security. Yet a world in which large numbers of individuals and small groups are capable of launching attacks on essential platforms whose security the state cannot assure is a world which may not meet the minimum security conditions to support long-term growth. And that possibility raises a deeply uncomfortable question that we are going to have to address as a political and legal community: Might we be innovating our way to an environment that is actually toxic to innovation and growth, and can we innovate our way out? What sort of innovation might it take to manage security in such an environment? And can the legal system foster such innovation? Put another way, can we grow more securely, and what innovations would secure growth require?

---

[1] Phillip Bobbitt, *Terror and Consent: The Wars for the Twenty-First Century* (New York: Alfred A. Knopf, 2008).

My purpose in this chapter is to advance the notion that anyone serious about long-term growth needs to think hard about the security of the platforms on which that growth will be predicated. We need as a society to begin incentivizing the development of more secure platforms that minimize our vulnerability to disasters. Toward this end, I mean to sketch out three broad legal approaches, some of which can reasonably be expected to inhibit short-term growth to a degree and some of which will deeply challenge the libertarian ethos of, in particular, the online world. First, I shall argue, we need to develop clear rules assigning liability for platform vulnerabilities recklessly introduced or maintained in the system. Second, we need to develop a comfort level with a certain degree of platform surveillance. And third, and most challenging, we need to come to grips with the fact that certain companies by dint of their businesses may have unique *affirmative obligations* to the security of platforms. These companies will inherit certain security functions we traditionally associate with the executive branch and—just as BP was the so-called "responsible party" that had to defend the Gulf Coast against its own oil—may necessarily be called upon to act accordingly. This may happen even in situations in which the companies, unlike BP, are not the sources of the disasters to which they alone can react.

THE PROBLEM

Dwelling on high-impact, low-probability events may seem like a dissonant note to strike in a volume broadly concerned with the more optimistic subjects of fostering growth and innovation and thus improving human happiness and well-being. There is, in fact, no dissonance at all. Growth and innovation require a measure of stability over time. There's nothing quite like mayhem to undermine confidence in the systems, governments, and institutions on which growth depends. An environment in which the technologies our economic lives depend on become systemic platforms for devastating attacks simply will not support the kind of sustained robust growth which the authors of this volume all wish to see.

The goal, which bears emphasis, is to maximize *sustained* growth. It is not to create bubbles. Just as individuals and business happily pay insurance premiums to hedge against disasters that would otherwise ruin them, we should be willing to grow more slowly to ensure that the growth in question is sustainable. Investing in the security of platforms seems to me essential to making sure that we do not depend for our growth on conditions that will prove highly vulnerable to bad actors, enemies, and accidents. Jonathan Zittrain has made this point eloquently with respect to the Internet. The generative nature of the Internet, he argues, has given rise to security problems that, if not addressed, threaten to move us away from generativity, which he regards as one of the Internet's chief virtues.[2] But the point, I suspect, is broader, encompassing platforms far beyond the Internet.

The technologies which pose the greatest concern for national security these days are, perhaps unsurprisingly, also the same technologies that offer the greatest promise in general. The concern and the promise emanate from the same source: these are technologies of mass empowerment, and delivering enormous new capacity to large numbers of individuals creates the certainty that some of those individuals will use that capacity to do evil. In the absence of particularly resilient systems, these technologies magnify the cost of accidents, and they both facilitate the activities of those with ill intent and magnify the consequences of their behaviors as well. The same technologies that can, say, allow two engineering students to start Google or let biotech entrepreneurs sequence the human genome also can create a permissive environment for the creation of what Lawrence Lessig calls "Insanely Destructive Devices."[3] These can take the form of anthrax bacte-

---

[2] Jonathan Zittrain, *The Future of the Internet and How to Stop It* (New Haven, CT: Yale University Press, 2007).

[3] Lawrence Lessig, "Insanely Destructive Devices: Trying to Defend against Self-Replicating Weapons of Mass Destruction," *Wired* 12, no. 4 (April 2004), accessed November 15, 2010, http://www.wired.com/wired/archive/12.04/view.html?pg=5.

ria sent through the mail, cyberattacks on critical infrastructure, or most likely something we have not even thought of yet.

Stewart Baker, former policy chief at the Department of Homeland Security, elegantly described in a recent book cycles of technological innovation, social excitement about the new technology, exploitation of that technology, and dependence upon it—all with inadequate appreciation of the degree of vulnerability this dependence generates. We build airplanes and fly them all over the world, for example. We dramatically lower the price of commercial air travel until long-distance travel is a norm for people's day-to-day lives. And nobody spends much time considering the possibility that someone smart and creative can make missiles out of our commercial jets using nothing but box cutters and ruthlessness. "Technology—cheap commercial jet travel—made the [September 11] attacks possible. In fact, it made attacks like September 11 more or less inevitable," Baker writes.[4] The more dependent we become on technologies available universally, the more we make ourselves vulnerable to the devastating misuse of those technologies. This is not a Luddite argument against technological development, just recognition that innovation that creates dependency also creates exposure. A society that stakes its future on the Internet, as the modern world has, makes itself enormously vulnerable to those with the will and the capacity to use its communications architecture to disrupt, say, its banking or military operations.

Technologies of mass empowerment—of which biotechnology and globally networked computers are the paradigmatic examples—have certain common characteristics that bear emphasis. First, they are widely disseminated technologies that depend on readily available training and materials. Unlike nuclear technologies, they did not develop principally in classified settings at government-run labs with the government's controlling access to the key materials. Rather, they developed in public in open dialogue

---

[4] Stewart Baker, *Skating on Stilts: Why We Aren't Stopping Tomorrow's Terrorism* (Stanford, CA: Hoover Institution Press, 2010), 12.

with nonmilitary purposes in mind. Scientists did not discover the double helix or sequence the human genome in order figure out how to design viruses to kill people. Nor did engineers build the Internet so that terrorists or foreign governments could seize control of the Hoover Dam—or even so that our intelligence agencies could seize control of some other country's dams. Yet in the cyber arena, attacks have grown up alongside the platform. And in the biotech arena, a public literature now exists to teach bad guys how to do horrific things—and the materials, unlike highly enriched uranium, are neither scarce nor expensive.

Second, the destructive technologies are virtually inseparable from the socially beneficial innovations that give rise to them. In the wrong hands, the research on how to use genetics to cure and prevent disease can be used to cause and spread disease. A paper on how to shield computers against viruses necessarily involves analysis of viruses that one can use to write stronger ones. Defensive research in this space will potentially empower the bad guys too.

Third, the use of these technologies blurs the distinction between foreign and domestic threats and, indeed, makes attribution of any attack extremely difficult. As every student in a biological laboratory and every individual on his home computer becomes a possible threat to national security, traditional techniques of surveillance, deterrence, and nonproliferation become increasingly ill suited to detecting and preventing terrorist activity. Large numbers of cyberattacks already take place with attribution impossible or long delayed. In the case of the anthrax attacks in the wake of September 11, attribution took seven years and remains to this day contested. Indeed, often in these cases, a targeted entity will not be able to determine whether its attacker is another state, a political group, a criminal group, or a lone gunman.

The life sciences present a prototypical case of this type of techno-logical development, threatening realistically to put the power of a WMD attack in the hands if not of the average person, certainly of many above-average people with relatively inexpensive equipment and basic training in genetic engineering. Biological weapons are unique among weapons of mass destruction in that they have the capacity, like nuclear weapons, to produce truly catastrophic damage, yet like chemical weapons, are comparatively inexpensive and easy to produce. The technology required for their production is generally the same as the technology used in legitimate life sciences research; indeed, it is the bread-and-butter stuff of the biotech revolution that has done so much good throughout the world. Precisely because modern biotechnology has so much promise and offers so many benefits in so many walks of life, the materials and skills required to develop these weapons are not rare. Just run a Google search on "gene synthesis companies" and you'll see a whole industry that will make DNA sequences for order over the Internet. While it may be difficult for even a highly trained individual to build his own nuclear weapon, an individual with relatively modest expertise and resources could potentially obtain or develop his own biological weapon with worldwide consequences. As costs continue to fall, the number of people whom governments around the world have to regard—at least in theory—as capable of having their own personal WMD programs grows commensurately.

The vulnerability of the world's network infrastructure similarly illustrates the growing capacity of small groups to become players in international relations and global security issues. The information technology underlying today's computer and communications networks, like biotechnology, is inherently dual use. Military IT depends largely on commercial IT developed in the private sector.[5] According to one estimate, 95 percent of the U.S. military's information transfers occur on civilian networks.[6] The expertise to launch cyberattacks is widely distributed

---

[5] William A. Owens, Kenneth W. Dam, and Herbert S. Lin, ed., *Technology, Policy, Law and Ethics Regarding U.S. Acquisition and Use of Cyberattack Capabilities* (Washington, DC: National Academies Press, 2009), 2.2.1.

[6] Vida M. Antolin-Jenkins, "Defining the Parameters of Cyberwar Operations: Looking for Law in All the Wrong Places?" *Naval Law Review* 51 (2005): 133.

throughout the world among states, organized criminal gangs, and individuals.

Most cyberattacks, of course, are the equivalent of street crime. Computer crime and identity theft are big business, after all. A National Science Foundation report in 2006 stated that "nearly all indicators of frequency, impact, scope, and cost of cybersecurity incidents show a continuously worsening picture. This is true whether one considers the losses due to IT-based fraud and theft, identity theft and attacks on personal information, incidence of viruses and malicious code, number of compromised systems or other types of impact."[7] Challenging though this climate is, the challenge is generally akin to life in a bad neighborhood. It presents personal-security and business-security concerns more than national security concerns. Like all crime kept at manageable levels, cybercrime limits growth, but it does not profoundly threaten it.

But cybersecurity has a more menacing side as well—one that brings it squarely into the national security arena. At the low end, this is an espionage problem, and it is going on every day. As Jack Goldsmith writes,

> For the past few decades, and with increasing frequency, many thousands of foreign agents …, sitting before computer monitors abroad, have "entered" the United States to steal or to destroy valuable digital assets. They have raided the Pentagon and other government agencies to disrupt their communications and to lift sensitive or classified information. They have attacked American corporations and taken or destroyed untold millions of dollars worth of data or intellectual property. They have contacted CEOs and credibly threatened to destroy their businesses unless the CEOs met the extortionists' demands. And they have planted mali-

---

[7] Seymour E. Goodman and Herbert S. Lin, ed., *Toward a Safer and More Secure Cyberspace* (Washington, DC: National Academies Press, 2007), 32.

cious software—known ominously as malware—inside government and corporate headquarters, and in critical infrastructure systems such as electrical grids and power plants. Some of this malware allows them to monitor activities in these places; other malware, called "logic bombs," enables them to trigger a destructive attack years later, if doing so would be useful.

If this were happening before our eyes—if thousands of foreign agents were physically entering our borders, breaking into brick-and-mortar buildings, and removing or destroying billions of dollars of proprietary information and monetary assets—the government would declare a national emergency. But it is happening largely out of public sight, on computers and computer networks, and so most people are not worried.[8]

At the higher end, the problem involves still-hypothetical attacks aimed at disabling society's civilian or military functionality. A cyberattack could aim at a nation's military operations or seek to disrupt its social and economic activity. An attack also could target critical infrastructure, like power-generation facilities.

As with biological attacks, it is hard to estimate the probability of a truly catastrophic cyberattack; the subject is a matter of earnest and legitimate debate among experts. The National Science Foundation wrote in 2006 that "high-level threats—spawned by motivated, sophisticated, and well-resourced adversaries—could increase very quickly on a very short time-scale, potentially leading to what some dub a 'digital Pearl Harbor' (that is, a catastrophic event whose occurrence can be unambiguously traced to flaws in cybersecurity)—and that the nation's IT vendors and users (both individual and corporate) would have to respond very quickly when such threats emerge." (Goodman & Lin 2007, 49). Similarly, former Director of National Intelligence Admiral

---

[8] Jack Goldsmith, "The New Vulnerability," *The New Republic*, June 7, 2010, accessed November 15, 2010, http://www.tnr.com/article/books-and-arts/75262/the-new-vulnerability.

Michael McConnell has repeatedly warned of an electronic Pearl Harbor involving an artificially induced collapse of confidence in the banking sector.[9] And Richard Clarke, the former National Security Council staffer who most presciently anticipated the threat posed by Al-Qaeda, writes that "the most likely targets are civilian in nature. The speed at which thousands of targets can be hit, almost anywhere in the world, brings with it the prospect of highly volatile crises." Clarke describes how coordinated cyberattacks could paralyze the United States on a number of levels simultaneously.[10]

Clarke seems to treat a cyberdisaster as a virtual certainty, and McConnell likewise talks about it with evident alarm as an immediate and very realistic threat. Cybersecurity expert Bruce Schneier, by contrast, regards the treat of cyberterrorism as overstated:

> I believe that fears about cyberterrorism, or the likelihood of a "Digital Pearl Habor," are largely the result of companies and organizations wanting to stoke the fears of people and of the news media looking for sensationalist stories. Real terrorism—attacking the physical world via the Internet—is much harder than most people think, and the effects of cyber attacks are far less terrorizing than might seem at first. Cyberterrorism is simply not a problem that we have to worry about....
>
> While people overplay the risks of cyberterrorism, they underplay the risks of cyber-crime....
>
> And someday, cyberterrorism will become a real threat. But that day is not coming soon, and even then the same terrorist would probably have a much easier time

---

[9] I was present at one such speech, a keynote address at the *Texas Law Review*'s annual symposium in February 2010.

[10] Richard A. Clarke and Robert K. Knake, *Cyberwar: The Next Threat to National Security and What to Do About It* (New York: Ecco, 2010).

killing the same number of people in a physical attack.[11]

My point is not that Clarke and McConnell are necessarily correct in this debate; Schneier may well prove to have the better of the argument. The point, rather, is that one cannot correctly plan for growth without at least taking into account the possibility that they may be correct. And that raises a difficult question: what percent likelihood does one have to assign to Clarke's and McConnell's being correct before one regards the security of the cyber- and bioplatforms as a serious threat to growth against which one must hedge one's bets?

It is important to emphasize that cyber- and biosecurity problems are *examples* of a class, not by any means the list of members of that class. One can only assume that the class of technologies that these examples typify will grow as the pace of innovation grows. Technologies will continue to develop in the civilian sector that magnify the power of individuals; those technologies will compound one another; and the magnitude of the damage we can thus reasonably expect individuals to be capable of bringing about will grow as well. It was once unthinkable that an individual might kill dozens of people with a single machine gun or that a single company with a single oil well could despoil the Gulf Coast. The more technology develops and the more dependent on it we become, the more it will not merely be conceivable but inevitable. The broad point is that we must face the possibility that the innovations that we rightly celebrate have created for us major new security problems. And we have to consider the possibility that those problems might in the long run poison the atmosphere for further growth. Just as we innovated our way to a massive, uncontrolled oil spill in the Gulf, we should confront that possibility that we might innovate our way as well to global

[11] Bruce Schneier, *Overview of the Cyber Problem—A Nation Dependent and Dealing with Risk*, testimony and statement for the record for the House Committee on Homeland Security, Subcommittee on Cybersecurity, Science, and Research and Development, 108th Cong., 1st sess., June 25, 2003, accessed November 15, 2010, http://www.schneier.com/testimony-commerce.html.

pandemics, financial crises, and significant assaults on critical infrastructure.

The Erosion of the Government's Monopoly on Security Policy

It rather understates the matter to say that current governance of technologies of mass empowerment is hopelessly inadequate to the task of preventing the disasters one might reasonably fear from them. This is not chiefly a function of the fact that changing governance in a fashion that carries real costs in the absence of some dramatic precipitating event is always difficult—though that fact plays a big role as well. It also reflects the fact that the ideal governance approach is far from obvious. Indeed, nobody quite knows how to attack the problem or even whether effective governance is possible. Even if one could, for example, classify all of the relevant now-public literature related to biosecurity and slap strict controls on the technologies in question, who would want to? The biotechnology revolution is a wonderful thing, and it has depended pervasively on precisely the open culture which has created the vulnerabilities I have been describing. In any event, this cat isn't going back in the bag. Too many people have too deep an understanding of how genetic engineering works. This point is even more acute in the cybersecurity arena, where most of us already are constantly using several connectivity devices to manage much of our day-to-day lives.

The problem with current governance is not that we don't have laws prohibiting abuse of these technologies. We do. The law, in fact, over the past two decades has developed rather admirably, and nobody now could do anything horrible without running afoul of it—at least not domestically. Nonetheless, current law isn't likely to do much more than inconvenience someone seriously committed to developing or releasing a biological agent that could do great damage. Nor will it do much to prevent overseas sources of cyberattack. More fundamentally, the law does not—and probably cannot—address the attribution problems at work here effectively.

The lack of promising options gives rise to what I suspect will be the most profound impact of this class of technologies on our law, one that touches the very structural arrangements of power in American life—and the lives of most other states as well. That is, it stands to bring about a substantial erosion of the government's monopoly on security policy, putting in diffuse and private hands for the first time responsibility for protecting the nation.

There are people who would write that sentence with joy in their hearts. I am not one of them. My views on executive capacity— notwithstanding the excesses of the Bush administration—are unapologetically Hamiltonian. The Constitutional assumption that the political branches, particularly the executive branch, are both responsible for national security and have the tools neces- sary to fulfill that responsibility is a comforting one, the destabi- lization of which I find scary. "Power to the people!" is a slogan that has always rung to me of gridlock at best, mob rule at worst.

The Constitution contains very few textual exceptions to the notion that national security is a federal responsibility. One, the Second Amendment, embodies the Framers' reverence for state militias, both as a means of fending off native attacks and as a means of preventing federal encroachments on state prerogatives. The other, the Letters of Marque Clause of Article I, contemplates a limited role for the private sector in military engagements— under Congressional supervision. Both involve institutions that have long since lapsed into disuse. The broader and more lasting presumptions in the document were that Congress would make the rules of security and that the president would lead the armed forces and the larger executive apparatus in a military or other crisis.

I'm not sure how these presumptions hold in the face of rapid development of these technologies. This point is perhaps most vivid in the cyber arena, where huge amounts of traffic into and out of the United States—including government traffic—now takes place over privately owned lines and the government *quite literally does not control the channels through which attacks can occur.* But it's also true in the biotechnology sphere. Because the revolution has taken place largely in private, not government, hands, the government employs only a fraction of the capable individuals. And the capacity to respond to or prevent an attack is therefore as diffuse as the capacity to launch one.

This point is crucial and provides the only real ray of hope in an otherwise bleak picture. The advent of technologies of mass empowerment has given enormous numbers of people the capacity to do great harm, but it has also given enormous numbers of people and organizations the capacity to work to prevent that harm. The proliferation of defensive capability has been as rapid as the proliferation of offensive capability—only exponentially more so since the good guys so vastly outnumber the bad guys. The individual scientist had no ability to prevent the Soviet Union from launching a nuclear attack against the United States or invading Western Europe. But the individual scientist and engineer, and groupings of individual scientists and engineers, have an enormous role in bio- and cybersecurity—from driving the further innovations that can wipe out infectious diseases, to developing security applications that will make the bad guys' jobs harder, to spotting the security implications of new research, to reporting on colleagues engaged in suspicious activities out of sight of authorities. It will, in short, take enormous innovation to save us from the consequences of some of our most exciting innovations. And the question then becomes how to incentivize people and companies to defend the platforms that innovation has created.

This question pulls the mind toward themes and ideas eloquently articulated by scholars such as James Boyle and Lawrence Lessig in the context of the debate over intellectual property. A major current of this body of thought involves the protection of legal space for communities of various sorts to use and borrow one another's ideas and work in collaborative efforts to build things. Boyle's recent book, for example, contains a spirited defense of distributed applications like file sharing, of the open-source software movement, and of Creative Commons licenses.[12] Indeed, the world has seen amazing demonstrations of what large groups of people can do when they pool expertise—even with very limited coordination. The most famous example is Wikipedia, but this is far from the only one. Anyone who has used Open Office—an open-source alternative to the Windows Office application suite—knows that it doesn't take a major software company to produce a major piece of software. Indeed, it is an interesting fact, highly salient for our purposes here—that open source software tends to be more stable and secure than proprietary code.[13] While this point has its dissenters, the famous line in the open-source software movement that "given enough eyeballs, all bugs are shallow" may have real application not just to computer bugs but to viral ones as well.[14]

Given that security will be, to borrow a term from this lexicon, a more distributed application than it has been in the past, we ought to start thinking about it as such. Collectivized individual security arrangements are nothing new. We see them in neighborhood expectations that people will put locks on their doors and keep an eye out for suspicious loiterers. Private innovations from burglar alarm companies to security camera operations to inexpensive fake security cameras are all part of noncoordinated distributed security applications for residential neighborhoods and business. As a child, I witnessed a particularly striking example of this sort of distributed security in the absence of a strong executive presence in New York City in the 1970s. I was crossing Columbus Avenue with my father. As we were crossing the street, a young man snatched the purse of an older woman crossing toward us and sprinted northward up the street. The woman

---

[12] James Boyle, *The Public Domain: Enclosing the Commons of the Mind* (New Haven, CT: Yale University Press, 2008).

[13] Bruce Schneier, *Secrets and Lies: Digital Security in a Networked World* (New York: John Wiley & Sons, 2000).

[14] Eric S. Raymond, "The Cathedral and the Bazaar," 2000, http://www.catb.org/~esr/writings/cathedral-bazaar/cathedral-bazaar/.

yelled, and spontaneously and with no coordination, half a dozen men in the immediate vicinity (my father among them) sprinted after him. They ran him down a few blocks later and held him until the police arrived. This sort of combination of technical impediments to intruders, an aware citizenry, and both formal and informal systems of collective action can combine to secure platforms to one degree or another. The question is how to enhance this sort of combination in the new platforms we have created.

Steve Martin, explaining to an audience once how they could become millionaires while paying no taxes, described the initial step as, "first, get a million dollars." It is, no doubt, similarly glib—and similarly abstract—to describe the initial step in the project at hand as "first, develop distributed platform security." It is a hypothesis, not a certainty, that such development is really possible. And I, for one, do not claim to know in any detail what it would look like. The initial challenge is more modest: it is to create legal incentives and structures that will encourage the sort of innovation that, in turn, stand to increase the security of these platforms. We need, in short, to think about platform security as a security vulnerability against which our laws need to focus the energies of everyone from system designers to end users.

INCENTIVIZING PLATFORM SECURITY

Even this more modest vision of the project is dauntingly difficult to imagine implementing. Conditioning a few large state actors not to use their nuclear weapons is hard enough. Conditioning billions of individuals against destructive uses of highly proliferated technologies presents a vastly deeper challenge. Anyone who doubts this proposition should reflect momentarily on firearms. The most the law has ever been able to accomplish is to discourage prospectively and create retroactive accountability for the illegal discharge of firearms. It has never come close to stopping firearms use. The United States alone suffers thousands of gun homicides per year, despite a range of significant federal and state disincentives to fire weapons at people. That fact alone offers a sense of the magnitude of the challenge.

Moreover, while platform security is a useful way to think about the general category of security problem I have described, the platforms in question differ markedly—a fact that has both theoretical and practical implications. Computer technology has proliferated to a degree that bioengineering has not, and it involves a degree of networking that does not characterize the biological sciences to date. We all carry around multiple devices that are connected to the worldwide network of such devices. And in the cyber arena, the platform is that network, each node being at once a potential target, a potential weapon, and a potential attacker. By contrast, in the biological arena, the platform and the network are literally us; there is no distinction between the platform and the humans which an attack seeks to injure. What's more, many fewer people (though still a great and rapidly expanding number) are capable of launching or threatening attacks. While biological attacks have taken place, they have been underwhelming in impact so far and are in any event far from the sort of routine events that cyberattacks have become. The debate thus lies in a different place. In the cyber arena we ask whether the proper analogy for the problem is pervasive street crime, whether we have a modest national security threat that's largely about espionage, or whether we are facing a major national security threat that can realistically expose us to significant attacks on the country whose impact is felt far beyond the online world. Nobody doubts that there is some problem. In the biological arena, by contrast, we ask whether we really have a problem at all.

The platforms of concern both today and in the future, in fact, will differ significantly enough that policies that might make a significant difference with respect to one may be of less relevance to others. The kind of specific policies that stand to render offshore oil drilling safer, for example, may have little relevance to biosecurity. And the kinds of policies that stand to insulate critical infrastructure from cyberattack will look nothing like the sorts of policies that may allow long-term sustainable growth of industries developing nanotechnology. It is thus impossible in practice—and highly undesirable even in theory—to identify a uniform set of rules for this class of technologies. The specific rules will have to emerge so as to be responsive to the unique circumstances different technologies will pose.

Yet there are, I suspect, certain high-altitude legal principles that can and should govern platform security in general, and to which a technology-independent focus on the security of platforms tends to lead. These principles will apply differently to different platforms; indeed, some are obvious with respect to certain platforms yet deeply challenging with respect to others. However, they seem to me to provide some basic building blocks of governance of this difficult space.

The first is that a party negligently introducing vulnerabilities onto a platform should be liable for the damages that result. It may seem difficult to object to this point, stated this simply and in the abstract. And applied, say, in the biosecurity arena, it is something of a no-brainer. A company or laboratory that, say, accidently released a pathogen would undoubtedly risk ruinous liability in tort from those the pathogen harmed. Similarly, there is no dispute about BP's general liability as the "responsible party" in the Gulf oil spill; it is liable both for the costs of the cleanup and for damages to individuals and the ecosystem.

The principle, however, is deeply controversial with respect to software manufacturers and Internet service providers. In fact, the general state of liability law for those whose insecure products expose others to damage is exceedingly protective. As Michael D. Scott has summarized, "software vendors have traditionally refused to take responsibility for the security of their software, and have used various risk allocation provisions of the Uniform Commercial Code (U.C.C.) to shift the risk of insecure software to the licensee. There were a few early cases in which licensees sought to have courts hold vendors liable for distributing defective software. These cases were unsuccessful."[15]

A number of key roadblocks stand in the way of reasonable liability rules for software vendors. The damages that software vulnerabilities cause tend to be economic in nature, not physical injuries, and are thus barred in tort by the rule against recovery for economic harms. There is some question as to whether software is even a product, or whether it's a service. And perhaps most fundamentally, the contracts to which users agree as a condition of licensing generally contain broad liability shields. The result, as Schneier puts it, is that "today there are no real consequences for having bad security, having low-quality software of any kind. In fact, the marketplace rewards low quality. More precisely, it rewards early releases at the expense of almost all quality."[16] Liability, Schneier argues, "will immediately change the cost/benefit equation for companies, because they will have to bear financial responsibility for ancillary risk borne by others as a result of their actions.... The insurance industry will step in and force companies to improve their own security if they want liability coverage at a reasonable price."[17]

The case for liability standards for software is not new. Back in 2002, an expert panel of the National Research Council urged the consideration of "legislative responses to the failure of existing incentives to cause the market to respond adequately to the security challenge" of vulnerable software. "Possible options include steps that would increase the exposure of software and system vendors and system operators to liability for system breaches and mandated reporting of security breaches that could threaten critical societal functions."[18] Calls for this sort of policy change go way back.

---

[15] Michael D. Scott, "Tort Liability for Vendors of Insecure Software: Has the Time Finally Come?" *Maryland Law Review* 67 (2008): 424.

[16] Bruce Schneier, "Liability and Security," *Crypto-Gram Newsletter*, April 15, 2002, accessed November 15, 2010, http://www.schneier.com/crypto-gram-0204.html#6.

[17] Schneier, "Overview of the Cyber Problem," 2003.

[18] National Research Council, *Cybersecurity Today and Tomorrow: Pay Now or Pay Later* (Washington, DC: National Academies Press, 2002), 14.

We should be candid about the consequences of such policies, for they are by no means cost free and, indeed, in the short term, will diminish growth, not enhance it. Forcing software vendors to take responsibility for the security of their products will reduce the pace of software innovation. It will make software manufacturers take longer to get products to market and probably will make software less rich with features—each of which adds complexity and, therefore, vulnerability. It may also make software run more slowly. All of which could strike the reasonable skeptic as profoundly antigrowth, antithetical to everything the rules in this volume are supposed to be cultivating. Unless, that is, one believes that the contemporary growth of the software industry on the unaccountable terms we have allowed it to date has created the equivalent of a building boom on a seismic fault line using substandard materials. In that case, one might choose to view liability standards as the rough equivalent of imposing reasonable building codes before the earthquake.

The specifics of such a policy are vexing. What does a standard of care in this arena look like? Given that perfect security is impossible, what separates mere imperfection from negligence? What degree of protection should vendors be able to arrange for themselves contractually through license agreements, particularly when they are effectively giving licenses away for free? And what happens if the United States imposes liability standards and other countries do not? Does this constitute a form of unilateral disarmament that will merely encourage innovation elsewhere and discourage it domestically?

Even the broad contours of the principle are contested. It is possible, after all, that a zero-liability regime is actually the optimal one because the benefits of growth and innovation on the platform so outweigh the risks that the best way to manage those risks is simply to let growth overwhelm them. This theory would explain why, despite decades of warnings about computer security vulnerabilities, the problem has remained manageable. And it offers a seductive logic for its remaining so perpetually—and a plausible basis to believe that a liability regime of the type I suggest here may offer only costs and no benefits. Indeed, if this logic is correct, liability rules might even make disasters more likely by slowing down growth of the sort that ultimately constitutes our best protection.

Ultimately, however, this is not the logic the law has followed with respect to earlier innovations, which it has tended to give a period of great liability protection and then tighten the reins. Ultimately, the law tends to settle on the notion that the risk of using products should be shared between the manufacturer and the user. And that principle seems appropriate for software as well. The user of software—the banks, the critical infrastructure operators, and the individual users—should not bear *all* of the risk associated with the platform; rather, those who introduce new vulnerabilities to the system should bear some of that risk.

This principle has a flip side. It is a responsibility on the part of those who use a platform to do their part to keep it secure. Most school systems do not permit children who have not received age-appropriate vaccinations to show up at school. Yet we think little of engaging with unsecured computer systems that may be propagating malware to the systems with which they interact. Companies that do not take reasonable steps to secure their own steps should be liable for the damage those systems cause.

For that matter, the system should incentivize *individuals* to take reasonable steps to protect the platform as well. This is not, as it may seem, the equivalent of a seatbelt law or other such nanny-state interventions in people's individual risk management decisions. An individual's failure to wear a seatbelt or a motorcycle helmet, after all, affects only his own risk of death or injury. But the failure to secure a networked computer makes that computer available for hijacking by an attacker and for use as a weapon against others. Many of the most common forms of cyberattack involve distributed, automated attacks by armies of infected computers around the world. So the individual who does not take reasonable precautions to secure his own computer undermines the integrity of the system as a system. Operationalizing an individual's duty of care is tough, since one cannot make every end user liable for the malicious use by others of his computer. One can, however, erect strong legal presumptions against recovery from software vendors who might otherwise have significant exposure by end users who do not take reasonable steps to secure their own systems. The broad rule should be that everyone can minimize his legal and financial exposure by doing what he can to make his piece of the system as secure as possible.

The second broad principle is that platforms have no privacy rights. Individuals have privacy rights and may have them in their use of platforms, but the platforms themselves are the sometimes-literal and sometimes-metaphorical analogues of public spaces and commons that authorities should patrol. A few examples make this point vivid. Consider first a playground, a park, or a neighborhood. Individuals use these spaces in various ways, and the police cannot simply stop and search anyone at any time for any reason on them. On the other hand, it is perfectly appropriate, even expected, for a cop on the beat to monitor general use of the platform—in other words, to hang out and keep his eyes open and thus both deter wrongdoing by his presence and also be in a position to stop bad things from happening. If such a policeman has with him, say, a dog trained to sniff for explosives or drugs, that is fine as well. If the dog gets excited about a particular person, that might justify a search of that person. In any event, such a cop would need some predication to search or detain an individual of whom he develops suspicions.

But as long as he's merely monitoring the use of the platform and not investigating any particular individual, we don't see his presence as threatening privacy but, rather, as protecting a public space designed for general use. Indeed, we often complain that inadequate monitoring of such spaces leaves them available for usurpation by the bad guys.

Platform surveillance can be more intrusive under certain circumstances without raising profound legal problems. For example, to secure the platform of commercial air travel, passengers must submit to baggage and personal screening; such surveillance is lawful because one has no legal entitlement to get on an airplane, so authorities can require the surveillance as a condition of travel. If an individual doesn't like it, he can drive or stay home. Similarly, following the 2001 anthrax attacks, the U.S. Postal Service began screening letters for anthrax at the giant sorting stations through which mail gets routed. Because postal workers do not open the mail or look at its contents, and because they are not investigating any individual but merely monitoring use of the platform itself, this raises few hackles—even though individuals have a strong Fourth Amendment interest in the privacy of their mail.

The legitimacy of platform surveillance hinges on several interrelated factors. The most important is that the surveillance does not target any particular individual. The cop on the playground is watching everyone. The anthrax mail screening system does not look specifically at whether *your mail* is giving off spores; it looks at whether *mail in general* is exuding spores and only then identifies the offending packages. Everyone goes through a minimum level of airport screening. Second, platform surveillance is not concerned with investigation but with deterring and stopping activity that threatens the platform. The cop does not patrol the playground in order to investigate a crime. He does it to establish presence and make the playground an unattractive site for criminal activity. Airport security screeners are not investigating any particular plot; they are preventing people from bringing dangerous materials onto airplanes. Third, platform surveillance loses legitimacy when it is abused or comes to focus in a discriminatory fashion on some group or other; airport security officials constantly are fending off allegations that Muslims or people from particular countries get a tougher look, and police forces get pressured when they give disproportionate attention to those "driving while black." Platform surveillance only gets accepted when it is perceived to focus in a nondiscriminatory fashion on all platform users, not on individuals, and when it is focused only on conduct that threatens the use of the platform itself. But in such circumstances, it gives rise to a social comfort level with surveillance we might otherwise find troubling under the Fourth Amendment or other privacy norms.

This distinction between individual surveillance and platform surveillance seems to me to be key to developing secure platforms for growth over time. We need to develop a comfort level with certain programmatic surveillance of new technological platforms that parallels the sort of platform surveillance I have described here. A system of sensors that scans Internet traffic in real time for malware but does not otherwise examine the content of communications, for example, is much more similar to, than different from, the anthrax scanning of physical mail. As long as it does not focus on any individual or group and is operated to protect the network, not as part of any investigation, the analogy seems quite close indeed. Yet such ideas, when even suggested, are treated with horror by many in the business and civil liberties communities, who regard such surveillance as per se threatening to privacy.[19] This is wrong. Rather, our analysis of such programs should focus more narrowly. What are the chances of false positives and what are the consequences of them? Is the system prone to abuse, and are the protections against abuse adequate? Is the system treating all users alike or is it targeting individuals or disfavored groups for special scrutiny? If these questions can be answered adequately, such systems should be acceptable.

Similarly, it is possible to imagine technological means of frustrating to some degree the use of gene synthesis equipment for illicit or unauthorized creation of pathogens. Currently, the major gene synthesis companies—which sell gene sequences by mail, phone, and Internet order—screen orders for sequences associated with certain dangerous agents and refuse to sell such sequences to those who are not registered to work with those agents.[20] At least in theory, this should prevent a bad actor from buying, say, the

---

[19] Siobhan Gorman, "U.S. Plans Cyber Shield for Utilities, Companies," *Wall Street Journal.* July 8, 2010, accessed November 15, 2010, http://online.wsj.com/article/SB1000142405274870454 5004575352983 850463108.html.

smallpox virus genome or sizable segments of it and then assembling them in his or her own laboratory. Yet this system would do nothing to prevent that same bad actor from using low-cost gene synthesis equipment in his or her own laboratory to build the sequence himself. In an article published early in 2009, Ali Nouri and Christopher Chyba proposed building the screening system directly into the gene synthesis equipment. Manufacturers would program the computers that drive the machines to decline to produce sequences associated with certain dangerous agents unless the user was registered to work with them. The software, in this proposal, could automatically update its list of prohibited sequences much the way antivirus software updates the list of malware it identifies and purges.[21] One can imagine further developments of the technology that would make it far more robust as a prevention tool. What if gene synthesis equipment alerted authorities whenever an unauthorized person tried to create a proscribed sequence? More intrusively, what if the equipment reported constantly on its own activities, so that authorities would have an ongoing audit trail that enabled them to monitor who was creating what gene sequences? Such approaches may or may not have promise as prevention methods, but we should not preclude them in the name of privacy.

The third broad principle is perhaps the most challenging: Certain companies by dint of their businesses, their technological capabilities, and their control over certain infrastructure *acquire affirmative national security obligations that have traditionally resided with the state.* We can see this point vividly in the Gulf oil disaster, particularly if, as I hypothesized at the outset, we imagine the spill being the result of an attack, rather than an accident. But the point, as I have argued, goes well beyond oil drilling. If we accept that the traditional state monopoly on security policy will erode

---

[20] H. Bügl et al., "DNA synthesis and biological security," *Nature Biotechnology* 25 (June 2007): 627-629. See also Jeremy Minshull and Ralf Wagner, "Preventing the misuse of gene synthesis," *Nature Biotechnology* 27 (September 2009): 800-801.

[21] Ali Nouri and C.F. Chyba, "Proliferation-Resistant Biotechnology: An Approach to Improve Biosecurity," *Nature Biotechnology* 27, no. 3 (March 2009): 234.

as more and more private entities develop functions and capabilities essential to security and yet absent from government, it follows that the law will and should come to oblige these companies to take responsibility for certain security functions. We already see this happening to a degree in the surveillance arena. The 1994 Communications Assistance for Law Enforcement Act (CALEA), for example, created obligations on the part of telecommunications companies to ensure that law enforcement, with an appropriate warrant, retained the technological capacity to conduct wiretaps as networks went digital.[22] The 2008 FISA Amendments Act required telecommunications carriers to share with the intelligence community large volumes of communications traffic concerning targets believed to be overseas—as did a temporary earlier statute and, before that, the Bush administration's warrantless surveillance program.[23] But the principle may extend far beyond surveillance.

Consider, first, the previously mentioned fact that the federal government literally does not own or control the channels through which cyberattacks take place. The trunk lines into the country, rather, are private, and the domestic routing infrastructure is private as well. This is the rough equivalent of letting a group of private entities both monitor the border and manage the interstate highway system and all local roads. A foreign intruder can—at least in a digital sense—invade the country and steal or sabotage valuable property, and it can do so without coming into substantial contact with government-controlled defenses. If then, in the digital sense, our border is patrolled not by the Department of Homeland Security or the military but by Verizon and AT&T, what obligations to national security do these companies have? The answer cannot be that they have none. Rather, it has to be that the fact of control of the pipelines of attack creates some duty to at least assist in protection against that attack.

---

[22] *Communications Assistance for Law Enforcement Act of 1994*, Public Law 103-414, 103rd Cong., 2d sess. (1994).

[23] *FISA Amendments Act of 2008*, Public Law 110-261, 110th Cong. 2d. sess. (2008).

Now consider a subtler example, one that involves both the cyber- and bioplatforms at once.[24] Imagine a deranged graduate student who decides to release a pathogenic organism. Such a person likely would begin by running a Google search or a search in one of several scientific research databases for published papers on the pathogen's genome. It follows that companies operating such databases have in their users' search histories a unique window into who is conducting the research about which government should be most concerned. There is no doubt that if the government were investigating this student and sought his search history with appropriate evidence, any company would be obliged to turn it over. But imagine that authorities produced an algorithm (or more likely a set of algorithms) to identify prospectively highly dangerous work in biotechnology. The algorithm would flag any IP address or account which requested certain patterns of information highly suggestive of non-innocent biotechnology research. And imagine that authorities asked database companies and, more broadly, search engines to deploy this algorithm and notify the FBI whenever a particular group of searches triggered an alarm. Most people who triggered an alert would be legitimate researchers, of course, but a quick check would verify that. Some would be the merely curious. A small number of others would be the proverbial needles in the haystack.

In some sense, of course, this is merely a species of platform surveillance of the type I have discussed already, but there's a twist: government would be coordinating the surveillance but not conducting it. It would be the database and search engine companies who would be policing the platform. And that raises the critical question of what, if any, responsibility these companies have to act affirmatively in the interests of national security? In a traditional environment, the answer to that question is easy. They have none. That is the government's job. Their job is to maximize value for their shareholders. Yet in an environment of radically distrib-

---

[24] I am indebted to Roger Brent for this example.

uted responsibility for collective security, a more communitarian ethos seems necessary. By storing users' search histories, Google has amassed the largest dataset anyone ever has collected on what people around the world are thinking. That fact may give it a role to play in identifying those people plotting to do grotesque and terrible things. Over time, the law should evolve to require that companies take on the national security responsibility their businesses enable.

It is easy to anticipate many objections both to these proposals and to the fatalism that lies beneath them. Luddites always see disaster in technological development, the critic will say. Without any real ability to quantify the risks or estimate the problem's magnitude, proposals that will constrain growth may not serve to protect long-run growth but may *only* stymie it in the short- and medium terms. Besides, people have been predicting these catastrophic events for decades now and they have never materialized—a fact which suggests that the predictions have involved a measure of hyperventilating exaggeration. Perhaps the risk is lower and our systems are more resilient than we imagine, and a major investment in what amounts to insurance is a waste. The argument is seductive because the events in question seem so much more like science fiction than like the reality to date of the Internet or the biotech revolution.

Yet it seems to me unwise to bet as a society against the occurrence of the concededly technologically possible. It makes as little sense to say that the difficulty of quantifying a risk should cause us to assume that risk as zero as it did for then-Vice President Dick Cheney to reportedly declare in 2001 that "If there's a 1 percent chance that Pakistani scientists are helping Al-Qaeda build or develop a nuclear weapon, we have to treat it as a certainty in terms of our response."[25] We cannot avoid attempting to quantify risk and acting on our admittedly imperfect probabilistic judgments. In the case of new technologies that radically empower

[25] Ron Suskind, *The One Percent Doctrine: Deep Inside America's Pursuit of Its Enemies Since 9/11* (New York: Simon & Schuster Paperbacks, 2007).

everyone from states to disaffected individuals, that means moving toward accountability for insecurity, a certain transparency in and oversight of the use of platforms, and a set of duties for those who have custody or control over significant pieces of the architecture. Sometimes, if something seems inevitable, it's because it is.

19: Legal Process and the Discovery of Better Policies for Fostering Innovation and Growth

Henry N. Butler and Larry E. Ribstein*

O ur topic concerns how legal process can lead to efficient policies for fostering innovation and growth. Future innovation will depend at least as much on how laws are made as on *a priori* analyses of the optimal content of those laws. Of particular importance, as we discuss in this chapter, is whether the U.S. legal system promotes an efficient market for law.

Our analysis supports three suggestions for improving the law to support growth. First, the rules governing the selection of the jurisdiction whose law governs productive activity can significantly affect growth and innovation. Second, any proposal aimed at increasing growth through a change in law or legal institutions should take account of the existence of multiple jurisdictions and parties' ability to choose the jurisdiction whose law controls their transactions. Third, we suggest harnessing the power of jurisdictional competition among the states through a federal law enforcing contracting parties' choice of law except to the extent that

* Henry N. Butler, a leading public policy analyst and specialist in law and economics, is a Foundation Professor of Law and Executive Director of the Law & Economics Center at George Mason University. He has devoted much of his career to improving the country's civil justice system through judicial education programs. Larry Ribstein is Associate Dean for Research and Mildred Van Voorhis Jones Chair, University of Illinois College of Law.

states legislatively override the choice of law and regulate local transactions.

LINKING LAW MARKET PROCESS WITH INNOVATION AND GROWTH: THE INFORMATION PROBLEM IN INSTITUTIONAL DESIGN

Our analysis begins with Frederick von Hayek's insight in his famous article on the "The Use of Knowledge in Society"[1] that experts, academics, and lawmakers lack the necessary knowledge to make decisions about which legal and regulatory structures maximize welfare. Even the most brilliant and thoughtful policy-makers cannot take account of the enormous number of political, social, technological, and economic variables that determine how their plans will operate in the unknowable real world of the future. In order to deal with this knowledge problem, Hayek championed the market system as a vast network that can process the necessary information. Consistent with this approach, consideration of how to alter laws and regulations to increase innovation and economic growth must include an analysis of how to harness market-like mechanisms to create an information network that leads to the discovery of better policies over time.

To understand the scope of the information problem involved in regulatory design, consider the broad array of potential legal rules governing contracts—mandatory versus default rules, opt-in versus opt-out, disclosure versus substantive duties. In general, legal rules must be designed to solve specific problems in the market while permitting parties to engage in value-increasing transactions. These rules sometimes should restrict opportunistic conduct in order to encourage trade or investment, while at other times they should enable the parties to craft their own agreements. It is also necessary to promulgate legal rules that reduce information costs or transactional frictions or increase property

---

[1] Frederick von Hayek, "The Use of Knowledge in Society," *American Economic Review* 35, no. 4 (1945): 519-530.

rights. Individual policymakers, however, lack the knowledge or foresight to see all the potential alternatives or figure out which should be adopted. Among other things, they cannot determine all of the immediate costs of regulation, the interaction among rules, the effect on incentives, or the long-run value of prohibited conduct.

In order to solve the knowledge problem and create efficient legal technologies, the lawmaking process should encourage innovation in the creation of legal rules. It is logical to use the same competitive process that encourages innovation in the private sector—that is, competition among suppliers—subject to rules and institutions regulating this competition. As we will see, this entails enforcing contracts among the parties regarding the applicable law.[2]

Jurisdictional choice and competition is particularly important to establishing a legal regime that promotes growth. First, the Hayekian "knowledge problem" is particularly challenging with respect to the rules appropriate to encouraging growth. There is much more certainty and information about the rules likely to maximize wealth over the short term than about those that maximize wealth over time. For example, even if intellectual property rights clearly promote innovation now, the effects of locking up ownership rights in those innovations for long periods may be less clear. The greater the knowledge problem, the more necessary it is to unleash markets to solve the problem.

Second, encouraging growth necessitates supplementing the "voice" of the political process with the power of exit, drawing from Albert O. Hirschman's famous analysis.[3] The political process inherently favors the interests of today's economically powerful firms over the small and not-yet-existing innovators of tomorrow's potentially leading firms. Incumbent firms not only have significant resources to fund political activities but also a

---

[2] Erin A. O'Hara and Larry E. Ribstein, *The Law Market* (Oxford: Oxford University Press, 2009).

[3] Albert O. Hirschman, *Exit, Voice and Loyalty* (Cambridge, MA: Harvard University Press, 1970).

strong incentive to spend those resources so as to block innovation. After all, these firms are threatened much more by potential extinction by brand-new industries and technologies than they are by their competitors' potential erosion of their market share. It is difficult to give future firms more voice without significantly altering the political system. However, these firms can influence policymaking by deciding where to locate their businesses. More specifically, firms' exit or potential exit can activate interests in the state who would be injured by this exit, including suppliers, customers, lawyers, and workers. These groups would then enter the political mix in opposition to the incumbent proregulatory interest groups. This process translates exit into political voice.

Critics of our approach may stress the imperfections of jurisdictional competition. Instead of racing to the top and enacting more efficient pro-growth laws, states may race to the "bottom" and enact laws that favor particular parties. If the rules on jurisdictional choice emphasize enforcement of the parties' contracts for the applicable law, laws might favor expert and economically powerful manufacturers and sellers, and undermine efficient state laws aimed at these parties. This could simply replace the defects of political choice with a different set of defects associated with exit. On the other hand, as discussed below, if states can override these contracts, the applicable state law effectively could be determined by plaintiffs' trial lawyers' decisions where to sue. This could introduce different but equally perverse legislative incentives. More jurisdictional choice also could mean more confusion and regulatory overlap.

One response to these criticisms is that a system that favors the dynamic growth potential of the firms empowered by greater jurisdictional choice necessarily increases social welfare compared to a system that focuses on avoiding static inefficiency caused by wealth-transferring regulation. To be sure, economically incumbent powerful firms could gain from greater ability to avoid regulating states. However, these firms already have a say in crafting regulation, and sometimes use this say to increase costs for potentially innovative competitors. Increasing the ability of innovative firms to choose the applicable law therefore may increase the political power of these firms relative both to incumbent firms and to other proregulatory groups.

A stronger response is that criticism of jurisdictional choice must proceed against a background of inevitable jurisdictional choice and competition in a multijurisdictional world. No single jurisdiction can reach all transactions in a global economy. Nor would we want it to, since the result would be duplicative regulation and chaos. Economic actors therefore inevitably can choose the jurisdiction whose laws govern their transactions. The relevant question is how to establish the best possible system of jurisdictional choice for maximizing growth in a multijurisdictional system. Our proposal discussed in Part II, and its application in the contexts discussed below, tries to balance the benefits of exit and jurisdictional competition against the benefits of empowering governments to efficiently address local problems. In other words, what system best channels jurisdictional competition toward efficient results? Criticism of our proposal should proceed against this backdrop of inevitable and necessarily imperfect jurisdictional competition.

RULE CHANGES THAT COULD BOOST INNOVATION AND GROWTH THROUGH THE LAW MARKET

Regulating jurisdictional competition involves developing efficient rules regarding courts' choice of the law applicable to particular disputes, the role of federal law, and the development of alternative adjudication mechanisms. These are the "meta" or systemic changes we propose. We also examine applications to specific areas, and discuss the major pros and cons of each idea.

State Choice of Law Rules

Choice of law rules focus on two types of decisions. Under conventional choice of law rules, courts choose which law applies to a particular transaction *ex post* when litigating a case arising out of the transaction. The courts apply vague rules whose applica-

467

tion the parties cannot reliably determine prior to litigation. Courts often apply local law, which effectively lets whoever controls the litigation forum—usually the plaintiff—choose the law. Plaintiffs' lawyers have an incentive to promote rules that encourage lawsuits in the states where they are licensed, and perhaps also rules that make these suits more costly for defendants. Courts and legislatures, in turn, have an incentive to come up with rules that cater to this powerful interest group.

By contrast, *ex ante* choice involves entering into a contract that chooses the governing law when the parties make their deal. Jurisdictions still would have an incentive to design their rules to encourage litigation. However, under this choice of law rule jurisdictions would attract litigation through rules that do not unfairly burden either plaintiffs or defendants generally. Regardless of whether states do not change their laws in response to competition from other states (perhaps because they want to apply the laws to relatively immobile local parties), mobile firms at least would be able to be subject to the law of their choice wherever they choose to do business.

Changing choice of law rules to give greater recognition to the *ex ante* approach than is now the case could encourage innovation and growth. Rules that consider the interests of tort defendants as well as plaintiffs may constrain the development and liberalization of new causes of action that can inhibit technological innovation. Also, *ex ante* choice of law can encourage lawyers to develop new property rights and legal technologies by enabling the parties to ensure that the case is heard by a court that is likely to enforce the rights. For example, the choice of law rule that ensures application to business associations of the law of their formation states has been instrumental in encouraging the development of the limited liability company as well as arbitration and other informal methods of adjudicating business disputes.

Choice of law contracts might enable evasion of rules intended to protect the contracting parties or nonparties. The competition facilitated by *ex ante* choice of law therefore may turn into a "race to the bottom" where jurisdictions adopt socially inefficient rules to appeal to the parties that control the contracting process.

On the other hand, if courts do not enforce choice of law contracts they will apply default choice of law rules with the potentially perverse result discussed above, that the choice is made by plaintiffs' lawyers. In other words, given multiple jurisdictions, somebody must choose the applicable law, and potential problems arise no matter who this is. Moreover, parties might react to a jurisdiction's non-enforcement of contractual choice of law by physically avoiding that jurisdiction altogether. As discussed generally above concerning the effect of exit, this could activate exit-affected interest groups in the state and motivate the state to change its policy.

Regardless of whether enforcement of choice of law contracts is efficient, states have the constitutional power to block erosion of their regulatory authority through choice of law, and trial lawyers and other interest groups inevitably influence how this power is exercised. Accordingly, it is necessary to find some mechanism for deciding to what extent individual states may regulate or impose liability on multistate firms and/or transactions that touch several jurisdictions.

Federal Substantive Regulation

The most obvious approach to resolving the above problems with state law might seem to be to apply federal law and thereby eliminate both the chaos of regulation by multiple states and the potential for a race to the bottom. But federal statutes inhibit the potential for state law competition and discovery.

Federal statutes are not necessarily wholly inimical to Hayekian processes. Even after Congress passes a federal law, courts must interpret the statute. Some types of statutory provisions provide a broad scope for legal evolution through a sort of common-law process that performs some market-type discovery functions. Statutes can be designed with this process in view.[4]

However, even the best-designed federal statute may allow for less Hayekian discovery and may be less conducive to growth than state law dealing with the same subject. The evolution of common law under federal statutes does not entail the sort of competition among multiple jurisdictions that can occur under an efficient state law system. Moreover, even a federal law designed to enable evolution may involve the antigrowth problem of protecting incumbent firms. Moreover, a federal statute designed to maximize common-law development may provide less certainty than state legislation coupled with a federal choice of law statute as discussed in the next section.

Federal Choice of Law Statutes

Instead of providing for specific regulation, federal law can promote Hayekian discovery by harnessing the state law process while ameliorating its worst problems. This could be done through a federal statute that provides for the enforcement of contracts regarding the applicable law. One approach is federal legislation designating the types of choice of law contracts that are or are not enforceable. But designing this regulation would implicate the knowledge constraints on policymaking discussed above.

Federal law could instead impose procedural constraints on state laws blocking enforcement of choice of law contracts. In particular, a federal statute could specify that choice of law contracts can be invalidated only pursuant to state legislation and not by judicial decisions.[5] This would serve two purposes. First, using the legislative process would promote robust competition among interest groups, which in turn can maximize welfare.[6] Specifically, as discussed above, interest groups who are hurt by

---

[4] Keith N. Hylton, *Antitrust Law: Economic Theory and Common Law Evolution* (New York: Cambridge University Press, 2003).

[5] O'Hara and Ribstein, *The Law Market.*

[6] Gary S. Becker, "A Theory of Competition Among Pressure Groups for Political Influence," *Quarterly Journal of Economics* 98, no. 3 (1983): 371-400.

firms' exits would join in opposition to the regulation with those more directly injured by it.

Second, because legislation tends to be more transparent than judicial decisions, requiring restrictions to be embodied in legislation would better enable firms to select jurisdictions in which to do business based on their enforcement of choice of law contracts. This would encourage jurisdictions to take firms' interests into account when deciding on enforcement.

The federal choice of law solution could encourage interstate recognition of contractual choice of law if the federal law were backed by an implicit threat of federal regulation, and preemption of state law, if the states insist on promoting parochial local interests and refuse to enforce even reasonable sister-state laws that parties select in their contracts.

A potential problem with the above proposal is that giving legislatures the exclusive opt-out power foregoes the benefits from judicial decisions whose random mutations can spur efficient legal evolution.[7] However, these beneficial mutations are more likely with respect to complex substantive issues than for the relatively simple question of whether or not to enforce contractual choice of law. In any event, these potential benefits of judicial mutation must be balanced against the costs of lower predictability, notice, and political transparency.

Federal Choice of Forum and Arbitration

Parties can help ensure enforcement of their choice of law contracts by avoiding non-enforcing courts. They can do this not only by avoiding contacts with non-enforcing jurisdictions, but also by contracting for adjudication of their disputes by pro-enforcement courts or arbitrators. As with choice of law contracts, choice of forum and arbitration contracts help motivate courts to maximize

---

[7] Henry N. Butler, "*Smith v. Van Gorkom*, Jurisdictional Competition, and the Role of Random Mutations in the Evolution of Corporate Law," *Washburn Law Journal* 45, no. 2 (2006): 267-282.

the welfare of all contracting parties rather than just the party that makes the *ex post* litigation decision.

Choice of forum and arbitration contracts may seem to raise the same issues as choice of law contracts in that courts that do not want to enforce the latter also will not enforce the former. However, contracting for the forum adds two new dimensions to jurisdictional choice. First, some courts that are not willing to enforce law-choice contracts may be willing to enforce forum-choice contracts because the latter do not require the court to choose between two competing state policies.

Second, federal law enters the picture with respect to forum choice through the Federal Arbitration Act, which itself was a response to global trade competition. Arbitration has become a powerful mechanism for supporting jurisdictional choice and furthering the Hayekian discovery process. However, prolitigation and consumer groups are now lobbying to reduce the role of arbitration, particularly of consumer contracts. Regulation of arbitration should take account of arbitration's benefits in promoting the law market.

State Initiatives

Federal law is not the only way to improve state legal competition. Individual states have incentives to engage in process innovations that attract firms to locate headquarters or factories in their states in order to increase the possibility that their cases will be litigated in the innovating state's courts. The innovators here are legislators, individual lawyers, and bar associations who essentially serve as legal entrepreneurs. Arbitration and business association law have developed partly as a result of this legal entrepreneurship. Several states have adopted choice of law statutes clarifying that choice of law clauses will be enforced in certain types of contracts, mainly large commercial contracts.

A Delaware court rule[8] indicates the potential for process innovation by the states. The rule essentially turns Delaware's respected Chancery Court judges into private arbitrators. Contracting parties can agree to have their case governed by the new procedures before a Delaware chancellor with direct appeal to the Delaware Supreme Court. The new rules represent a convergence of private arbitration and public judicial procedures. This process theoretically could be taken a step further by Delaware judges retiring from Delaware public life and going private. Other states also might hire the judges and adopt Delaware law, thereby competing with both Delaware law and infrastructure. Perhaps a central agency could be developed for accrediting roving judges. As more states have an opportunity to become viable competitors in the law market, they have greater incentives to change the choice of law rules to better accommodate state competition.

SPECIFIC APPLICATIONS OF THE MARKET FOR LAW

This part applies the above general principles to a few areas of the law that significantly affect innovation. The following discussion attempts to capture the range of applications in terms of the feasibility of applying law-market principles.

Restricted Choice of Law: Noncompetition Clauses

Contracts restricting competition by former employees can significantly affect innovation and growth. On the one hand, noncompetition agreements protect employers' rights in intellectual property, and thereby potentially encourage investments in creating that property and therefore innovation. On the other hand, noncompetition agreements can inhibit the movement of knowledge, skills, and information between firms, and thereby discourage innovation that depends on new combinations of these resources. Individual firms may be tempted to ignore the effect of their contracts on innovation because they incur all of the costs of losing control over intellectual property while capturing only some of the benefits of innovation.

---

[8] Delaware Chancery Court Rules (February 1, 2010), 96-98.

The problem of determining the appropriate regulatory approach to noncompetition agreements illustrates how the law market can promote innovation while allowing space for reasonable regulation. The dynamic and long-term social costs and benefits of rules protecting property rights or encouraging the spread of knowledge are beyond the knowledge or foresight of any individual lawmaker. Indeed, it is likely that no single rule is appropriate. California's law making these clauses unenforceable has been heralded as spurring the growth of Silicon Valley.[9] On the other hand, non-competes may be critical in industries in which developments take longer and patents and copyrights are less available to protect intellectual property. The law market provides a way to experiment with a variety of regimes to achieve the optimal pro-growth/pro-innovation policy.

Full Enforcement of Contracts: Business Associations

Efficient business structures are vital to innovation. For example, capital-intensive firms need outside investors. These investors want rules that balance the benefits of empowering managers to run the firm against the need to hold them accountable for their actions. Given the almost infinite combinations of rules that are possible in structuring the governance of a business association, the market for state law is especially important in designing business structures. Since large firms can have owners in many states, each of which can exercise jurisdiction over suits regarding the firm's governance, any market for corporate governance law would be infeasible in large firms unless firms could choose a single state's law to control their governance. Also, in long-term contracts where parties' needs may change and litigation may arise multiple times during the life of the firm, parties have strong reasons for choosing not only a particular law, but a particular jurisdiction with reliable courts, lawyers, and legislature.

---

[9] Ronald J. Gilson, "The Legal Infrastructure of High Technology Industrial Districts: Silicon Valley, Route 128, and Covenants Not to Compete," *New York University Law Review* 74, no. 3 (1999): 575-629.

These conditions justify the strong U.S. rule providing for enforcement of firms' choice of the state law applicable to their governance contracts.[10] Under the so-called "internal affairs doctrine," the parties to a firm can organize in any state and have the rules of the state of organization apply to their firm's internal organization regardless of where they live or where the firm is based. The internal affairs doctrine has facilitated the evolution of the corporation from the era of special chartering, when firms had to seek legislatures' permission to form, to the adoption throughout the United States of general incorporation laws giving the parties full contractual freedom to decide on applicable governance rules.[11] Broad application of the internal affairs doctrine to small and unincorporated firms has facilitated efficient contracting for incentives and governance in these firms. This is significant for present purposes because small firms are an important source of innovation and growth.

These considerations support continued encouragement of the corporate law market not only by enforcement of the internal affairs doctrine at the state level, but also by limiting the effect of federal securities and tax laws that can constrain the state law market. A positive development along these lines was the promulgation of the "check the box" tax classification rules, which permitted small firms to choose their business form irrespective of their tax status as corporations or partnerships.[12] On the other hand, the expansion of federal law into the details of corporate governance in both the Sarbanes-Oxley Act of 2002 and the Dodd-Frank Wall Street Reform and Consumer Protection Act of 2010 significantly reduced the ability of the state market for law to experiment with governance provisions and discover the most efficient provisions.

---

[10] Larry E. Ribstein, *The Rise of the Uncorporation* (Oxford: Oxford University Press, 2010).

[11] Larry E. Ribstein and Erin A. O'Hara, "Corporations and the Market for Law," *Illinois Law Review* (2008): 661-729.

[12] Treas. Reg. § 301.77011-3 (2004).

Innovation in the Legal Profession

Law firms are an important exception to firms' general freedom to choose the state governance law. As part of their power to regulate the legal profession, states limit the types of business structures lawyers practicing in the state can use for the practice of law. Because these rules apply to all lawyers practicing in the state, lawyers may not choose to organize under the law of State A while practicing in State B. National law firms therefore must abide by the laws of all of the states in which they practice. This rule effectively requires the legal profession to function under uniform laws proposed by the American Bar Association. Uniformity, in turn, bars law practice from the competitive lawmaking process that has enabled the evolution of business associations discussed in the previous section.

The purported rationale for having a distinct choice of law rule for law practice is that states have a special need to regulate the legal profession. Even if this is true, however, it does not clearly justify regulating law firms' structure, as distinguished from lawyers' and law firms' conduct. Firms generally are free to choose their business structure to best facilitate their business operations, including the firms' compliance with applicable regulation of business practices. It is not clear why the same principle should not apply to law firms.

The availability of a competitive market for law firm governance is particularly important now because of the pressures facing law practice. Law firms confront unprecedented challenges to their business model because of, among other things, changes in technology and increased global competition. Innovations in business structure facilitated by legal competition would enable the legal services business to better respond to these challenges.[13] This, in turn, would not only facilitate growth of the legal services industry but provide incentives for the development of more efficient

---

[13] Larry E. Ribstein, "The Death of Big Law," *Wisconsin Law Review* 2010, no. 3 (2010): 749-815.

legal information and services that could support growth throughout the economy.

An important example of the need for innovation in law firm structure concerns the sale of equity shares in law firms to non-lawyers. In the United States, only lawyers may own law firms.[14] This means that law firms, the largest of which are multibillion-dollar operations, can obtain financing only from their lawyers and bank loans. This limitation effectively forces firms to operate hand-to-mouth, and can result in their swift unwinding under financial pressure. It also prevents law firms from financing new lines of business such as investments in research and the development of new legal technologies, and from fully realizing potential synergies from combinations with nonlawyer professionals.

A competitive law market for law firm governance would promote the development of financing structures that would meet the special challenges of nonlawyer financing of law firms. Law firms need new structural rules that balance outside investors' demands for power to protect their investments against lawyers' need for sufficient control to assure clients and regulators that the firm will maintain professional standards. These structures raise new issues and the potential problems are unforeseeable. Effective solutions call for the same sort of Hayekian discovery process as the competition for business association laws under the internal affairs doctrine. At the same time, it is necessary to preserve some role for efficient state regulation of law firm structure. These objectives could be accomplished through a default rule of enforcing interstate law firms' choice of state law subject to each state's power to enact laws regulating local lawyers.[15]

Internet Law

The Internet can be a powerful medium for communicating and gathering information. Because websites place unique identifying

---

[14] Model Rules of Professional Conduct Rule 5.4.

[15] Larry E. Ribstein, "Ethical Rules, Law Firm Structure and Choice of Law," *University of Cincinnati Law Review* 69, no. 4 (2001): 1161-1203.

numbers called "cookies" on the hard drives of consumers who browse the Internet, web operators can gather information from consumers who visit their sites. This enables the operators to know which pages consumers visit and how long they spend on each page, and potentially to link this information with customer identifying information such as e-mail addresses, passwords, and credit card numbers. This technology offers significant opportunities to reduce transaction costs and increase information. At the same time, it poses potential problems by enabling sellers to invade consumers' privacy.

Balancing these competing concerns raises issues as to what the applicable rules should be, whether they should be default or mandatory, whether it is enough to let consumers opt out of default rules, or whether consumers should have to opt in to rules that enable sellers to invade their privacy. The answers to these questions depend to some extent on how individual consumers weigh privacy interests against the convenience of visiting websites that know their preferences. Different types of transactions and goods and different types of consumers may call for different rules.

Developing a competitive legal process would enable experimentation and discovery necessary to determine the mix of rules that would enable efficient innovation. Each firm could choose the set of rules that best fits its business model. The industry could grow and innovate based on these secure and suitable legal platforms.

A fully competitive legal process in this area entails enforcement of choice of law contracts. If each state can apply its law under general common-law choice of law rules to transactions that are connected to the state (which connections states can determine through modern geographic filtering technologies), sellers might not know which law applies to any of their transactions and may have to comply with the strictest rule.[16] This would discourage

---

[16] Bruce H. Kobayashi and Larry E. Ribstein, "State Regulation of Electronic Commerce," *Emory Law Journal* 51, no. 1 (2002): 1-82.

legal innovation and deny firms the secure legal platforms they need for growth.

The National Conference of Commissioners of Uniform State Laws attempted to achieve interstate enforcement of choice of law contracts by promulgating the Uniform Computer Information Transactions Act (UCITA), section 109(d) of which would enforce a choice of law clause in electronic consumer sales unless the contract would vary a mandatory rule in the seller's state. Like the internal affairs doctrine applicable to business associations, the choice of law contract would be enforceable without regard to the seller's or transaction's relationship with the state whose law is selected in the transaction. This would free sellers to choose the law of any state. If there is a restrictive law in the seller's home state, the seller can avoid the restriction simply by relocating to another state. A similar rule could be applied to the "cookies" context.

Only two jurisdictions adopted the UCITA provision and several adopted "bomb shelter" provisions that explicitly invalidated choice of law clauses choosing UCITA-based laws. This leaves firms subject to more open-ended default choice of law rules. This result arguably indicates the futility of relying on the uniform lawmaking process to encourage the efficient evolution of state law. States rejected contractual choice of law that was tied to an objectionable uniform law. Contractual choice might work if states were free to develop laws that met sister-state objections rather than being bound to a single "uniform" solution.

The states' rejection of contractual choice in the Internet setting also might reflect the states' inherent inability to coordinate on this issue, perhaps because local business interests are able to override those of out-of-state firms competing on the Internet. The appropriate solution might be a federal law mandating enforcement of choice of law clauses except to the extent enforcement is explicitly prohibited by a state statute. This could enable a competition among state laws, which discovers the right balance between permissive and mandatory rules.

Insurance

The insurance industry would seem to be ripe for innovation of numerous kinds of contracts that protect from a variety of risks. However, the industry is particularly stymied by the choice of law problem. The McCarran-Ferguson Act of 1945 prohibits federal regulation of the insurance business, thus leaving regulation up to the states. The states, for their part, are particularly reluctant to cede their regulatory power through enforcement of choice of law contracts, given concerns about the complexity and take-it-or-leave-it nature of insurance contracts and consumers' inability to judge insurers' solvency. Moreover, many states prohibit arbitration clauses in insurance contracts, thereby blocking an important mechanism for promoting enforcement of choice of law and choice of forum clauses.

There currently is a move toward repealing McCarran-Ferguson and federalizing insurance law. This would protect insurers from duplicative state regulation and consumers from inadequate state regulation. However, as discussed throughout this chapter, federal regulation would eliminate the potential for experimentation and discovery of superior regulatory solutions through state competition. Dodd-Frank made a move toward federalization but stopped with the creation of some oversight through a new Federal Insurance Office.

As with the other contexts discussed above, the various relevant interests could be addressed through a federal law that requires state courts to enforce choice of law provisions in insurance contracts unless a statute in the state where the policy is sold explicitly bars such enforcement.[17] This would enable firms to choose the law that suits their business and would encourage states to adopt the laws firms prefer. States could compete to lead the competition, which is significant in this area given the complexity of insurance law and the need for regulatory expertise. States' ability to specialize may increase the quality of regulation compared

[17] Henry N. Butler and Larry E. Ribstein, "A Single-License Approach to Regulating Insurance," May 18, 2008, http://ssrn.com/abstract=1134792.

to the current system of regulation under which parties cannot choose the applicable law. Also, states' power to adopt legislation applying local law to local insureds would help prevent a "race to the bottom" in insurance law. At the same time, repealing McCarran-Ferguson and paving the way for potential federal regulation would discipline the states by exposing them to the threat that excessive regulation could lead to broad federalization of insurance law.

Property Law

Rights concerning real property—including rules regarding use, ownership, and transfer of the property—are subject only to the law of the state where the property is located. This clear "situs" rule at least reduces the potential for applying multiple state laws at the time of litigation to a single transaction. However, the application of a single rule also prevents the operation of a competitive process that can lead to the discovery of the most efficient menu of rules. As land use is subject to increasing stresses of laws relating to such matters as the environment, historic preservation, and restrictions on growth,[18] there is a special need for a discovery process with respect to the development of new legal technologies for real property.[19] A competitive law process could further this development by making it easier for property owners to choose among rights available in various states.[20]

Conservation easements illustrate how such a lawmaking process could facilitate property rights innovations.[21] These instruments enable property owners to lock in particular uses of their property in perpetuity. Many states have adopted laws providing for these easements, spurred by a federal tax break for conservation

---

[18] Nicole Garnett, *Land Use Regulation, Innovation, and Growth*, this volume, chapter 12.

[19] Andrew P. Morriss, "The Role of Offshore Financial Centers in Regulatory Competition," in *Offshore Financial Centers in Regulatory Competition*, ed. Andrew P. Morriss (Washington, DC: AEI Press, 2010), 116.

[20] O'Hara and Ribstein, *The Law Market*.

[21] Larry E. Ribstein, "The Market for Conservation Law," May 17, 2010, http://ssrn.com/abstract=1609793.

easements. The complexity and novelty of these property rights and the federal tax law have induced states to widely adopt the Uniform Conservation Easement Act. Letting property owners enter into easements provided for by the law of states other than where the property is located could spur a competitive lawmaking process and legal innovations. As with the other areas discussed above, states would retain the ability to legislatively block local property owners from adopting certain types of laws. This combination of competition and mandatory rules could lead to the discovery of more efficient rules regarding this relatively new property right.

Products Liability Litigation

Nowhere is there a greater need for legal process to pave the way for innovation than in the area of products liability law. Manufacturers may be significantly discouraged from innovating because new products pose new risks of liability to consumers for product injuries. The expansion of tort law is sometimes viewed as a failure of state law that calls for federal safety regulation to preempt the states. But before sacrificing the benefits of the market for state law, it is worth trying the choice of law alternative.

Current choice of law rules generally let plaintiffs choose to litigate in states with the most pro-plaintiff laws. Changing the prevailing rule to one that always applies the law where the product is manufactured could be too favorable to manufacturers. Applying the law of the state where the product is first sold might be a reasonable compromise because firms could determine their prices based on the product liability laws in each state where the product is sold. However, no states apply such a rule.

A possible solution, as with the other areas discussed above, is a federal law enabling the parties to contract for the applicable state's product liability law. Consumer groups might fear that this would cause a "race to the bottom" toward the laxest standards because consumers could be expected to shop on the basis of the applicable state law. However, states would have an interest in protecting their own residents from unsafe products rather than just being states chosen in product liability contracts. Also, manufacturers of high-quality goods have an incentive to avoid choosing very lax laws because of the negative signal this could send as to product quality. The press, blogs, and consumer watchdogs could be counted on to alert the market of very pro-manufacturer state laws and the large consumer product firms that adopt them.

Even if consumers cannot rely fully on the market, the system applied throughout this chapter—that is, enabling states to enact statutes blocking enforcement of contractual choice—could provide fallback protection. States could decide whether they want to adopt relatively lax product standards and enforce contractual choice in order to attract manufacturers into the state or adopt strict laws that protect consumers. The federal government could provide discipline by standing ready to supplant state law if states prove too obedient to trial lawyers or manufacturers.

This approach would enable states to experiment with various legal rules and discover policies that optimally balance the costs and benefits of product innovation. Although this system may not yield perfect results, it is important to keep in mind the costs of the alternatives—a chaotic state system that exposes manufacturers to the rules of all of the states in which they sell products, or a one-size-fits-all federal rule that preempts state law and precludes experimentation.

Franchise Regulation

Franchising is a potentially valuable form of contracting and an important pathway for innovations in distributing products and services. However, state regulation has limited the usefulness of franchising by restricting franchisors' ability to terminate franchisees, thereby undercutting franchisors' most important mechanism of policing franchisees' attempts to cheat on quality. Proponents of the regulation argue that the laws are necessary to prevent franchisors from opportunistically using termination provisions to take over the locations that prove most profitable (i.e., "cream skimming").

State franchise regulation has been tested in the market for state law. Franchisors have struck back against the regulation by inserting choice of law and choice of forum clauses in their contracts that avoid the most onerous state regulation. Regulating states counterattacked by enacting laws invalidating these provisions. Theory predicts that franchisors would then avoid the states that insist on applying the most onerous laws. This, in turn, could set off a political backlash by workers, suppliers, and customers in the state who are injured by the departure of the franchises.

Indeed, there is direct evidence of the reduction of outlets in regulating states, and indirect evidence of this reduction based on reduced employment in franchise industries. These effects are greatest in states that invalidate choice of law and choice of forum contracts.[22] These data indicate that the market for state law can enable innovation by limiting the effect of regulation.

Our proposed federal law mandating enforcement of choice of law clauses subject to state opt-out through legislation again provides a useful compromise between the market for law and state regulatory interests. This approach is particularly valuable in a context such as franchise regulation where the interest groups that would face off in the legislature are closely matched and the threat of franchisor exit could influence the legislative decision. As discussed in the article footnoted above, franchise regulation went through a period of back-and-forth between judicial decisions and legislation that left the law unclear and muted interest group competition. A clear rule providing for enforcement of choice of law clauses subject to state legislative opt-out could have shortened the period of uncertainty, encouraged growth-enhancing developments in franchising, and helped ensure a regulatory outcome that best reflected all political interests.

---

[22] Jonathan, Klick, Bruce H. Kobayashi, and Larry E. Ribstein, "The Effect of Contract Regulation: The Case of Franchising," December 13, 2006, http://ssrn.com/abstract=951464; Klick, Kobayashi, and Ribstein, "Federalism, Variation, and State Regulation of Franchise Termination," *Entrepreneurial Business Law Journal* 3, no. 2 (2009), 355–379.

CONCLUSION

Innovation and growth depend on the existence of a legal environment that allows room for these developments to occur. At the same time, society demands reasonable regulation even if this regulation could have the effect of inhibiting some innovation and growth. Individual lawmakers lack the necessary knowledge to determine just where to draw the line. This supports the need for a market-type legal process that enables discovery of optimal rules. This chapter suggests how the market for state law could be designed to produce such a process. Even if the suggested approach is not adopted, the main lesson of this chapter is that any regime for encouraging growth must take account of the existence of multiple jurisdictions and the potential for jurisdictional choice and competition.

20: The Political Economy of Reform: Some Concluding Thoughts

Robert E. Litan*

The preceding chapters have outlined an ambitious, thought-provoking, and we hope useful guide to the many possible ways that U.S. laws and legal institutions might be reformed to generate higher rates of innovation and growth. As we noted at the outset, the list of legal ideas is hardly exhaustive. Nor does it include many ways in which expenditures and tax systems at all levels of government might be changed to generate similar outcomes. Perhaps most important in this respect, given the legal focus of this effort, we do not address some of the major long-term domestic challenges facing the country, notably how to best bring governmental budgets closer to balance over the long run; reforms needed to improve education; issues related to climate change; and the highly controversial problem of illegal immigration, primarily of individuals with few job skills. Still, while the authors of the foregoing chapters might not agree with each and every suggestion that has so far been outlined, we all agree that the ideas proposed here, if implemented in part or in whole, would increase the rate of innovation and growth.

---

* Robert E. Litan is Vice President for Research & Policy at the Ewing Marion Kauffman Foundation and Senior Fellow in the Economic Studies program at the Brookings Institution.

The ambition of the book, however, extends beyond the list of specific proposals—important though we think they are. The collective essays in the book propose a new way of thinking about the legal system. Over the past forty years, legal scholars and judges have paid increasing attention to the economic effects of the law and of legal institutions that have succeeded in converting our understanding of the law from serving solely moral goals to serving instrumental goals. To date, however, this instrumental view has been limited to achieving what we called in Chapter 1 "static efficiency": efficient employment of currently available resources, but nothing beyond.

The essays in this book seek collectively to expand our vision of the economic effects of the law and legal institutions to consider how the law has in the past, and how it might in the future, stimulate innovation and economic growth. The normative ambition of this vision—which, as explained in Chapter 1, is hardly controversial—seeks to move economic analysis of law beyond static efficiency in order to more concretely advance societal welfare for all citizens through innovation and economic growth.

We appreciate that the book is incomplete. It represents just the beginning of the study of the effects of law on innovation and economic growth. But we hope that it is an important beginning. The policy proposals of each chapter are illustrative of this hope.

In this concluding chapter, we address, albeit briefly, this important question: how and under what circumstances might some of these ideas be adopted by the appropriate decision makers. At the outset, we can safely say that not all of the suggestions will be implemented in any form, and certainly, even the "best of the list" will not be adopted at once, simultaneously. Our political system, with its checks and balances provided by different branches of government, purposely was created to prevent any such outcome, no matter how good the ideas.

Indeed, with rare exceptions, government policymaking is inherently reactive, and almost never creative. Congress has a history of adopting statutes primarily in response to crises, often banking or economic crises, or when political forces align in a way so that elected officials believe they must respond to perceived or actual action-forcing political pressures. Examples of the former, of course, include the large body of post-Depression era legislation and regulation, which transformed the nation's financial, labor, and housing laws, and laid the foundation for the modern administrative state; the more modest changes to financial laws after the savings and loan and banking problems of the 1980s, and later the financial disclosure and accounting scandals (notably Enron and MCI) of the late 1990s and early twenty-first century; and most recently, the almost total overhaul of the nation's financial regulatory system following the financial crisis of 2007-8. Outside the economic/financial arena, examples where the political stars have aligned to induce congressional action include the adoption of Medicare in 1965; transportation, environmental, and occupational safety statutes adopted in the 1960s and 1970s; deregulation of the transportation sector in the 1970s and 1980s (though much of this was done by administrative action and not just by statutory change); tax reform in 1986 (though this subsequently has been undone by a series of tax bills); welfare reform in the mid-1990s; and, again most recently, comprehensive health reform legislation adopted in 2010.

Regulatory and judicial decision making also, by design, are reactive. Regulators take their cue from Congress, which often directs agencies to write rules to flesh out broadly or vaguely worded statutes (as in the case of the health care and financial regulatory reform bills enacted in 2010), or from problems that private citizens or companies, acting alone or through the media, bring to regulators' attention. Rarely do regulators anticipate issues and try to get ahead of them. There is not likely to be sufficient scientific and/or political consensus for them to be proactive.

Judges are even more reactive since, again by design, they are not policymakers. How often is it said during judicial confirmation proceedings (especially for the Supreme Court) that "judges should not legislate from the bench"? Of course, to the extent that judicial decisions establish legal doctrines that fill in the interstices of statutes, regulations, or the common law, judges do perform the functional equivalent of legislative or regulatory functions. But all such decisions grow out of the cases that the judicial system passively accepts. Judges do not have the luxury or the charge to write on a blank slate and affirmatively reach out to "fix" social or economic problems they may see in their midst and want to address. Likewise, some judges may not see it within their charge to conduct, or ask the parties and their counsel who come before them to conduct, cost-benefit analyses of what the optimal rules would be to govern situations that happen to be litigated in particular cases. To the extent that judicial doctrines change over time, and they do, this happens incrementally, case by case, and generally not in response to political pressures to act one way or the other.

Despite these differences in the way the three key decision-making institutions in our democratic capitalist society make or are presented with decisions, there is one common element among them. In many or most cases, when changes in policy are made, decision makers draw upon ideas on the proverbial shelf. More often than not, the ideas are put there through the research or writings of academic scholars, researchers in think tanks, or intellectual thought leaders writing for themselves or housed in some other kind of institution (principally the media), or some combination of these. The famous economist John Maynard Keynes is well-known for his many quips, but surely this one ranks among his best: "Practical men, who believe themselves to be quite exempt from any intellectual influence, are usually the slaves of some defunct economist." We would modify that thought only to cover defunct (and living!) scholars from the other social and physical sciences and, pertinent to the subjects addressed here, from the legal academy as well.

This book has been written in that spirit. First, our authors want to put still more ideas on the policy shelf, hopefully to be picked up at various points in the future by decision makers in each of the three branches of government. Second, at the same time, we hope to stimulate policymakers and professors to reorient their thinking about the possibilities of law, to move beyond identifying and promoting how law can achieve static efficiency into a new approach:

to examine how law has in the past and can in the future improve social welfare by stimulating innovation and growth.

The prior chapters necessarily take as a given, however, the current legal and institutional framework in each of the areas covered, and seek to improve upon it. The authors were not charged with writing on a blank slate as it were, as economist Paul Romer has suggested through his proposal for countries (or smaller jurisdictions) to establish "charter cities"—jurisdictions with only a few necessary rules to maintain social and economic order, but otherwise highly facilitative toward growth—by selling or extending long-term leases to the land to other nations or even corporations to make this idea happen.[1] We in the United States are not likely ever to do something as radical as that, although we do have special, limited "free trade zones" and "enterprise zones" that resemble Romer's idea. But it is unlikely, at least for the foreseeable future, that policymakers are going to be any more adventurous than that.

Working with the existing set of institutions, then, imparts a heavy bias against change. Indeed, as the late economist Mancur Olson argued, and as journalist Jonathan Rauch has popularized, as societies and economies age, they harden not only with the growth of incomes and wealth but also with the number and strength of different interest groups.[2] To some extent, the groups can offset each other, but the more evident pattern is one of growing complication. Two analogies come to mind: from the health arena, societies come to resemble plaque-filled arteries in an aging patient; and from water navigation, one might say that societies grow to resemble streams with an ever-expanding number of rocks that make navigation increasingly difficult. Pick whatever metaphor you like, the key point is this: societies, like most people, get more rigid and set in their ways as they age.

---

[1] For an excellent guide to this idea, its pluses and minuses, see Sebastian Mallaby, "The Politically Incorrect Guide to Ending Poverty," *The Atlantic*, July/August 2010.

[2] Mancur Olson, *The Rise and Fall of Nations* (New Haven, CT: Yale University Press, 1982); and Jonathan Rauch, *Government's End* (New York: Public Affairs, 1999).

Just look around at some of the major social and economic challenges that the United States has been confronting—or, increasingly, not confronting or resolving—for the past decade or more: restoring fiscal sanity at all levels of government, fixing our nation's broken immigration system, and addressing climate change in the most cost-effective way. At this writing, resolution of each one, let alone all, of these highly contentious issues seems impossible, or at the least highly remote.

But then there are exceptions. Incremental changes in policy— mostly implemented through regulations and judicial interpretations of those rules or statutes, or even the common law—happen all the time, in response to new fact situations often driven by changes in technology. The rise of the Internet, for example, has aroused concerns about privacy that would not have existed without this new technology (just as the development of telephones and wiretapping technologies did nearly a century ago). The genetics revolution, likewise, is raising not only policy issues relating to privacy, but also moral and ethical questions. Ben Wittes in Chapter 18 wrestles with the new and unanticipated consequences, especially the downsides, of technological change and innovation. Nonetheless, the clear consensus of the authors in this volume is that whatever else they do, law and policy should not preempt innovation out of fear of what could go wrong, but instead fix things that do go wrong when that happens. It is these incremental "fixes" that continue to be made by decision makers in different branches and at different levels of government all the time.

And yet, as suggested at the outset of this chapter, there are cases where, either in response to a crisis or due to a confluence of events, Congress has enacted major legislative reforms. Are any of the ideas outlined in this book likely to be adopted in a similar fashion?

Since relatively few of the ideas in this book call for legislation, a crisis is not likely to be necessary for any to attract wide popular attention, with one possible exception: proposals to liberalize U.S. immigration laws for high-skill immigrants, especially those with

entrepreneurial intentions. Although immigration reform generally seems to have become the "fourth rail" that U.S. politicians seek
to avoid at all costs (the "third rail" being the two popular entitlement programs, Social Security and Medicare), a proposal to create
a new visa just for immigrant entrepreneurs eventually could
prove to be politically attractive, especially if the economic recovery from the Great Recession continues to be sluggish. In that
event, a crisis—the recession and its aftermath—eventually may
serve as the trigger for useful legislative reform.

One other major legislative reform suggested here—the replacement and/or augmentation of the federal income tax with some
kind of consumption (or value-added) tax—is not likely to emerge
from a future budget crisis, since either raising taxes or reforming
them is unlikely to be popular in the midst of another recession.
Nor would such a measure make economic sense, unless it were
advanced as part of a plan to fix the nation's long-run fiscal problems, in which case it would help reduce long-term interest rates
and thus facilitate the recovery. It also is possible, if unlikely, that
elected officials from both parties will muster the political courage
to enact a comprehensive budget bill before any debt-market crisis.
Such a bill could very well include a consumption tax, along with
reform of entitlement benefits.

The rest of the ideas proposed in this book are more incremental in
nature, and thus are better suited for the regulatory or judicial arenas, where decision makers constantly are required to adapt or
develop new rules in response to new factual circumstances. It also
is possible that the few ideas presented that require some incremental legislative change—such as the antitrust reforms offered by
Priest—may be packaged together, at an appropriate time, with
other related reforms that Congress may consider.

Alternatively, or in conjunction with policy changes adopted by
federal decision makers, states may be best positioned to compete
with one another to offer growth-friendly legal environments. This
is more easily done by legislators and regulators who may have
this explicit or implicit mandate than by judges who make case-by-

case rulings where the advancement of economy-wide growth may not be uppermost in their minds (or even legally permissible). Alternatively, and most far-reaching, Ribstein argues in Chapter 19 that the Congress should explicitly allow and even encourage states to compete in multiple arenas in adopting pro-growth policies or changes in rules. It is not clear whether a crisis of any form is necessary to achieve this objective, but the notion that states should be allowed greater freedom to experiment has been a long-standing one, and even recently was embodied in the financial reform legislation enacted after the Great Recession (which permits states to enact and enforce more restrictive consumer protection rules than those issued by the new federal consumer financial product regulator).

In the end, almost all of the pro-growth proposals advanced in this book have one important political virtue in common: they cost little or no government money to implement and enforce. At a time when government resources are scarce—and, if anything, spending growth needs to be reined in as part of long-term deficit reduction—this is a feature that should be highly attractive to legislators and regulators (albeit less so with judges, whose rulings rarely involve or require government spending). Given the continuing need for growth, not just to lengthen the recovery but to sustain improvements in living standards over the long run, it is the collective view of the authors in this book that the ideas for enhancing innovation and growth outlined here should attract serious attention and consideration by policymakers, ideally sooner than later. Moreover, it is our collective view that this recovery, plus the stimulation of economic growth into the future, will benefit from a reorientation of the study of law in order to consider carefully how it can be defined to promote innovation and economic growth and thus enhance the welfare of Americans, and perhaps eventually citizens throughout the rest of the world.